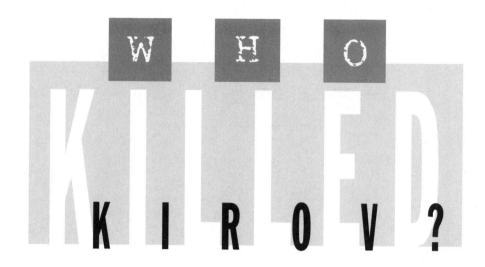

WHO KILLED KIROV?

Also by Amy Knight

Spies Without Cloaks: The KGB's Successors

Beria: Stalin's First Lieutenant

The KGB: Police and Politics in the Soviet Union

WHO KILLED KIROV?

The Kremlin's Greatest Mystery

Amy Knight

Hill and Wang
A division of Farrar, Straus and Giroux
New York

Hill and Wang
A division of Farrar, Straus and Giroux
19 Union Square West, New York 10003

Copyright © 1999 by Amy Knight
All rights reserved
Distributed in Canada by Douglas & McIntyre Ltd.
Printed in the United States of America
Designed by Lisa Stokes
First edition, 1999

Library of Congress Cataloging-in-Publication Data
Knight, Amy W., 1946–
    Who killed Kirov? : the Kremlin's greatest mystery / Amy Knight.—
1st ed.
        p.   cm.
    Includes index.
    ISBN 0-8090-6404-9 (alk. paper)
    1. Kirov, Sergei Mironovich, 1886-1934. 2. Revolutionaries—
Soviet Union—Biography. 3. Soviet Union—Politics and
government—1917–1936. I. Title.
DK268.K5K58 1999
947.084'1'092
[B]—DC21   98-48989

To Viola Brudno

Contents

Illustrations

1. Sergei with his sisters, Anna and Elizaveta, and his grandmother, Melaniia Avdeevna, Urzhum, 1904. (Courtesy of Kirov Museum, St. Petersburg)

2. Police photograph of Sergei, 1907. (Courtesy of Kirov Museum, St. Petersburg)

3. Mariia L'vovna Markus at the editorial offices of the paper *Terek*, Vladikavkaz, 1910. (Courtesy of Kirov Museum, St. Petersburg)

4. Kirov and Sergo Ordzhonikidze, 1920. (Courtesy of Kirov Museum, St. Petersburg)

5. Kirov and Stalin on the platform of Moscow Station, Leningrad, April 1926. (Courtesy of Kirov Museum, St. Petersburg)

6. Site of the Kirovs' home in Leningrad. (Author's photograph)

7. Stalin and Kirov with Leningrad party officials at the Smolnyi, April 1926. (Courtesy of Kirov Museum, St. Petersburg)

8. Kirov with a delegation of metalworkers at his office in the Smolnyi, July 1929. (Courtesy of Kirov Museum, St. Petersburg)

9. Kirov and Maxim Gorky among factory workers, Leningrad, July 1929. (Courtesy of Kirov Museum, St. Petersburg)

Preface

. . . .

This book recounts one of the most controversial episodes in Soviet history—the murder, in December 1934, of Leningrad Communist party chief Sergei Kirov. Few events have drawn such attention from historians and yet been so little understood. The thousands of books and monographs that have been written about the Soviet Union often contain discussions of the murder, but usually with the caveat that no conclusions can be drawn about who was really responsible. Although most historians would agree that the Kirov murder was one of those defining moments that cast a long shadow over the Soviet era, there is little consensus regarding the crime itself. Was Kirov murdered by a lone assassin or was his death the result of a conspiracy, perhaps involving Stalin? The circumstances of this terrible crime, which served as the catalyst for the massive and bloody purges that reached their peak in 1936–38, have remained a mystery that needs explaining.

In writing this book, I do not expect to end completely the controversy over who really killed Kirov. As with other political murders, including here in the United States the exhaustively investigated John F. Kennedy and Martin Luther King, Jr., assassinations, there will always be unanswered questions and unresolved puzzles. But, drawing on the compelling new evidence that has emerged since Mikhail Gorbachev initiated glasnost and Russian authorities began to open up their archives, I have provided what I consider to be a convincing version of the Kirov murder and the momentous events surrounding it. This is not a simple story; in order to understand what really happened, the reader must learn what kind of a man Kirov was, how he rose to the top of the Soviet political system, and how that system came to be dominated by Stalin. Thus, much of the book is devoted to the personal story of Kirov, his role in helping to forge the Bolshevik regime, and his relationships with key party leaders, especially Sergo Ordzhonikidze, Nikolai Bukharin, and of course Stalin. Kirov's murder and its tragic aftermath are the focal point of the narrative, but the larger purpose of the book is to broaden our understanding of the phenomenon of Stalinism.

Historians have devoted a tremendous amount of study to Stalin's dictatorship, and yet the fascination with it never seems to end. This is as it should be, given the enormity of Stalin's crimes and those committed in his name. In the West, much of the initial interest in studying Stalinism was motivated by the Cold War and the desire to understand the roots of a regime that posed a grave threat to democracy. Now, at least for the time being, that political imperative is no longer so urgent, but the reasons for our continued fascination with the Stalin period are no less compelling: we have at our disposal a vast amount of new material that offers the opportunity for a deeper understanding of one the bloodiest regimes in world history.

Just as Russia's ongoing struggle to enter the arena of democratic nations captures our attention, so too does its past. Russia, its fate always seeming to hang in the balance, is a country of profound contrasts—of endless possibilities and lost opportunities, glory and doom, hope and despair. The Stalin period, terrible as it was, epitomizes this duality. A few years ago I had the rare opportunity of visiting Stalin's dacha outside Moscow at Kuntsevo. Here in this wooden fortress, unfortunately still closed to the public, nestled in a birch forest was where Stalin held his infamous all-night dinners, which members of his entourage were compelled to attend, consuming at Stalin's behest copious amounts of vodka and dancing together for Stalin's amusement. Here too was where Stalin died in 1953, under circumstances that have never been fully explained. Nothing had been moved since Stalin's death: his shaving utensils still rested above the sink in his bathroom; his phonograph, a gift from Churchill, still sat next to the long dining table, with all the chairs in place.

His books and papers were still on his desk. As I sat on the sofa bed where Stalin took his last breath and looked out at the silver trees, glistening in the brilliant sunlight, I was struck by the contrast between the beauty and softness of the natural surroundings and the stark, dreary interior of the house. The thought that this evil tyrant, guilty of killing millions of innocent people and of inflicting unbearable hardships on millions of others, had lived here, had made his cruel decisions while looking out at the same beautiful scenery that I was seeing, sent chills down my spine.

This was Russia, the land of paradoxes. It could produce Ivan the Terrible, Stalin, the GULAG, the pollution-filled industrial cities with miles of gray apartment blocks, the miserable collective farms. But it was also the homeland of Pushkin and Dostoevsky, Tchaikovsky and Rachmaninov, the reforming Tsar Alexander II, spectacular forests and mountains, and cities like St. Petersburg (formerly Leningrad), which is unparalleled for its magnificence. As I sat in Stalin's dacha, it occurred to me that the way Kirov was murdered, brutally gunned down in an elegant building overlooking the curving, gracious Neva River, which flows through that beautiful city, was another such paradox. These contrasts, and the mysteries that surround them, are what make Russia and its history so fascinating.

I would like to express my gratitude to the many people who have helped me in the preparation of this book. My first thanks are due to my friend Viola Brudno, whose help and encouragement were indispensable. She spent long hours deciphering letters and documents handwritten in Russian, and she read and commented critically on the manuscript. I am also deeply grateful to my husband, Malcolm, who gave so generously of his time to read the manuscript in its entirety and provide incisive critical analysis. And this book could not have been written without the invaluable and painstaking editing of Lauren Osborne, my editor at Hill and Wang.

Special thanks are due to my daughter Molly and my friend Rod Barker for their encouragement and advice in the initial stages of the project. I also owe my appreciation to David Brandenburger and Steve Guenther for their assistance in obtaining materials for me in Russia.

Several others were tremendously helpful to me while I was conducting research in Moscow and St. Petersburg: Tat'iana Sukharnikova at the Kirov Museum in St. Petersburg gave generously of her time and expertise, as did Alla Kirilina, a leading Russian researcher on Kirov. I am also grateful to Ina and Valentin Bliumenfel'd, Nina Chernysheva, Nadezhda Kodatskaia, Valentina Tiucheva, and Ludmilla Gorskaia. And I want to thank the International Research and Exchanges Board for providing financial support for my research in Russia.

Harry Leich at the Library of Congress responded kindly and efficiently to my many requests for help in tracking down sources, as did the late David Kraus, and the reference librarians in the European Reading Room. Among the others to whom I am grateful are Lesley Rimmel, Miklosh Kun, Robert Conquest, Robert C. Tucker, Mark Kramer, Christian Ostermann, Nadia Zilper, Richard King, E. A. Rees, and Catherine Newman. Finally, thanks to Diana and Alexandra for so patiently enduring their mother's preoccupation with Kirov.

Author's Note

The dates used in the text for events before February 1918 are those of the Julian, or "old-style," calendar, which was used in Russia until that time. In the nineteenth century, the Julian calendar was twelve days behind the Gregorian calendar used in the West; in the twentieth century, it was thirteen days behind.

I have used the Library of Congress system of transliteration from the Russian, except for well-known names, which appear in the more familiar Anglicized forms.

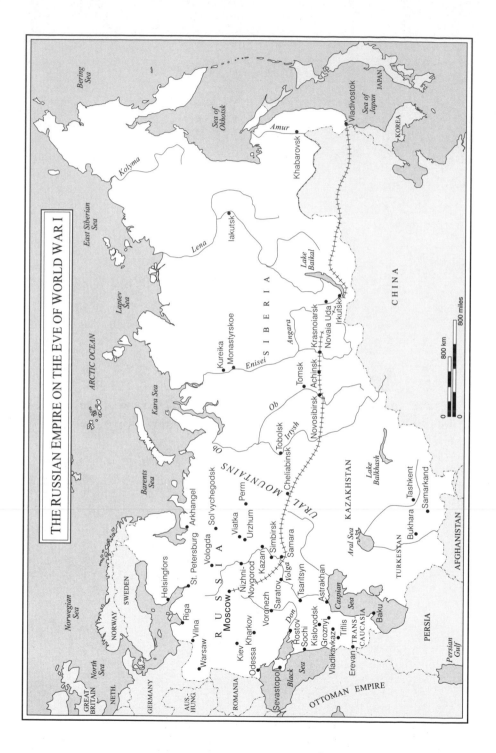

THE RUSSIAN EMPIRE ON THE EVE OF WORLD WAR I

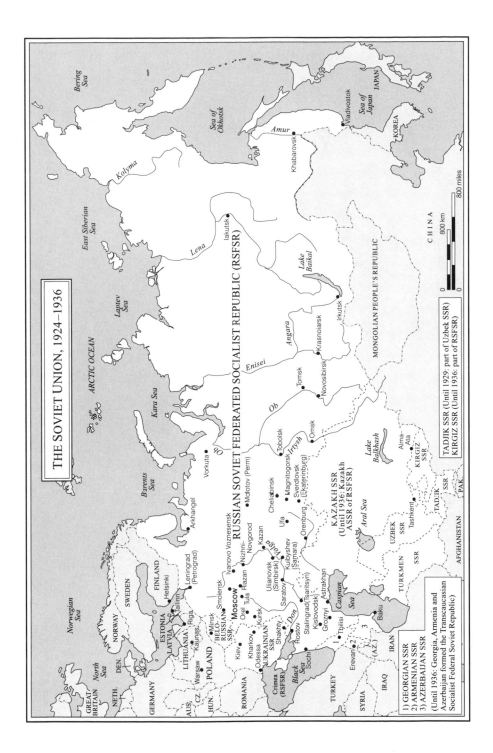

THE SOVIET UNION, 1924–1936

A December Tragedy

In the first days when Leningrad was orphaned, Stalin rushed there. He went to the place where the crime against our country was committed. The enemy did not fire at Kirov personally. No! He fired at the proletarian revolution.

—Pravda, *5 December 1934*

On 4 December 1934, with a freezing, damp dawn breaking over Moscow's October railway station, a large delegation of workers, summoned for the occasion by the party, watched in shivering silence as the Red Arrow from Leningrad pulled up and a coffin was lowered onto the platform. Inside was the bullet-scarred body of Sergei Kirov, former Leningrad party chief, Politburo member, and prized orator of the Stalin regime. As workers shouldered the coffin, a group of Kirov's former colleagues, led by Stalin, stepped off the train, doubtless weary after the all-night journey from Leningrad. Their faces, all but hidden in the thick folds of their coat collars and the heavy fur of their hats, were expressionless.

Kirov had been murdered late in the afternoon on 1 December, in the Leningrad party headquarters at the Smolnyi Institute, an imposing neoclassical building that had once been an aristocratic girls' school. That same day, immediately after learning the news of the tragedy, Stalin had ordered several leading party officials to accompany him to Leningrad.[1] After a perfunctory visit of consolation to Kirov's distraught widow, Mariia L'vovna, Stalin and his subordinates began an investigation of the crime. It was highly unusual for the top political leadership to abandon the capital to oversee a case that the NKVD, the powerful and efficient secret police, was presumably well equipped to handle on its own. But this was no ordinary crime. The victim was one of Stalin's closest comrades. Since the death (by apparent suicide) of Stalin's wife, Nadezhda Allilueva, two years earlier, Kirov had become an indispensable companion to Stalin, vacationing with him in the South and even having the rare privilege (given Stalin's extreme self-consciousness about his physical appearance) of accompanying him to the sauna. Though separated by hundreds of kilometers, they talked often on the telephone—sometimes, given Stalin's erratic work habits, in the middle of the night.

Leningrad, moreover, was no ordinary city. Just a few years earlier it had been rife with party oppositionists who took the side of the "leftist" Grigorii Zinoviev in his quarrel with Stalin. As a member of the Politburo, the Communist Party's leading body, and head of the Leningrad government, Zinoviev had joined with the prominent Bolshevik Lev Kamenev in opposing Stalin's economic and political leadership. After Zinoviev had been ousted from Leningrad in 1926, Kirov, as the new party chief, had waged a difficult struggle to rid the Leningrad party of loyal Zinovievites. Stalin had never trusted Leningraders, whose city, built by Peter the Great in the early eighteenth century to serve as Russia's "window on the West," he detested. The home of Russia's most prominent intellectual and cultural figures, Leningrad seemed more European than Russian. Thus he would personally see to it that justice was wrought for Comrade Kirov.

The investigation produced surprisingly quick results. On 3 December, just one day after Stalin and his group arrived, *Pravda* cited an NKVD communiqué: "The preliminary investigation has established that the name of the villain, the murderer of Comrade Kirov, is Leonid Vasil'evich Nikolaev, born 1904, a former employee of the Leningrad RKI [Worker-Peasants' Inspectorate]. The investigation continues." Further details emerged the next day. Citing the NKVD, the papers claimed that Kirov had been preparing a report to give at a party meeting at the Tauride Palace that evening. Nikolaev stood near Kirov's office at the Smolnyi, where he usually received visitors, and when Kirov "walked by into his office," Nikolaev came from behind and shot him in the neck. The murderer was caught on the spot. Kirov was carried unconscious into his office, where doctors found him without a pulse and not breathing. Efforts to resuscitate him proved fruitless. The bullet lodged in the victim's neck was the type used in a Nagan revolver, which had been established as the weapon. The circumstances of the attack and the path of the bullet indicated that the victim had been shot at close range.

As would later emerge from documents on the case, the report contained some curious anomalies. First, the alleged assassin, Nikolaev, was identified only as a "former employee of the RKI." But he had worked at the RKI (a government monitoring agency) in 1932–33; his last place of employment, from which he had been fired in April 1934, was the Institute of Party History. Why would only the RKI be mentioned? Second, the papers implied that Kirov had been working at the Smolnyi that day, when in fact he had been writing his report at home and had turned up unexpectedly at the Smolnyi late in the afternoon. He was not shot outside his office, but a good fifty-five feet away, outside the office of the second secretary, Mikhail Chudov. It was into Chudov's office, not Kirov's, that his body had been carried. In addition to the bullet that hit Kirov so accurately at close range, another had been fired, lodging in a cornice near the ceiling. And finally, no mention was made of the fact that Nikolaev had been taken unconscious to a special NKVD medical unit for treatment before being interrogated.

Such inaccuracies might be understandable in a country with independent newspapers that sent out reporters to the crime scene and hurried to publish the news. But the Soviet press did not allow for mistakes. By 1934 the Soviet Union had become, under Stalin, a state where all forms of public expression were controlled by the party and the secret police. Even the smallest detail was subject to intense scrutiny before being printed, making it unlikely that these errors had crept in by chance. Was the public being deliberately misinformed?

Another important piece of information that never appeared in the press was that a key witness, Kirov's bodyguard M. D. Borisov, was killed in an alleged accident a day after the crime, while on the way to be questioned by Stalin. Although news of the accident spread quickly around Leningrad, the newspapers ignored this unfortunate event completely, devoting their pages instead to the glorification of Kirov.

The slain leader became a saint overnight. News about the funeral plans and Kirov's lying in state were interspersed with poignant statements about the loss from stricken workers and party members. According to one observer, a young Soviet diplomat named Alexander Barmine: "The papers at the time of Kirov's death were filled with his praises, and with expressions of grief, actually far exceeding those which followed the death of Lenin. For at least twelve days all Soviet newspapers were devoted from the first to the last line to the life and death of the beloved leader Kirov."[2]

With astonishing speed, *Pravda* had managed by 5 December to locate and print extensive biographical details about Kirov, including a secret dossier from the tsarist police archives. By this date also, entire books about Kirov, with reminiscences by former comrades, stories about his childhood, and reproductions of his speeches, had gone to press. It was almost as if someone had assembled all the material beforehand and was waiting for the go-ahead to put it together.

Kirov's murder resounded abroad as well, making the front page in *The New York Times* on 2 December. *Times* Moscow correspondent Harold Denny reported that Kirov's death was declared dramatically the night before in the midst of an 11 p.m. news broadcast: "The announcer interrupted the program to say that he had an announcement of a dastardly deed to make. Then he read communiqués of the Central Committee of the party and the Council of People's Commissars of the government. The orchestra played the funeral march from 'Tannhäuser,' and all broadcasting ceased."[3] The next day, Denny reported, "a stunned Moscow, draped with black-bordered red flags, waited silently but anxiously for any fragments of news about yesterday's murder."[4]

The funeral was set for 6 December. The day before, people streamed into the Hall of Columns in Moscow's House of Soviets all day to view Kirov's open casket. At 10 p.m. access was restricted to family and high party and government officials. Kirov's widow, Mariia L'vovna, sat to the right of the coffin with her two sisters at her side. She was in bad shape. Her health had been deteriorating for some time, and the shock of her husband's death had rendered her incoherent and barely able to walk. With them sat Lenin's widow, Krupskaia, his sister Mariia, and Kirov's two sisters, who had traveled hundreds of miles to attend the funeral. Although they had been close to Kirov growing up, his sisters had not seen him for thirty years. They had only corresponded. Now they were seeing him for the last time—dead, his face "greenish-yellow" with black-and-blue bruises from his wound and his face-down fall to the floor.[5]

Stalin's sister-in-law, Mariia Svanidze, who was sitting with the women, described the scene in her diary:

> The air had a heavy funereal scent, mixed with the smell of flowers, earth and evergreens. Despite the full light, it seemed, through my tears, that it was dark, gloomy and painfully uncomfortable. . . . At 11 o'clock

everyone became tense, looking every minute toward the corner from which the great ones would appear, our leaders. . . . Finally their steps, firm and resolute. . . . Iosif [Stalin] stood at Kirov's head. Chopin's funeral march was playing. . . . Iosif climbed up the platform of the casket, leaned over and kissed the forehead of the dead Sergei Mironovich. The picture tore my soul, knowing as I did how close they were, and the entire hall sobbed. I heard, through my own sobs, men sobbing.[6]

Mariia L'vovna by this time had begun to faint. Doctors surrounded her, gave her some drops. During the commotion, the leaders silently slipped out of the hall and the coffin was closed, ready for its journey to the crematorium.

The next day, 6 December, was a day, in *Pravda*'s words, "which will go down in history as a day of great mourning for the party, the whole country, all the workers, the day of the funeral of the best son of the socialist motherland—Sergei Mironovich Kirov." That morning Mariia L'vovna, supported on the arms of Kirov's sisters, entered the Hall of Columns, where Stalin and other political and military officials waited. At noon the hall was closed to the public and an hour later the funeral march began. Stalin and others carried the urn with Kirov's ashes to Red Square, where over a million workers stood, bearing the dank December cold in hushed silence.[7]

After two hours of eulogies, Kirov's closest comrade, the famed Georgian Bolshevik Grigorii (Sergo) Ordzhonikidze, placed Kirov's remains in the Kremlin Wall. Flags were lowered, heads were bared, as the funeral sounds of a trumpet broke the silence. In just a little over two years Sergo's own ashes would be placed in the wall. He too would be felled by a bullet, but in his case it would be alleged that he himself, not an assassin, had fired the shot. Sergo was a tried revolutionary, a Bolshevik who had enforced Soviet rule in his native Transcaucasia with all the calculated ruthlessness required of the best defenders of the Soviet state. Nonetheless, he was fiery-tempered, sensitive, and emotional, and it must have been difficult for him to keep his feelings inside during the lengthy ceremony. When he heard of the murder, he had said to his wife: "I thought that Kirych would bury me, but it has turned out the opposite." He was so overcome that he lost his voice completely, which may explain why he unexpectedly failed to speak at the funeral.[8]

Sergo and Kirov had worked together as trusted comrades throughout the bloody civil war that followed the Bolshevik seizure of power in 1917 and during the early 1920s, when the Bolsheviks were consolidating their rule. After their duties took them to separate places, they corresponded almost daily, vacationed together, and saw each other as much as possible. Their bond had been one of deep trust and affection, going beyond that of traditional party comradeship. Given the atmosphere of intrigue, denunciations, and factional strife that came to characterize party life by the late 1920s, this friendship was especially important. Now Sergo would have to face the difficulties of working under Stalin's increasingly dictatorial and arbitrary rule without Kirov.

▪ THE LOSS OF A BOLSHEVIK

The murder of Kirov not only devastated his family and friends. It sent shock waves throughout the Soviet Union. The forty-eight-year-old Kirov had been a popular leader in party circles—handsome, charismatic, and a highly effective public speaker. With his youthful face and a lack of pretensions, Kirov had a forthcoming and approachable demeanor that made people feel they could trust him. In contrast to Stalin, who rarely left the confines of the Kremlin and was uncomfortable with spontaneity, Kirov was a man of the people, who would leap out of his chauffeur-driven car to shake hands on the street. Whereas Stalin spoke Russian with a heavy Georgian accent, Kirov's words rang out in the clear, forceful tones of a native Russian, a real muzhik, a man of the soil.

Like Stalin, Kirov had experienced a childhood of poverty and deprivation. Born Sergei Mironovich Kostrikov in 1886 in the small Russian town of Urzhum (in Viatka Province), he was the son of a minor clerk, whose drinking bouts prevented him from holding down a job. Kirov's father subjected family members to beatings, just as Stalin's alcoholic father had done, and abandoned the family when Kirov was five. Two years later, when his mother died of tuberculosis, Kirov was parentless. He was then separated from his two sisters and spent the rest of his childhood in the local orphanage.

One might have expected little from a life with such inauspicious beginnings, but Kirov's keen intellect and intense ambition marked him as a survivor. After excelling in the local school, Kirov was able to get funds to study for a diploma in mechanical engineering in the city of Kazan in 1901. He moved on to the Siberian city of Tomsk in 1904, intending to continue his education, but he soon got caught up in revolutionary fervor. By 1905, the year of the first revolution, he had become a Bolshevik.

His subsequent career as a professional revolutionary fighting the regime of Tsar Nicholas II put an end to his formal education. But his thirst for knowledge continued to be intense, and he read voraciously, especially when he was spending time in tsarist prisons for illegal revolutionary activities. Kirov did not limit his prison reading to Marxist literature, but read works by Dostoevsky, Chekhov, Tolstoy, Herzen, Victor Hugo, and Anatole France, and even tackled Hegel, Descartes, and Spinoza. He also read the Bible, where he found "much that is interesting."[9] His passion for books never diminished. When Kirov died he left a personal library of over 20,000 volumes.

Kirov loved to write, as his long letters from prison to his wife, Mariia L'vovna, attest, and he expressed himself well on subjects ranging from philosophy to literary criticism. In 1909, when the revolutionary movement had ground to a temporary halt, he got a job as a journalist on a liberal newspaper in Vladikavkaz, a city in the North Caucasus. For the next eight years, with interruptions for arrests and exile, he was a regular contributor to—and from 1915 a senior editor of—the paper.

By all accounts, Kirov did not fit the Bolshevik stereotype of single-minded ruthlessness. His tolerant attitude toward different political views set him apart from those who rose to positions in the leadership in the 1920s. He did not shy away from friendships with those from other political parties, such as the Socialist Revolutionaries, and up through the 1917 Revolution he worked so closely with the Bolsheviks' main competitors, the Mensheviks, that later his political rivals accused him of having been a Menshevik himself.

Kirov's humanity stands out especially in comparison to Stalin, whose lack of scruples and apparent indifference to other people's suffering was already evident in the prerevolutionary period. In a 1911 letter to Mariia L'vovna from prison, Kirov described an execution and his own reaction to it: "What a terrible mood I am in! I have good reason to suppose that tonight I will witness a nightmarish, simply horrible event. It seems that I am just about to hear the sound of the executioner's axe. . . . When you are free you do not experience a horror like this so directly. Here when such a 'routine event' occurs almost in front of your eyes—it is indescribably difficult. But how boundless is the human soul! People get used to such executions and carry them out with amazing indifference."[10]

Stalin, by contrast, was said to have little reaction to the executions that went on when he was in prison before the revolution. According to one biographer, Isaac Deutscher: "In the tension of such moments, Koba [Stalin] would, if an eyewitness is to be believed, fall sound asleep, astonishing his comrades by his strong nerves, or else he would go on with his unsuccessful attempt to master the intricacies of German grammar."[11]

However atypical Kirov might have been, he joined the Bolsheviks and, by the end of the civil war in 1921, they all had blood on their hands. Their ruthless suppression of those who opposed the Bolshevik seizure of power in 1917 cost well over a million lives, including those of innocent civilians. Justice was sacrificed in the name of the revolutionary cause, and Kirov became a standard-bearer of that cause. He first attracted the attention of Lenin and Stalin when he served as chief of the Bolshevik Revolutionary Committee in Astrakhan, a key stronghold at the foot of the Caucasus, and successfully put down an anti-Bolshevik rebellion there in 1919. Later he was a member of the Revolutionary Military Council of the Eleventh Army, which invaded Azerbaijan in 1920 and then moved into Armenia and Georgia. As chief of the Azerbaijan Communist Party from 1921 to 1926, Kirov enforced Soviet rule over unwilling Azerbaijani nationalists, whose country had enjoyed a brief period of independence before the 1920 invasion. Kirov's letters and telegrams to his chiefs in Moscow make it clear that he was doing everything in his power to bring the republic into line.

In 1926, when Stalin wanted once and for all to rid the Leningrad apparatus of Zinoviev's sympathizers, he chose Kirov for the job. It must be said that Kirov did not relish his new appointment as Leningrad party chief. Indeed, he complained bitterly in letters to his wife and friends about how difficult and unpleasant the job was. But he could not refuse Stalin. Although he kept sanctions against the former Zinovievites to a minimum, trying instead to bring them back into the Bolshevik fold, he delivered fiery speeches against them in public and presided over endless meetings where they were denounced.

In the process of revamping the Leningrad organization, Kirov earned a few enemies. In 1929 a group of Old Leningraders even took their complaints about him to the party leadership in Moscow, dredging up some of his prerevolutionary newspaper articles in an effort to show that he had bourgeois leanings. In the end, Kirov survived the attack, but not without a black mark on his record.

The early 1930s were taken up with implementing Stalin's First Five-Year Plan, begun in 1928. The plan called for industrialization at a break-neck pace, accompanied by collectivization of agriculture. Millions of peasants all over the Soviet Union were removed from their individual landholdings and forced into collective farms. Peasant resistance led to bloody clashes with the authorities, as well as to famine. Well over a million peasants perished in the process. Kirov was not enthusiastic about the policy of forced collectivization—and in fact the process was implemented at a much slower pace in the Leningrad region than in other parts of the country. Nonetheless, he went along with Moscow's directives. Open resistance was not Kirov's style, and to challenge Stalin on this issue, as his Bolshevik comrade Nikolai Bukharin did, would have meant the end of his political career.

We do not know what kind of ethical equations Kirov was making at this point, how he justified to himself the loss of life and the repression for which he was responsible. He still deserved his reputation as a "moderate" Bolshevik; he was not a vindictive dogmatist, and he exhibited no penchant for wanton cruelty. But in aligning himself with Stalin and professing support for his leadership, he had entered upon a life of moral compromise.

Indeed, in the context of Stalinist Russia, popularity was a highly relative term. Kirov was "popular" only insofar as a leading member of a brutal, repressive government could be. Recently declassified secret informational reports from local party officials reveal that the Leningrad proletariat was deeply dissatisfied with the economic situation, especially the proposed end to bread rationing. Some workers and peasants from the Leningrad region blamed Kirov for their dismal plight and thus reacted to the news of his death by expressing indifference or scorn.[12]

But the majority of party members held Kirov in high esteem. The regime was still young, and many Communists believed the incessant propaganda—that they were suffering now to build a brilliant socialist future. Kirov was part of a leadership that had been portrayed by the press as wise, omnipotent, and devoted to the public's cause. Moreover, he radiated the kind of energy and authority that made people look up to him.

Even nonparty members reacted with profound grief at the news of Kirov's death. According to one Leningrader, who was in his late teens at the time, everyone cried. The feeling of loss was tremendous.[13] Russian historian Roy Medvedev, who was a child living in Leningrad in 1934, reports that, on the night of the murder, the workers of Leningrad led a massive torchlight procession along the Neva River, culminating in a memorial gathering at the Winter Palace.[14] Similar ceremonies were held all over the Soviet Union in the days that followed. According to *The New York Times*: "Factories and other organizations held special memorial meetings where speakers extolled the dead man, while people wept for Kirov, the smiling popular figure. . . . In the industrial centers of the nation the grief and indignation of workers were freely manifested."[15]

Beneath the grief, however, some also felt fear, which was to prove well founded, that the murder would bring about a change for the worse in the already oppressive political environment. Nadezhda Kodatskaia, the daughter of Ivan Kodatskii, head of the Leningrad City Executive Committee (equivalent to the city's mayor), whose family lived in the same building as Kirov and his wife, recalled the sense of foreboding that pervaded their household after the murder. Her father, she said, was not only grief-stricken but terribly afraid.[16]

▪ A CONSPIRACY UNCOVERED

For all the mourning of Kirov, who continued to be the object of intense adulation in the press throughout the month of December, no one lost sight of the Great Leader, who was portrayed as deep in sorrow. As diplomat Alexander Barmine observed: "In the pages surrounded with a great black band of mourning we were told of the dreadful grief that had seized our country, our leaders and, most heart-stricken of all, Stalin."[17] Typical of the outpouring of public sympathy for Stalin was a communication to him from Leningrad workers, reprinted in *Pravda*: "By the coffin of Sergei Mironovich we give you, Iosif Vissarionovich, our proletarian oath that we will fight with all our energy for the great course, to which our Kirov devoted his crystal pure life. We know how difficult these days are for you personally, we know what a true friend and faithful helper our Mironich was to you."[18]

However great his sorrow, it was impossible to find even a trace of emotion on Stalin's face as he was pictured in the press, standing impassively beside Kirov's coffin in Leningrad. And several of those who attended the funeral in Moscow reported that he was remarkably calm, seemingly absorbed in his thoughts. But, then, he had a lot to think about. It soon transpired that, according to the Soviet press, the murder was not the work of a single assassin, but rather part of a much larger conspiracy. The public, which had probably assumed that Nikolaev was a mentally unbalanced malcontent who had acted from personal motives, first learned about the conspiracy on 22 December, when another terse NKVD announcement appeared in the press: "The investigation has established that the perpetrator of the abominable crime in the Smolnyi on 1 December 1934, L. V. Nikolaev, was a member of an underground terrorist anti-Soviet group established by members of the former Zinoviev opposition in Leningrad." The report named thirteen other members of the group and claimed that they had the goal of "disorganizing the leadership of the Soviet government by means of terrorist acts" in order to "change the direction of policy back to the Zinoviev-Trotsky line." They also had the more personal motive of revenge against Kirov.

The case of the "Leningrad Center" was heard by the Military Collegium of the Supreme Court a few days later. Nikolaev and the thirteen other defendants, several of whom had known Nikolaev in his childhood or had been connected with him in the Komsomol (Communist Youth League), were found guilty and shot. The sentences, announced in the press on 30 December, had been carried out the day before in accordance with a new law passed on Stalin's orders on the day of Kirov's death. The law gave those accused of terrorism a mere twenty-four hours to acquaint themselves with the case against them, provided for a closed hearing without a defense lawyer, and authorized the court to carry out the death sentence immediately. The new antiterrorism law was not intended for just a few isolated cases. On the contrary, it provided the backbone for an NKVD witch-hunt for terrorists and conspirators that would eventually engulf the entire country.

In Leningrad, the witch-hunt had begun on 2 December, extending to all those who had any connection with Nikolaev, including members of his family, who were all arrested. Soon these connections led to faraway places. Elizabeth Lermolo was a young woman from an aristocratic Russian family, who some years earlier had been exiled to a remote part of northern Russia because her husband, a member of the tsar's army, had been arrested as a "counterrevolutionary." Lermolo had the unfortunate luck of having lived in exile with an aunt of Nikolaev and had met the assassin briefly when he came for a visit. This, together with her "bourgeois" lineage, was enough to brand her a criminal. She was hauled to Moscow to be interrogated endlessly, sometimes for twenty hours at a stretch, by the NKVD. The sessions were accompanied by brutal torture. One night, in an effort to get Lermolo to confess to her participation in the plot to kill Kirov, an NKVD officer placed her hand on a doorjamb and then closed a heavy door on it. After losing consciousness from the excruciating pain, Lermolo was revived by a bucket of cold water, only to be beaten so severely that she lost several teeth and her clothes, drenched in blood, were torn to shreds.[19]

Meanwhile, the NKVD in Moscow went after the "bigger fish," Zinoviev and his ally Lev Kamenev, both of whom had disavowed their oppositional views some years back and had recently been reinstated in the party. In mid-January, Zinoviev and Kamenev, along with seventeen others, were "tried" for membership in an anti-Soviet terrorist group, the so-called Moscow Center. The defendants were charged with responsibility for the Kirov murder on the grounds that the Moscow Center had allegedly guided and inspired the Leningrad group. All were given lengthy prison terms. On 18 January the Central Committee sent out a secret letter, "On Lessons of the Events Tied to the Evil Murder of Comrade Kirov," to the local party organizations. The letter condemned all former Zinoviev followers, tying them to the murder of Kirov and demanding that they be arrested and isolated.[20]

The country was getting its first taste of a terror that in a year and a half would sweep the country, ultimately claiming millions of victims, a terror that would not, as in the past, restrict itself to bourgeois class enemies or party heretics, but would lash out indiscriminately and arbitrarily at all elements of Soviet society.

The exiled Bolshevik leader Leon Trotsky once said of Stalin that he was "like a man who wants to quench his thirst with salt water." Every vanquished enemy, every victim of his revenge made him lust for more enemies and victims. But after December 1934 the entire country was drinking salt water, for the Kirov murder ignited a chain reaction of suspicion and paranoia that made the people unwilling accomplices in Stalin's vendetta against them. At his behest, they searched for spies and enemies among themselves with a vengeance. It mattered little whether or not they actually believed that a vast conspiracy was behind the Kirov murder, because they were guided not by reason, but by fear.

In fact, as Roy Medvedev pointed out, the claim that Kirov's murder was organized by Zinoviev and his followers seemed quite plausible at the time: "Everyone knew that Kirov had succeeded the Zinovievist Grigory Yevdokimov as leader of the Leningrad Party organization. It is therefore not surprising that right after the murder the thoughts of many people turned toward the former Leningrad opposition."[21] But, as Medvedev goes on to emphasize, "it is just this obvious plausibility that obliges us to have doubts about Stalin's story. The Zinovievist opposition would have gained no political benefit from the murder of the man who was at that time the most popular party leader after Stalin."[22]

Clearly the person who gained the most from the murder was Stalin himself, because it offered him an ideal pretext for eliminating all remnants of the former opposition and launching the purges. Back in 1929 Trotsky had observed prophetically: "There remains only one thing for Stalin: to try to draw a line of blood between the official party and the Opposition. He absolutely must connect the Opposition with assassination attempts, preparations for armed insurrection, etc. . . . The impotent policy of maneuvering and evading problems, the growing economic difficulties, the growing distrust within the party toward the leadership have made it necessary to stun the party by putting on a large-scale show. He needs a blow, a shock, a catastrophe."[23]

That shock came on 1 December 1934, enabling Stalin not only to draw a blood line between his party followers and the opposition but to unleash a terror that was rivaled in its ferociousness only by that of Hitler's Germany. Today, even in Russia, it is generally acknowledged that Stalin used the Kirov murder for political purposes, ordering the NKVD to trump up false charges of conspiracy against the opposition. Indeed, the USSR Supreme Court reached this very conclusion in 1988 when it reviewed the evidence in the case of Zinoviev, Kamenev, and the Moscow Center, which resulted in a highly publicized show trial, and found all the defendants innocent of the charges. But their findings by no means resolved the mysteries surrounding the Kirov case. If the Zinoviev group did not organize the crime, did this mean that Nikolaev acted on his own? Or were others involved in a conspiracy?

The most obvious suspect was Stalin himself. Indeed, many Western historians have long suspected that he ordered the NKVD, headed by Genrikh Iagoda, to arrange the murder. In a 1989 book, *Stalin and the*

Kirov Murder, Robert Conquest pulled together the available evidence on the case and came up with some compelling arguments in favor of Stalin's guilt.[24] In Conquest's view, Stalin had strong reasons for having Kirov assassinated. Not only did the murder give him an excuse for embarking on his bloody purges; it also got rid of a political rival who might have stood in the way of his plans. Although Stalin was the unquestioned party leader by 1934, there was reportedly disillusionment with him among party activists, who had become concerned by his increasingly ruthless and repressive policies and the excesses of his campaign to force peasants into collective farms. Kirov, according to Conquest, was being considered by influential party officials as a replacement for Stalin. Thus, if he had not been killed, he might have become General Secretary. And had he assumed the party leadership in the Soviet Union, the history of that country and the world might have taken a very different course. Although by no means a democrat, Kirov was not the crazed, paranoiac tyrant that Stalin was and thus would have been incapable of launching the bloody purges that decimated his country.

▪ UNANSWERED QUESTIONS

Whatever the evidence presented against Stalin, however, it has been far from conclusive. Even Stalin's bitter enemy Trotsky, who predicted from his exile abroad that Stalin would use the murder to launch a bloody vendetta, never accused him of arranging it beforehand. There are still quite a number of historians, both in Russia and in the West, who do not believe that Stalin was guilty of this crime. Their doubts have centered mainly on the question of motives. Was Kirov, who had spoken out so enthusiastically for Stalin and his policies, really a "moderate" who offered an alternative to Stalin? Or was this simply a myth, created by émigrés abroad who were hostile to Stalin and anxious to blame him for Kirov's death? Even if he did disapprove of Stalin's policies, it was not clear that Kirov would have been a serious obstacle to him. Stalin had already succeeded in suppressing several leading Bolsheviks who were opposed to his ruthless policies. Would not Kirov have succumbed to party discipline just as the rest of his comrades did?[25]

Furthermore, arranging an assassination was not without risks. As one Stalin biographer observed: "In September 1936 Stalin dismissed Yagoda, suspecting him of protecting people who were against him. In 1938 he sent him to death. Could he in 1934 have entrusted him with such a terrible mission? . . . It is a very clumsy and dangerous way to get rid of somebody. . . ."[26] And why would Stalin have had Kirov killed during working hours in the Smolnyi Institute, where someone might have interfered with the plan, rather than out on the street?

Also, establishing the precedent of an assassination of a high Soviet official created the danger of giving others the idea of attempting it themselves. Indeed, secret party reports quoted workers and students as saying things like "They have killed Kirov; now let them kill Stalin."[27] Worry about his safety may have been one reason why Stalin shunned contact with the people and made only rare public appearances.

Most important, there is the indisputable fact that Stalin was personally close to Kirov. He had seemed to prefer Kirov's company more than that of other Politburo members. Just a few months earlier Kirov had visited Stalin at Sochi in the Crimea, and immediately upon his return from Sochi in October, Stalin had called Kirov in Leningrad and urged him to come to Moscow. Kirov was a favorite of Stalin's daughter Svetlana, who would entice him into her games of make-believe when he visited.[28]

Stalin's sister-in-law Mariia Svanidze, who saw Stalin almost daily, notes repeatedly in her diary how grief-stricken he seemed over Kirov's death. She writes: "His cheeks were sunken, he was pale and there was hidden suffering in his eyes. . . . After Nadina's [Stalin's wife] tragic death he [Kirov] was the closest person to Stalin, able to approach him sincerely and simply and give him the warmth and comfort he needed."[29] Was Stalin really playacting, feigning grief for the benefit of those around him so as not to arouse suspicion? How could he spend so much time with Kirov and be so seemingly devoted to him if he was harboring plans to have him killed? Is it not possible that the loss of Kirov was so devastating to Stalin, who may already have been mentally unbalanced, that it drove him to a bloody vendetta against his people?

The idea that someone other than Stalin would have masterminded a conspiracy to kill Kirov can be dismissed out of hand. By 1934 the Soviet Union was a totalitarian society with Stalin at the helm, and it is hard to imagine that Iagoda or other NKVD officials would have undertaken such a mission without their master's knowledge. Not only did they have no obvious motives to kill Kirov on their own; they also would have had great difficulty keeping their crime a secret from Stalin. On Stalin's orders, numerous NKVD officials in Leningrad were dismissed and arrested after the murder, but this was ostensibly because they had not been vigilant in protecting Kirov. As for Iagoda, he was not arrested until almost two years after the crime, when Stalin decided to purge the NKVD and bring in a new group of officials who he felt were more trustworthy.

So, aside from Stalin himself, Nikolaev was the only possible perpetrator of this terrible act. Is it unreasonable to suggest that he could have acted alone, motivated simply by personal feelings of inadequacy or vengeance? He was, after all, out of a job, and it was reported at his trial that he had allegedly written letters to both Stalin and Kirov to complain about his plight. Judging from what was revealed about him, Nikolaev seemed to fit the pattern of an unbalanced malcontent, not unlike John F. Kennedy's assassin, Lee Harvey Oswald.

With the Kennedy assassination too, there were several unexplained circumstances that made people suspect a conspiracy. Like Nikolaev, Oswald was able to shoot his victim despite the heavy police guard all around. Both Oswald and Nikolaev were deemed guilty before an investigation. In both cases, a key figure in the drama, whose testimony would have been crucial, was killed immediately after the crime. And finally, questions arose in each of the murders about a second bullet.

▪ OFFICIAL SECRETS

Although there are still those who claim that the Kennedy assassination was part of a conspiracy, for many people the issue was put to rest by the extensive investigations into the case. With the Kirov murder, however, official attempts to get to the bottom of the mysteries have been halfhearted at best. No one even raised the issue publicly until Soviet Communist Party chief Nikita Khrushchev spoke out at the Twenty-second Party Congress in 1961: "We must still devote a lot of energy to finding out for sure who is to blame for Kirov's death. The deeper we delve into the materials related to his death, the more questions arise."[30]

Clearly this was a tantalizing hint that some sort of conspiracy, probably involving Stalin, was behind the murder. But Khrushchev was far from a neutral observer. He had a political agenda that included dismantling Stalin's cult and discrediting some of Stalin's former colleagues, while at the same time preserving his own legitimacy as a former member of Stalin's entourage. Khrushchev was thus performing a delicate balancing act when he appointed a succession of commissions to look into the case. Although they interviewed witnesses who had survived Stalin's purges and accumulated vast files of documents, they did not publish their findings.

Twenty-five more years went by. Glasnost arrived, people began talking and writing openly about the Kirov murder, and another commission, headed by the KBG and the prosecutor's office, was established to examine the case. The conclusion was that Nikolaev was the sole murderer. Gorbachev advisor Aleksandr Iakovlev objected, saying in a 1990 letter to the Politburo that the report was inadequate and that further investigation was required, but the matter was dropped.[31]

The top secret reports of all the commissions investigating the assassination remained classified, forcing historians to rely primarily on secondary sources and thirdhand accounts until the Soviet Union was disbanded in 1991. Then the authorities began to release archival materials. The Soviets were meticulous record keepers. Every letter, every note, every transcript of a party meeting, and every police interrogation was duly kept in the files. With many of these documents now declassified, it is time to take a new look at the Kirov case and attempt to unravel the mysteries surrounding it.

It must be said that Russian authorities have not yet released all the documents on Kirov and his murder. But, in making some of the archival sources available, they have opened the door to a new understanding of this pivotal historical event. The large personal archives of both Kirov and Sergo Ordzhonikidze (which include a great deal of correspondence) are now available, along with copies of the handwritten testimonies of several persons who were at the Smolnyi that fatal December day; the original stenograms of key party meetings; and even a daily record, over several years, of all the persons who visited Stalin's office. Copies of Nikolaev's letters and excerpts from his diary are also available, as are memoirs of persons who knew Kirov well and were in contact with him up until his death.

We can now document Kirov's story—what sort of a man he was and how he rose in the Bolshevik party. Was Kirov really a moderate, who offered an alternative to Stalinism, as the famed Bolshevik theoretician Nikolai Bukharin did? Or was this only a myth that arose after his death? Bukharin and Kirov shared similar views on many issues, but, unlike Kirov,

Bukharin actively pushed his ideas and thus clashed openly with Stalin. Kirov's views on policy and his relationship with Stalin—a key part of the puzzle surrounding his murder—have never been fully understood. Now, as a result of new evidence, they become much clearer. Was the attachment between Stalin and Kirov genuine or were there tensions? What role did Ordzhonikidze, who was also very close to Stalin, play in this relationship? For the first time it is possible also to learn about Nikolaev. Did he have a plausible motive for killing Kirov on his own? And, finally, the circumstances of the murder itself—and the bizarre criminal investigation that followed—emerge in a new light.

An important part of the story is the question of why Russian authorities have continued to this day to cover up the circumstances of the crime. The Kirov case is a key not merely to the Stalin period but also to the present, because it must be understood in order for Russians and all former citizens of the Soviet Union to come to terms with their history. If Stalin had no role in the murder, it is important to put those suspicions to rest and shift attention to Nikolaev and the phenomenon of an individually motivated terrorist act. If Stalin was the culprit, however, we are talking about a crime of unprecedented dimensions in terms of its meaning and impact, a crime, as Robert Conquest pointed out, that involved not only murder but also hypocrisy in the extreme. That Stalin would have been able to dupe an entire nation, to get away with punishing thousands, millions, of innocent people for a crime that he himself committed out of personal motives of jealousy and the desire for power, would be astounding, to say the least. As Aleksandr Iakovlev expressed it: "If the murder of Kirov was organized [by Stalin], it means this was our native variant of the Reichstag fire. It means that what happened occurred, not by ignorance, not by confusion, not by inevitable circumstances, but by evil will. . . . This is why learning the truth is for us more than satisfying curiosity. This is why the question still has such political importance today and will continue to be politically important until we have convincing answers."[32]

On 21 December 1934, less than three weeks after Kirov's murder, Sergo Ordzhonikidze and his wife, Zina [Zinaida], were invited to Stalin's "nearby dacha" at Kuntsevo to celebrate Stalin's fifty-fifth birthday. The usual group of Politburo colleagues, friends, and family was there.[33] The festivities began at 9 p.m., with the customary four-hour dinner, and then

Stalin turned on his phonograph, playing his favorite Georgian songs. At his insistence, the ladies and men formed a circle, Georgian style, for dancing and singing. Mariia Svanidze noted that "Iosif was in a good mood."[34] During the first half of the dinner, party official Anastas Mikoyan was toastmaster (*tomada*), after which Sergo took over. He made a toast to Kirov, saying that "some villain killed him, took him away from us." Everyone got tearful and for a few minutes there was silence. Then someone shouted: "The toastmaster can't be heard!" The silence was over and the toasts resumed. Life would go on without Kirov, but for some in this room, it would end within two or three years. The murderous act of 1 December was to have repercussions that few of Stalin's guests could have imagined.

Had he not been killed, Kirov might well have been at Stalin's table that night. He died a premature and tragic death, but at least he escaped the denunciations, arrests, trials, and executions that many of his comrades suffered in 1936–38. Indeed, Kirov's image remained sacrosanct all the way through the purges and well after Stalin's own death in 1953. Even when the Stalinist myth was deconstructed by Khrushchev, Kirov remained a hero, with towns, squares, streets, and monuments in his name all over the Soviet Union.

Once the Soviet Union collapsed in 1991, however, the entire Soviet past—including such icons as Lenin and Kirov—fell under a cloud. Leningrad was renamed St. Petersburg, as a symbol of the city's prerevolutionary roots. The Kirov Ballet became the Mariinskii Ballet and Kirovskii Prospekt was renamed Kamennostrovskii Prospekt. *The Boy from Urzhum*, the romanticized story of Kirov's youth, was no longer required reading in the schools. The Kirov Museum, in Kirov's former Leningrad apartment, is still there, but it has seen better times. The building's façade is grimy, and the elevator going up to the fourth-floor display is often broken. Old ladies sit in the museum's rooms, guarding the Kirov memorabilia and watching the clock impatiently for teatime. Visitors are rare.

Nonetheless, the people of St. Petersburg have not forgotten the man who was once their city's leader or the mystery of his murder. When asked whether or not they think Stalin was behind the crime, some will say: "Impossible—Stalin and Kirov were best friends." Others will say: "Of course, it could not be otherwise." Still others will respond: "Who knows, difficult to say." They might profess indifference, asserting that it doesn't matter anymore, but their eyes make it clear that it does.

2

The Boy from Urzhum

.   .   .   .

Der Mensch bleibt immer was er ist.
[Man always stays who he is.]

—*Goethe*

.   .   .   .

One early August morning in 1904, Sergei Kostrikov stood on the deck of a riverboat outside the Russian town of Urzhum, waving his black service cap to his two sisters and the three friends who had come to see him off on his long journey to the Siberian city of Tomsk. Dressed, as always, in his double-breasted student's jacket with gold buttons down the front, Sergei had long, unruly hair and a scraggly black mustache, which made him look older than his eighteen years. He carried only a small basket of belongings with him, but it was all that he owned. Inside the basket was just enough money for the trip of over a thousand miles by boat and train.[1]

At the dock Sergei's sisters had noticed that he was upset. It was not easy for him to say goodbye to his family and to the town he had grown up in, especially with such an uncertain future ahead of him. And it had been an emotional morning. Before they left for the dock, his grandmother, Melaniia Avdeevna, had made everyone sit down and pray. Making the sign of the cross on Sergei, she kissed him several times and blessed him. She then stood alone watching as Sergei walked away with the others. She would never see him again.

Nor would Sergei ever see his sisters, his friends, or Urzhum again. He may not have realized it at the time, but as the boat pulled away from the dock and started down the Urzhumka River toward the Volga, his youth had come to a close. Ahead were his life as a student radical and his decision to change his name to Kirov. Ahead too was his career as a revolutionary, a journalist, and a Bolshevik leader. Behind him forever were the memories of growing up in Urzhum.

▪ EARLY YEARS

Those memories were far from carefree. Indeed, according to the numerous Soviet biographies of the man who became Kirov, his childhood and youth were fraught with hardship. His experience was hardly unusual in Russia at the time. Tsarist society at the end of the nineteenth century was still backward in terms of economic development. Industrialization was underway and Russia was developing capitalist markets, but it was still predominantly a rural, agriculturally based society, plagued by poverty and illiteracy. The focus of economic modernization, neglected for decades and now taking place as a crash program under the auspices of Russian Finance Minister Sergei Witte, was on heavy industry and urban factories. The production of consumer goods and improvements in the agricultural sector were neglected, and the burden of financing industrialization by taxation was placed on the peasantry. Enlightenment and prosperity were visible only in large cities like Moscow and St. Petersburg, or on the vast country estates of Russia's landed gentry. For the rest of the country, life was mainly a matter of survival, with few rewards.

Urzhum, a typical Russian merchant town, was located in a heavily forested region about five hundred miles northeast of Moscow. Its unpaved streets were lined with shabby wooden houses, interspersed with a few large homes belonging to prosperous timber merchants. The town was eighty miles from a railway line, so its rapidly developing commerce was served by the Urzhumka River, which fed into the Volga. The town's 5,000 inhabitants included not only Russians but also the ethnic peoples who had lived in that area for centuries—Tatars, Mariitsy, and Udmurts. The weather was extreme: winters in Urzhum were harsh, with temperatures far below zero Fahrenheit; summers were hot and mosquito-infested. The contrast between rich and poor was also striking: some merchants were millionaires, while other families barely had enough to eat.[2]

Sergei's family belonged to the latter category. His father, Miron Kostrikov, never could make ends meet. The son of a peasant clerk who died young, Miron was raised in the household of a landowner, where his mother was employed as a nursemaid. Having learned to read and write,

Miron elevated himself to the status of a *meshchanin* (petty bourgeois), working as a clerk in an Urzhum timber yard. When he married the pretty, fair-haired Ekaterina Kuzminichna and moved into the log house where she lived with her father, it seemed like a good match. But Miron resented the fact that his father-in-law had leased a plot of land outside town and compelled him to quit his clerk's job to take up farming. He aspired to the life of a gentleman and hated working on the land. It was peasant's labor, and he was no longer a peasant. When his father-in-law died Miron refused to farm anymore and took a job as a forester.

The farm was left on the shoulders of Ekaterina, who by this time had several children to look after. She bore seven in all, giving birth to one under a wagon in the fields, but the first four died in infancy. The eldest of the three surviving children was Anna, born in 1883, followed by Sergei in 1886 and Elizaveta in 1889. Seven pregnancies and three young children underfoot eventually forced Ekaterina to give up the farm. She then worked as a seamstress, took in peasant travelers to lodge for the night, and rented out half of her house, but there was still not enough income to feed the family. To make things worse, Miron began to drink heavily and soon lost his job.

Sergei's childhood friend Aleksandr (Sasha) Samartsev, whose family rented in the Kostrikovs' log house, recalled that when Miron would return home from his binges, his violence terrified the whole family: "'Miron, Miron has arrived!' they would whisper fearfully when he appeared, and then they would scurry off somewhere so he wouldn't see them."[3] Soviet biographers have attributed Miron's drinking to his inability to find satisfying work and his frustration at not being able to support his family. But Sergei's sisters judged their father more harshly:

> He did not in any way suffer. He did not want either a wife or children. How could this "suffering man," coming home drunk, mercilessly and for no reason whatsoever beat his hardworking and gentle wife, and throw his children, including his son Sergei, out on the street in any weather? Father frightened and horrified us with his drinking.[4]

As Miron increasingly "sought solace" in vodka, the family sank further and further into poverty. In the words of Anna and Elizaveta: "Father drank away the one horse left by Grandfather. Then the harness and the wagon went. Then our household things. Finally he dealt a terrible blow to our family—he took away the sewing machine."[5] Then one day Miron announced that he was leaving, going off to the Urals to seek a new life. He did not return to Urzhum for over twenty years and never communicated with his family during this time.

When he did reappear in Urzhum, Miron was an old man, dressed in a convict's uniform and part of a prisoners' convoy. By this time Sergei was far away in the North Caucasus. Sergei's mother had long since died and his grandmother was also dead. The local administration called Anna and Elizaveta, who were still living there, but they were not about to reclaim their father: "What could we do? Miron Ivanovich gave us life and then made our life unhappy. Because of him Sergei had to leave home and go into an orphanage. Because of him we had to scrounge for every meal— breakfast, lunch, and dinner. He was one of the reasons for our mother's early death. Having left home, he left us a memory of him that was only unpleasantness and fear. Miron Ivanovich was a complete stranger to us."[6] The town administration sent Miron to an almshouse, where he stayed until he eventually found work as a carpenter in a small village. But his years of drinking had destroyed his health, and he soon died of a heart attack, alone in a peasant hut, in 1912.[7]

Sergei was around five years old when his father deserted the family. He was a sturdy, robust boy with an adventurous spirit. Poverty did not deprive him of the joys of nature, which were plentiful in Urzhum. He did not go to school, so when the weather was warm he played outside for the entire day, building castles of stones and fishing and swimming in the river. Winters were a different story. Then he had to stay inside the log house, where, according to his friend Sasha Samartsev, "the air was dank, dirty, and smoky from the stove and the filthy footclothes hung up to dry by their peasant lodgers." Sergei and Sasha cut a hole in their joint wall, so they could talk and stick their hands through. When the cold let up they would go tobogganing.[8]

In order to feed her children, Ekaterina hired herself out as a house-maid and laundress for local merchants. Although she worked herself to the bone, she earned only enough to put bread and potatoes on the table. Meat was a luxury, reserved for holidays. The hard work took its toll, and within a short time Ekaterina was bedridden with tuberculosis. She died several months later, in December 1893. Before she died she kissed each of her children, and told them not to cry, to work hard and be honest.

Sergei and his sisters would have been completely destitute had it not been for their *babushka,* Melaniia Avdeevna, Miron's mother. At age eighty, she came to live with her grandchildren and care for them. But her pension and the money from the renters was not enough for the family to survive, and they went into debt. The police came and confiscated their samovar and other possessions. Desperate, Melaniia decided to put the children in the local orphanage, where at least they would be fed and clothed. But there were not enough places for all of them because a famine, followed by a cholera epidemic, had swept over Urzhum two years earlier and left many children without parents.

Finally, she managed to get Sergei accepted and told him that he would have to go. Sergei, eight years old at the time, took the news badly, as did his sisters. They all cried, including Melaniia. Sergei begged to be allowed to stay, promising that he would earn enough money to pay his contribution to the family. Melaniia could only laugh through her tears at his unrealistic proposal. Later, when she took him to the orphanage, Sergei refused to go inside. He gained a respite of one night, but the next day they returned and he reluctantly agreed to stay.[9]

After a few days Elizaveta and Anna went to visit their brother. They found him sitting on a windowsill, clasping his knees and looking out distantly. The life had gone out of him. Whatever moments of lighthearted happiness he had enjoyed were now over. Financed by donations from the town's wealthy merchants and well-to-do intelligentsia, the Urzhum Children's Home was a grim, cruel place. The regime was strict and the food was sparse, mostly Lenten fare, and the children were consequently pale and emaciated. They slept on cots covered by thin gray mattresses in a large barrackslike room. They had no toys and little time to play, because they had to earn their keep. Sergei knitted socks and tended the garden. According to his sisters, he developed a passion for flowers that stayed with him throughout his life. As an adult he never went for walks in the country without returning with a bouquet of flowers.[10]

▪ EDUCATION

Sergei attended school at the orphanage and later went to the parish school along with the other orphans. His older sister, Anna, had already taught him to read, and now he learned the basics of grammar. But, as was typical throughout Russia at the time, the main emphasis at school was on religion, Russian Orthodox Christianity, and the law of God. At the orphanage too, religion predominated over all else. The children were required to say prayers and go to confession every morning and to attend church—the prison church rather than the town one—at least twice a week.[11]

Fortunately Sergei's life was not devoid of adult affection and concern. Thanks to his exceptional brightness and appealing nature, Sergei attracted the attention of his teachers. Iulia Konstantinovna Glushkova, who taught the children ethics and religion, was especially fond of Sergei and, according to his sisters, became almost a mother to him. A deeply religious and cultured woman who adored children, Iulia Konstantinovna instilled in Sergei strong moral principles, a strict work ethic, and a love of learning. She remained close to him throughout his youth and frequently helped him out financially. Another important figure in Sergei's life was Father Konstantin Ponomarev, who was in charge of religious education in the schools and also taught at the orphanage. He was pleased when Sergei was able to recite by heart a religious parable he had heard only once and was so impressed by Sergei's singing ability that he induced him to join the church choir. As a lonely widower who was estranged from his only son, Father Ponomarev sought out the company of young Sergei, taking him fishing and on nature hikes.[12]

In 1897, at age eleven, Sergei began attending the town school (*gorod-skoe uchilishche*) in Urzhum. One of his teachers at the parish school had persuaded the Urzhum Charitable Society to pay for his tuition and school uniform because he was such a promising student. The school was close to his house, so he was able to stop off and visit his sisters after lessons, which included history, geography, physics, natural sciences, and religion (taught by Father Ponomarev). Although he excelled at his studies, Sergei found school difficult. First, he was overburdened with chores at the Children's Home, so it was hard to find time to study. Second, there was a stigma to being an orphan, and the other children, some from wealthy families, beat up on Sergei and his fellow students from the Children's Home. Sergei took it upon himself to organize a self-defense group among those who were being persecuted, and the problem was resolved.[13]

Sergei did so well at the town school that Iulia Konstantinovna prevailed upon the Urzhum Charitable Society to finance his education further. This was no easy task, because it meant sending Sergei to Kazan, about eighty miles to the south, and the society had never before paid for an indigent student to study in a different city. But Iulia Konstantinovna insisted that they could not permit a boy with Sergei's gifts to abandon his education, and the society finally agreed. Sergei was beside himself with joy, as were his grandmother and sisters, who immediately began gathering together the things he would need. Iulia Konstantinovna gave him money "for the road." In the autumn of 1901, after tearful farewells to his family, Sergei set off for Kazan, where he enrolled at the Kazan Industrial School, taking courses in mathematics, physics, religion, and mechanical engineering.[14]

He stayed at the home of Liudmila Sundrem, who ran a boarding house for students from Urzhum. Sergei disliked it there, not because he had to reside in the kitchen and thus postpone his studying until after the dinner meal was over, but because his impoverished circumstances made him feel out of place. His stipend of five rubles a month was not enough to live on, and the other student boarders were much better off. They paid for their meals, for example, whereas he received his meals "out of charity." He felt that they looked down upon him.[15]

In his second year of study Sergei moved, sharing rooms with two fellow students who were equally poor. The Charitable Society, low on funds, discontinued Sergei's monthly stipend, and the occasional money that Iulia Konstantinovna sent was insufficient to keep him from going hungry. To make matters worse, Sergei, along with several classmates, contracted malaria. Finally, at the suggestion of two teachers, he sent an appeal to the Student Aid Society. His teachers endorsed the appeal: "Deserves a stipend . . . He is very poor. He receives nothing. How he lives, no one knows." The society granted Sergei five rubles a month.[16]

Grateful though he was for the money, Sergei hated the fact that he was a supplicant, forced to rely on charity. He was loath to admit to anyone, even his family, that he was in bad straits. His letters home—which were rare because he could not afford stamps—never gave a hint of his hardships. If he ever made references to problems he always made light of them. Only when Sergei came home for the summer of 1903 and they saw how much weight he had lost did his sisters and grandmother realize how he had suffered.[17]

His studies were also difficult. Middle-level technical education was just beginning in Russia, and the Kazan Industrial School had been operating for only three years, so it had little experience in establishing a curriculum. The young students were overwhelmed by the amount of work—eight hours of classes every day, together with at least three hours of homework at night—and many could not handle it. Although he found the workload excessive, Sergei was not about to give up. In the words of one of his teachers: "The absence of family or close friends, the bad living conditions and the constant hunger might have suppressed all desire to learn in another student. But this was not so with Sergei. He was interested not only in his studies but also in expanding his horizons by reading literature. In conversation he displayed a sharp, critical mind."[18] As usual, Sergei excelled in school. By the second year, as reported in the local Kazan newspaper, he was ranked among the top eight out of 300 students. When he graduated in the spring of 1904, his diploma in mechanical engineering carried seven marks of five (the highest possible) and five marks of four.[19]

▪ POLITICAL AWAKENINGS

In the view of his sisters, the three years in Kazan were a milestone for Sergei: "In the late summer of 1901 a fifteen-year-old boy left Urzhum for Kazan. In June 1904 that boy returned from Kazan to Urzhum as the young man Sergei Kostrikov, a specialist in mechanics." As his grandmother observed proudly, "he stood now on his own feet."[20] But Sergei acquired more than a diploma in mechanical engineering during his time in Kazan. He also gained a political education.

This was a period of intense political ferment in Russia, culminating in the Revolution of 1905, when nationwide strikes and public protests threatened to bring down the regime of Tsar Nicholas II. Toward the end of the nineteenth century, the tremendous economic and social inequalities in Russia had given rise to widespread discontent among peasants and workers. The tsar's failure to institute reforms had also alienated him from the intelligentsia and liberal entrepreneurial classes. As a result of the deepening gulf between the population and the conservative autocracy, terrorism and violence were reaching alarming proportions. A sense of crisis was brewing by the time Sergei arrived in Kazan in 1901.

The radical unrest had deep roots, extending back to the 1860s, when Tsar Alexander II had initiated his Great Reforms, which abolished serfdom. Dissatisfied with the failure of the reforms to improve the lot of Russian peasants, young members of the intelligentsia started a populist movement, the goal of which was a socialist revolution. By the late 1870s the movement had bred terrorists, who assassinated the "reforming tsar" Alexander II in St. Petersburg in 1881. The monarchy reacted by clamping down on liberal reforms, thereby fueling even more radicalism among its subjects. By the 1890s, in addition to the populists, who focused on the peasantry and called themselves Socialist Revolutionaries, a Marxist movement had sprung up in Russia, competing with the populists, while at the same time borrowing elements of their philosophy. In 1898 Russian Marxists, who called themselves Social Democrats, formed the Russian Social Democratic Labor Party (known by the Russian acronym RSDRP), which, under the leadership of Vladimir Lenin, soon gained wide appeal among the radical Russian youth and factory workers.

Sergei had, of course, experienced firsthand the poverty and frustration of the downtrodden classes, so he was especially receptive to critics of the autocracy like the Social Democrats. His contacts with radical fellow students and his observations of the deplorable conditions and low wages at factories in Kazan increased his political awareness and sense of alienation from the tsarist regime. At home during summer vacations, Sergei fell under the influence of the numerous political exiles who were sent to Urzhum as punishment for their illegal activities. Together with his boyhood friend Sasha Samartsev, who was two years older and had also been away to study, Sergei became acquainted with the exiles, attending meetings of their underground discussion group and reading their revolutionary literature. He and Sasha even reproduced some of the exiles' illegal pamphlets on a makeshift hectograph and distributed them in Urzhum.[21]

Sergei returned to Kazan in the autumn of 1903 with the address of a student revolutionary in his pocket and joined an underground student discussion group. The members had no party affiliation and did nothing except meet and talk until November, when an explosive incident occurred. A student who belonged to the Kazan Committee of the Social Democratic Labor Party, or RSDRP, had been arrested and died of an illness contracted during police detention. His death galvanized students into action. On 14 November they organized a large demonstration, which had to be broken up by the police. Sergei, who attended the demonstration, barely escaped expulsion from school.

This incident was typical of what was happening among students all over Russia. As Richard Pipes points out in his history of the Russian Revolution, Russian institutions of higher learning had been the main source of opposition to the autocracy since the 1860s. As a result, even innocuous student activities drew the suspicious attention of the authorities, who cracked down on the slightest pretext, thus giving students more reason to protest and radicalizing them further. Pipes notes that the general university strike of 1899, an event brought on by a tactless and threatening warning to students at St. Petersburg University against organized activity, was the catalyst for mounting unrest in the early 1900s. By 1903 confrontations between students and police were becoming everyday occurrences, and students were often more interested in politics than in academics.[22]

At Sergei's school the students were especially radical, because they were from working-class or petty-bourgeois families and felt a sense of solidarity with each other, as well as with their teachers, who had similarly modest backgrounds. A week before the demonstration Sergei had run afoul of the school authorities when he and other students in his religion class refused to write a composition on why Christ was not recognized as the messiah by his contemporaries, and would not answer the questions posed by the teacher. The Academic Council of the institute considered expelling Sergei but, in view of his excellent academic record, decided to punish him with twelve hours in the *kartser* (detention room) instead.[23]

Although Sergei's experiences in Kazan had a profound effect on his political views and made him feel a strong allegiance with the revolutionary young people who opposed the monarchy, he was not ready to commit himself fully to their cause. His first priority was a personal one—he wanted to continue his studies. His diploma in mechanical engineering did not qualify him to enroll in a university or institute. He would first have to complete a two-year course of general study. At home in Urzhum during the summer of 1904, as he and Sasha Samartsev went on picnics, sang duets, recited the verses of Russian poets Nekrasov and Lermontov, and enjoyed the outdoors, Sergei mused over this problem. Sasha introduced him to Ivan Nikonov, who was a student at the Tomsk Technological Institute in Siberia. Nikonov told Sergei that if he pursued his two-year general course of studies in Tomsk, he could be admitted to the technological institute there. Sergei, much to his grandmother's dismay, decided on a move to Tomsk.[24]

▪ SIBERIA

Tomsk was in some ways similar to Urzhum. It had a large non-Russian population of Tatars and other Asian ethnic groups, and, as in Urzhum, herds of sheep and cattle filled the muddy streets. Tomsk was also a transit point for prisoners who had been sentenced to hard labor in Siberia. But, with a population of around 70,000, it was much bigger than Urzhum and, although it was far away from cities like Moscow and St. Petersburg, it was a center of political radicalism. From the moment he arrived Sergei faced a conflict between his academic ambitions and his political concerns. He had intended to enroll in evening classes as soon as possible, but, as it turned out, he did not even apply for the certificate of reliability necessary for enrollment until mid-December, four months after his arrival, and did not receive formal admission until February, by which time he had already been arrested for illegal political activities. In the meantime, however, he audited evening courses.[25]

Sergei moved in with Ivan Nikonov, his friend from Urzhum, and after about a month, during which he relied on funds given to him by his sister Anna, he found a job as a salesman for the Rossiia Insurance Company. Through a neighbor in a nearby flat Sergei met members of the RSDRP and was soon attending their illegal meetings. The Tomsk RSDRP committee, which was founded in 1901 as a subcommittee of the Siberian Social Democratic Union, based in Irkutsk, had lost most of its leaders because of arrests in the spring of 1904. Among those who stepped in to take over was G. I. Kramol'nikov, who arrived in Tomsk about the same time as Sergei and set up a Marxist study group, which Sergei attended. Later the group became a propaganda subcommittee of the Tomsk committee. Kramol'nikov, who was to be a prominent historian and professor in the Stalin period, became one of Sergei's mentors in the party committee, giving him responsibility for printing propaganda and for agitating the workers.[26]

Another patron in the Tomsk committee was Aleksandr Smirnov, who had set up the party's "fighting squad" (*boevaia druzhina*), a conspiratorial group that was preparing for the possibility of an armed uprising. Smirnov made use of Sergei's mechanical skills by putting him in charge of maintaining the arsenal. In November 1904 Sergei was officially admitted into membership in the RSDRP and given the party name Serzh.[27]

By this time, the RSDRP leadership had, at its second congress in Brussels in 1903, split into two separate wings because of disagreements over tactics and organization. The Bolsheviks, led by Lenin, favored a centralized, highly disciplined party organization composed of full-time revolutionaries working to overthrow the tsar. The Mensheviks, by contrast, favored a looser, more democratic party structure with less emphasis on conspiratorial, militant tactics and more on a gradualist approach to Marxism. At the time the disagreements between Lenin and the Menshevik leaders may not have seemed all that significant, but they reflected a difference in outlook and temperament that would become more profound as the Social Democratic movement developed. In the mind of Bolshevik leaders, Mensheviks became synonymous with "conciliators" and "liquidators," who opposed underground activities and wanted to restrict Social Democratic politics to what was legal. Eventually, after the Bolsheviks triumphed in 1917, Mensheviks would be branded as criminals.

Although they were members of what was a nationwide movement, Sergei and his colleagues were far removed from the political center of the Social Democratic Party, the leaders of which were living abroad. It is true that in July 1904 the Siberian Union declared itself in favor of the Bolsheviks, but the Siberian committees themselves, concerned with their day-to-day operations, did not pay much attention to the split. Sergei's associations with Kramol'nikov and Smirnov placed him among the more militant, leftist members of the Tomsk committee, so it is not surprising that he chose to adhere to the Bolshevik faction. But the Tomsk committee remained united, and Bolsheviks and Mensheviks worked together without the acrimony that characterized relations between the two factions at the top.[28]

If Sergei was still harboring plans to go to university, these plans were abandoned once and for all after the crisis of January–February 1905. The events began with Bloody Sunday on 9 January, when tsarist troops fired upon crowds of workers demonstrating in St. Petersburg. There were at least 200 casualties, and disorder spread throughout the city. Before this tragedy, which caused revulsion and indignation throughout the country, the revolutionary movement had been limited primarily to students and the intelligentsia, but now it became a mass phenomenon. The monarchy was under siege, and the country verged on civil war.

In Tomsk, Social Democrats seized the initiative, resolving to stage a demonstration at a political banquet organized by Tomsk liberals on 12 January. Led by Sergei, in his capacity as a member of the fighting squad, a group of 400 workers and students stormed into the banquet hall and disrupted the meeting. A Bolshevik member of the Siberian Social Democratic Committee gave a speech in which he called for armed rebellion to bring down the autocracy. Sergei and his comrades then spent the next several days planning a demonstration of workers and distributing weapons. On 18 January a group of 300 workers, students, and radicals, including Sergei, began marching in columns toward the center of the city, singing the "Marseillaise" and displaying banners that called for the overthrow of the tsar. When Cossack troops broke up the demonstration, Kirov's friend Iosif Kononov, the eighteen-year-old standard-bearer for the Social Democrats, was among those killed. This was a blow to Sergei, who had been in the thick of the fighting but managed to escape. When he found out from a local doctor where Kononov's body was, he went there in the middle of the night and retrieved from the pocket of the deceased the party's standard, drenched in blood.[29]

After a subsequent demonstration on the occasion of Kononov's funeral, a group of forty Social Democrats met on 2 February to plan yet another protest. Suddenly the police burst into their headquarters and arrested everyone, including Sergei. They later searched his flat, finding illegal literature and compromising correspondence, and arrested Sergei's roommate, Nikonov. According to the police report, Sergei refused to cooperate by talking to investigators and "during his incarceration was very rowdy, not following the orders of the prison authorities."[30] Nonetheless, because prosecutors were not able to establish a firm case against him, Sergei was released in early April.

Sergei had gone through his baptism of fire during these early months of 1905. He was now a revolutionary, dedicated to the overthrow of the tsar by any means necessary. After the experience of bloodshed and prison, the breach between him and the established order was complete. There seemed to be no turning back. As he later expressed it in a short autobiographical sketch, "from this moment my real revolutionary activity, soon to become professional, began."[31] Sergei's reaction was far from unique. All over Russia young people were coming to the conclusion that they had to join the cause of the revolution, becoming Social Democrats, Socialist Revolutionaries (who espoused terrorism), or simply anarchists. After Bloody Sunday, disillusionment with the tsar was such that radical groups were attracting youth in much greater numbers than were the liberals, who wanted gradual reform.

Upon his release from prison, Sergei found a job as a draftsman for the city administration—apparently they did not check on his background—but spent every free moment working on the party's underground printing press. The press reproduced articles from Lenin's paper in Geneva, *Vpered*, along with leaflets devoted to propaganda against the increasingly unpopular Russo-Japanese War. The leaflets, written in simple, emotive language and directed at soldiers, were distributed by the thousands all over Siberia.

By the summer of 1905 the militant Bolshevik wing of the party, to which Sergei adhered, no longer represented a majority in the Tomsk organization, and the Mensheviks predominated. This did not prevent Sergei from being elected in July 1905 to membership in the Tomsk RSDRP committee. Apparently the committee members valued his skills as a revolutionary enough to overlook differences over tactics and theory. As for Sergei, according to the memoirs of a comrade, Mikhail Popov, he was disappointed that the Bolsheviks had lost their decisive influence in the committee, particularly since it meant that the committee no longer endorsed the strategy of armed rebellion against the government.[32] But Sergei's desire to work for the party cause led him to minimize differences with the Mensheviks. Indeed, during the entire period up to 1917 Sergei would never again work in a Social Democratic committee where Bolsheviks predominated, but his open-mindedness was such that he was always able to have smooth relations with his Menshevik comrades. The only Menshevik who may have alienated Sergei was Leon Trotsky, a leader of the Siberian Social Democrats and a virulent critic of Lenin's policies. Sergei's opposition to Trotsky in later years, at first halfhearted but eventually vehement, may have been rooted in his Siberian experiences.[33]

In August 1905 the Social Democrats assigned Sergei the task of organizing a strike among railway employees at the Taiga station, where he was joined by his friend Mikhail Popov and another young party member. The Taiga station, which employed about a thousand men, was fertile ground for radical propaganda. Working and living conditions were deplorable, the hours were long, and the pay was low. Many of the employees were former soldiers who had returned from the Russo-Japanese War with reports about the ineptness of the Russian military leadership and demoralization within the ranks. Sergei and his comrades held a mass meeting at the depot, with Sergei as the speaker. It was his first experience as an orator, and it went exceptionally well. The workers appreciated his simple, direct style and his forceful presentation. They voted to declare a strike right away, but Sergei urged restraint. He wanted to lay a solid groundwork and make thorough preparations, so the workers would be motivated not just by hatred of the tsar but by a deeper understanding of their goals. Sergei worked day and night at Taiga, returning only occasionally to Tomsk, where he stayed with the mother of his deceased friend Kononov. Known simply as Serezhka to the workers, he always dressed neatly, with a double-breasted jacket and a scarf around his neck. He spoke simply, but with conviction. Soon he was a popular and respected figure at Taiga.[34]

▪ THE FIRST RUSSIAN REVOLUTION

By October 1905 a wave of strikes that had begun in Moscow and St. Petersburg was sweeping Russia. Once the railway workers joined in, the country was brought to a standstill. On 11 October workers at the Taiga station declared a strike, and the strike committee, under Sergei's direction, issued a list of demands to the railway administration. A few days later the committee confiscated arms from the railway police and seized control of the station. Even after the tsar was forced to issue his manifesto of 17 October, in which he committed himself to a constitution of sorts, the Bolsheviks at Taiga remained intransigent. Sergei told the workers that the manifesto was a deception on the part of the tsar, who wanted only to prevent them from resorting to armed rebellion.[35]

Despite the efforts of the Bolsheviks, however, the October Manifesto put an end to the general strikes in the major cities, as well as the strike at Taiga, and calmed much of the antitsarist unrest in the country. But the manifesto also unleashed a violent backlash from conservative, often anti-Semitic elements of society, angry over the tsar's concessions. When Sergei returned to Tomsk on 20 October he witnessed this violence firsthand. Armed gangs from the Black Hundreds—an extreme right-wing political movement that arose in the early 1900s—were roaming the city beating and killing Jews and anyone they associated with the radicals. In anticipation of the violence, the Bolsheviks had reconstituted their fighting detachment, recruiting and arming around seventy men, who then headed for the building of the Siberian Railway Administration for a meeting of workers, Social Democrats, and students. The building had been surrounded by Black Hundreds and Cossack troops, and a fiery battle ensued.

Inside were terrified employees, as well as railway workers and their wives, who had come to collect their pay.

At that point Sergei arrived from Taiga, armed with a revolver. According to one source, the fighting detachment was just about to surrender its weapons when Sergei persuaded the men to continue the battle. The Black Hundreds then threw burning wood into the building. People tried to escape the flames amidst the bullets of the Black Hundreds. Some began to jump out of a third-floor window. Eyewitness accounts have Sergei entering the building at great risk and shooting at the attackers as he helped people to escape. The building burned to the ground, and many of those inside perished. According to Tomsk newspapers, the death toll at the end of this day of violence was 300, with another 160 wounded or severely burned.[36]

Perhaps one reason why Soviet historians have downplayed this tragic incident is that militant Bolsheviks, including Sergei, contributed to the escalation of the violence in Tomsk by gathering arms and inciting workers to continue their rebellion after the issuance of the manifesto. To be sure, the Black Hundreds had initiated the conflict, and the Bolsheviks saw it as their job to fight the aggression. But in the end they made the situation worse.

The tragic result of their efforts did not deter Sergei and his fellow Bolsheviks, who became more determined than ever to bring down the autocracy through an armed struggle. Sergei began to work on restoring the fighting detachment and also on the Social Democrats' printing press. By January 1906 the tide of the revolution had turned. Siberia was under military law, and the Tomsk police were cracking down heavily on the Social Democrats, whose ranks were decimated by arrests. Sergei and Mikhail Popov had moved to a conspiratorial apartment on Nechaevskaia Street. When they returned home late one night police were conducting a search there, and they quickly fled, spending the night on the streets. Both of the Social Democrats' printing presses had been confiscated, so the committee decided to send Sergei to St. Petersburg and Moscow to purchase new printing equipment. On the eve of his departure, 30 January, he was arrested at the apartment of the treasurer of the Tomsk organization, and charged under article 126 of the Russian Criminal Code for possessing illegal literature with the intention of distributing it. When they searched Sergei's flat, the police had confiscated a substantial amount of subversive literature to support their charge, including Lenin's "Letter to a Comrade Concerning Our Organizational Tasks" (1902) and works by European socialists.[37]

It is a testimony to how much Sergei was valued by the Tomsk Social Democrats that they secured his release from prison on bail in April 1906. After organizing the escape of five comrades who had been arrested with him, Sergei began constructing a new printing press. He was determined that this time the police would not find the equipment, so he and his comrades spent arduous days and nights digging a deep recess for the press underneath the floor of a rented house. In mid-July 1906, just as the press was ready to operate, police raided the house and although they did not discover the equipment, they arrested Sergei along with Popov and three others. When Sergei's residence was searched the next month, the police again found compromising literature and correspondence.[38]

This time bail was out of the question, and Sergei spent almost two years in prison. He had been sentenced to three years, but the term was shortened because he was not yet twenty-one years of age. According to his cellmate, Popov, the prison regime for them, as "politicals," was fairly lax. They could receive books and newspapers from the outside, and he and Sergei even built (with the help of a dentist who procured the necessary chemicals from the prison pharmacy) their own printing press. They published an underground journal called, appropriately, *Prison* (*Tiurma*), which contained short articles on social and political subjects, poetry, and a chronicle of prison life. On the front page there was a notation: "The editorial office is open for personal discussions daily from after the first walk until the beginning of the second one. Manuscripts are accepted anytime."[39]

The journal was smuggled out of the prison and sold by university students to raise funds for political prisoners. A problem arose, however, when an assistant to the prison administrator who was taking courses at Tomsk University saw a copy of the journal and alerted his chief. A search was carried out in all the cells. Although the press, hidden in a lavatory underneath a brick stove, was not discovered, Sergei and his comrades had to cease publication.[40]

Later, when the prison administration attempted to "tighten up" the regime, the prisoners rioted. They took bricks from their stoves and threw them through doors and windows, compelling the warden to call in army troops. Sergei and Popov were then moved to a large communal cell, with over forty inmates. The always enterprising and indefatigable Sergei established a "constitution" for the cell, so that there would be some order among them, and started to conduct lessons in politics. The prisoners also produced several plays under Sergei's direction. At his suggestion, a small group of political prisoners began staying up all night to read Marx's *Das Kapital,* which required too much concentration to be read amidst the noise during the day. They would then sleep in the morning. Sergei was not happy with the two Russian translations that he had of Marx's work, so he started to teach himself German.[41]

When Popov and his comrades were released for lack of evidence after several months, Sergei moved into a cell by himself, which he jokingly called his "winter apartment," and threw himself into intensive reading and study. Taking advantage of the excellent prison library, he studied economics, philosophy, and belles lettres. Sergei's solitude was relieved by weekly visits from a young female student, who posed as Sergei's fiancée but was really an emissary from the local Social Democrats.[42]

When Sergei, at age twenty-two, was released from prison in June 1908, the monarchy was back on its feet. As promised by the October Manifesto, Russia now had a parliament, or Duma. But restrictions on suffrage eventually led to the Duma's domination by conservatives, and in any case the monarchy never granted the Duma real constitutional power. By 1908 counterrevolution was in full swing, and the police had driven the radicals underground. Bad news awaited Sergei upon his release. The Tomsk Social Democratic organization had fallen apart, and, after all his hard work, no one had been able to use the printing press because the house it was hidden in was occupied by strangers. The Kononovs, the family of Sergei's friend who had been killed in 1905, had letters for Sergei from his sisters, warning him not to return to Urzhum. The police had come to their home in July 1907 and, in the process of a search relating to Sergei's case, had ransacked the place. Melaniia Avdeevna had sat the entire time on a chest in the kitchen, crying and refusing to allow the police to open it. They took away all Sergei's letters. Worse still, Melaniia Avdeevna had fallen ill, and Elizaveta had been expelled from the Urzhum *gymnazium* (secondary school)—apparently in connection with Sergei's arrest—just before her final examinations. She could not find work, so they had to sell their house.[43]

Sergei's family had clearly suffered on account of his revolutionary activities, but he did not try to help them, probably because there was little he could do. Instead, he took their advice and stayed away from Urzhum. Sergei was too well known by the police in Tomsk to remain there either. He had spent almost four years in Tomsk—two and a half of which had been in prison—but in terms of revolutionary experience it must have seemed even longer. Sergei moved several hundred miles northwest to the district town of Novonikolaevsk, where he took charge of a local Social Democratic group. In order to keep the ubiquitous tsarist police off the track, he circulated a rumor in Tomsk that he was heading for the Far East. But the police soon caught up with him and were watching him closely in Novonikolaevsk. It was time to move on, this time to Irkutsk, about 750 miles southeast of Tomsk. On his way he wrote a postcard to Anna and Elizaveta, imploring them to write to him in care of general delivery, Irkutsk. He also informed them that he was in "splendid spirits."[44] Although he had no plans for the future, and the outlook for Social Democracy was grim, at least he was free.

Sergei arrived in Irkutsk in the autumn of 1908 and made contact with local Social Democrats. Their situation was unfortunate. A police crackdown had sent those who were not arrested into hiding, and they had no printing press. Sergei moved from place to place, living from hand to mouth and attending the occasional secret meeting. He did not stay long. In April 1909, just as the Social Democratic movement there was beginning to regain strength, Sergei heard that police in Tomsk had finally discovered the underground press. They had arrested Popov and other comrades and would soon be after Sergei. Before he left Irkutsk, Sergei obtained a passport under a new name, Sergei Mironov. (His middle name was Mironovich, son of Miron, following the Russian custom of the patronymic.[45])

▪ VLADIKAVKAZ

Since avoiding the police was foremost in his mind, Sergei chose a far-off destination—the city of Vladikavkaz in the mountains of the North Caucasus. The administrative center of the Terek region, Vladikavkaz was dominated by the Cossack aristocracy, tsarist military officers, bureaucrats, and merchants. There was little industry, aside from a few small factories, and the working-class population, which consisted of Russians, Armenians, Ossetians, Georgians, Ingushes, and Chechens, lived in squalor on the outskirts of the city.

Upon his arrival in Vladikavkaz in May 1909, Sergei sought out a Social Democratic friend whom he had earlier helped to escape from the Tomsk prison—Ivan Fedorovich Serebrennikov. Serebrennikov was living with a young dental surgeon from Tomsk, Nadezhda Germanovna Bliumberg, whom he later married. It was fairly typical for men and women from the radical intelligentsia in Russia to live together without marriage at this time. The rejection of the political regime went hand in hand with disregard for established social norms. Equality of the sexes, moreover, had been a fundamental tenet of all the radical groups since the 1860s. This meant in practice that men and women were comrades in the struggle for the liberation of the country from autocracy, sharing tasks as revolutionaries and sometimes sharing beds. When intimate relations developed they were often fleeting, because the cause of the revolution took precedence over personal feelings, and the underground was not conducive to long-term commitments. On the other hand, it was not uncommon for revolutionaries to enter into platonic, "Tolstoian" marriages. (Tolstoy wrote that lust was the root of all evil and advocated asceticism, although he himself did not adhere to it.)

Whatever the basis for their partnership, Serebrennikov and Nadezhda Germanovna gave Sergei a place to stay and befriended him. They also introduced him to the local Social Democrats and helped him to obtain employment with the regional newspaper, *Terek*. It is not clear how long Sergei lived with them before renting a room of his own, but it was long enough for Sergei to develop a close friendship with Nadezhda Germanovna. They corresponded and occasionally saw each other for over a decade. Although it is impossible to say for sure, Sergei's letters to her suggest that at one point their relations may have been intimate.

At the same time Sergei also became acquainted with the woman who was to become his wife—Mariia L'vovna Markus. The daughter of an impoverished Jewish watchmaker from the Caucasian region of Dagestan, Mariia L'vovna worked as a cashier and clerk at the offices of *Terek*. She was older than Sergei, probably by three or four years—her date of birth was never revealed—and, judging from her pictures, pretty and slightly plump. The eldest of four children, she completed only the first two classes of formal schooling before quitting to help support the family. Mariia L'vovna improved her reading and writing skills at home, and also learned how to play the piano, an accomplishment that Sergei greatly admired. After a series of minor jobs, she moved to Vladikavkaz and found employment at *Terek*. Although she was not a member of the Social Democratic Party, she had ties with members of the Bolshevik underground and in 1905 had acted as a liaison between the Central Committee abroad and the local party organization. She had also helped families of Bolsheviks who were imprisoned for underground activities. Both her sister Sof'ia L'vovna, who had completed *gymnazium* and was living in St. Petersburg, and her brother Iakov, who was a teacher, were Bolsheviks.

According to Sof'ia L'vovna, her sister was "a serious, thoughtful and industrious girl, who had lived through a great deal for her years."[46] Sergei had also been through a lot in his twenty-three years and he doubtless found in Mariia L'vovna a kindred spirit. The date of their marriage is uncertain. According to one Soviet source, it took place in the spring of 1912, against the wishes of Mariia's parents, who, as Jews, objected to her marrying a Russian. In any case, by 1910, less than a year after Sergei's arrival in Vladikavkaz, they were living together in a small, two-room flat.

As attested to by the intimate and intense correspondence that they maintained when Sergei was imprisoned and when they were otherwise separated, Sergei and Mariia were deeply in love, at least in the early years of their marriage. Yet, while mixed marriages between Russians and Jews were not uncommon among radicals and revolutionaries, the Kirovs' marriage went against the grain of both their backgrounds. If she was at all typical of her social and ethnic group, Mariia L'vovna would have been raised in a strict patriarchal family, where disobeying her parents and marrying a non-Jew was an act of extreme rebellion. As for Sergei, he had no family to answer to, but he was the product of intensive exposure to conservative Russian Orthodoxy, a religion which, in stressing great Russian nationalism, was not friendly to Jews. Like most Bolsheviks, Sergei doubtless discarded Russian Orthodoxy when he accepted Marxism. But in marrying a Jew he also demonstrated that any latent prejudices instilled in him as a result of his religious upbringing had been discarded as well.

Although love propelled them to overcome these obstacles, their radical politics also played a role in their union. Indeed, Sof'ia L'vovna's portrayal of the relationship between Sergei and her sister was one of shared ideals and revolutionary commitments rather than passion: "Sergei Mironovich became friends with Mariia L'vovna precisely because she was close to him spiritually and ideologically. She followed his work and helped him. She considered various revolutionary parties and then went with the Bolsheviks."[47]

One gains the same impression from Mariia L'vovna's own brief recollections about Sergei, written shortly after his death and entitled "In Memory of a Dear Friend and Comrade." She began by observing: "The name of Sergei Mironovich in my life is closely linked to his tireless revolutionary work. The personal life of S. M. Kirov was always subordinated to the revolutionary cause," and followed with a description of a man devoted to Lenin and Bolshevism. She recalled how, when her sister Sof'ia came to visit in 1910, Sof'ia and Sergei stayed up all night talking about party affairs. "This," she said, "showed one of Sergei Mironovich's characteristic traits. He became acquainted with my sister not as he would with a relative, but as with a revolutionary."[48]

Of course, Mariia L'vovna was writing at the height of the Stalin period and her words were for public consumption, despite the fact that they were never published. So it is not surprising that she would focus on her husband's qualities as a Bolshevik rather than as a mate. But the absence of even the slightest reference to their personal feelings toward one another suggests that their union might have evolved eventually into a marriage similar to that of Lenin and Nadezhda Krupskaia, whose main role was that of a loyal helpmate to her husband. The fact that Mariia was older and that the Kirovs, like Lenin and Krupskaia, remained childless reinforces this impression. Kirov may also have permitted himself the occasional extramarital affair (as, perhaps, with Nadezhda Serebrennikova). Whatever the truth about their level of intimacy, the Kirovs' devotion to each other appears to have remained strong until the end.

▪ FROM REVOLUTIONARY TO JOURNALIST

Despite his dedication to the revolutionary cause, Sergei found little opportunity to further his political goals in Vladikavkaz. A police crackdown had decimated the revolutionary ranks in the city, and even underground propaganda circles did not exist. Sergei turned his energies to journalism, a calling for which he displayed considerable talent. After being hired initially at *Terek* as a proofreader, Sergei soon advanced to the job of reporter on political and economic affairs. Later he was promoted to "literary contributor" and by 1915 he was a senior editor. The newspaper, which had a distinctly liberal bent, had a circulation of about 10,000. Although tsarist censorship was especially severe during this period, the publisher and proprietor of the paper, Sergei Iosifovich Kazarov, allowed the contributors considerable latitude, even when they wrote critically about tsarist politics and social conditions.[49]

The Bolshevik leadership categorically forbade party members from using the legal "bourgeois" press to debate party issues. On the other hand, it was not a violation of party ethics for Bolsheviks to publish articles in the legal press for propaganda purposes, which is essentially what Sergei did. Lenin himself in 1909 had urged party members to spread revolutionary ideas by any means possible, legal or illegal. The Bolsheviks' decision to participate in the Third Russian Duma, convened in 1907, was just such an example of the use of bourgeois institutions for revolutionary purposes. Nonetheless, the fact that Sergei wrote for *Terek* on a regular basis, and eventually became an editor, made his journalistic activities questionable from the Bolshevik point of view. Indeed, his work on *Terek* was to come back to haunt him years later, when his political opponents would accuse him of collaboration with the bourgeoisie.[50]

Sergei's rather constrained revolutionary activities during his first years in the North Caucasus offered these detractors further grounds for questioning his Bolshevik credentials. Conditions in the city of Vladikavkaz and in the Terek region as a whole were not favorable to the growth of Social Democracy, mainly because the population was overwhelmingly rural, with the proletariat only a small minority. When Sergei arrived in 1909, "there was no organization whatsoever. There were only individual comrades."[51] He set to work trying to revive the Bolshevik organization suppressed in 1906–8 and creating a network of contacts to build up an infrastructure for their activities. He also began teaching mechanics, technical drawing, political economy, and the Russian language to groups of workers and organized free theatrical performances for them. But his efforts at fomenting revolution were on a much smaller scale than in Tomsk. Only fifteen people were present at the first *massovka* (mass meeting) that he organized in the autumn of 1910.[52]

Being forced to concentrate more on his work as a journalist than on that as a revolutionary suited Sergei well. He enjoyed the fact that he was now a bona fide member of the Russian intelligentsia and realized that by shaping public opinion he could be just as important to the revolutionary cause as he had been leading an underground organization. His writing was prolific, to say the least: according to one Soviet biographer, he contributed, under a variety of pseudonyms, more than 3,000 articles, reviews, commentaries, and other materials to *Terek* during the period from 1909 to October 1917.[53]

Because only a few of these writings have been preserved in full, we are forced to rely on the extracts that have appeared in Soviet accounts. As might be expected, these sources are at pains to portray Sergei as an orthodox Bolshevik during his period in Vladikavkaz and thus provide examples that reinforce this image. In fact, Sergei was working under conditions of strict censorship, and his writings did not display revolutionary inclinations. They were limited to critical analyses of the political, economic, and social situation in Russia.

Although he was to become a sharp and incisive critic of the tsarist regime, Sergei got off to a cautious start. His first article, written under the pseudonym "Terets" and entitled "On a New Way," appeared on 29 August 1909. He discussed the ongoing construction of a railway and, in reminding readers of what had to be done to ensure its success, stressed the need for public initiative. In further articles Sergei focused on problems such as the low living standards of the local working class, drunkenness, and the lack of educational opportunities for the population. He also touched upon international subjects, with an article called "Crisis in the English Parliament." Similar themes appeared in his writings in 1910–11, along with discussions of the agrarian question, the problem of national minorities in the Russian empire, and the Russian Duma. For all of these articles, Sergei did background research, using extensive facts and figures to buttress his points. Although he refrained from mentioning the Social Democrats, Sergei borrowed ideas and subjects from the Bolshevik press and used a Marxian approach to analyzing Russia's economic problems.[54]

In his literary criticism Sergei demonstrated not only the wide breadth of his knowledge of literature and philosophy but also his disdain for the tsarist bureaucracy. Writing in 1911 to commemorate the hundredth anniversary of the birth of the celebrated Russian literary critic Vissarion Belinskii, he characterized the era in which Belinskii wrote as follows:

> The heavy stamp of bureaucracy, recognized as the alpha and omega of the state's wisdom, lay everywhere. . . . There could be no mention of public opinion in that epoch. Social, literary, artistic, and scientific

activity was subjected to strict bureaucratic tutelage and anything that did "not accord with the values of the government, or with the existing order," was relentlessly banished.[55]

It is ironic that twenty years later this passage would aptly describe the censorship introduced by the Stalinist regime, in which Sergei had a key role. But in 1911, as a writer subjected to censorship, Sergei placed a high value on intellectual freedom and viewed constraints on literary expression as a sign of Russia's backwardness. In fact, his intellectual views seemed more in tune with those expressed by the Russian liberals or the Mensheviks than with those of the Bolsheviks, whose authoritarianism and intolerance for other opinions were characteristic traits. Sergei admired Belinskii because he was a freethinker and a so-called Westernizer, who believed that Russia should look to Western Europe as a model for its development. Although Sergei still thought of himself as a Marxist and a Bolshevik, he was clearly open to broader intellectual currents.

He was also open to adventure. Not long after he arrived in Vladikavkaz, Sergei took up mountain climbing. He joined a climbing club and soon developed into an avid mountaineer, making expeditions that provided him with material for his articles in *Terek*. In September 1910 he described an expedition he made to the top of Mount Kazbek, a formidable peak in the Georgian Caucasus. It was an arduous climb, through snow, heavy winds, and oxygen-deprived air, and at least one member of the group turned back. When they finally reached the top it was a thrilling moment for Sergei: "It is impossible to describe the grandeur that unfolds from up there. You want to fall on the snow and kiss it from the joy that envelops you in seeing the magnificent richness of nature and the boundlessness of its majesty. . . . What space! What captivating beauty in all these snow-covered peaks, mightily rising toward heaven! What a variety of colors and tones in the rocky cliffs of the endless chain of mountains, disappearing somewhere far in the distance."[56]

Sergei was in his element—literally on top of the world. He thrived on outdoor adventures and the thrill of physical challenges. Even in his later life, when he no longer had the opportunity to mountain-climb, he would always seek out every opportunity to experience the wilds of nature with comrades.

▪ SERGEI BECOMES KIROV

Vladikavkaz, which Sergei had initially considered a temporary refuge from the police, had become his home, a place where unexpected opportunities had unfolded before him. He was thriving in his new career as a journalist. He was one of *Terek's* most popular writers and was highly respected by his colleagues. According to a former contributor to the paper, "the issues with articles by Kirov sold like hotcakes, they made a tremendous impression."[57] He had forged a relationship with the woman who was to become his wife. And he had experienced the joy and adventure of climbing some of the world's most spectacular mountains. But the heavy yoke of Nicholas II's authoritarian regime again clamped down upon Sergei. On 31 August 1911, just a month after he and a friend had triumphantly reached the summit of Mount Elbrus, he was arrested in Vladikavkaz for his earlier role in running the underground printing press in Tomsk.

Sergei's arrest sent shock waves throughout the editorial offices at *Terek*. Two of his colleagues and fellow mountaineers, who had already been in trouble with the police for radical underground activity, fled Vladikavkaz. The editors imposed a regime of self-censorship on the paper as a precaution against further reprisals. In a letter written to Mariia L'vovna from his prison cell, Sergei expressed his dismay at their reaction: "I did not expect that my arrest would cause such a panic among the editors. Am I really so terrible a figure? The clowns! So now *Terek* appears without leading articles. This is awful. But never fear. Don't make any suggestions and don't jump to any conclusions. Let's just wait and see."[58]

Sergei spent three weeks in a Vladikavkaz prison and then was transferred to Tomsk to await trial. Despite the fact that he had already survived one prison ordeal, Sergei found his second incarceration difficult to bear. He missed Mariia L'vovna, who was able to visit him only once before he left for Tomsk. In one of his letters to her he confided: "You cannot imagine how touched I am by your concerns about me. I have never been in this position in my life. . . . If anyone had been watching us it would have appeared that you were in prison rather than me." He implored her not to worry about him: "Serozhka is a strong fellow, he can endure anything, whatever injustice befalls him."[59]

Nonetheless he soon found his confinement intolerable. Frustration resonated in his soulful and philosophical letters to Mariia L'vovna. "Dear Marusia," he wrote at the end of September:

Today it will be exactly a month since I was taken out of circulation. Thirty days! In comparison with eternity this is an imperceptibly small amount; in comparison with a man's life, it is hardly appreciable. But it seems to me like eternity. If it were not for your letters, I don't know how I would pass the time. The boring day often ends with a holiday, when in the silence your letter arrives. I read it once, reread it, and it seems like I am talking with you directly.[60]

For Sergei time was no longer a valuable commodity but a curse:

How nice it would be to live in freedom! At times you begin to understand a person who, because of one moment that can thrill him, can fill his entire soul and heart, his thoughts, his whole being, he can sacrifice even his life. Indeed. People face a dilemma: either a gray, like autumn, monotonous to the point of nausea, long, endlessly boring life and an equally unnoticed, unnecessary and senseless death; or a bright, like the first light of the rising sun, lovely, divinely brilliant, full life of trepidation and of delight for a single moment and only a moment, after which, like a finale, death. I would prefer the latter.[61]

After the arduous trip in a prisoners' convoy to Tomsk, Sergei was placed in a cell by himself. He was desperate for communication with the outside world. In a November 1912 letter to Nadezhda Serebrennikova, he talked about his loneliness and chastised her for not answering his letters: "I asked you to write but you for some reason don't." In a postscript he added that he had just received a letter from her: "I was overjoyed. I had thought that you had forgotten me. Thank you, many thanks. From today onward I will be completely alone both spiritually and physically. So please write often."[62]

Alone with his thoughts, Sergei began to question his calling as a writer and a journalist. He wrote to Mariia L'vovna that same month: "It is strange: it is a long time since I have written to you and there is nothing to say. Once you used to say that I am a 'writing man.' Take your words back as wrongly addressed."[63] In February 1912, he observed to her: "You know, the saving virtue of all dilettantes is that they fulfill the role of a gramophone: they are alive when something is singing in them. Dilettantes cannot perform their own arias. But many of us have a large supply of records, sung by others. Such dilettantes are called 'talented.' Substitute the word 'journalist' for 'dilettante' and you will understand my tragic situation: all my records are used up and broken." And in another letter: "It is very difficult to start writing! What to write? That is the question that torments me no less than the Danish prince was tormented by the question of whether to act or just to be indignant."[64]

At this point Sergei thought of himself as a writer rather than a professional revolutionary, and his main concern was his lack of inspiration. Resourceful as always, he did in fact find subject matter to write about in his observations of prison life. Some of these observations, including the earlier-mentioned description of an execution, he imparted to Mariia L'vovna in letters. He also began a more ambitious project, a group of literary sketches, which he planned to publish as a book. Some forty pages of this manuscript, existing in his personal archives, portray the tragic fate of individual prisoners, the grim reality of life behind bars, and the harrowing details of executions.[65]

Before Sergei could finish the manuscript, his prison confinement came to an end. On 15 March 1912, the day after his twenty-sixth birthday, the fifth such occasion that he had spent in prison, Sergei was released. The next day he faced trial in Tomsk, defended by a lawyer named Noi Levin, who had successfully defended other Tomsk Social Democrats. According to Levin, Sergei denied to the judge that he was Sergei Kostrikov, who had been arrested in 1906 and charged with operating an illegal printing press. When the officer who arrested him six years earlier failed to recognize Sergei, the judge had no choice but to dismiss the charges for lack of evidence.[66]

Sergei left Tomsk immediately and headed for the town of Cheliabinsk to visit his old friend Mikhail Popov. He then proceeded to Moscow, with the intention of finding work there as a journalist. He apparently thought that the police would be on his trail if he returned to Vladikavkaz, but, more importantly, he felt that Moscow would offer better opportunities for his journalistic career and intellectual interests.

Once he arrived, he was overwhelmed with how much the city had to offer culturally and intellectually. He wrote to Popov from Moscow: "The impression is such that . . . it is essential to move here, especially for me, considering my profession." Unfortunately, however, his hopes of finding a job had been dispelled: "But alas! It is not easy or simple to achieve this harmless goal. I was in the literary-artistic circle. I saw almost the entire school of writers and journalists. They all gave me the same answer: here it is difficult to find something. There are too many of your colleagues."[67]

Sergei expressed his bitter disappointment in a letter to Nadezhda Serebrennikova: "Ahead lies 'Terek' with all its dregs and mud. Can it really be that it is closing in on me and my dream of Moscow did not become a reality?"[68] He apparently felt that he had no choice but to return to Vladikavkaz, where he was sure of gainful employment. He had been in Moscow only a little over a week, but that was enough to convince him that he would not be able to make a career for himself there. This was a blow, given how successful his journalistic endeavors had been in Vladikavkaz. But Vladikavkaz was provincial compared to Moscow, where the circle of journalists and writers that Sergei aspired to was much more sophisticated than any he had encountered.

Significantly, it was precisely at this low point in his career that Sergei adopted the name that he would go by for the rest of his life—Kirov. In order to conceal his identity when he wrote, he needed a new nom de plume. After returning to Vladikavkaz, he happened to see the name Kir on a calendar of saints' names and it brought to mind the Persian warrior-king Kir he had read about in his childhood.[69] So Sergei Kostrikov became Sergei Kirov, named after a saint and warrior. This name change appropriately marked the beginning of a new phase in his career, when his writings would become more radical and he would turn his attention back to Social Democracy and the revolutionary cause.

3

The Triumph of Bolshevism

Men are in general *divided by a law of nature into two categories, inferior (ordinary), that is, so to say, material that serves only to reproduce its kind, and men who have the gift or the talent to utter* a new word. . . . *The second category all transgress the law; they are destroyers or disposed to destruction according to their capacities. The crimes of these men are of course relative and varied; for the most part they seek in very varied ways the destruction of the present for the sake of the better. But if such a one is forced for the sake of his idea to step over a corpse or wade through blood, he can, I maintain, find within himself, in his conscience, a sanction for wading through blood.*

—*Raskolnikov in Dostoevsky's* Crime and Punishment

B y the time Kirov had made his reluctant way back to Vladikavkaz in the spring of 1912, the Russian revolutionary movement was beginning to revive. Reacting to the April shooting by tsarist troops of several hundred strikers at the gold mines of Lena in Siberia, Russian workers protested with widespread strikes, which were to continue sporadically until the outbreak of World War I in 1914. The substantial economic progress that Russia had achieved since 1905 was not enough to quell labor unrest. By 1914 Russia had become the fifth-ranking industrial power in the world, and its economic growth rate was one of the highest, but in terms of per capita production it still ranked low in comparison with the West. Russia's governmental and social structures remained fragile, and it retained many characteristics of a feudal society, with no significant middle class. The experiment with a quasi-constitutional government had not succeeded in resolving the intense societal conflicts among the 170 million inhabitants of the Russian empire. Over 80 percent of the population were poor peasants, and Russia's vast territories included many non-Russian peoples, who resented Russian domination.

Had it not been for the outbreak of the war, which disorganized Russia's already weak political structures and exposed its economic and military unpreparedness, Russia might possibly have overcome its problems and gradually evolved into a liberal constitutional monarchy. But the strain of military conflict caused popular unrest to mount. Rising food prices and fuel shortages led to strikes in urban areas. Military reversals and the incompetence of the army command, taken over personally by Tsar Nicholas II in 1915, created disaffection among the largely peasant army, and desertions became widespread. By 1917, as shortages became more acute, the monarchy would lose all its credibility, leaving Russia ripe for revolution.

Russia's problems during this period were grist for the mill of the Social Democrats, whose leaders remained abroad, planning their revolutionary strategies and engaging in intense theoretical debates. At the Prague Conference of Social Democrats in early 1912, Lenin's Bolshevik faction had made its final break with the Mensheviks and formed itself as a separate party. The Bolsheviks' Central Committee included two new members—Stalin and Ordzhonikidze, both of whom had served on the Social Democratic committee in Baku, Azerbaijan, a stronghold of radicalism and worker unrest. Neither Stalin nor Ordzhonikidze was particularly prominent, but Lenin wanted to include in the Central Committee practical underground workers who could implement the Bolsheviks' agenda in Russia.

Stalin and Ordzhonikidze, who would be the two most important figures in Kirov's career as a Bolshevik leader, were both Georgians and had been friends since the early 1900s, when they met in Tbilisi. Ordzhonikidze, or Sergo, as he was known in radical circles, was born in the same year as Kirov, 1886, to parents of the petty nobility. He studied to be a doctor's assistant, but abandoned this career in order to become a full-time revolutionary. Stalin's background was more modest. Seven years Sergo's senior, Stalin (born Djugashvili) was the son of a poor shoemaker and former serf, who, like Kirov's father, was prone to drunkenness and beat both Stalin and his mother. He left the family for good while Stalin was still a young boy. Thanks to the perseverance of his mother and to his abilities as a student, Stalin gained an elementary and middle education in his native town of Gori in Georgia and was then able to attend the Theological Seminary in Tbilisi for four and a half years. The seminary, a breeding ground for radicalism, was where Stalin first became exposed to radical ideas.[1]

As his biographer Isaac Deutscher pointed out, Stalin was one of the few leaders of the 1917 Revolution who did not come from the intelligentsia, the gentry, or the middle class. Like Kirov, he had been born a member of the oppressed masses in whose name the Bolsheviks were attempting a revolution. Lenin and other radicals from the more privileged classes, such as Lev Kamenev, Grigorii Zinoviev, and Nikolai Bukharin, joined the revolutionary struggle in large part because of a moral impera- tive. Talented enough to have had successful professional careers else- where, they had no reason to feel inadequate or socially inferior. Not all were brilliant theoreticians like Bukharin or Trotsky (who was initially a Menshevik and joined the Bolsheviks in 1917). But they brought with them to the radical movement inherited cultural traditions and values, along with intellectual refinement. As for Stalin:

> These were precisely the qualities that life had not been kind enough to cultivate in Djugashvili. . . . Young Djugashvili had plenty of acumen and common sense; but imagination and originality were not his charac- teristics. He could lecture coherently on socialism to small circles of workers; but he was no orator. Nor, as time was to show, was he a brilliant writer. . . . Circumstances inevitably bred in him a certain sense of inferi- ority, of which he would not rid himself even in the Socialist under- ground.[2]

Kirov was of course much closer in background to Stalin than to the other Bolshevik luminaries, who had experienced the evils of the tsarist system only at a distance. But there was a difference. Stalin's parents had been born serfs and never managed to raise themselves above the status of illiterate peasants. Kirov's parents, though equally impoverished, belonged to the ranks of the lower middle class. Both could read and write, and Kirov's sister Elizaveta had even attended *gymnazium*. To be sure, Kirov was ashamed of his poverty when he was a student in Kazan, and his brief experience of trying to find a job as a journalist in Moscow made him real- ize that his limited education and intellectual background placed him on the fringe of the Russian intelligentsia. But Kirov did not have the sense of social inferiority that Stalin seems to have had, and he was able to rise above the parochialism of his upbringing and strive to broaden his intellectual horizons with a certain amount of confidence. It was this con- fidence, doubtless encouraged by mentors like his teacher Iulia Konstanti- novna, that allowed him to develop into a talented writer and orator.

▪ TEREK BEFORE THE REVOLUTION

The Terek region of the North Caucasus, where Vladikavkaz was located, had been conquered by the Russians in the first half of the nineteenth century after long and bloody conflicts. Its population of around 1,200,000 in 1912 was heterogeneous, including Russian Cossacks, who had originally inhabited the region as military guards for the tsar and had gained over the centuries a privileged social status and an abundance of land; and those who had arrived more recently from Russia, the so-called *inogorodnye*. There were also the native mountain peoples—Chechens, Ossetians, Ingushes, Kabardians, and others—who had no ethnic or cultural unity and were isolated from one another by the mountain ranges. Although they shared a common resentment toward the monarchy and the Russian Cossacks, their ethnic diversity and competition for land made efforts to unite them politically difficult. In short, the economic and cultural situation in Terek—as in other regions of the North Caucasus—presented a tremendous challenge to Russian radicals who sought to channel the social ferment into a concrete movement.[3]

These difficulties may help to explain why Kirov continued to devote most of his energy to journalism upon his return to Vladikavkaz in 1912. Given that he had just been through a second term of imprisonment, he might have been expected to be cautious in his writing for *Terek*. In fact, Kirov's articles reflected a new boldness, which soon drew the attention of tsarist censors. One article, entitled "Simple Manners" (*Prostota nravov*), got him into serious trouble. Kirov castigated the Fourth Duma, elected in September 1912, for presenting itself as an institution representative of the population. In reality, he wrote, the deputies were reactionary "buffoons" with no ties to the people: "they swing in the direction that the political wind is blowing."[4] Kirov was referring to the fact that an electoral law passed in 1907 had severely restricted suffrage so that the majority of deputies would be conservative landowners and bureaucrats loyal to the tsar. In early January 1913, because of this article, judicial proceedings were instituted against Kirov and the publisher of *Terek* for "arousing hostility on the part of the population towards the highest popular assembly of the empire."[5]

The proceedings were dropped in February 1913 as a result of a general amnesty granted by Nicholas II to commemorate the 300th anniversary of the Romanov dynasty. But the publisher was fined repeatedly for printing Kirov's articles. Kirov's sharp criticism of Vladikavkaz's governmental administration in an article entitled "Still a Panama" aroused "strong indignation" on the part of city officials and led to a fine of 100 rubles in November 1912. A fine of 200 rubles was imposed the next month for two pieces about the exploitation of the working class. Further fines came in January 1913 because of Kirov's writings, and the paper was threatened with closure.[6]

None of this deterred Kirov, who continued to focus on the serious failings of the tsarist regime, discussing everything from the educational system to Russia's backward economic state. As usual, he read assiduously to keep himself informed, spending more on books than his modest income could afford. In October 1912, he wrote to Mariia L'vovna, who was visiting her family in Derbent (about 200 miles southeast of Vladikavkaz, on the Caspian Sea). After chiding her for not writing—"I was so naive as to expect a letter today. I absolutely forgot that you are now on the banks of the wide Caspian, and under these conditions there is no place for writing letters"—he reported that he was in debt to a publisher for a history book and was "very worried" about it. He went on: "Maybe you would like to know what I am doing? I have a very useful occupation: I am reading. I must be up to date concerning the Balkans. Just as before, I don't go out. (How frugal I am!) . . . In a day or two I will try to beg for a sum of money. These office bureaucrats just cannot realize that there is sometimes a crucial need of money."[7]

But the focus of Kirov's writing in these prerevolutionary years was not exclusively political. He also wrote about literature and social problems, not always adhering to a strictly Marxist approach. As one Western historian pointed out, Kirov at this time did not "display those traits of vindictive dogmatism which are considered to have been the professional deformation of the Bolshevik conspirator, and which form part of the 'Stalinist' stereotype, but who, equally, is free of the doctrinaire and occasionally intransigent cast of mind which is observable in the case of Lenin."[8] Thus, for example, Kirov seemed to be arguing in favor of art for art's sake when he wrote in *Terek* on 1 August 1915: "I once knew an *esdeka* (Social Democrat), an inveterate Marxist, for whom even the migration of birds had to be viewed from the point of view of class interest, and who used to assert that ideas were best looked upon as paving stones."[9]

Although Kirov was preoccupied with journalism in the years before 1917, he did not neglect revolutionary activities entirely. On the contrary, he worked hard at reviving the local Social Democratic Party and establishing contacts with Social Democrats elsewhere in Russia. This proved a difficult task, given the remoteness of Vladikavkaz and the fact that it had such a small working-class population. Aside from Kirov, the Bolshevik organization in Vladikavkaz had only seven members in 1912–14, and by 1917 total membership had dropped to six, including Kirov's brother-in-law, Iakov Markus, who had arrived in Vladikavkaz in 1916.[10]

With the assistance of a comrade, Kirov set up a Marxist study group among workers at a lead factory. He spoke at several *massovki*, which were organized secretly out in the countryside, with the goal of drawing workers into the effort to overthrow the tsar. He also taught at "Sunday Schools," special courses set up for workers, usually with members of the radical intelligentsia as their teachers, and he organized strikes among printing workers in Vladikavkaz. One such strike even took place at the press of *Terek* in February 1914.[11]

According to Soviet sources, Kirov established ties with Bolshevik organizations in the nearby cities of Groznyi and Mineral'nye Vody, which had much larger working-class elements. In August 1913 he helped to initiate a strike among oil workers in Groznyi, which lasted for almost a month and resulted in a victory for the workers. Kirov made periodic visits to Groznyi and Mineral'nye Vody to discuss strategies concerning the war and to exchange illegal literature with other Social Democrats. The Bolsheviks at this time were actively agitating against the war effort, and a good deal of their propaganda was directed toward soldiers heading for the Caucasian Front. Kirov himself had managed to avoid conscription, but it is not clear how. He had registered with the territorial reserve in Urzhum in 1907, and the Urzhum authorities apparently tracked him down in 1915, but nothing came of it.[12]

Meanwhile, Mariia L'vovna had been forced to leave Vladikavkaz in 1915, when, because of the war, the government there had ordered all Jews, Austrians, Germans, and Hungarians out of the city. She moved to Derbent to live with her family. As usual, Kirov found her absence difficult and grew impatient when he did not hear from her. In one letter he complained:

> The situation is such that your presence is essential. The most absurd thing is that I don't know your plans. Do you intend to go to Tiflis [Tbi-

lisi] to appeal to the vice-governor [presumably about returning to Vladikavkaz] or do you have another solution? It seems to me that you discussed this question with Iasha [her brother Iakov] and reached a decision. In the meantime, I hear nothing from you. In any case the question needs to be decided immediately. And, finally, write![13]

Left on his own, Kirov made frequent trips to the mountains, where his climbing expeditions brought him into contact with the mountain peoples of the North Caucasus and familiarized him with their customs and grievances. He soon came to recognize their revolutionary potential. There was considerable discontent among these peoples, especially among the Kabardian peasants of the Nal'chik district, where a new land law had deprived them of some of their traditional pasturelands. In the spring of 1913 they staged an insurrection, which had to be suppressed by government forces. Kirov, dressed in alpine clothes, visited several of the peasant villages during the uprising and afterward made contact with the participants. In particular, he met Betal Kalmykov, a young herdsman and a leader of the revolt, who later created a movement that supported the Bolsheviks in 1918.[14]

Kirov's understanding of the importance of drawing the mountain peasants into the struggle against the monarchy was to be a key element in the establishment of a Soviet republic in the Terek region in 1918. He realized that ethnic nationalism was a strong source of opposition that could be tapped by the Social Democrats in arousing the mountain peoples to revolt. It is possible that Kirov was influenced by Lenin's 1913 publication "Critical Remarks on the Nationality Question," which maintained that Social Democrats should provide limited support for "bourgeois nationalism" in its fight against oppressors of other nationalities. But Kirov had already shown an interest in the nationalist sentiments expressed by representatives of the intelligentsia from some of these non-Russian peoples. He enjoyed the poems and essays of Ossetian and Chechen writers and published translations of them in *Terek*. These nationalist writers gave the Bolsheviks their support in 1917–18.[15]

The Bolsheviks in the Terek region had few links with their comrades in Moscow and St. Petersburg (renamed Petrograd at the outbreak of World War I to Russianize the Germanic name), aside from the fact that they used Social Democratic literature from the center. Kirov is said to have been in contact with party organizations in Baku and Tbilisi and he also visited his old comrade Mikhail Popov in Rostov-on-Don, but the Terek Bolsheviks acted primarily on their own initiative. Of course, the bulk of the Bolshevik leadership, including Lenin, was still abroad, or, as in the case of Stalin and Ordzhonikidze, exiled in Siberia. Although Lenin was following events in Russia and in the Caucasus, it is doubtful that Kirov's name was familiar to him at this point.

In the North Caucasus, however, Kirov was gaining renown as a radical journalist. During 1915–16 his antiwar rhetoric became increasingly strident. As Kirov stressed in his articles, the war was bringing great hardship to the Terek region, as to other parts of the Russian empire. Industrial production had almost ground to a halt, and prices had risen by over 400 percent. "Hunger rebellions" (*golodnye bunty*) and strikes spread to the Terek region in 1916. Kirov met with striking workers in April of that year and published their demands in *Terek*. The mountain peasants of Ossetia, Chechnia, and Kabardia also rose up in protest against the monarchy and the war. In May 1916, Kirov wrote about the coming revolution in Russia, which he said was inevitable because of the continuous defeats of tsarist forces, the colossal losses at the front, and the universal indignation and disgust with the monarchy. Nine months later the first phase of that revolution occurred.[16]

▪ THE FEBRUARY REVOLUTION

Popular discontent with the monarchy, manifested by increasing labor unrest, reached alarming proportions by 1917. The disorders that set off the revolution began in Russia's capital, Petrograd, where unusually harsh winter weather had compounded transportation difficulties caused by the war and led to severe food and fuel shortages. When the temperature in Petrograd rose in late February 1917, the crowds took to the streets to protest. The tsar ordered troops into the city on 26 February, and for a time it appeared that order had been restored, but a mutiny in the 160,000-man Petrograd garrison, comprised mainly of peasant soldiers, brought the monarchy down, and power reverted to a Provisional Government formed by moderate progressives in the Duma. Socialist Duma deputies (Mensheviks and Socialist Revolutionaries, or SRs) and representatives of the trade unions meanwhile formed a Soviet (Council) of Workers' Deputies, which initially competed for power with the Provisional Government. During March soviets modeled after that of Petrograd emerged in cities all over Russia. By the spring of 1917, the Mensheviks and SRs decided to cooperate with the Provisional Government, joining its leadership in a coalition, with the SR Aleksandr Kerenskii at its head.

The Bolsheviks, by contrast, were determined to bring the Provisional Government down. Their leader, Lenin, who was said by Trotsky to be "raging like a caged animal" in Switzerland at the time, outlined Bolshevik policy in a telegram sent to Petrograd on 6 March: "Our tactics: complete mistrust, no support for the new government. We especially suspect Kerenskii. The arming of the proletariat provides the only guarantee. Immediate elections to the Petrograd Duma. No rapprochement with the other parties."[17] On his return to Russia in early April, Lenin elaborated his views further in his famous "April Theses," a statement of the Bolshevik program. In contrast to the Mensheviks, who believed, as Marx did, that Russia had to go through a prolonged "bourgeois-democratic" phase before the proletarian revolution could be accomplished, Lenin urged in his April Theses that there be an immediate transition to the second phase of the revolution. This novel interpretation of Marxism meant toppling the Provisional Government as soon as possible and transferring all power to the soviets, which the Bolsheviks would attempt to gain control of. According to Lenin, there also should be no question of reuniting with the Mensheviks.

In Vladikavkaz, as elsewhere in Russia, Lenin's policies were slow to take hold. News of the events in Petrograd reached Vladikavkaz in early March. On 5 March the Vladikavkaz City Duma met in an extraordinary session and set up a Civil Executive Committee to replace the tsarist administration. Similar committees were established in the other major towns in the Terek region. At the same time, however, representatives of the working class and the military garrisons set up soviets of workers' and soldiers' deputies. Bolsheviks represented only a small minority of delegates to the soviets, which were dominated by Mensheviks and Socialist Revolutionaries throughout the Terek region.[18]

According to the Bolshevik Elena Poliakova, she and her comrades in Vladikavkaz were at a loss as to what strategy to pursue. The sudden abdication of the tsar and establishment of a liberal government in Petrograd had caught them by surprise. Judging from an article that appeared in *Terek* on 5 March 1917, Kirov might have been surprised, but he was also elated: "What an astonishing paradox Russia has achieved! Within 24 hours an enslaved country of many millions, which represented an unlimited ground for tyranny and arbitrariness, where the city and land captains considered themselves absolute pharaohs, this country has suddenly become free. . . . World history knows of no such examples. Obviously, our motherland is indeed a country of unlimited possibilities."[19]

It is significant that Kirov actually addressed the session of the Vladikavkaz Duma that set up the "bourgeois" city government. Whereas his fellow Bolsheviks may have been hesitant about supporting the new government, Kirov was not. His willingness to appear at that forum and his subsequent commentaries in *Terek* leave no doubt that, unlike Lenin, he favored unconditional Bolshevik support for the Provisional Government and its local branches. He described the program of the new government as "more persuasive and majestic than anything that was ever written in the offices of the autocracy over centuries." Later he wrote that the old order had to be buried "as if it had never existed, and let the day of its funeral be a day for us of historical birth. This is precisely how our Provisional Government views it."[20] In subsequent articles he referred to the Provisional Government and its local organs as the "people's regime" and called for universal support for its policies.[21]

As his Soviet biographers acknowledged, Kirov's stance was a clear deviation from Leninism. But then, even Stalin had initially favored support of the Provisional Government, as well as cooperation with the Petrograd soviet, dominated by Mensheviks and Socialist Revolutionaries. Although Stalin soon accepted Lenin's views, other Bolshevik leaders in Petrograd, Zinoviev and Kamenev in particular, continued to disagree with Lenin's demand for an immediate socialist revolution. Lenin's views eventually prevailed in Petrograd, but the party's rank and file was slower to fall in line, especially on the sanction against cooperation with the Mensheviks. As late as September–October 1917 twenty-eight regional party committees remained joint Bolshevik-Menshevik organizations.[22]

The Vladikavkaz Social Democratic Committee, which did not split until October 1917 (and perhaps even later), was one of them. Kirov's decision, which his Bolshevik comrades accepted, to ignore Lenin's demands to stop cooperating with the Mensheviks and the Provisional Government was determined by several considerations. Although a committed Marxist, Kirov was acutely aware of the inexperience of the Russian people at self-government and of their need to get used to their new freedom and to prepare themselves adequately for the transition to socialism. Like the Mensheviks, he did not think it expedient to rush the revolutionary process. Thus, he wrote on 8 March: "The main problem is to adjust to freedom, to learn how it can be utilized more effectively. . . . The bureaucracy thought that the secret of governing the country belonged to it alone. Our task is to prove that the bureaucracy was wrong, that democracy is the true, the most perfect form of government."[23]

Another consideration for Kirov and his comrades was the numerical weakness of the Social Democrats in Terek, where over 90 percent of the population was employed in agriculture. Under such conditions they could ill afford to engage in factional strife. Also, in all the towns and cities except Groznyi, which had a substantial proletariat because of the oil industry, the Mensheviks predominated among Social Democrats. Thus it is understandable that Kirov would encourage cooperation with them. On 9 March he wrote in *Terek*: "Comrades, the time has come when our party must harmoniously close into mighty ranks in order to take a most decisive role in the great hour of building a new Russia."[24]

Although expediency was probably the main motive for Kirov in forging an alliance with the Mensheviks, it was also characteristic of Kirov to take a flexible approach toward his fellow Social Democrats. He had, after all, been open to cooperation with the Mensheviks ever since he joined the RSDRP in 1904. It would not have made sense to Kirov to stir up factional strife at this crucial juncture of the revolution.

▪ THE ROAD TO OCTOBER

No longer forced to operate in the underground, the Vladikavkaz Social Democrats set up a unified party organization on 5 March 1917, with an executive committee of two Bolsheviks and three Mensheviks, including a chairman, the Menshevik N. P. Skrynnikov. Kirov, who was attending a municipal duma session at the time, was added to the executive committee a few days later, as a deputy chairman. Despite setbacks and strains, the Social Democrats managed to wrest control of the city's joint Soviet of Workers' and Soldiers' Deputies from the Socialist Revolutionaries in May 1917. Kirov was one of four Social Democrats to be elected as a delegate to the Caucasian Regional Congress of Soviets, which convened in Tbilisi in May.[25]

In Kirov's absence, a Georgian Bolshevik, Samuil Buachidze, arrived in Vladikavkaz from Petrograd. He had been sent by the Central Committee—possibly by Lenin himself—for the purpose of persuading the Vladikavkaz Bolsheviks to accept Lenin's April Theses and split with the Mensheviks. Buachidze created a storm of controversy when he delivered a speech endorsing Lenin's line at a party meeting, which took place after Kirov returned from Tbilisi. Although some Soviet historians would have us believe that Kirov had come around to the correct Leninist position by this time and that he backed Buachidze unreservedly, in fact, in a report delivered in early June, he still called for united Social Democratic action. On 8 June, when the Social Democrats chose an eight-man presidium to take over policy functions from the party's executive committee, Kirov was elected a deputy chairman, serving again under the Menshevik Skrynnikov, who was elected presidium chairman.[26]

The other deputy chairman was the Georgian Bolshevik Mamia Orakhelashvili, who had recently arrived in Vladikavkaz with his wife, Mariia Pavlovna, also a Bolshevik. Orakhelashvili, a former physician, supported Kirov on the Menshevik issue—a stance which came back to haunt him in the mid-1930s, when he was publicly labeled a "collaborator"—and became Kirov's lifelong friend. He later wrote: "To divide or conquer the organization. This was the main question which at this time, in the summer of 1917, had to be decided in our struggle with the Mensheviks. Kirov took the point of view that the organization had to be conquered."[27]

Although they eventually won over the majority of Social Democrats in the towns and in the workers' settlements of North Caucasia, the Bolsheviks were still weak in the countryside. Orakhelashvili recalls how pragmatic Kirov was in dealing with this problem:

> We had to find a link to the peasant masses. And this link was found. In Ossetia the peasant party "Kermen," named after the legendary Ossetian hero Kermen, had been founded. Its program was extremely backward, with SR leanings. But this did not bother Kirov. "They will come over to communism in any case," said Kirov. "That's how it will be." He fully believed that sooner or later all workers would unite under the communist banner.[28]

Although Kirov and the Vladikavkaz Bolsheviks marched to their own drums during the months leading up to October 1917, guided by their special regional circumstances rather than by instructions from Petrograd, they were by no means unaffected by the tumultuous events taking place in Russia's capital. During May and June, revolutionary fever was mounting in Petrograd, where the Bolsheviks, with their calls for an end to the "imperialist" war, were becoming masters among the working class. They suffered a setback during the "July Days," when spontaneous street demonstrations by workers shouting Bolshevik slogans led to violence and bloodshed and forced Lenin into hiding. But by August the Bolsheviks were regaining their influence in the Russian capital.

In the Terek region, as elsewhere in Russia, local Bolsheviks were encouraging chaos and discontent with calls for immediate peace and distribution of land to the peasants. They also exploited the growing tensions between the mountain peoples and the Cossacks, who owned most of the arable land and were heavily represented in the regional organs of the Provisional Government. Kirov himself put great store in the revolutionary potential of the mountain peoples, helping to establish a Bolshevik paper, *Red Banner,* which spread propaganda among them and published the program of the Kermen Party, the base of which was among the mountain peasants.[29]

The newly established Terek Civil Executive Committee was in the hands of the Cossacks. Alarmed by the growing influence of the Bolsheviks and their encouragement of unrest in the countryside, the Cossack-dominated government tightened military control over the region. In response to these local events and also to the news of the suppression of the July uprising in Petrograd, Kirov finally initiated a break with the Provisional Government and its local representatives. In a speech before the Vladikavkaz soviet on 7 August 1917 he passionately condemned the government for its repressive measures: "The Cossacks talk about the absence of authority and demand the introduction of the death penalty, which means that they want a virtual dictatorship. Everyone must struggle against the ensuing reaction, for freedom, equality, and brotherhood can easily slip away."[30]

A few days later Kirov made a trip to Moscow, where he attended as an observer at least one session of a so-called State Conference, convened on 14 August by Russian Prime Minister Kerenskii to rally public support for the Provisional Government. Kirov probably witnessed the sensational appearance at the conference by General L. G. Kornilov, commander-in-chief of the Provisional Government, who was greeted by tumultuous cheers. Just days later Kornilov attempted to restore order and suppress the Bolsheviks in Petrograd by bringing in troops. Kornilov carried out a mutiny against the government after Kerenskii decided that Kornilov was going too far and dismissed him from his post as commander-in-chief. In order to defeat Kornilov, Kerenskii appealed for help from the Bolsheviks, with whom the socialists in the government began to cooperate. The Kornilov affair ended up discrediting the Kerenskii government, especially in the eyes of the military, and rehabilitating the Bolshevik Party. In elections to soviets held throughout the country in September and October the Bolsheviks won majorities.[31]

When Kirov returned to Vladikavkaz in early September he made maximum use of the Kornilov affair for propaganda on the Bolsheviks' behalf, and he launched a stinging attack against the Mensheviks, singling out Menshevik leader Skrynnikov for defending the Provisional Government and Menshevik participation in it.[32]

Nonetheless, Kirov and the other Vladikavkaz Bolsheviks did not split with the Mensheviks until the eleventh hour—after Mamia Orakhelashvili attended a Bolshevik congress in Tbilisi in early October. The congress came down adamantly against organizational ties with the Mensheviks and passed a resolution demanding separate Bolshevik organizations in all places where Bolsheviks were united with Mensheviks. According to one account, the Vladikavkaz Bolsheviks broke with the Mensheviks at a party meeting on 12 October, at which Kirov reportedly spoke. By this time, the Mensheviks were in a small minority within the Social Democratic committee, so they walked out of the meeting in protest. The Vladikavkaz organization then unanimously declared itself a Bolshevik one.[33] Another source, however, puts the date of the split even later, claiming that Vladikavkaz Bolsheviks did not create a separate organization until November 1917.[34]

Given the initial weakness of the Bolsheviks in Vladikavkaz, the delay in splitting from the Mensheviks was understandable. Nonetheless, the policy set men like Kirov and Orakhelashvili apart from Bolsheviks like Lenin and Stalin, for whom the very idea of persuasion and conciliation was anathema. By the 1930s, when the history of the revolution was being rewritten under Stalin's auspices, it became treason.

▪ THE OCTOBER REVOLUTION

Although the Terek region, as elsewhere in Russia, was seething with revolutionary discontent, the center of events was of course Petrograd, where Lenin and the other Bolshevik leaders were planning an insurrection. In order to legitimize their coup they decided to convene a Second All-Russian Congress of Soviets, which, because it would be dominated by Bolsheviks, would endorse their actions and serve as a symbolic body of authority. Kirov was among the 650 delegates who attended the congress. In early October he had been elected by the Vladikavkaz soviet as its representative and was later selected to represent the Nal'chik and Piatigorsk soviets as well.[35]

Kirov's mandate, however, was not entirely clear. When he was elected as a representative from Vladikavkaz, the Bolsheviks, while dominating the local party committee, may not have had a majority in the local soviet. It is not clear when they won a majority—one source claims that it was in the first half of September, at which time Orakhelashvili was elected chairman and the Bolsheviks were able to dominate the executive committee. This would have meant that they were in a position to push through their resolutions without Menshevik support.[36] Other sources report, however, that the Bolsheviks did not gain a majority until later, possibly not until 20 October.[37] This was after Kirov, accompanied by the Bolshevik delegate from Groznyi, N. A. Anisimov, left for Petrograd, where the historic congress was scheduled to open on the 20th. The opening was then postponed until the 25th in order to allow all the provincial delegates time to get to the capital. If the Bolsheviks did not gain control of the Vladikavkaz soviet until after Kirov left, this would explain why, when he filled out the questionnaire for delegates, Kirov described the official stance of the soviet he represented as "all power to democracy" (a Menshevik demand), rather than the Leninist formula "all power to the soviets."[38]

On the night of 25 October the Bolsheviks occupied all important points in the capital, except the Winter Palace. The congress delegates had been assembled in the Smolnyi building all day, but the opening was held off until late in the evening to give the Bolsheviks time to seize the Winter Palace, which they finally did a few hours after the congress began. The congress, in session for two days, approved the formation of a provisional workers' and peasants' government, to be called the Council of People's Commissars, or Sovnarkom, which would have power until the convocation of a Constituent Assembly. With Lenin as its head, the Sovnarkom was all Bolshevik in composition. The Bolshevik leaders' decision to seize power was made without any consultation with the provincial organizations, which in most cases had to act on their own, without instructions from Petrograd. But within a few weeks the Bolsheviks were in control of most of the important towns and cities of Russia.[39]

After Kirov arrived back in Vladikavkaz, he reported to the local soviet on 4 November about events in Petrograd. Unfortunately, the full text of Kirov's remarks was not preserved, and the only available record of what he said is from a local newspaper account, first reproduced in a 1935 collection of Kirov's speeches and writings. According to this version, Kirov was remarkably cautious in his assessment of the Bolshevik coup. He condemned the Provisional Government, which "did not hide its aggressive plans toward the Congress of Soviets. . . . The ease with which the Provisional Government collapsed shows that it was sitting on sand, that in general it had no definite agenda, that each minister had the right to do what he wished." And he portrayed the Bolsheviks as the true defenders of the revolution, who had the solid support of the Petrograd proletariat. But he made no mention of the manifesto adopted at the congress and drafted by Lenin calling for a transfer of all power in the country to the soviets.[40]

In an introduction to the 1935 edition, Boris Pozern, a former Leningrad colleague of Kirov, commented on this rather surprising speech: "We cannot consider it to be an accident or attribute to a bad manuscript the exceptional cautiousness of the wording, and at times the complete reticence." He went on to explain that Kirov correctly understood that conditions in the North Caucasus were not yet ripe for a complete transfer of power to the soviets and that, had the Vladikavkaz Bolsheviks called for this, they might have alienated themselves from the workers and peasants.[41]

Kirov's November speech was reproduced in an expanded form for a second Kirov collection in 1936, again with an introduction by Pozern.[42] But by 1938, when yet another Kirov collection appeared, the purges had been going on for over a year, accompanied by a complete rewriting of revolutionary history. It could not be acknowledged that Kirov, who had been elevated to Bolshevik sainthood after his death, had such a lukewarm reaction to the October coup. In the 1938 publication there was no introduction by Pozern, who had been arrested by the NKVD, and a new version of the speech contained fiery tirades against all who did not agree with the Bolsheviks and unqualified endorsements of Lenin's slogan "all power to the soviets."[43]

However much Kirov's editors tried to cover up his heresies posthumously, the fact remained that the Vladikavkaz soviet passed a resolution endorsing Kirov's report and failing to advocate a takeover of power. The reluctance of Vladikavkaz Bolsheviks to attempt an overthrow of the local government and assert Soviet control marked a sharp contrast to the attitude of Bolsheviks elsewhere. In Groznyi, after hearing a report from their congress delegate, Anisimov, who had returned from Petrograd with Kirov, the soviet voted solidly in favor of supporting the new Sovnarkom in Petrograd and also of transferring local power to the soviets.[44]

Led by Kirov and his comrade Buachidze, Vladikavkaz Bolsheviks continued to take a cautious policy well after Lenin forcibly dissolved the Constituent Assembly (where the Bolsheviks were in a minority) in Petrograd in early January 1918 and declared the Petrograd soviet as the sole organ of power. By this time civil conflict, fueled by animosities among the Cossacks, the Chechens and Ingushes, and the Ossetians, was spreading over the Terek region, and the local government was losing control rapidly. In Vladikavkaz itself, civil disorder and violence forced many Bolsheviks, including Kirov, to flee the city in the second week of January.[45]

Those who remained in Vladikavkaz, including the Bolshevik Buachidze, decided that their only option amidst the violence of civil war was to form a bloc, uniting the Bolsheviks with Mensheviks, SRs, the nationalist Kermen Party, and other socialists. Kirov readily agreed with the idea and tried to persuade Bolsheviks in Piatigorsk, where he was residing at the time, to unite similarly with other socialists. At the first session of the People's Congress of Terek, convened in the Caucasian town of Mozdok at the end of January 1918, Kirov gave an impassioned speech endorsing unity, despite the protests of a group of "left" Bolsheviks:

> It is essential for us to speak for the entire region, so that democracy will be unified, to stop picking each other to pieces. If we don't do this, we will fall apart. . . . Here they say that if we recognize the authority of the Council of People's Commissars [Sovnarkom], all burning issues, including the land question, will resolve themselves. But before determining the authority of the Council of People's Commissars, we must establish how to create an order which will above all respond to the interests of democracy. There is only one way to do this—to consolidate a true regime of the people. . . . Not soviets, which are far from us right now, but true democracy.[46]

In sharp contrast to Lenin, who had insisted that the civil war was not only inevitable but desirable, Kirov emphasized the need for peaceful solutions to the conflicts that had beset the Terek region: "If we recognize the regime of the soviets only to disperse arms among different nationalities, then it is better not to recognize this regime."[47]

It is hardly surprising that after 1936 this speech was either "revised" or omitted entirely from Kirov's collected works.[48] His remarks amounted to an open disregard for the decrees of the Bolshevik leadership. Unswayed by what was happening in Petrograd, Moscow, and elsewhere, Kirov realized that the Bolsheviks in Terek would be embarking on a highly risky venture if they attempted at this moment to seize power in the name of the Sovnarkom and the soviets. He also seems to have been genuinely motivated by a desire to be responsive to the wishes of the different nationalities and social classes of the region.

Kirov's speech won the day for the Socialist Bloc. On 30 January 1918 the Terek People's Congress unanimously accepted a statement drawn up by Kirov on ending civil conflict in Terek. The statement called for the establishment of a democratic government representing various national delegations. According to two Menshevik delegates, Iakov Marschak and his sister Frania (both of whom later emigrated to the United States), Kirov made a tremendous impression on the congress. Marschak had met Kirov some weeks earlier and judged him to be "a man of great warmth, kind among friends, not overbearing, and certainly absolutely honest." At the congress, according to Marschak, "Kirov was probably the most prominent. He would make very fiery speeches—even his diction was significant. . . . And then some sort of resolution would be adopted. The picturesque tribesmen were so terribly enthusiastic that they actually came up to kiss his hands." His sister Frania concurred, adding: "We didn't forget that Kirov was a Bolshevik, but we were not concerned, and I think that he was not concerned himself. We were all interested mainly in pacification, and we felt that it had to be done and could be done."[49]

Kirov's pivotal role at this congress elevated him to a new political stature. To be sure he was still a minor figure, little known outside the North Caucasus. But he was earning a reputation beyond his revolutionary journalism and was becoming a politician. Perhaps befitting his new stature, Kirov now took part in the rituals of politicians: according to Marschak, Kirov and other members of the Socialist Bloc, living in a luxury train throughout the session, engaged every evening in excessive drinking bouts. They drank *araka,* a strong Caucasian liquor. Marschak's sister took a dim view of this ritual: "He [Kirov] was a drunkard. It doesn't mean much in Russia, but . . . after he had a success we had to celebrate. I was the only girl there; I had a small cup of my own and they had big cups. Kirov drank more than anyone else."[50]

Whatever his drinking habits, Kirov did not lose sight of the goal of establishing a Bolshevik regime in the Terek region. Realizing that the issue of Soviet power could not be ignored forever, Kirov and other Bolsheviks began behind the scenes to agitate for recognition of the central Soviet government among the national groups. Once most of the other issues had been resolved, they called upon delegates at a second meeting of the Terek People's Congress, convened in Piatigorsk two weeks later, to recognize the authority of Lenin's government. Inevitably, the moderate socialists objected, and the socialist coalition fell apart. After endorsing the new regime in Petrograd, the congress elected delegates to a Terek People's Soviet, which in turn elected a Council of People's Commissars for Terek, the chairman of which was Buachidze. On 7 March the entire congress traveled by train to Vladikavkaz, while remnants of the local Provisional Government quickly evacuated the city. Two days later the congress declared the formation of the Terek Republic, as part of the Russian Federation, thus formally establishing Soviet power throughout Terek.[51]

- ## CIVIL WARRIOR

Whereas the Bolsheviks' October Revolution was relatively bloodless, subsequent resistance to their seizure of power led to violent conflict. Bolshevik support was primarily urban-based and thus secure in cities like Moscow and Petrograd, but throughout the empire social and political forces opposed to the new regime arose, often forming anti-Bolshevik regional governments. Elements dissatisfied with the Bolsheviks and their policies set up centers of resistance in southern Russia and in Siberia. The so-called Whites, anti-Communist forces led by former officers from the tsarist army, set out to defeat the Bolsheviks' Red Army, led by Commissar of War Leon Trotsky. From early 1918 to the end of 1920, Russia would endure one of the bloodiest civil wars in history.

Military intervention by outside powers—including France, Great Britain, the United States, and Japan—gave the Whites much needed supplies and munitions. By the summer of 1918 the very survival of the

Bolshevik regime was in doubt. The Germans occupied Ukraine and the western borderlands, while the Whites controlled much of the Volga region to the east and southeast, as well as Siberia. In the words of one historian: "Russia had been reduced to a size roughly the same as medieval Muscovy. Seemingly it would not be long before a foreign power reached Moscow and overthrew the Bolsheviks."[52] With key transportation lines cut, the towns were deprived of crucial food supplies from the countryside. The peasants in any case had little incentive to produce for urban areas, so the Soviet regime extracted grain by force—a policy known as war communism, which led to even more bloodshed.

The North Caucasus was an especially volatile area, because it was the home of so many non-Russians, who saw the revolution as an opportunity to defend their national interests and resented the continued imposition of Russian rule. The new Terek government soon began to lose its political authority when open conflict broke out between the mountain peoples and the Cossacks. By June 1918 the area was in a state of anarchy. According to one source, Soviet rule in the North Caucasus "existed only in name, having among the population neither weight nor authority."[53]

Kirov's efforts at achieving peace among the peoples of Terek had thus proved fruitless, and, from the point of view of his political career, perhaps misguided. Although he soon showed himself a staunch defender of the Bolshevik regime, his hesitations during the early months of 1918 did not go unnoticed in Moscow. A Bolshevik from Piatigorsk who had attended the Mozdok congress complained directly to Lenin that Kirov had encouraged "counterrevolutionary enemies" to form a bloc with Bolsheviks.[54] And later, in July 1921, the Bolshevik Iurii Butiagin, who knew Kirov well and attended the drinking bouts that took place during the Mozdok congress, sent a damning report on Kirov to the Central Committee. Butiagin claimed that Kirov was known in the Caucasus as a Menshevik who was not particularly active in party work and who wrote for bourgeois newspapers in the Caucasus. Butiagin went on:

> Comrade Kirov, as an orator, enjoyed wide popularity among the masses, but he had almost no experience in practical party and soviet work, which he either was not able to do or carefully stayed away from, restricting himself mainly to appearances at factories and at large meetings. Before 1918 he was a Menshevik. . . . He wavered and maneuvered for a long time. He did not officially join the party until 1919.[55]

Butiagin, it must be said, had a falling-out with Kirov in 1920, when Kirov reprimanded him for misconduct in his capacity as a military commander, thus causing his dismissal. So Butiagin had a strong motivation to besmirch Kirov's reputation. He was of course not speaking truthfully when he said that Kirov was a Menshevik before 1918. Although always willing to cooperate with Mensheviks, Kirov had affiliated himself with the Bolsheviks well before this time. But the fact that Butiagin would make these statements about Kirov suggests that Kirov's Social Democratic past was murky in the eyes of others and that his independent and flexible approach to politics had early on in his career raised questions about his commitment to Bolshevism.

Reinforcing the impression that he was a waverer, Kirov held no formal position in the new Soviet government in Terek, when it was established in Vladikavkaz in March 1918, although he did serve as a troubleshooter on its behalf, negotiating with the various nationalities to prevent warfare among them. He also started up a newspaper, *Narodnaia vlast'* (People's Power), which served as the official organ for the Terek soviet.[56] Kirov's seemingly disparate local activities abruptly ceased, however, when, in May 1918, the Terek Sovnarkom dispatched him to Moscow on an important mission—to obtain money and military equipment from the central Soviet government. Henceforth, a new Kirov began to emerge—resolute and ruthless in the Leninist mold.

When Kirov said his goodbyes to Mariia L'vovna, who had returned to Vladikavkaz sometime in early 1918, he assumed he would be gone for only a few weeks. As it turned out, he would not be reunited with his wife for almost two years. The trip to Moscow was tedious, taking longer than expected. Kirov wrote Mariia L'vovna from Tsaritsyn (Volgograd) on 20 May, saying that he had been detained there because of a crash of two earlier trains on the line to Moscow.[57]

Soon after his arrival Kirov had his first meeting with Stalin, who was Commissar of Nationalities. Stalin arranged a room for him at the Second House of Soviets (formerly the Metropol Hotel) and issued him a certificate of identification.[58] On 30 May, Lenin received Kirov personally, and Kirov delivered a request from the Terek Sovnarkom for millions of rubles for the support of Red Army units in the North Caucasus, for the repair and rebuilding of the Groznyi oil industry and the railways, and for medical care. Kirov also gave Lenin a report of his own, written after he arrived in Moscow. The report pointed out that the North Caucasus was a stronghold of Soviet power in political, economic, and military terms, in that the adjacent regions—Stavropol, the Kuban, the Volga Basin, and Baku—could offer significant help to the Soviet Republic with grain, coal, and oil. But the army there was desperately in need of money and supplies.[59]

After Lenin agreed to an advance of fifteen million rubles and to the provision of supplies and weapons, Kirov began organizing an expedition to the North Caucasus. This required him to remain in Moscow for several weeks. During this time the Cossacks in Terek began a full-scale revolt, precipitated by Chechen-Ingush demands for their lands. Buachidze, the head of the new Soviet government, was assassinated in mid-June. Kirov was devastated by the news of Buachidze's death and all the more anxious to return to the North Caucasus. Before he left, however, he managed to write an article for *Pravda*—making his debut as a journalist of national stature—on the situation in Terek. Bending the truth, Kirov scoffed at those who spoke of anarchy there and claimed that strong forces were being mobilized to secure the Soviet hold on the region.[60]

Accompanied by the military representative of the Terek Sovnarkom, A. V. Vologodskii, Kirov set off from Moscow on 20 July with two trainloads of arms and equipment for Bolshevik troops in the North Caucasus.[61] Vologodskii later gave a detailed description of the mission, which came close to a calamitous ending.[62] They got as far as Tsaritsyn, but could not proceed further because the Whites, or White Guards, under the command of General Anton Denikin, had cut off the railway line to Astrakhan, a city situated strategically at the mouth of the Volga on the Caspian Sea. Leaving Vologodskii in charge of the supplies, Kirov headed for Piatigorsk to deliver the money to the Terek government. (He could not get through to Vladikavkaz, because the way was blocked by anti-Communist forces.) In his absence, Vologodskii went to the Military Council of the North Caucasian district to seek help in transferring the supplies to barges so they could be shipped down the Volga to Astrakhan. He immediately ran up against Stalin, who was now in Tsaritsyn arranging the transport of grain from the North Caucasus to Moscow and was already overstepping the bounds of his authority. Stalin had cabled to Lenin: "I am driving and scolding everybody who needs it. Rest assured that we shall spare nobody, neither ourselves nor others, and that we shall deliver the bread."[63]

Rather than helping with the transport, Stalin demanded that Vologodskii's cargo be handed over to a Red Army division from the Donbass in order to defend Tsaritsyn from Denikin's army. Vologodskii, unaware that Tsaritsyn was threatened with imminent attack, refused. Stalin thereupon issued an order to have him shot. Vologodskii was rescued by the intercession of a military commander, who explained the situation to him and persuaded him to agree to Stalin's demand. When Kirov returned to Tsaritsyn in early August, he was dismayed to learn that the trainloads of supplies he had worked so hard to secure had been handed over, on Stalin's orders, to the division defending Tsaritsyn. According to Vologodskii, Kirov managed "with great trouble" to retrieve part of the equipment and have it put on barges for shipment to Astrakhan.[64]

It is not clear whether Kirov had to confront Stalin directly in order to do this, but in any case they were operating at cross-purposes, and the incident probably left a lasting impression on both of them. In fact, Kirov had good reason to be upset with Stalin for diverting the military materials. Soviet historians later admitted that Stalin's actions in Tsaritsyn were harmful to the Bolshevik military effort in the North Caucasus. Stalin ran afoul of several Red Army commanders there, and Trotsky eventually managed to have him recalled to Moscow.[65]

After accomplishing his mission to Astrakhan in mid-August, Kirov moved on to Piatigorsk, where he helped to form armed units against the Whites in the North Caucasus. Later, he was a delegate to the Sixth Congress of Soviets of the Russian Republic, which convened in Moscow in November 1918. Significantly, Kirov was accompanied to Moscow by Georgii Atarbekov, chief of the Cheka of the North Caucasus. The Cheka was Lenin's political police, established in December 1917 to help suppress opposition to Bolshevik rule. Its ruthless methods, which included summary justice and random executions, soon earned the Cheka a reputation as a notoriously savage Bolshevik institution. Atarbekov himself did much to further this reputation in the next several years, but this did not deter Kirov from forming a close association with him that was to last until Atarbekov's sudden death in 1925.[66] Indeed Kirov's friendship with Atarbekov marked the beginning of a new stage in his career, when he not only devoted all his energies to establishing Soviet power throughout the former Russian empire but also accepted the Bolsheviks' tenet that they were above the law and that anything done to further their cause, including taking the lives of others, was justified.

While in Moscow, Kirov met with Lenin and the president of the Russian Republic, Iakov Sverdlov, to request additional military supplies for the North Caucasus. His request was granted. In late December 1918,

Kirov left Moscow with a military supply train and fifty million rubles in boxes. He was accompanied by Atarbekov and two representatives of the Terek government. They arrived in Astrakhan on 16 January 1919 to discover that the Eleventh Army, fighting in the North Caucasus under the command of Sergo Ordzhonikidze, was in disarray and was retreating north toward Astrakhan.[67]

Kirov and his party then headed southwest toward the North Caucasus with their equipment on trucks, traveling across the Kalmyk Steppes toward Vladikavkaz. They were forced to turn back, however, after having problems getting through the snow and encountering sick, wounded, and dead soldiers from the Eleventh Army along the way. When they crossed the Volga to return to Astrakhan the ice had already begun to melt and the truck with the boxes of money sank into the river. Kirov was in a panic. They enlisted divers to retrieve the boxes, but the task took eleven days. Meanwhile, the chairman of the Revolutionary Military Council of the Caspian-Caucasian Front, A. G. Shliapnikov, who was headquartered in Astrakhan, accused Kirov of misappropriation of government funds and held him in detention while he launched an investigation.[68]

Not surprisingly, the incident infuriated Kirov, who was already indignant over the collapse of the Eleventh Army and the failure to prepare adequately for its retreat—for which he reportedly reproached Shliapnikov. Kirov was also angry at the Soviet leadership in Moscow. In response to a telegram sent to the Revolutionary Military Council in Astrakhan from Moscow, requesting the reasons for the Eleventh Army's collapse, Kirov did not mince words. Addressing his comments to Trotsky with a copy to Lenin, Kirov reminded Trotsky that he, Lenin and "other responsible workers" in Moscow had been repeatedly warned about the grave situation of the army in the North Caucasus and the severe problem with supplies. He complained that only fifteen million rubles had been designated for the troops and that only part of the supplies had reached Terek because the rest had been "unloaded" at Tsaritsyn (by Stalin) and Astrakhan. As late as December, Kirov wrote, he and his colleagues had told Trotsky face to face that the situation was close to a catastrophe and had insisted on urgent measures.[69]

We have no way of knowing what Trotsky and Lenin—or for that matter Stalin, who bore much of the blame—thought of Kirov's telegram. But, despite the fact that Kirov requested permission to return to White-controlled Terek to do underground work, the Central Committee and the Central Executive Committee sent him the following instructions: "In view of the changed circumstances we suggest remaining in Astrakhan to organize the defense of the city and the region."[70] Shliapnikov was recalled and replaced by Konstantin Mekhanoshin, a member of the Revolutionary Military Council of the Russian Republic.[71]

▪ RED TERROR IN ASTRAKHAN

Astrakhan, both the city and the surrounding region, was in desperate straits. With the influx of refugees accompanying the retreating Red Army, food shortages had reached a critical point, typhoid gripped the city, and speculation was endemic. Discontent with the Bolshevik political-military command was widespread, especially among the workers, who resented the "tyranny of the commissars, their constant threats with their revolvers," and the long delays in payment of wages. They began organizing for a strike.[72] On 25 February 1919 an extraordinary session of the city and provincial executive and party organs was held, together with the Military Council. Mekhanoshin proposed the creation of a body with dictatorial powers, a Revolutionary War Committee. As the highest power in Astrakhan, it would use every means to suppress unrest. The session approved the proposal, and designated Kirov as the committee's new chairman, with Iurii Butiagin his deputy.[73]

It soon became clear that Kirov's high-flown speeches at workers' meetings, where he tried to explain the class struggle and the world proletarian revolution, could not quell the discontent. Kirov became a dictator overnight. On 4 March his war committee announced "bread only to those who work," and three days later declared martial law. When thousands of Astrakhan workers, supported by a Red Army rifle division, went on strike on 10 March, waving banners that said "Down with the Communists and commissars!" Kirov ordered the punitive organs of the Cheka into action, with Atarbekov in charge. Together with Mekhanoshin and the commander of the Caspian-Caucasian Front, he issued a directive declaring that "all bandits, marauders, and those opposing Soviet power will be shot on the spot." Food would be distributed only to supporters of the Soviet regime, and the Special Department (of the Cheka) would conduct an investigation and send all those responsible to the military tribunal.[74]

By 11 March the rebellion had been quelled by bullets and grenades, but this was by no means the end of the violence. Although the main cause of the unrest was the desperate material circumstances of the workers, Kirov and the war committee portrayed it as a "White Guard conspiracy," "inspired by the gold of British imperialists," and referred to "self-seekers wearing the honored shirt of the proletariat, who attacked the invincible might of socialist Russia." Reprisals began immediately, as Atarbekov's Special Department began rounding up those suspected of instigating the rebellion. Close to 1,500 strikers, the majority of whom were young men with families, were shot within a few days. Anyone suspected of even the slightest disloyalty to the Soviet regime was imprisoned. By April almost 4,000 people had been killed by the Cheka's Special Department, some shot personally by Atarbekov without any investigation or trial.[75]

Atarbekov's behavior was so bloodthirsty that it raised eyebrows even in Moscow. In July 1919 he was arrested and sent to Moscow for an investigation by the Central Committee. Kirov reportedly had to acknowledge Atarbekov's outrageous deeds. But at the last moment Stalin intervened, and Atarbekov was exonerated and allowed to continue his work in the Cheka.[76]

Whatever Atarbekov's crimes, Kirov unquestionably bore a great deal of responsibility for the bloodletting in Astrakhan during March and April 1919. He was issuing the orders, and there is no evidence that he urged restraint upon Atarbekov or tried to limit the reprisals. On the contrary, the archives contain a report, dated 18 March, on the case of the "bourgeois homeowner Pimenov," who had been hiding his furniture and his valuables (now the property of the Soviet state) at the home of his gardener. On the bottom of the report was an order signed by Kirov: "Send this case to the Special Department."[77] This meant, of course, that the unfortunate Pimenov would be shot, merely for trying to hold on to his possessions.

How is it that Kirov, who just a few years earlier had been tormented by the sound of an execution in a tsarist prison, could have become so inured to people's suffering and so contemptuous of human life? One might, of course, ask the same question about Lenin, who had written to a Bolshevik commander in December 1918: "Use all forces to hunt down and shoot Astrakhan speculators and thieves. With this swine it is necessary to carry out reprisals that will be remembered for years."[78] This was the Bolshevik mind-set, the new revolutionary morality, born of the desire to establish Bolshevik rule at any cost. We can only surmise that Kirov accepted this morality because he had, since the beginning of 1918, seen a great deal of bloodshed and human cruelty. He was living on the edge, in charge of a city that was threatened by the White Army and filled with starving, hostile citizens. Coercion was a condition for survival. This was not a time for human feelings, but a time for single-minded, resolute action.

Yet he had not suppressed his human side entirely. Exactly a month after the rebellion, on 10 April, Kirov wrote to Nadezhda Serebrennikova:

> Now I am living in Astrakhan, probably soon I will be transferred. I work like a slave here, with not even a minute of free time, because the situation is very difficult. On 10–11 March there was a substantial White Guard revolt. It was liquidated successfully, but it was plenty of trouble. I wish so much just to have one line from you. Try to send something by post if you don't find any other way.
>
> I burn with the desire to be in Moscow, but it seems that I won't manage soon. In any case I have not lost hope.
>
> . . . The revolution goes literally like clockwork. Earlier it seemed like we tried to shape events, but now events outstrip us. But we will catch up. With my warmest greetings
>
> Yours, Sergei
>
> Write a few lines, without fail. I'm waiting.[79]

Although he wanted desperately to get out of Astrakhan, Kirov was compelled to remain there for close to a year. It was during this time that the civil war reached its climax. While Denikin's troops were pressing northward, General Nikolai Iudenich was marching on Petrograd, coming close to capturing the city in May 1919 and again in October. Fortunately for the Bolsheviks, although the White forces were backed strongly by the British and the French, with both air and naval power, their effort was never concerted.

At the end of April 1919, Kirov was appointed head of the Political Department of the newly reconstituted Eleventh Army and then in early May was named a member of its Revolutionary Military Council. In June

1919 Trotsky sent an order for Astrakhan to be evacuated and abandoned to the Whites, but Kirov resisted and appealed to Lenin. Sergo Ordzhonikidze was in Astrakhan briefly and, after meeting Kirov for the first time, agreed to speak to Lenin on Kirov's behalf. Denikin occupied Tsaritsyn at the end of June, thereby cutting Astrakhan off from communications along the Volga; the city was threatened from the west by the White Army and was bombed from the air by the British, but Kirov held fast. Lenin finally endorsed Kirov's decision in August when he sent a message saying: "Defend Astrakhan until the end."[80]

By the autumn of 1919, when the tide began to turn in favor of the Bolsheviks, the Eleventh Army, now under the command of Valerian Kuibyshev, joined forces with the Tenth Army east of Tsaritsyn to begin a counterattack. Meanwhile Kirov was pressing the Bolshevik leadership to transfer him to Terek. In early September he wrote to Central Committee secretary Elena Stasova: "There [in Terek] my experience and knowledge of local conditions would bring significantly more value than here, where I have stayed too long."[81]

He had others plead his case for him as well. In November 1919 a member of the Political Department of the Military Council of the Eleventh Army wrote to Moscow recommending that Kirov be sent to the Caucasus because of his knowledge and experience in that region:

> Comrade Kirov lived and worked in the Caucasus for a long time, enjoying popularity there, and he knows the Caucasus. He repeatedly conciliated the warring tribes in Dagestan. In 1918 he brilliantly conducted the Mozdok congress, creating a unified Socialist Bloc. . . . Although not participating in the Terek Sovnarkom, Kirov was the main initiator of this body and its policy, which was a dictatorship of the proletariat in conformity with the special features of the Caucasus. This policy undoubtedly was what preserved until now the Caucasus for Soviet Russia.[82]

Although this letter praised Kirov, it also reminded the Bolshevik leadership that he had not followed Lenin's dictum about severing ties with the Mensheviks. This may have been one reason why Kirov's requests were ignored.

Sergei with his sisters, Anna and Elizaveta, and his
grandmother, Melaniia Avdeevna, Urzhum, 1904

Police photograph of Sergei, 1907

Mariia L'vovna Markus at the editorial offices
of the paper *Terek*, Vladikavkaz, 1910

Kirov and Sergo Ordzhonikidze, 1920

Kirov and Stalin on the platform of Moscow Station, Leningrad, April 1926

Site of the Kirovs' home in Leningrad

Stalin and Kirov with Leningrad party officials at the Smolnyi, April 1926

Kirov with a delegation of metalworkers at his office in the Smolnyi, July 1929

Kirov and Maxim Gorky among factory workers, Leningrad, July 1929

Kirov with Soviet naval officers on the Baltic Sea, 1929

Kirov (far right) with other leaders at
Stalin's birthday celebration, December 1929

Kirov (far right) on holiday, sitting with Medved (on far left),
N. P. Komarov, and an unidentified woman. Leningrad region, circa 1929

We know for certain that Stalin opposed his transfer. In mid-September 1919 a colleague of Kirov's sent him a letter in which he told him about a meeting he had in Moscow with Lenin, Trotsky, and Stalin:

> In our conversation about Astrakhan you were discussed. Stalin for some reason was not particularly nice toward you. Of course, he did not say anything that was outright critical, but he thinks that you are weak-willed toward the Caucasus. Why he thinks this I was not able to find out. It was not convenient because the conversation took place in front of Il'ich [Lenin] and it concerned possible candidates for work in the Caucasus. . . . Stalin apparently considers you not "especially strong" for work in the Caucasus. But what this means I don't know.[83]

Why would Stalin consider Kirov too weak for a job in the Caucasus, especially after his brutal and decisive suppression of the Astrakhan revolt and his sponsorship of Atarbekov? Was Stalin simply getting back at Kirov for the ruckus he raised about military supplies in the summer of 1918? It is more likely that Stalin objected to Kirov's tolerant views toward Caucasian nationalists, whom Stalin detested. While Kirov advocated a cautious approach in dealing with them, Stalin pushed for a ruthless struggle against all manifestations of local patriotism. Despite, or perhaps because of, his Georgian nationality (which he saw as a political drawback), Stalin was aggressively pro-Russian.[84]

A case in point was that of Armenia, Azerbaijan, and Georgia, which had been part of the Russian empire since the nineteenth century and had all declared themselves independent states in 1918. Although internationalism was a fundamental precept of Marxism, Social Democrats in Transcaucasia had strong feelings of national pride and identity. Armenian Bolshevik Anastas Mikoyan, who in 1918–19 headed the illegal Bolshevik organization in Baku, Azerbaijan, urged Moscow to make concessions to nationalist sentiments in Transcaucasia, if only for the purpose of quelling fears of Soviet domination. In principle, of course, all Bolsheviks opposed the idea of "bourgeois autonomy" because it ran counter to the socialist premise of internationalism. But, as Mikoyan argued, it was necessary to demonstrate sensitivity to the nationalists' concerns in order to shore up support for the Soviet regime.[85]

Mikoyan had, by means of correspondence, won over Kirov, who was acting as a go-between in communications with Moscow, and also Ordzhonikidze, head of the Caucasian Regional Committee. Both were persuaded of the necessity for adopting the slogan of independent republics for Armenia, Georgia, and Azerbaijan as part of the future Bolshevik program. Back in June 1919, Kirov had forwarded to Lenin (with a copy to Stalin) a report from Mikoyan laying out the basis for his policy. In the report, which Kirov endorsed, Mikoyan pointed out that the local Muslim Communist organization in Azerbaijan enjoyed popularity among the masses and that by giving it recognition and promoting the idea of continued independence for Azerbaijan, Moscow would win much needed support.[86]

In October 1919, Mikoyan met Kirov for the first time in Astrakhan. He was favorably impressed: "A lively, inquisitive and intelligent man, with a clear, precise mind, Kirov could grasp the subtleties of an issue in an instant. His positive attitude toward our policy on issues was encouraging and convinced me that questions of concern to us would be successfully examined in the Party Central Committee. He astonished me with his efficiency and drive, and his ability to make decisions on the spot."[87]

After meeting with Mikoyan, Kirov wrote a letter to the Central Committee asking its members to review their positions on the Transcaucasian states and to recognize nationality-based Communist Party organizations.[88] Lenin and the Politburo backed Mikoyan and Kirov but not without objections from Stalin, who delayed the implementation of the proposals for several months.[89]

It would be misleading to make too much of these disagreements in policy among Bolshevik leaders because all, including Mikoyan and Kirov, had the same ultimate objective—the centralization of Bolshevik leadership and the Sovietization of all three independent states of the Transcaucasus. Their dispute concerned only short-term strategy. Whereas Mikoyan and Kirov understood local sensitivities and wanted to pay obeisance to them, Stalin, who craved vengeance upon Caucasian nationalists, advocated a Sturm und Drang approach. But the controversy revealed a side of Kirov—as a compromiser and a conciliator—that was anathema to Stalin and may have contributed to Stalin's hesitations about approving Kirov for a position in the Caucasus.

At this point, however, Stalin's opinion was not decisive. It was Lenin who had the final say, and he apparently overcame his reservations about

Kirov. At the end of December 1919, just before the Red Army recaptured Tsaritsyn, Kirov was finally granted an appointment to the North Caucasus, as deputy chairman of a special bureau, chaired by Ordzhonikidze, to reestablish Soviet power there. When the Eleventh Army was able to advance into the North Caucasus in March 1920 Kirov left Astrakhan, returning to Vladikavkaz and to Mariia L'vovna for the first time in two years.[90] He was a very different man.

4

Building Soviet Power

· · · · · · · · · · · · · · ·

*Comrades, we Communists are people of a special cut. We have been
cut out of peculiar stuff. . . . There is no loftier title than that of a member
of the party, of which Comrade Lenin has been founder and leader.*

—*Stalin,* Collected Works, *Vol. 6, p. 46*

· · · · · · · · · · · · · ·

By the time the Bolsheviks launched an offensive against Denikin's
White forces in the North Caucasus, the White Army was retreating
on all fronts, and a Bolshevik victory in the civil war was only months
away. As an organizer of the offensive, along with Sergo Ordzhonikidze,
Kirov, residing in Vladikavkaz, acted as liaison between the army and the
Central Committee in Moscow, passing on to Lenin and Stalin reports
from the front and arranging for the delivery of supplies and money to the
army command. Judging from Kirov's correspondence during this time, he
was overwhelmed with responsibilities. Only thirty-four years old, with no
military or national-level political experience, he had been catapulted onto
the stage of leadership politics during a bloody civil war. Like Sergo (who
was the same age) and many other Bolsheviks who were emerging in leadership roles, Kirov was suddenly feeling the intoxication of real power.

According to comrades like Mikoyan, Kirov had the organizational
skills, intellect, and ambition necessary to carry out his work successfully
and win the respect of his colleagues. He was also able, it seems, to overcome moral scruples about enforcing Soviet rule with ruthless and violent
repression. But in entering the arena of Bolshevik leadership he encountered a world of intrigue and infighting where ethnic, class, and genera-
tional rivalries often interfered with the straightforward business of

military and political conquest. This was a world in which men like Stalin, who could shift his loyalties and change his policies with the political wind, thrived. Kirov lacked the political acumen of Stalin and he had not completely shed the earnestness and idealism that had characterized his prerevolutionary days. He also had a tendency to form intense personal bonds, which sometimes clouded his political judgment.

One example was his relationship with Iurii Butiagin, who had served as his deputy in Astrakhan and then became a temporary commander of the newly reconstituted Eleventh Army in the spring of 1919. Kirov and Butiagin became close friends during the months that they worked together. As a result, when the Moscow leadership decided to replace Butiagin with an officer named M. I. Vasilenko as head of the Eleventh Army, Kirov launched an outspoken campaign to keep Butiagin on. He sent several letters to Moscow stressing Butiagin's exceptional qualities and pointing out the inefficacy of changing commanders. On 27 November 1919, for example, he wrote to Lenin and Trotsky:

> Comrade Butiagin has been commander of the Eleventh Army for three months. It is my duty to observe that in this time the army has definitely grown and become stronger. . . . Butiagin's main virtues are energy, good management, and organizational talents. . . . Unfortunately, Butiagin's work has not been sufficiently valued by the military leadership, since recently the former division chief Vasilenko was appointed commander. In my opinion this change is not only uncalled for, but also risky.[1]

In another letter, to a member of the Revolutionary Military Council of the Russian Republic, Kirov wrote: "I have no formal right to criticize the decisions of the high command, but I nonetheless think it essential to note that the Eleventh Army continues to be in a state of instability, especially in terms of the command. . . . Unfortunately the appointment of Vasilenko as commander must be reconsidered."[2]

Kirov's outspoken support for Butiagin not only did not sway Moscow; it proved to be misguided. In early 1920 Butiagin overstepped his bounds by not complying with the orders of his superior, Vasilenko. Kirov reproached him strongly for this in a letter: "Iurii, a corps is completely and absolutely subordinate to an army and obviously the army commander bears full responsibility for the corps. Your behavior is not only unacceptable, it is even criminal."[3] As it turned out, Butiagin was blamed for an outbreak of typhus that spread through his staff and for a disastrous defeat of his corps at the hands of Denikin's army. Despite his strong pleas to be allowed to remain in his post, Kirov told him in no uncertain terms that he had to go: "I personally am convinced that it is impossible for you to continue with the Eleventh Army. There will be no compromises on this matter."[4] Kirov's misplaced confidence in Butiagin must surely have raised doubts in Moscow about his judgment, although there is no evidence of the reaction. As for Butiagin, he was, as already noted, bitter enough to denounce Kirov to the Central Committee a year later.

The Butiagin incident did not deter Kirov from voicing his opinions forcefully and making recommendations to the Central Committee, as shown by his daily communications to Moscow. Nor did he shy away from forging deep alliances with some of his fellow Bolsheviks, the most important of which was with Sergo Ordzhonikidze. As a deputy to Sergo in the Bureau to Reestablish Soviet Power in the Caucasus (later called the Caucasian Bureau, or Kavburo), Kirov developed a close rapport with him, and they began to communicate almost daily. The correspondence between the two, which continued until Kirov's death fourteen years later, covered not only politics but also personal matters. Supporting each other unswervingly on almost every issue, they became an inseparable pair in people's minds.

Kirov and Sergo formed part of a group of Bolshevik politico-military commissars concerned with the affairs of the Caucasus (the North Caucasus and Transcaucasia), which developed into a Caucasian leadership cadre that ran this area on Moscow's behalf. Kirov was one of the few non-Caucasians to be a part of this group, but this was not a particular handicap. His years in Terek had given him experience in dealing with non-Russians, especially Muslims, and his affable and approachable manner made him popular among Caucasian Bolsheviks.

As a Georgian and Commissar of Nationalities, Stalin was the overseer of the Caucasian group from Moscow. Whatever his reservations about Kirov in 1919, they should have been overcome after Kirov embarked with the Eleventh Army on its offensive in the spring of 1920. In contrast to his earlier approach to national questions, Kirov showed no lack of resolve in the establishment of Soviet power in Transcaucasia, which marked the final victory for the Red Army in the civil war. He and

Sergo Ordzhonikidze took over the entire direction of the ruthless Bolshevik conquest of the three Transcaucasian states and their incorporation into Soviet Russia. Azerbaijan was the first republic to fall into Soviet hands. On 28 April 1920, after several weeks of intensive preparation, the Red Army entered the capital, Baku. Kirov and Sergo arrived there with Mikoyan on an armored train a few days later.[5]

Although nominally supported by the native Bolsheviks, the Soviet occupation of Azerbaijan was a bloody business, because of widespread resistance on the part of the predominantly Muslim population. An uprising, led by the Muslim Mussavat Party, in the city of Giandzha at the end of May took the Bolsheviks six days to suppress and resulted in the massacre of 1,000 citizens. Kirov's role in the Giandzha affair is not entirely clear, but we know that he and Sergo were monitoring the situation from Baku and presumably giving orders. The fact that Giandzha was renamed Kirovabad in 1935 suggests that Kirov was given some credit for suppressing the rebellion.[6] In early June 1920 another rebellion occurred in Karabakh, the Armenian enclave in Azerbaijan that has continued to be the subject of territorial dispute to this day. Again the rebellion was quelled only by a fierce Red Army onslaught.[7]

Although Sergo's name is most strongly associated with the repressions in Azerbaijan—he reportedly had many members of the Azerbaijan nationalist movement executed—Kirov clearly bore responsibility as well. How did he rationalize his actions? He was not innately cruel or sadistic, but the brutalities of World War I and over two years of civil war were apparently enough to inure him to human suffering. As a Socialist Revolutionary leader later observed, such experiences "wiped out the value of human life—both of one's own and of others. It hardened people not to care about the death of millions. The right to spill blood and take away life ceased to be a tragic problem."[8]

- KIROV THE DIPLOMAT

By the time of the Karabakh rising in June, Kirov was already in Moscow, where he had been summoned suddenly and appointed Russia's new ambassador to the still independent state of Georgia. Although Sergo Ordzhonikidze had more than once cabled Lenin and told him that the Eleventh Army would soon be in Georgia's capital, Tbilisi, Lenin had ordered him to desist and negotiate a treaty arranging for a peaceful recognition of independent Georgia, as well as to hold back from "liberating" Armenia. A Polish offensive against Russia that began in April 1920 led the Soviet leadership to adopt temporarily a "soft" policy toward Georgia and Armenia, but it did not abandon plans for an eventual military-diplomatic offensive against both countries.[9]

Kirov must have been pleased to receive this prestigious new post, which involved setting up a mission of dozens of Bolsheviks in Tbilisi. In preparation for his job, he visited a tailor in Moscow and outfitted himself in appropriate diplomat's attire. He had always taken special pride in the simple way he dressed, but now it was time to exchange his peaked cap, leather jacket, and boots for a dark blue suit, a mackintosh, a soft hat, and gloves. Kirov's new status conferred upon him a diplomatic passport written in both Russian and French, and the privilege of traveling by train in a special lounge car, stopping along the way in Rostov-on-Don.[10] From there he sent a telegram, dated 19 June, to the Soviet Commissar of Foreign Affairs, Georgii Chicherin, with a copy to Lenin. He reported the latest news about Georgia, which did not bode well for the Soviet mission. The Georgian government, controlled by the Mensheviks, had agreed to diplomatic relations with Moscow and to the legalization of the Communist Party there. But, according to Kirov, the Mensheviks were allowing their territory to be used as a base for subversive operations against the new Soviet regime in Azerbaijan.[11]

Upon his arrival in Tbilisi a few days later, Kirov observed in a letter to Sergo that the Georgian government representative had received them hospitably.[12] But he found the atmosphere tense. It became apparent that the Georgians were highly distrustful of the Bolsheviks—with good reason—and were not inclined to be cooperative. Before Kirov's arrival, the Georgian government had arrested a number of Bolsheviks and closed several of their newspapers. This, of course, greatly hindered Moscow's efforts to spread propaganda and undermine support for the Menshevik government in Georgia. The suspicion and hostility of Georgian authorities were directed specifically toward the Soviet mission, which frustrated Kirov's efforts at diplomacy. He described his problems in a July 1920 letter to Stalin: "Dear Koba . . . it is difficult to imagine the situation here. One has to live here, to talk to Zhordania, Gegechkori [Georgian leaders], and others, to breathe the air, in order to assess completely the government

regime here." He went on to complain that he and his colleagues were con-
stantly spied upon and that every step they took aroused suspicion.[13]

Kirov sent similar reports to Chicherin and Lenin, pointing out the
many obstacles that prevented him from establishing "normal" relations
with the Georgian government. Ignoring the undeniable fact that the
Bolsheviks harbored plans to take over Georgia, Kirov expressed indignation over the hostility toward him. "I have given the Georgian government
no grounds for acting so aggressively toward us," he complained to
Chicherin.[14] Writing to Lenin, Kirov was also ingratiating: "Dear Vladimir
Il'ich, Your predictions about my work have been brilliantly confirmed
with every step. Chicherin has undoubtedly told you about the position of
our government here. . . ."[15] And in another letter to Lenin: "I have followed your advice exactly. . . . I have read an account in *Pravda* of your
report to the Second Conference of the Third International on our
relations to backward peoples in capitalist countries and think that this
[enclosed] article would interest you. It confirms, it seems to me, your
outstanding analysis of the question. I will not take anymore of your
time . . ."[16]

However deferential he was toward Lenin, Kirov did not hesitate to
press his views upon him and to make demands upon the leadership. One
matter of particular concern to him was the increasingly volatile territorial
disputes between predominantly Christian Armenia and Azerbaijan,
which was mainly Muslim. Kirov reported in his letters to Moscow that he
had held numerous meetings with representatives of both sides, but that
nothing had been resolved. The only solution, he insisted, was to have
Moscow decide these territorial questions as soon as possible. Otherwise,
he said, the Bolsheviks would be discredited and their policies attributed
either to weakness or to evil intentions.[17]

It is not clear how, if at all, Lenin and the Politburo responded to
Kirov's persistent requests, because Kirov soon set aside the problems of
Transcaucasia when he received another diplomatic mission—as part of a
delegation from Russia to Riga, Latvia, for peace talks with the Poles.
Chicherin, it seems, had been so impressed by Kirov's diplomatic skills in
Tbilisi that he insisted on including Kirov in the delegation.[18] Kirov left
for Riga in September 1920, stopping on the way in Moscow. He probably
took the opportunity to see Nadezhda Serebrennikova, to whom he had
written in July, voicing his despair over not hearing from her: "I will wait

for even the smallest bit of news from you. . . . Again, I strongly implore you to write."[19] Mariia L'vovna, meanwhile, was still in Vladikavkaz, apparently waiting for her husband to settle someplace permanently so that she might join him.

Upon arriving in Moscow, Kirov found himself immersed in the first of many scandals involving his comrade Sergo Ordzhonikidze, who was quick-tempered and emotional. Sergo was dedicated to his work and an able administrator, but was prone to impulsiveness and intolerance of others' views. Thus, although he had gained the respect of Lenin and the other Bolshevik leaders, he also had made enemies. This was not just because of Sergo's personality. The Caucasus and Transcaucasus, where his work was concentrated, were seething with ethnic strife, fueled by centuries-old grievances among the various national groups and deep resentment of Russia. As Kirov himself discovered, it was difficult for any representative of Moscow to administer this area, even with the might of the Red Army and the Cheka behind him.

Then, of course, there was the rapidly developing habit among Bolsheviks of denouncing colleagues and superiors behind their backs every time there was a dispute. The Bolshevik Party had never been a democratic organization. Once in power, Bolshevik leaders became even more authoritarian and intolerant of diverse views within their midst. Decisions were reached by behind-the-scenes machinations and unilateral decrees from the top. There was no room for open exchange of opinions or consensus. This situation caused resentment among the party members whose recommendations were not followed or who did not receive desired appointments. Often they vented their anger by denouncing those whose views had won out. The Moscow leadership, lacking a system of accurate and objective reporting and accountability, tended to encourage such denunciations as a means of following what was going in the localities and keeping local leaders on their toes.

It is not entirely clear what precipitated the attack on Sergo, who, as head of the Kavburo, was now based in Baku. But sometime in the summer of 1920 a group of Communists from the mountain regions of the North Caucasus came to Moscow to complain about Sergo to the Central Committee. He acted in a heavy-handed manner, they said, without taking into consideration their views. He made threatening and insulting remarks about their peoples. They also claimed that Ordzhonikidze had protected subordinates who had stolen money.[20]

Although Sergo was the main target of the attack, Kirov, as Sergo's deputy in the Kavburo, also came under criticism, and he found the pressure difficult to withstand. Writing to Sergo on the eve of his departure for Riga, Kirov told him:

> The gossip against all of us is unbelievable. They say that many of these fabrications come from someone in the Special Department [the secret police in the Red Army]. . . . Today I had a long talk with Il'ich and put the issue directly—it is impossible to work in the Caucasus under the conditions that have developed. Il'ich thinks that I should return quickly from Riga and go to work in the Caucasus, where you, in his opinion, also must remain for sure. In addition Il'ich suggested that I write my observations about how the story concerning the Caucasus is nothing but a White Guard plot to discredit or somehow get rid of influential workers. . . . Il'ich says that under these conditions it is especially important to have people in the Caucasus who know local customs. I, of course, did not object.[21]

Lenin's flattering reassurances mollified Kirov. He was persuaded to return to the Caucasus after Riga, but not without Sergo there. He ended a letter to Sergo the following day with these words: "I hope that in a month and a half I will find you in the Caucasus. If, despite my expectations, you are not there, then I too will not go."[22] It may seem odd that Kirov, who since his youth had been daring and independent, would feel that he could not stand on his own. But the Caucasus was now dangerous political terrain, and he needed Sergo to help him navigate. Kirov's decision to bind his fate to Sergo's was not without its drawbacks, however. Sergo would prove to be a loyal and devoted friend, but he would also draw Kirov into some bitter political controversies.

- CONFLICTS IN THE CAUCASUS

Indeed, upon finishing his diplomatic stint in Riga—about which we know little, except that a treaty was signed with the Poles—Kirov found himself defending Sergo at a stormy meeting of regional Caucasian party officials in late October 1920.[23] The meeting was held in Vladikavkaz to discuss a report to the Central Committee in Moscow containing a number of accusations against Sergo. Some of the charges were those Kirov had heard about when he was in Moscow in September, but the report also mentioned other things. Sergo had, it seems, placed a Georgian in command of a mountaineers' division to fight the Whites in the North Caucasus some months back. This commander was then arrested for some offense by the Special Department, but he escaped and fled to Georgia. Sergo had allegedly tried to protect him only because he was a countryman. The report went on to conclude that politics in the Caucasus had been reduced to pettiness and "zigzags" under Sergo's leadership.

Sergo himself was present at the meeting, but Kirov, who had been appointed chairman of the Terek Revolutionary Committee (in addition to being a deputy chairman of the Kavburo), led the defense. Eloquent and persuasive as always, he did a good job. He opened with an amusing story about how he himself had once been arrested in Astrakhan on the grounds that he was the famous monk Iliodor, to whom he bore a resemblance. He was released only after it was revealed that the White Army had started the rumor as a deliberate provocation. Drawing an analogy to the accusations against Sergo, he observed: "I see, comrades, that many of you are smiling. Unfortunately, I did not notice these smiles when Comrade Dzhatiev [one of Sergo's accusers] was talking." Kirov then went on to dismiss the various charges against Sergo as "White Guard provocations" against a Bolshevik of the highest integrity. Because the meeting was closed to outsiders, the local press did not report the speeches, but it did state that a resolution by Kirov "on the political situation in the North Caucasus" was adopted by the attendees, which meant that Kirov was successful in his efforts to refute the charges against his friend.[24]

Significantly, the press also mentioned that Stalin was in attendance, and another source had him "directing the work of the conference."[25] Although we have no record of what Stalin said, his mere presence there served as a sign that the charges were to be taken seriously. In fact, he had fueled the controversy by soliciting a written report from Sergo's critics and then showing it to Sergo, who was highly incensed: "When I received this vile paper from Comrade Stalin I at first laughed. When I read it for a third time it became clear to me that we are dealing with an undoubted agent of the White Guards and the Georgian Mensheviks."[26]

Already at this point, Stalin had learned how to take advantage of controversy within the party and use it to bolster his own power. As he observed what took place at this meeting, he must have learned a great deal about the weaknesses of his Bolshevik comrades, especially Sergo. Indeed, according to Anastas Mikoyan, Sergo "became unrecognizable when he came up against lies, intrigue or rank injustice. Then he would explode with indignation and rage and was capable of things he would later sincerely repent." In this instance, Sergo had slapped the face of his accuser and got himself into trouble with Lenin, who wanted him to be punished for "indulging in that hot temper."[27]

At the same time, however, Stalin was cultivating both Sergo and Kirov, giving them encouragement and support so that they would feel a sense of loyalty to him. Thus when he reported back to Lenin and the Central Committee in Moscow about uprisings that had erupted in Terek and neighboring Dagestan that month, he noted: "There is no doubt that the Kavburo and Ordzhonikidze conducted our policy skillfully, uniting the mountain people with the Soviet regime."[28]

Stalin had in fact been in Vladikavkaz since 21 October and had attended a meeting of the Vladikavkaz soviet, where Kirov reported on the Polish peace talks. Stalin left for Baku at the end of the month but returned on 16 November 1920, to speak at the Terek People's Congress. Although Stalin and Kirov had met on numerous occasions and had corresponded a great deal, Stalin's visit to the North Caucasus marked the first time that he had extended contact with Kirov. From this point onward they became much closer, although theirs was hardly a relationship of equals. As Commissar of Nationalities and of the Worker-Peasants' Inspectorate, as well as a Politburo member, Stalin already wielded considerable power. Kirov, young and ambitious, was anxious to please him, whatever their earlier differences had been. As Trotsky later observed: "On the surface relatively a second-rater himself among Bolshevik leaders, he [Stalin] had already begun convincing a growing group of Bolshevik politicians eager for advancement that he was able to reward the faithful with political plums."[29]

Kirov saw Stalin again in December 1920, when he attended the Eighth Congress of Soviets in Moscow and was elected to the All-Russian Central Executive Committee, the highest state body. This was shortly after the Red Army had invaded Armenia, a move that Stalin and the Kavburo had been advocating for some time, despite the reservations of Lenin and Trotsky. In fact, one reason why Stalin had been courting Kirov and Ordzhonikidze was that they agreed with his view on the necessity for the Bolsheviks to extend their power immediately and were willing to do all they could to persuade Lenin to go along with them. Although it was atypical of Kirov to advocate such a heavy-handed approach, in this instance he apparently felt an invasion was worth the risk of damaging Moscow's relations with non-Russian Communist nationals.

Once the "Sovietization" of Armenia had been accomplished, Kirov and Sergo concentrated their efforts on Georgia. In early January 1921, they sent a letter to the Central Committee outlining the reasons why it was necessary for the Red Army to move in. The thrust of their argument was that the Georgian Menshevik government was undermining the stability of Armenia, Azerbaijan, and the North Caucasus by instigating anti-Soviet uprisings on their territories. Georgia, they wrote, served as a base for counterrevolution in the entire area. Answering the arguments of Trotsky, who wanted to delay the invasion in order to prepare an uprising within Georgia, they insisted that it was pointless to wait for this to happen: "Georgia cannot Sovietize itself without our help."[30]

Lenin responded negatively to their calls for an invasion, but Stalin and the Kavburo were not to be deterred. Using the pretext of an insurrection within the republic, which had actually been organized by the Kavburo, Sergo Ordzhonikidze summoned the Eleventh Army to march into Georgia from Baku on 11–12 February 1921. Kirov, who was still in Vladikavkaz, apparently did not know about the invasion immediately, for he wrote a letter to Sergo on 14 February in which he said nothing about it.[31] But once he heard the news he organized a transfer of troops to Georgia from the North Caucasus and then he went to Tbilisi to participate in the takeover. On 2 March 1921, *Pravda* announced in Moscow: "The flag of the proletariat is flying over Tbilisi."

Less than a week later Kirov was again in Moscow, this time as a delegate from Terek to the Tenth Congress of the Russian Communist Party. Probably at the instigation of Stalin, who wanted to show his gratitude for Kirov's cooperation in the matter of Georgia, he was elected a candidate member of the Central Committee, which was a significant step in his climb up the party ladder. Kirov was realizing how it could pay off to side with Stalin. Unfortunately, however, Kirov had to listen to more criticisms of Sergo, with whom he was now closely associated in everyone's mind. Sergo himself did not attend the congress because he could not leave Georgia so soon after the Bolshevik invasion. During elections to the

Central Committee (held at every congress) several delegates, military officers from the North Caucasus, openly expressed their opposition to Sergo's candidacy. According to Anastas Mikoyan, who was present at the congress, one officer went to the podium to report that Sergo shouted at everyone, ordered people around, and did not consult with local party workers. Therefore, the officer went on, he should not be in the Central Committee.[32]

Speaking in a calm, soft voice, Stalin came to Sergo's defense, discussing his work in the underground before the revolution and his accomplishments in the civil war. But this was not enough to sway the recalcitrant delegates. Then Lenin came to the podium. He had apparently forgiven Sergo for his earlier display of temper, for he told the delegates that he had known Sergo for many years and considered him to be an able and dedicated revolutionary and a talented organizer. Lenin said that he could agree with only one of the criticisms raised against Sergo—that he shouted at everyone. This was true, Lenin acknowledged, but he shouted because he was deaf in his left ear and thought that people could not hear him. Therefore this fault should not be considered. Lenin's remarks made everyone laugh and convinced more than the necessary majority of the delegates to approve Sergo's membership in the Central Committee during the secret vote.[33] But it had been a close call, and Sergo was indebted to Stalin and Lenin for their support. As for Kirov, this incident provided further evidence of how precarious the career of a Bolshevik politician was.

▪ THE REGIME UNDER THREAT

The dispute over Sergo Ordzhonikidze was minor in comparison with the crisis that occurred during the March 1921 congress and threatened the entire Bolshevik leadership—a rebellion against the government that broke out at the Kronstadt naval base near Petrograd. The insurgents, of worker and peasant origin and supporters of the Bolsheviks in 1917, demanded an end to the Communist dictatorship and the immediate institution of economic and political freedoms. The rising caused such alarm among Bolshevik leaders that they interrupted the congress and sent a cohort of its delegates, led by Trotsky, to accompany the Red Army in storming the fortress and executing the leaders of the rebellion. The Soviet regime was shaken to its core. As historian Leonard Schapiro observed:

"The revolt of the proletariat against the dictatorship of the proletariat was something for which Marxist doctrine had made no provision. The Tenth Party Congress when it met on 8 March was dominated by the plain evidence of the growing unpopularity of Communist rule over those whom it claimed to represent, of which the Kronstadt revolt was only the culminating proof. As Lenin admitted to the congress, 'we have failed to convince the broad masses.'"[34]

The official party propaganda line was that the Kronstadt revolt was a "counterrevolution" instigated by "White Guardists" and foreign enemies. But Kirov chose to be more candid in reporting to the party rank and file. He doubtless realized that some plausible explanation of this traumatic event was necessary, especially since most people knew full well what had happened and would not be convinced by feeble references to foreign interference. Addressing party and trade union workers in Tbilisi in early April, he admitted that the peasants, who formed the bulk of the population, could no longer tolerate the economic hardships and deprivation they had endured since the civil war and suggested that their discontent found its expression at Kronstadt: "As comrade Lenin correctly observed about the events at Kronstadt: it is difficult to say what happened there. Whether it was from those to the left [politically] or to the right of us, or in another place. But one thing is clear—Kronstadt was the focus, the sum of all the sentiments existing in Russia."[35]

Kirov went on to explain that, in order to alleviate the situation, the leadership had decided to cease its policy of forcible requisitioning of grain from the peasants and to introduce an economic system that would allow market forces to operate in the countryside. "In a military situation," he said, "it was easy to conduct a grain monopoly. In peacetime things are different. Obviously, we have to change our economic relations in the country."[36]

This change was reflected in what was known as the New Economic Policy, or NEP, which was basically a mixed economy, with free enterprise operating in agriculture and trade, while the state retained ownership of large industry. At the same time, however, this liberalization of economic life was accompanied by tighter political control in the country and greater discipline within the party. At Lenin's instigation the Tenth Party Congress passed a resolution on party unity, which set strict limits on criticism of policy by party members and conferred full disciplinary powers on the Central Committee. Henceforth, debate within the party would be significantly curtailed, while infighting and behind-the-scenes conflicts would become more intense at all levels.

Kirov left Vladikavkaz for good in May 1921 and assumed duties in Tbilisi as a member of the presidium of the party's Kavburo. He spent the next month and a half working on a railway project, meeting with Kavburo members to discuss a range of pressing political and economic issues affecting the Caucasus and speaking at various party and trade union forums. By this time he had established a considerable reputation as an orator. The leading party newspaper in Georgia, *Pravda Gruzii*, described the audience's reaction when Kirov spoke at a meeting:

> Kirov slowly approached the footlights. The audience settled into a dead silence. The comrades love to listen to Comrade Kirov. They love his always beautiful and vividly constructed speeches, with sparks of genuine humor, but always rising to the heights of real pathos. In his speech Comrade Kirov combines mild, purely Slavic humor with lashing scorpions of revolutionary rage.[37]

Kirov also had gained a reputation as a skilled organizer and a hard worker. Thus when Lenin and the Politburo decided in June 1921 that it was imperative to find an able official to run the party in Azerbaijan, they chose Kirov for the job, appointing him secretary of the Azerbaijan Communist Party. A prime consideration was the need to rescue the faltering oil industry, consisting of more than 250 plants that had formerly belonged to private companies but were now under Soviet control. Apparently, the choice was made on the recommendation of Stalin, who headed a special Central Committee commission on the oil industry, and was in Tbilisi in June and early July, while Kirov was there.[38] Kirov's technical training and his experience with the oil fields in the North Caucasus made him well suited for the position. Also, he had demonstrated his ability to deal effectively with ethnic problems and mediate conflicts among non-Russian nationals, which would be crucial in administering Azerbaijan. Finally, and most importantly, he was Russian and thus could be counted on to have Moscow's interests at heart.

Although the appointment was a promotion for Kirov, he can hardly have been uplifted by his surroundings after he moved to Baku in July 1921. According to Mikoyan, Baku was "a dirty, trash-filled, litter-strewn city, which was always covered with a fine—almost microscopic—coating of sand from the hurricane winds blowing in from the north."[39] The writer Maxim Gorky had a similar impression when he saw the city shortly before the revolution:

> The oil fields left in my memory a brilliant picture of dark hell. I do not joke. The impression was stunning. . . . Amidst the chaos of derricks, long, low workers' barracks, built of rust-colored and gray stones and resembling very much the dwellings of prehistoric peoples, pressed against the ground. I never saw so much dirt and trash around human habitation, so much broken glass in windows and such miserable poverty in the rooms, which looked like caves. Not a single light in the windows, and around not a piece of earth covered in grass, not a tree, not a shrub.[40]

Now, after the destruction wrought by the civil war, Baku was in even worse shape. Judging from a letter he wrote to Nadezhda Serebrennikova in August 1921, Kirov assumed that his appointment in Baku was only temporary: "I have been living in Baku for two months and probably will stay for that much longer. Then, then, I don't know where I will be—probably in the Caucasus. I hope to be in Moscow at the first opportunity, but unfortunately I don't foresee that for the time being."[41] As it turned out, Kirov was deluding himself. He would remain in Baku for the next four and a half years.

▪ PARTY CHIEF IN BAKU

Mariia L'vovna soon joined Kirov. She may have found Baku dreary, but at least she was finally able to live with her husband, enjoying the benefits of his prestigious new position. As one biographer observed: "In the atmosphere of eastern servility and adulation Mariia L'vovna felt in Baku like the revered wife of an all-powerful deputy from the center."[42] It would have been out of character for her to remain at home doing nothing, however. In the spirit of the "liberated" Bolshevik women of the 1920s, she started a campaign to eliminate homelessness among children and organized a women's soviet (*zhensovet*), which had as its slogan "Down with the chador."[43]

Mariia L'vovna saw little of Kirov, whose job as Azerbaijan party leader was extremely demanding. (At one point his friend Sergo was so concerned about him that he telegraphed Stalin: "Kirov is absolutely exhausted. Without a vacation he is not fit for any work."[44]) World War I and the ensuing civil war had devastated the Azeri economy. Transportation and agriculture were in ruins; unemployment was rife; and oil production was at about a third of what it had been before 1914. The Baku oil fields were crucial to the economy of the entire Bolshevik empire, and Lenin was thus desperate to raise oil production. "Because of insufficient drilling, we will perish and will destroy Baku," he wrote to a leading Bolshevik engineer in 1921.[45] Thus, for Kirov, the top priority was the "battle for oil."

After a weeklong inspection of the oil fields, which reportedly looked like graveyards, Kirov understood why five party secretaries had come and gone from Azerbaijan in the past year and a half. But he rose to the challenge and threw himself into his work. Kirov's prerevolutionary comrade Mamia Orakhelashvili, who came from Tbilisi to visit him, commented: "I observed Kirov in a new situation. His style of work amounted to a personal, daily involvement in every detail. . . . Times were difficult. He had to develop the oil industry out of nothing, without equipment, without money, without people."[46]

A. P. Serebrovskii, head of Azneft (Azerbaijan Oil), described how Kirov approached his new job:

> I remember well the day of his arrival in Baku. He didn't call for anyone, didn't organize any kind of ceremonial reception. He came directly to us at Azneft and requested all the materials on the oil industry. And from that first day, for an entire week, he did not take up his [political] duties as secretary of the Azerbaijan Central Committee, but visited all the enterprises and learned all the details about the oil industry. . . . We went around with Sergei Mironovich to the enterprises. Not a bad mechanical engineer, he quickly grasped the tremendous significance of mechanizing oil production, of introducing rotary drilling and deep pumps, and he became a fierce advocate of all these innovations.[47]

As party leader of Azerbaijan, Kirov had responsibilities for both political and economic matters. Although the Soviet regime instituted state structures to run economic enterprises, the party had the ultimate say. Kirov made his top priority a complete technical renovation of Azerbaijan's oil industry, exchanging antiquated methods of drilling for modern ones within three years. In order to accomplish this, Azneft had to turn for help abroad. Lenin had authorized Azneft to give up part of its oil reserves to foreign concessions, but Kirov discarded this plan because it entailed relinquishing too much control to foreign capitalists. Instead Azneft sold its oil abroad and released credits in gold to pay for technical assistance and equipment, mainly from America. Such trade practices gave rise to protests in Moscow about "plundering" in Baku because the state was supposed to have a monopoly on foreign trade, but Lenin personally approved the transactions.[48]

The introduction of new machinery and mechanized equipment into oil production met with strong resistance from the Muslim oil workers. Fearing that the technology would make them redundant, they protested by declaring strikes. On one such occasion Kirov and Serebrovskii called a meeting of the strikers. Using a translator, because most workers spoke only Azeri, Kirov exhorted the men to go back to the oil wells: "Why are you against the deep pumps? Is it really easier for you to stand at bailing machines for eight hours? Is it not better to hold an oil can in your hand and press a pump, which bails for you, rather than to bail yourselves?"[49]

Despite assistance from abroad, the task of reviving Azerbaijan's oil industry was long, arduous, and fraught with unexpected setbacks. Shortly after Kirov's arrival in Baku an enormous fire broke out at a factory, igniting seven tanks of oil. The fire, which covered the entire city in smoke, took three days to extinguish. In November 1922, another fire broke out, this time damaging the pumping station that provided water for the city of Baku and making it inoperable. The population was in panic. For seventeen days men worked round the clock, under Kirov's direction, to repair the damage and restore water to Baku. Finally an exhausted Kirov was able to telegraph Lenin triumphantly: "There is water in the Baku region—and there will be oil in accordance with the quota given to us."[50]

By the autumn of 1922 oil production in Azerbaijan had increased substantially and was well above its prewar level. But Azneft continued to experience financial crises, making it necessary for Kirov to do continuous battle with the Moscow center, Stalin in particular, on Azneft's behalf. The archives contain numerous telegrams from Kirov to Stalin and the heads of various economic agencies protesting interference from Moscow in Azneft's trade ventures and imploring them to send money. Thus, in a January 1923 telegram to Stalin and other officials, Kirov wrote that further development of the oil industry could not be achieved without foreign trade. He went on:

The source of money is the sale of oil products on foreign markets. *Only by means of this trade can Azneft and the trading organs of the oil syndicate ensure regular and timely receipt of these monetary resources,* without which the realization of the 1922–23 production plan is inconceivable. Any interference in such trade by various agencies and or transfer of earnings [from Azneft] leads the oil industry back to the situation in 1921, when . . . oil extraction consistently fell and the number of workers declined.[51]

On 7 March 1923 Kirov wrote: "Azneft's financial crisis is growing every day. Earnings from the syndicate are barely enough for the workers' wages. There are absolutely no reserves for continuing work begun on drilling and for purchasing equipment. . . . Either we curtail our work and basically destroy our program or we immediately receive a loan of fifteen million [rubles in] gold."[52] That same day Kirov sent another dramatic message, marked "top secret," to Stalin: "I am requesting an immediate payment of a loan of three million for March. The money situation is so severe that Azneft is already in agony."[53]

As the desperate tone of his telegrams suggested, Kirov was under tremendous pressure, attempting to build up Azerbaijan's economy with a backward workforce, a weak technical base, and constant interference from Moscow. We do not have Stalin's replies, but, judging from Kirov's pleas, Stalin was not being cooperative. As in the past, Kirov was encountering Stalin's intransigence. He probably did not appeal to Lenin, however, because Lenin had just days before suffered his third stroke and was too ill to intervene effectively. Now Stalin had the ultimate say in Moscow's policies toward Azerbaijan. His views toward all three Transcaucasian republics, as mentioned earlier, were strongly pro-Russian, with little regard for regional concerns. Kirov was able to go along with Stalin's centrist approach until he himself, by virtue of his new post, became an advocate of Azerbaijan's interests vis-à-vis Moscow. Now he was seeing things in a different light.

▪ POLITICAL STRUGGLES

The push for centralization from Moscow also had a strong impact on internal politics in Azerbaijan, forcing Kirov into the no-win position of mediator between Azeri nationalists and pro-Soviet internationalists.

Baku had been a hotbed of political conflict well before Kirov arrived. But his arrival coincided with a new round of strife among party politicians there. In fact, it was Sergo Ordzhonikidze, backed by Stalin, who actually precipitated the conflict. In August 1921, at a meeting of the Kavburo in Tbilisi, he demanded a purge of all the "national deviationists" from the Transcaucasian Communist parties. National deviation was a pejorative term applied to those non-Russians who sought to defend the autonomy of their republics against the centralizing policies of Moscow. Kirov was thus faced with the task of implementing this purge upon his return to Baku.[54] He had no choice but to follow through with orders. By early January 1922 over 4,000 members had been excluded from the Azeri Communist Party. Not surprisingly, resentment toward Kirov ran high. According to one source, he even received death threats.[55]

The purge in Transcaucasia was carried out primarily to eliminate those who opposed a plan that was the brainchild of Stalin and Sergo—the unification of Armenia, Azerbaijan, and Georgia into a single federated Transcaucasian republic. When the plan was finally unveiled, as a fait accompli, to the party central committees of the three republics, there was great consternation among the native Bolshevik elites, who wanted at all costs to preserve the national integrity of their republics as independent entities. The Georgian nationalists—who referred to their countryman Sergo Ordzhonikidze as "Stalin's ass"—were especially vocal in their opposition, sending a letter of protest to Lenin about the federation, which officially came into being in December 1922.[56]

Lenin had initially gone along with the idea of a Transcaucasian Federation, but when he found out how heavy-handed Stalin and Sergo had been in implementing their plans, he was furious. They had, in his view, run roughshod over national sensitivities and exacerbated resentment toward Moscow. In early March 1923, already disabled by illness, he wrote to members of the Georgian Central Committee: "Respected comrades, I am following your affair with my entire soul. I am indignant at the rudeness of Ordzhonikidze and the connivances of Stalin and Dzerzhinskii [chief of the political police, who had headed a commission to look into the matter]."[57] Lenin appealed to Trotsky to defend the Georgian "deviationists" against Stalin and Sergo at an upcoming Central Committee plenum, which he himself was unable to attend. Trotsky, at Lenin's behest, requested that Sergo be suspended from membership in the party, but the plenum, which took place at the end of March, neither supported his request nor took any concrete measures to appease the Georgians. Nonetheless, the affair damaged Sergo's reputation, while at the same time making him more beholden to Stalin, who had lent him valuable support throughout the ordeal.[58]

Kirov, immersed in Azerbaijan's economic problems, was a background player in the "Georgian affair," although he was deputy chief of the Transcaucasian Regional Party Committee, and he and Sergo sent more than one telegram to Moscow during March 1923 regarding changes in the Transcaucasian party leadership. In typical fashion, Kirov took a cautious attitude toward the formation of a Transcaucasian Federation, coming down neither for nor against the idea. He even wrote a letter to the Central Committee in February 1922 expressing concerns about the rising tensions over the issue in Transcaucasia.[59] Unlike Stalin and Sergo, Kirov was not disposed at this point to handling his fellow Bolsheviks with an iron fist.

He also deeply resented the political surveillance of the Cheka, which served as Moscow's watchdog, over members of the Azeri party, himself included, and complained to Stalin about it. This prompted a letter to Kirov from the deputy chief of the Azeri Cheka, Lavrentii Beria, who went to great lengths to defend himself.[60] Beria's chief, the notoriously ruthless Mir Dzhafar Bagirov, was to cause Kirov even more trouble. Kirov, who had difficulty getting him to follow orders, even tried to have him dismissed from his post in 1925, but was unsuccessful. The police, as he increasingly realized, were controlled from Moscow.[61]

Kirov's relatively moderate stance did not prevent him from being viewed by some Azeris as Sergo Ordzhonikidze's lackey, willing to do his bidding at any cost. This was how the prominent Azeri Bolshevik N. N. Narimanov saw it. Narimanov had been strongly opposed to the creation of the Transcaucasian Federation, and, as a result, Sergo forced him out of his post as chief of the Azeri Sovnarkom in the spring of 1922. Feeling bitter and betrayed, Narimanov sent a letter to Stalin in 1924, with a copy to Trotsky, denouncing Sergo and Kirov for their duplicity and ruthlessness. Kirov, he claimed, had used military troops to prevent Muslims from practicing their religion. But Sergo was the real culprit: "In all probability, the inspirer of Kirov, Comrade Sergo, must answer for these actions, since he [Kirov] does nothing without the latter." Narimanov went on to say: "The center's representative Kirov will report to the Central Committee that the congress [in Baku] unanimously endorsed his policies in Azerbaijan and the center will believe him. . . . Thus we will live in self-deception until a catastrophe."[62]

But Narimanov's views were apparently not widely shared. An evaluation [*kharakteristika*] of Kirov sent from an unnamed official in the Baku Party Committee to Moscow in early January 1924 presented a completely different picture:

> Comrade Kirov is a strong political worker, virtually directing the operations of party, soviet, and economic organizations alike. He has great erudition in Marxism. He quickly grasps political situations and orients himself splendidly in the most difficult political circumstances. He is completely firm politically. Energetic, forceful in implementing decisions. Has tremendous initiative. Even-tempered, with great political tact, completely composed. A first-class, outstanding orator. Good organizer and administrator. Relations with others are correct, comradely. . . . When mistakes are made he quickly recognizes them and draws correct conclusions. He is not one of those who, because of egoism, is stubborn and does not want to admit mistakes.[63]

In Moscow, Kirov's political star was shining, despite the controversies that surrounded his mentor, Sergo. At the Twelfth Party Congress in April 1923 he was promoted to full membership in the Central Committee, thus gaining nationwide party stature. It was reportedly Stalin who put forth Kirov's candidacy. Stalin had done another one of his about-faces and was openly cordial to Kirov. In May 1924, he gave Kirov a book with the inscription "to my beloved brother and friend." And two months later—under the stewardship of Stalin, who, as head of the party Secretariat, controlled party appointments in the regions—Kirov was designated "first" secretary of Azerbaijan, thus formalizing his de facto leadership of the Azeri Communist Party.

▪ THE SUCCESSION ISSUE

Stalin had good reason to be courting Kirov, as he was other regional leaders, for he was engaged in an intense struggle over the succession to the party leadership, which began after Lenin's third and final stroke in

March 1923. With Lenin no longer physically able to govern, a "troika" of Stalin, Grigorii Zinoviev, and Lev Kamenev emerged to take up the reins of power and block Trotsky. But Lenin now had serious reservations about Stalin, not only because of the Georgian affair but also because of an incident in late 1922 when Stalin had called Lenin's wife, Krupskaia, on the telephone and berated her in a rude and offensive manner. In fact, in late December 1922 Lenin had dictated a letter to the party, harshly criticizing Stalin. In early January 1923 Lenin added a postscript in which he said: "Stalin is too rude, and this fault . . . becomes unbearable in the office of General Secretary. Therefore, I propose to the comrades to find a way to remove Stalin from that position and appoint another man."[64]

The contents of what came to be called Lenin's testament were kept secret, but members of the leadership, including Stalin and Sergo, learned about it. Realizing that he was now highly vulnerable, Stalin pushed ahead with his vigorous drive to gather the party apparatus in his hands while the Soviet leader languished on his deathbed. As General Secretary, Stalin was able to marshal forces by extending throughout the country a network of party personnel branches with the power of making appointments, not only of provincial party leaders like Kirov but of all government posts. When he described the work of the personnel department in the Secretariat to the Twelfth Party Congress, it was clear how many delegates there depended on him for their political careers.[65]

As Stalin began to stack the cards in his favor, even his closest Bolshevik allies became worried. In July 1923, Politburo members Zinoviev and Bukharin, vacationing together in Kislovodsk, a resort in the North Caucasus, decided to limit Stalin's power by proposing a reorganization of the party leadership: the Orgburo, a powerful Central Committee subcommittee that Stalin served on, would be abolished, and Zinoviev and Trotsky would join the Secretariat. Their plan was supported by several members of the Central Committee who were in Kislovodsk at the time, including Sergo Ordzhonikidze, who agreed to tell Stalin and Kamenev about their decision. As Zinoviev observed in a letter to Kamenev, Sergo's support for the proposal was surprising, especially since the reorganization was so clearly intended as a move against Stalin's authority:

> If the party is destined to go through a period (doubtless very short) of absolute rule by Stalin, then so be it. But I, at the very least, do not intend to cover up all these swinish tricks. . . . In fact, there is no troika, but

rather a dictatorship of Stalin. Il'ich was a thousand times right. Unless we find a serious way out, a period of struggle is inevitable. For you this is nothing new. You yourself have said the same thing more than once. But what surprises me is that Voroshilov, Frunze [a military commander], and Sergo think almost the same.[66]

It is difficult to say what motivated Sergo to participate openly in a move against his mentor, except that he had come to realize that Stalin's growing powers were a detriment to the party. Behind Sergo's devoted letters to "Dear Koba," his brotherly embraces and warm Georgian toasts, distrust was simmering. Did Kirov share Sergo's misgivings? Unfortunately, there is no record of who else was in attendance at the fateful meetings of Central Committee members in Kislovodsk. But, given Kirov's habit of spending all his free time with Sergo, he may well have been there. In any case, he was in constant contact with Sergo, so he at the very least was apprised of what had happened. Predictably, Stalin was furious when Sergo told him about the plan. He raised such a ruckus that a compromise was reached: the Orgburo was retained, with Bukharin, Zinoviev, and Trotsky becoming members. In backing down before Stalin, his comrades lost a crucial opportunity to limit his power. This was a mistake that would have tragic consequences for all of them.

A sharp conflict with Trotsky that began in the autumn of 1923 temporarily brought the troika members— Stalin, Zinoviev, and Kamenev— together again, and their disagreement was patched up (although not forgotten). Trotsky, for all his brilliance as a theoretician and military leader, was an unequal match for Stalin in the succession struggle. Lenin's testament had given Trotsky plenty of ammunition for an attack on Stalin at the Twelfth Party Congress in April 1923. But Trotsky did not use it, apparently because he did not want to endanger the stability of the party apparatus. He also was loath to create the impression that he was stepping into Lenin's shoes. Later, when Trotsky began to voice his criticisms of the troika publicly, carrying the debate into the press, Stalin forced him to retreat and vacillate time and again. In response to Trotsky's claims that party bureaucracy was stifling the freedom of its members and suppressing legitimate criticism, Stalin and the other triumvirs accused him of trying to revoke the very principles of party unity that Lenin had introduced.[67]

Lenin's sudden death on 21 January 1924 temporarily dampened the conflict with Trotsky, who, apparently because of illness, failed to attend the prolonged funeral ceremonies. Stalin and the other triumvirs used the occasion to inaugurate an elaborate cult of Lenin, while at the same time presenting themselves as the heirs of the great leader. This was especially true of Stalin, who was in the limelight throughout the several days of official mourning and who was pictured alone with Lenin in many published photographs. As Leonard Schapiro observed: "The purpose of the new cult was clear to all: if Lenin was Allah, then Stalin was his prophet."[68]

Although Kirov attended the funeral in Moscow, he either did not get the message of the new cult or did not wish to convey it. At a memorial meeting in honor of Lenin in Baku, Kirov discussed the political leadership in conjunction with an upcoming party congress, but he failed to offer even the slightest hint of Stalin's superior standing: "You know that, before every one of our congresses, everywhere the European bourgeoisie begins to guess who will be elected to the government, who to the Central Committee. They cannot in any way understand that for us this has no significance, that among us there is no difference whatsoever among Stalin, Rykov, Zinoviev, Kamenev. We elect into our leading organs only those whom the Communist world has anointed."[69]

Lenin's deathbed views of Stalin were still a closely guarded secret, but Kirov had doubtless heard about the testament from Sergo and thus knew that Stalin's status was in jeopardy. Indeed, in May 1924, the testament was read aloud at a plenary session of the Central Committee that took place before the Thirteenth Party Congress. It was a close call for Stalin. He was saved by the appeals of Zinoviev and Kamenev, who managed to convince the Central Committee members that Lenin's fears about Stalin had proved groundless and that he should remain General Secretary. Over Krupskaia's objections, the plenum decided not to publish Lenin's testament, but only to communicate it confidentially to selected congress delegates. Stalin now had an unshakable grip on the levers of power.

Trotsky sat through the plenum proceedings in silence. Although he was to continue opposing the triumvirs, he would be resoundingly denounced at the congress and by the end of the year removed from his post as Commissar of War. During 1924 the attacks against Trotsky rose to such a fever pitch that Kirov himself felt compelled to join the fray. He had never had cordial relations with Trotsky, and, along with the other regional party secretaries, Kirov owed his position to Stalin, so he had to lend his voice to the chorus of Trotsky's detractors. But he did so with strong reservations. Thus, in one speech to party activists he remarked: "It is important to appoint experienced and responsible comrades. This is why we say that Trotsky has more than once been capricious with the truth, but this does not mean that he should not be in the Central Committee. That's not right. I would be the first, who louder than everyone would say [that] here; I would be the first to protest against his exclusion from the Central Committee. He has played a great role in our party."[70]

In February 1925, Kirov reported to a party conference in Baku on the results of a Central Committee plenum in Moscow. Trotsky had been condemned yet again at the plenum, held in mid-January 1925, this time for his publication of an essay called "Lessons of October," in which he criticized Zinoviev and Kamenev for opposing Lenin's plan for an uprising in 1917. He was also denounced for his doctrine of "permanent revolution," which said that, in order to succeed, Russia's revolution could not be confined to Russia, but had to spread to Western Europe. This ran counter to Stalin's recently developed theory of "socialism in one country," which set forth the idea that the Russian revolution was self-sufficient and that socialism could be developed in a single isolated state such as Russia.[71]

Kirov told the Baku party elite that Trotsky had been the main topic of discussion at the plenum. The dispute, he explained, had much more than theoretical significance: "If we accept the view of Trotsky on so-called permanent revolution, then we would suffer the defeat of every revolutionary uprising in every country. . . . It must be said that, unless Trotsky completely renounces his position, we will not have peace with him in the party." Kirov criticized Trotsky's theories point by point, but he stressed that Trotsky himself was still a loyal Bolshevik: "It would be a grave mistake to say that Comrade Trotsky gives voice to all the feeble impulses of these [anti-party] elements. Comrade Trotsky, like all of us, is prepared to serve the revolution, but it has turned out in practice that all those who are against Bolshevism, against Leninism, and against the Communist Party have grouped around Trotsky, and people will resort to unbelievable things." Although Kirov claimed that the Mensheviks were quoting Trotsky's writings and using them for their anti-Bolshevik propaganda, he emphasized more than once that Trotsky bore "not the slightest degree of responsibility for this."[72]

Did Kirov's hesitations rankle Stalin? It must be said that Stalin himself, in an effort to appear above the unseemly harsh and strident behavior of the two other triumvirs, against whom he was about to turn, was taking a fairly moderate stand toward Trotsky in public at this point. At the January 1925 plenum, he resisted the demands of Zinoviev and Kamenev that Trotsky be expelled from the party. So in this sense Kirov was not going out on a limb. Nonetheless, Kirov's defense of Trotsky was apparently deemed so inappropriate by those who edited Kirov's speeches for publication after he died that they deleted the positive remarks he made about Trotsky.[73]

▪ MORE TROUBLES FOR KIROV

Soon after the February 1925 Baku party conference a terrible blow befell Kirov. His close comrade, Alesha Miasnikov, a secretary of the Transcaucasian Party Committee, was killed in a plane accident along with Kirov's notorious friend Georgii Atarbekov, who had worked with him in Astrakhan, and another police official. The plane blew up in midair not far from Tbilisi. Judging from his emotional speech at the official memorial ceremony, Kirov was devastated by the tragedy:

> I don't know how nature will choose in the future to play with the life of party members, but for all our Bolshevik steadfastness, all our battle scars, experienced through long, difficult agonizing decades, it is hard for us to speak, to repeat the names of those so precious to us. In Transcaucasia we experience this loss for the whole party twice as much. If terrible things happen in the life of the people, the state, the political party, then just such a terrible event took place on 22 March beneath the skies of the capital of Transcaucasia—Tbilisi.[74]

As Kirov told his audience, the cause of the crash was a mystery, and it remained so after three separate investigations. Rumors circulated that Beria, who had moved from Azerbaijan to become deputy chairman of the Georgian GPU, had plotted to have the plane blown up, possibly on behalf of Stalin. Adding to the mystery, Trotsky later revealed that the three men were on their way to see him.[75] Although Trotsky never questioned the assumption that the crash was an accident, Kirov himself suspected foul play. In a letter to Sergo, he observed: "The more I think about it, the more I think that it was not an accident. There was an interesting conversation between [name unclear] and one of the airport mechanics. Aleksian [apparently a party comrade] knows about it. Probably he told you."[76]

Kirov was clearly unnerved by the crash, even developing a stomach ulcer. Already at this early stage of the Bolshevik regime, accidents and deaths of public officials were shrouded in secrecy, so no one could be sure what really happened. Whatever suspicions Kirov may have had, they did not outwardly affect his relations with Stalin, which became increasingly close in 1925. Not long after the tragedy, Stalin sent a telegram to Kirov in Baku: "with warm greetings from an old Bakuite" in honor of the fifth anniversary of the successful Bolshevik invasion of the city. Stalin expressed his confidence in Kirov's leadership: "I have no doubt that the Communist Party of Azerbaijan will successfully transform the republic into a model for oppressed peoples of the East and a standard-bearer for their freedom from the imperialist yoke."[77]

In the summer of 1925, Stalin wrote Sergo, who was together with Kirov at Kislovodsk, known for its mineral baths: "And Kirov, what is he doing there? Is he recovering from his stomach ulcer with Narzan [a type of mineral water]? That is the way to do it. What quack is treating him? Will you be in Kislovodsk for a long time?"[78] Stalin was always very curious about the health of his subordinates. Both Kirov and Sergo suffered from a variety of chronic health problems—probably exacerbated by poor working and eating habits, heavy smoking, and stress—which stimulated Stalin's interest. As it turned out, Stalin, who was in Sochi at the time, decided to join Sergo and Kirov in Kislovodsk for several days' vacation.[79]

All the while, Stalin was focusing his attention on his relationship with Zinoviev and Kamenev. The anti-Trotsky campaign had been the glue that held the triumvirate together. Once Trotsky was forced to resign his post as Commissar of War, the alliance with Stalin fell apart. Zinoviev and Kamenev began to realize that Stalin was tightening his grip on the party and excluding them from control. Stalin was taking steps to undermine their influence, while forming a new tactical alliance with men from the right wing of the political spectrum: Nikolai Bukharin, Sovnarkom chairman Aleksei Rykov, and trade union leader Mikhail Tomskii. The rightists favored a slower pace of industrialization together with a conciliatory policy toward the peasantry, with the party abandoning its hostility toward the well-to-do farmers, the so-called kulaks. Zinoviev and Kamenev denounced this pro-peasant policy, claiming that it would give rise to a resurgence of capitalism.

The conflict came to a head at the Fourteenth Party Congress in December 1925. Zinoviev and Kamenev made strong protests against the dictatorial policies of the General Secretary and tried, unsuccessfully, to bring up the issue of Lenin's testament. But it was too late. Although Zinoviev controlled the Leningrad party organization, Stalin had the rest of the party apparatus in his hands. He leveled against Zinoviev and Kamenev the same accusations that his enemy Trotsky had earlier made against them and managed a reorganization of the top leadership that reflected the decisive defeat of their left opposition. Kamenev was demoted to candidate membership in the Politburo, and three new members loyal to Stalin were brought in—Molotov, Voroshilov, and Mikhail Kalinin.[80]

The Fourteenth Congress was Stalin's launching pad to a dictatorship. The term "leader" was applied to him for the first time, and some speakers, including Control Commission chairman Valerian Kuibyshev, who would later have misgivings about Stalin, flattered him unashamedly. Kirov, who headed the delegation from Azerbaijan and was elected to the presidium of the congress, was not among the overt flatterers. But he did recognize Stalin's wisdom in his report to the congress delegates: "Comrade Stalin correctly said that whoever has oil predominates." And, not surprisingly, Kirov sided openly with the anti-Zinoviev group, calling for "an end to all that is going on in the first Soviet capital, the birthplace of the Communist Party, Leningrad."[81]

Kirov, unwillingly it turns out, was to play a key role in Stalin's drive to eliminate Zinoviev's fiefdom in Leningrad. During the congress, on 29 December, the Central Committee sent him to Leningrad with Ordzhon-ikidze and Mikoyan to campaign against the left opposition. Kirov gave a speech to Communists in the Vyborg section of Leningrad, returning to Moscow the next day. There was already talk of his being sent to Leningrad on a permanent basis, but Kirov was trying his best to prevent this from happening. He wrote to Mariia L'vovna during the congress:

> I was expecting more from you than just a telegram. As I was leaving, I asked if there was anything you wanted me to buy, but you didn't answer. I wanted to get you a knitted jacket like the one you have, but a hundred times better. Not knowing the size and color, I decided against it. Our mood here is very bad. As you know from the newspapers, a terrible fight is going on here, as never before. Read *Pravda* closely and you will be

able to follow the events. In connection with this conflict, they are talking about sending me to Leningrad on a permanent job. Today they spoke about it quite definitely. Of course, I categorically refused. Sergo is also against sending me there. I cannot predict the final result.[82]

Unfortunately for Kirov, Stalin overruled his objections and those of Sergo. Kirov was thrown into despair. On 4 January he wrote again to his wife:

They are transferring me from Baku to Leningrad, where an unbelievable squabble is going on now. . . . I tried everything to resist it, but nothing helped. I don't know if I will be able to hold out there. If they dismiss me I shall return to Baku. My mood is awful. I have never felt so badly. I am ready to do the devil knows what. Now concerning yourself: for the time being stay in Baku. I will write to you from Leningrad and we will decide about your coming. . . . Maybe you should first come without any luggage to have a look at Petersburg [sic] (which you have not seen) and then we will return together to Baku and take our belongings. All of this on the condition that I shall be able to hold out in Leningrad, in which I have no faith. Dear Marusa, how difficult it is to realize that I am going to an awful world, to Petersburg! How I would like you to be near, I am absolutely alone! Well, let's see what happens. . . . Many kisses, Sergei.[83]

Why was Kirov so reluctant to make a move to Leningrad, a move that would have been a significant step up for him in his career? Although he was ambitious and wanted to play an influential role in the party, Kirov dreaded Leningrad because he knew that he would be in the midst of a political tempest, under fire from all sides. He was loath to engage in the kind of factional conflict that Stalin would demand of him as party leader there. Baku, for better or worse, was now his home, where he had achieved economic success and forged close relationships with Bolshevik comrades, and he did not want to leave. Kirov managed to elicit a promise from Stalin that his stint in Leningrad would last for only a few months, just long enough for him to eliminate the opposition. But Stalin later reneged on his word. Remaining in Leningrad until his death, almost nine years later, Kirov would gradually realize the fateful implications of his support for Stalin, but it would be too late.

Leader of Leningrad

I love you, Peter's creation, I love your stern
Harmonious look, the Neva's majestic flow
Her granite banks, the iron tracery
Of your railings, the transparent twilight and
The moonless glitter of your pensive nights.

—*Pushkin, "The Bronze Horseman"*

Although the bitter factional disputes within the party leadership in the mid-1920s centered on power politics, pressing economic issues formed the backdrop for these conflicts. By 1926 the country was coming close to returning to its prewar production levels, and the New Economic Policy (NEP), so enthusiastically endorsed by party leaders like Nikolai Bukharin, seemed to offer an alternative to the policies that had been promoted by Trotsky and the left opposition. Whereas the latter opposed concessions to the peasantry and advocated rapid industrialization, Bukharin wanted the Soviet Union to pursue a gradualist approach to building socialism. As a result of encouraging the peasants to produce more through economic incentives and thus expanding the consumer market, the necessary capital for industrial growth would be generated, but at a slow pace.

But the NEP never really operated as a full-fledged mixed economy. Increasingly the regime harassed the small private sector of entrepreneurs—along with the more productive kulaks in the countryside—with new taxes and regulations, thus discouraging market mechanisms. Faced with a decline in the supply of market goods and a lowering of grain procurement prices by the state, the peasants produced less, and by 1927 grain supplies to the urban areas had dropped precipitously. Bukharin's response to the crisis was to argue that further concessions should be granted to the peasantry in order to encourage confidence in the Soviet state and raise agricultural production. Initially, this seemed to be Stalin's response as well. Over and over, he condemned the policies of the left opposition, whom he managed to hound out of the party leadership by late 1927. But no sooner would he dispose of Trotsky, Zinoviev, and Kamenev than Stalin would do an about-face. In 1928 he embraced the theories of the vanquished left opposition and advocated forced requisitioning of grain from the countryside, which meant, in effect, a war against the peasants. The new enemies would become Bukharin and the so-called rightists.

When Kirov was sent to Leningrad in early 1926 to take on the left opposition on Stalin's behalf, he of course had no way of knowing that events would take this turn. He had every reason to assume that Stalin would continue to advocate the NEP and the policies of the right, policies which Kirov himself favored. But this did not make him any less apprehensive about his mission.

Kirov's worst premonitions about Leningrad were borne out. Upon his arrival on 5 January 1926, accompanied by a delegation from the Central Committee, he was immediately plunged into a torrent of political strife. Although Zinoviev's left opposition had been outmaneuvered by Stalin at the Fourteenth Congress in December, he still had a substantial party following in his former home base of Leningrad. Kirov's task, set for him by Stalin, was to rout out Zinoviev's supporters there as soon as possible, by speaking at meetings of workers and party activists all over the city and urging his audience to adhere to the decisions of the congress.

Living in the Evropeiskaia Hotel, just off Nevskii Prospekt, Kirov spent all his waking hours visiting factories and campaigning against the Zinovievites. He had little opportunity to appreciate the splendid beauty of Leningrad, a city of sumptuous palaces and magnificent churches, interspersed with canals. Leningrad was founded as St. Petersburg in 1703 by Peter the Great, who conceived the city as a gateway connecting Russia to the European world. Located along the winding Neva River on the eastern shore of the Gulf of Finland, it had remained a symbol of Russia's ties with the West, both cultural and economic, ever since. As the second-largest city in Russia, Leningrad was not only a major industrial center but also a hub of intellectual life, housing at least sixty higher educational establishments and countless theaters and museums.[1]

Stalin, with his characteristic xenophobia, felt nothing but hostility toward Leningrad, which he saw as a breeding ground for foreign ideas and oppositional tendencies. He refused even to visit the city. Instead he sent Kirov, one of his faithful, to do the dirty work of getting rid of his enemies there. Kirov was a persuasive speaker and, with his humble background and lack of pretensions, he was less likely than some of the other Bolshevik politicians to be enticed by the subversive Westernizing influences of Leningrad. Indeed, Kirov found Leningrad inhospitable and unpleasant from the start. In contrast to the balmy, primitive Baku, with its predominantly Muslim population, Leningrad was European and sophisticated. It was also harshly cold and, with a northern latitude of almost 60 degrees, under the cover of night much of the time during the winter.

All of this might have been bearable, however, if it had not been for the overwhelming stress of his new assignment. On 7 January, Kirov wrote to Mariia L'vovna in Baku: "We were received with extreme hostility. . . . The situation here is very difficult, and enough work for 24 hours a day. I am not sure about the future. I feel horrible."[2] And several days later: "The situation here is desperate, such as I have never seen before. I live in a hotel, together with members of the Central Committee, of which there are quite a few. Every day I am at meetings. And what meetings there are here! The party cells have 1,500 to 2,000 people!"[3] Kirov conveyed similar impressions to Sergo Ordzhonikidze in Tbilisi: "The provincial and district committee members are climbing up the walls. They want us to drive them away. But we think that this would destroy the basic principles of party democracy. In general the atmosphere is heated. I have to work a lot and shout even more."[4]

Sergo had done his best to make Kirov's reception in the city hospitable, writing from Tbilisi to his comrades in the Leningrad Party Committee with requests for them to help his friend. Thus, in a letter to Nikolai Komarov, S. S. Lobov, and I. M. Moskvin (all of whom were opposed to the Zinoviev group, which had run Leningrad), he wrote:

> Your row [with Zinoviev] has cost us dearly: they have taken Comrade Kirov from us. This is a very great loss for us, but as a result you will be reinforced. I have not the slightest doubt that you will manage there and that within a month or two everything will be finished. Kirov is a splendid fellow, except that, aside from you, he knows no one. I am sure that you will surround him with friendly confidence. From my soul I wish you full success. . . . Boys, settle our Kirov in, otherwise he will knock about without an apartment and food.[5]

Although they were anxious to defeat the Zinoviev supporters, Sergo's friends were not well disposed toward Kirov. As Old Leningraders, they considered themselves the rightful heirs to the city's political leadership and resented the imposition of an outsider. Thus, they treated Kirov coldly, tolerating him as a necessary evil but not being particularly helpful. In the words of Leningrad party official Mikhail Rosliakov, who survived the purges of 1937–38 to write memoirs: "They saw him as a 'Varangian' [one of the Norsemen who ravaged the Baltic area in the ninth century and imposed their rule on Russia], although they personally felt respect for him on account of his qualities as a political fighter. But they nonetheless stuck to their position: 'Kirov is a Varangian, who has come temporarily to help establish order; after that, we ourselves will lead our native organization.'"[6]

The Zinoviev people, by contrast, were blatantly hostile to Kirov, whom they considered, not without justification, to be Moscow's henchman. When the Central Committee in Moscow put forth his candidacy as first secretary of the Leningrad Provincial Party Committee (Gubkom) to replace Zinoviev's man, G. E. Evdokimov, they mustered enough opposition to prevent the nomination from being confirmed, despite the fact that Evdokimov had already been dismissed. Kirov was brought into the secretariat, but was not formally elected first secretary until mid-February. The Zinovievites tried to shout him down at meetings and made things so difficult for him that he appealed to the Central Committee to send more envoys to help him. They also spread rumors about Kirov's past, claiming that he was never a Bolshevik revolutionary, but had only been a liberal journalist. And they sneered at him, referring to him as "pockmarked, with bad teeth," as "one who smokes cheap tobacco and wears a coat made of coarse cloth."[7]

▪ OVERCOMING OBSTACLES

Of course, Kirov did have a few "rough edges," especially in comparison with Zinoviev, an intellectual and the son of a prosperous Jewish merchant. But many of the rank and file had found Zinoviev haughty. They were impressed by Kirov's unpretentiousness and his affable, approachable manner. And, by all accounts, his oratory skills were unsurpassed. In contrast to his Bolshevik colleagues, he had the unique ability to keep his listeners captivated, to convey his message in terms that they could understand. Mikhail Rosliakov, who heard Kirov the first time he spoke in Leningrad, recalled that he was "passionate, convincing, inspiring." In his view, "Kirov conducted the meetings with Leningraders brilliantly. His speeches were full of fire, reasoned argumentation, and conviction that the party's decisions were correct." Zinoviev, according to Rosliakov, "tended to get hysterical when he spoke, as well as didactic and preachy. Kirov tried to convince and reason with his audience."[8]

For all his doubts about his ability to cope, Kirov was a success in Leningrad. It was a herculean achievement. Day in and day out he addressed meetings of party members, winning them over to Stalin's line. As he implied in a letter to Mariia L'vovna, he was against the idea of forcing the Zinovievites out of the party. He wanted to put the question to a democratic vote. Thus, after over a month of "campaigning," he called a special conference of the provincial party organization and was finally confirmed by a solid majority as chief of both the Leningrad Gubkom and the Northwest Regional Party Bureau, which incorporated Leningrad and four other provinces. The supporters of Zinoviev, who had already lost his post as head of the Leningrad soviet, had suffered a resounding defeat.

On 13 February, Kirov wrote to Sergo Ordzhonikidze that the conference had been a success, although he added that a new conflict had arisen with the Old Leningraders, and as a result one of them, Lobov, had been transferred to Moscow. "I am swamped with work," he went on. "Not even time for a good sleep. In general, of course, now it is a little easier. . . . I am bored with all the discussion. If you wake me up in the night I will produce a speech about building socialism."[9]

Kirov's efforts took their toll. He grew exhausted and ill from overwork. In a late February 1926 letter to his close friend Levon Mirzoian, a secretary of the Azerbaijan Communist Party, Kirov wrote:

> Dear Levon, Thank you very much for your letters and I apologize even more for not responding to you in the necessary detail. But you must understand me and the real situation that I am in. As an illustration: I am writing these lines at 3 o'clock in the morning. And this is no exception, since I am busy the whole day. But I won't complain, since it will not cause you to burst into tears, right? . . . Everything has settled down now. The entire apparatus is in our hands. As a result, I have lost my

voice and my chest hurts. I have to chatter and be on edge here like I have never had to before.[10]

A few weeks later Kirov reported to Sergo: "I was in bed the whole week because of the flu. A crazy sickness. Temperature 40.6. Even now I have not completely recovered. This is a very fashionable illness here." Kirov went on to tell Sergo that he had been in Moscow the week before and had found Stalin also laid up with the flu. They had discussed Kirov's future plans:

> Stalin talked, probably on the basis of your information, about Baku— who he should send there. I said for the time being no one, since the problem will be resolved by itself when the terms of our agreement [about Kirov's temporary stay in Leningrad] are completed. Laughing, he said that Sergo must also be taken by force from the Caucasian slums, which, in his opinion, give nothing to the heart and mind of a person, but just sap his strength. . . . We talked a lot about the economy and finances. Many interesting things emerged, but it is better to hear about it from the chief. According to Soso [Stalin], things will definitely be straightened out. Of course we will have to struggle, but it is not the first time.[11]

Kirov was still hoping to return to Baku. Not only did he prefer it to Leningrad; his friends needed him there. Mirzoian had complained to him about financial problems and political intrigues, which had begun after Kirov's departure. Although Kirov wanted to help, there was little that he could do from Leningrad, except try to reassure him. "I understand your situation," he had written to Mirzoian. "Things are not especially merry for you either. The changes that have taken place in Baku could have been foreseen and should have been foreseen. . . . However [difficult] things are there, Baku is better. Good brother, you have an organization that is fine in all respects. You must protect it, no matter what, from anything harmful . . ."[12] At Mirzoian's request, he had asked the Central Committee for 500,000 rubles to be sent to Baku, but the request had apparently been turned down. "I think," Kirov wrote to Mirzoian about the money, "that you are destined to fail."[13]

Kirov was not in a position to influence things in Baku. Once he had left, new political forces began to take over, and those who had been close

to Kirov fell out of favor with Moscow. "Moscow doesn't have a high opinion of us," Mirzoian had observed in one letter to Kirov.[14] Such was the
nature of the Soviet system, devised by Stalin, a master strategist, who
could move regional party officials about like pieces on a chessboard. It
suited Stalin's purposes to operate this way. If an official was allowed to
remain in one region for too long, he might develop too much power and
influence there, creating for himself a sort of mini-fiefdom. The way to
reduce the threat was to transfer him after a few years.

This was probably one reason why Stalin decided to move Sergo
Ordzhonikidze, who, as first secretary of the Transcaucasian Party Committee, had become a powerful, if controversial, political force in the Caucasus. In July 1926, Stalin proposed to Sergo that he come to Moscow to
head the Central Control Commission and the Worker-Peasants' Inspectorate, two powerful watchdog agencies. Despite the fact that Stalin had
warned him, "Don't kick up a fuss, it won't do any good," Sergo refused flat
out to come to Moscow. As a native Georgian, Sergo was at home in the
Caucasus and, even given the internecine feuds among his subordinates,
he lived a good life there. He knew full well that the chairmanship of the
Central Control Commission, which disciplined party members, would
draw him into the struggle between Stalin and the opposition. Stalin
clearly wanted someone who was loyal to him to be in this key post when
he delivered his final blow to Zinoviev and Kamenev.[15]

Stalin devised a clever maneuver to get Sergo to comply with his
request. In August the Politburo announced that Sergo would replace
Anastas Mikoyan as first secretary of the North Caucasian party organization, a clear demotion. As Stalin had intended, Sergo was in a bind. He
could either accept the Moscow job or be relegated to this lesser post. He
tried to defend himself by having his supporters in Tbilisi appeal to the
Central Committee for him to remain there, but to no avail.

Stalin saw Sergo in early September while he was vacationing in the
Caucasus. He wrote to Molotov in Moscow that Sergo was deeply
offended by the wording of the Politburo decree, which implied that he
was inferior to Mikoyan politically. At Stalin's suggestion, the Politburo
then issued another announcement, stating that it agreed with members of
the Transcaucasian party organization in their assessment of Sergo
Ordzhonikidze's work, but that their request to have him remain as their
leader was denied. In mid-September, Stalin wrote to Molotov: "I didn't

tell you the details about Sergo the last time. Now I must inform you that both Sergo and Nazaretian [a colleague of Sergo's in Transcaucasia] made a very bad impression on me in connection with this incident about the 'recall' from Transcaucasia. I had a stormy quarrel with Sergo, called him petty, and stopped seeing him."[16] Sergo was finally pressured into accepting the job in Moscow. Like Kirov, he had been outmaneuvered by Stalin, and it would not be the last time. The quarrel between Stalin and Sergo was patched up, but not forgotten, at least on Stalin's part.

▪ LIFE IN LENINGRAD

For Kirov, Sergo's transfer from the South was a good thing. It meant that they could communicate more easily and see each other more often. They spoke on the telephone daily, and Kirov soon developed the habit of staying at Sergo's apartment on his visits to Moscow, which became more frequent after July 1926, when he became a candidate member of the Politburo. They never faltered in their devotion to each other. Later, after Kirov's death, Sergo told his wife, Zinaida, that, despite his quick temper, he never once said a harsh word to Kirov.[17]

Kirov's Politburo position was presumably a reward for his successful efforts against the left opposition. (In fact Stalin had already demonstrated his gratitude to Kirov by making an unprecedented visit to Leningrad in April 1926—his first visit since 1919—and speaking favorably about Kirov to Leningrad's party elite.) As a candidate Politburo member, Kirov did not have a vote, and he certainly did not attend Politburo meetings in Moscow regularly. Nonetheless, his appointment gave him a higher stature within the party hierarchy. Formally elected by the Central Committee, the Politburo was the top leadership body of the party. While the Secretariat was the main center of party administration, the Politburo was the center of decision making, deciding issues in the name of the Central Committee, which was convened only a few times a year.

At the time of Kirov's promotion, Stalin managed to have Zinoviev voted out of the Politburo, which now had a Stalinist majority. Zinoviev's main asset had been his control of the Leningrad party apparatus, which, thanks to Kirov and the Central Committee members from Moscow, he had lost. Trotsky, who had earlier followed Stalin's battle against Zinoviev and Kamenev with detached contempt, now allied himself with them in what was called the United Opposition. They declared their program at the July 1926 plenum, but by this time they had lost too much influence within the party to be a serious threat to Stalin. By October 1926 the Central Committee had ousted Trotsky from the Politburo and Kamenev from candidate membership in that body.

Meanwhile, Mariia L'vovna had joined her husband in Leningrad, since it was clear that Kirov was there to stay. They moved into a spacious apartment at numbers 26-28 Krasnykh Zor', a major street running across one of the city's large islands. Mariia L'vovna soon took up a new cause, a campaign against prostitution, and established the Women's Labor Center for Disease Prevention. She ran the center herself until 1930, when she became Kirov's full-time personal secretary.[18]

The Kirovs' fourth-floor apartment reflected Sergei Kirov's preoccupations. In addition to a study, with pictures of Lenin and Kirov's deceased Caucasian friend Miasnikov hanging on the wall, the apartment had a special "man's room," where Kirov kept his tools and made hunting equipment. With his love of the outdoors, Kirov discovered a new avocation in Leningrad—duck hunting, for which the marshes outside the city were ideal. He soon became a keen hunter, going on expeditions whenever he had free time and arranging his vacations to coincide with the opening of the spring and autumn hunting seasons. Sometimes he would go for several days, taking with him Leningrad party or government colleagues.[19]

Kirov also had a large library, which housed his massive book collection. It included writings on science, politics, history, economics, finance, literature, and art, as well as a set of the works of Marx and Engels, which Mariia L'vovna had bound in leather and engraved as a gift for Kirov. Kirov was an avid reader, despite the long hours he spent working. An insomniac—and a chain smoker, like many Bolshevik leaders—Kirov would often stay up reading much of the night, a pack of cigarettes by his side.

Taking advantage of his privileged status, Kirov took home banned émigré literature from the party's special collection—which included journals published by Mensheviks and former liberals in the Provisional Government, as well as a history of the Russian civil war by the White general Anton Denikin. (Later, he also obtained a Russian translation of Hitler's *Mein Kampf.*) The émigré publications, of course, condemned the Soviet government. The authors were in constant communication with comrades back home and followed events in Russia closely, perhaps hoping that the system would collapse and they could return. Their criticisms were incisive—they could say things that could never be repeated in the Soviet press.[20] One wonders what Kirov thought when they wrote of Stalin's accumulation of power and his dictatorial methods, of the party's growing reliance on the secret police. Kirov had, after all, been sympathetic to liberal democratic views when he was a journalist in prerevolutionary times.

If Kirov had any doubts about his mission in Leningrad he did not show it publicly. He continued his energetic campaign to win the loyalty of Leningraders on the General Secretary's behalf. In all, he made 180 speeches against the opposition at factories and party conclaves during 1926. Although he appeared to speak extemporaneously, he in fact prepared his speeches with the utmost care, painstakingly going over the facts and figures that he used to illustrate his points. Kirov kept a notebook with him wherever he went, so that he could record information and impressions. He did not read his speeches word for word, but would glance down occasionally at notes. The result was always impressive. Speaking with self-assurance and commitment, he rarely hesitated. He used simple yet colorful language and often asked rhetorical questions to make his points, raising and lowering his voice at intervals so as to keep his audience engaged.[21]

As Kirov spoke, a stenographer would record his words verbatim. Later Kirov would go over the stenogram carefully, checking his presentation for accuracy and correcting the phrasing before it appeared in the press. The published versions of Kirov's speeches were often significantly different from the originals, which are in the archives. What Kirov said spontaneously to party activists was often not suitable for public consumption and thus his speeches had to be "sanitized." Sometimes his busy schedule prevented him from going over the text, in which case the newspaper editors would make corrections. Not surprisingly, Kirov was angry when they made changes of which he disapproved. By the end of the 1920s, political discussions had become tightly constrained, and the Central Committee's Ideological Department was keeping a close watch on what regional politicians said, to make sure they adhered to the party line. Any deviation from that line, however slight, could be interpreted as a violation of party discipline. In 1931, to protect himself, Kirov had the Leningrad Party Committee issue an order saying that the press could not publish any speeches by members of the committee's secretariat without prior approval of the speaker.[22]

Kirov's speeches that appeared in the press gave no hint of unorthodoxy, adhering to the dictates of the Central Committee, which were in fact those of Stalin. Although Kirov had dreaded the vicious mudslinging campaign against the Zinoviev supporters that he knew was in store for him when he first went to Leningrad, after a few months he fell into his role as the scourge of the opposition. Indeed he became a leading advocate of strong sanctions against Stalin's critics. "I forgo my modesty," he had said proudly to a group of Leningrad party activists in October 1926. "I was that Central Committee member . . . who introduced the proposal to exclude Trotsky from the Politburo and Kamenev from candidate membership, and also the proposal to remove Zinoviev from his work in the Communist International [Comintern, an organization of Soviet and foreign Communist parties]."[23] By the next year Kirov's denunciations of Trotsky, Zinoviev, and Kamenev had reached a fever pitch. At a series of regional party meetings in late October 1927, Kirov recited over and over the evil deeds of the opposition:

> This is without doubt an underground, oppositional center of leadership. They have their own discipline, not just that of a faction but already of a party. They have an illegal publication, illegal presses, regular illegal meetings, taking place parallel to our legal meetings, in Moscow and wherever else. In Moscow there are meetings of the collective, where serious questions are discussed. But Trotsky has illegal meetings, inviting all his supporters. In a word, all the elements of a separate party are present in the Trotsky faction.[24]

A joint plenum of the Central Committee and the Central Control Commission held in October 1927 had just passed a resolution expelling Trotsky and Zinoviev from the Central Committee, an action that caused consternation within the party as a whole. Some members opined that Lenin would not have approved of such severe sanctions if he were still alive, but Kirov hastened to defend the plenum's decision: "If this had happened when Lenin was leader, then neither Zinoviev, Trotsky, nor Kamenev would have a single political rib left. And when they try to paint Lenin as some sort of an internal party liberal, this, comrades, is sheer slander against Lenin."[25] In one speech Kirov even suggested expelling Trotsky and Zinoviev from the party entirely. A month later, after the opposition had organized street demonstrations in Moscow and Leningrad on the tenth anniversary of the Bolshevik Revolution, the Central Committee did just that.[26]

At the Fifteenth Congress in December 1927, the remaining leaders of the left opposition were subjected to a virtual kangaroo court, with delegates hurling insults and accusations at them and cutting them off whenever they tried to respond. Kirov was Stalin's golden boy. From the speaker's rostrum he mocked prominent Bolsheviks who had sided with the opposition, Bolsheviks toward whom he had been deferential when he was serving under them during the civil war. He aroused laughter, for example, when he heaped scorn on the respected diplomat Kh. G. Rakovskii, demeaning his motives and referring to his "deceitful, oppositionist tears." Citing "Comrade Stalin" throughout his speech, Kirov backed Stalin's demand that the opposition capitulate completely and urged that those who did not agree with the policies of the General Secretary be "cut off in the most decisive, firm, and merciless way."[27]

Why had Kirov so willingly become a mouthpiece for Stalin in the latter's struggle with his opponents? Did he not realize the implications of suppressing the opposition to Stalin so ruthlessly and decisively? Kirov agreed with Stalin and the rightists in their endorsement of the New Economic Policy (NEP) and a gradualist approach to economic development. But the disagreements with the left opposition extended beyond economic policy or debates about "socialism in one country." A key objection of the oppositionists centered on the accumulation of political power in the hands of one man, Stalin, and his destruction of party democracy. In trampling on the oppositionists, Kirov and his party colleagues set a dangerous precedent, ensuring that they too would be trampled upon if they ever disagreed with the General Secretary.

▪ KIROV AND BUKHARIN

Unfortunately, we have no record of Kirov's private thoughts on the matter of Stalin's power. But some insight on his motivations can be gleaned by looking at Nikolai Bukharin's reaction to the attack on the left and at Kirov's attitude toward Bukharin. Although Kirov and Bukharin were not especially close, they respected each other and were on friendly terms. More significantly, their views on the country's economic development were at this point quite similar. Although their paths later diverged, their fates, both tragic, would remain intertwined.

As only a second-ranking politician, Kirov was hardly in a position to resist the overwhelming momentum of the campaign to crush the opposition, especially when such respected figures as Bukharin were actively taking part. Although he was not yet forty years old, Bukharin, the party's leading theoretician, was already editor of *Pravda* and head of the Comintern. Bukharin had been strongly in favor of appointing Kirov to run the Leningrad party. He went to Leningrad in October 1927 to justify to the party apparatus there the Central Committee's decision to expel Trotsky and Zinoviev. In tones similar to Kirov's, he denounced his former friends in the most scathing terms, saying that the opposition had gone over to the "liberal and Menshevik camp" and announcing that "we will fight with all our might against those who try to drag our comrades into the Menshevik swamp."[28]

Bukharin reportedly did all this with a heavy heart, however. One source relates how he called Trotsky on the telephone one day and moaned: "Lev Davydovich, it is not possible that they expelled you from the party. Do something."[29] According to Bukharin's biographer Stephen Cohen, "he participated in this final dance of vengeance undoubtedly still not 'relishing it' and 'trembling from head to foot.' . . . Bukharin was not without some empathy for 'this tragedy of the opposition leaders.' Nonetheless, he lent his authority to and abetted their destruction."[30]

Cohen attributes Bukharin's actions to his firm belief that the left opposition's economic policies would destroy all that the Bolsheviks had worked so hard to achieve. But also, as Cohen points out, Bukharin made "the perilous equation that persistent dissent augured a faction, a second party, and ultimately counter-revolution."[31] Although Bukharin had misgivings about Stalin and recognized his driving ambition to accumulate power, he believed that if party members opposed the decisions of the leadership they would threaten the party's very existence. But he should have known better. By this time, ominously, Stalin had already unleashed the political police, the OGPU, against the left opposition, listening in on their telephone conversations and opening their mail. Indeed, the OGPU had set up a special department for uncovering "deviationists" within the party.[32]

Kirov's reasoning was probably similar to that of Bukharin. Kirov hated dissension and factional strife, preferring to reach compromises. He did not enjoy his role as a "civil executioner" of Trotsky and the others at the Fifteenth Congress. In the words of one Soviet biographer of Kirov: "The Soviet people, applauding the fiery defender of the revolution, did not realize how exhausting, how repugnant this conflict was for Kirov."[33] But Kirov felt obliged to act out his part for the sake of preserving party unity.

Had he realized how quickly Stalin would reverse himself and launch an attack on Bukharin and the other rightists, Kirov might have been less strident in his condemnation of the left opposition. Soon he would be compelled to enter into a new conflict on Stalin's behalf, and the inexorable logic of Stalin's ruthless strategy of destroying any possible rivals would be impossible to ignore. Indeed, already at the Fifteenth Congress there were signs of tension behind the smiles of Politburo leaders as they posed together for photographs. And a protégé of Stalin even made a speech in which he criticized Bukharin's handling of the Comintern.[34]

The tension soon erupted into open disagreement, precipitated by the sudden drop in grain collection and a consequent decision by the Politburo in January 1928 to take "emergency measures" in the countryside. Bukharin and the rightists had gone along with the decision, on the assumption that the measures would be temporary and involve only selective confiscation of hoarded grain. But Stalin took charge of the operation, and it soon turned into an all-out war against the peasants, with widespread arrests and arbitrary grain seizures. In this context, the NEP was meaningless. By May 1928, Stalin was calling for the rapid development of industry and for the amalgamation of individual peasant holdings into state-owned collective farms, without any mention of collectivization being voluntary.

At a stormy Central Committee meeting in July 1928, Bukharin and his allies, Politburo members Mikhail Tomskii and Aleksei Rykov, actively campaigned for support by claiming that Stalin's policies of forced collectivization would cause a complete break with the countryside. Bukharin also indirectly challenged Stalin's leadership of the party by bringing up the taboo subject of Lenin's testament, although not referring specifically to what Lenin had said about Stalin.

The Bukharin group had the backing of the Moscow party organization, headed by Nikolai Uglanov, and strong support among the heads of various commissariats, but, as before, Stalin's total control over the Secretariat proved the decisive factor. In theory the elective principle still applied to party organizations, but in practice the Secretariat decided who would be "elected" to key party posts throughout the country. This meant that Stalin, as head of the Secretariat, could ensure that regional secretaries—who formed a large portion of the Central Committee—were loyal to him. Stalin's persuasive arguments also had an influence: he told Central Committee members that, unpleasant as it was, the Bolsheviks had no choice but to exact a tribute from the peasants. This was the only way that the Soviet Union could industrialize.[35]

By the end of the July plenum the right opposition had been reduced to minority status within the leadership and had lost its struggle for a policy of compromise with the peasantry. Bukharin was so alarmed by this turn of events that he took the unusual step of turning to Kamenev, his erstwhile leftist enemy, in an attempt to strike an alliance with him and Zinoviev against Stalin. In the course of their conversation, which Kamenev later recorded in notes that ended up in the Trotsky archives, Bukharin revealed how he had tried to win over members of the leadership but they had succumbed to pressure from Stalin and had changed sides. Speaking specifically of Ordzhonikidze, he said: "Sergo is not a knight. He came to me, cursed Stalin violently, but in the decisive moment betrayed us."[36]

Significantly, Bukharin also told Kamenev that they had counted on support from the Leningrad delegation. Among Kirov's subordinates in Leningrad were several outspoken Bukharinites, including Aleksei Stetskii, head of the agitprop (agitation and propaganda) department in the Leningrad party apparatus, and the editor of *Leningradskaia pravda,* Petr Petrovskii. Stetskii had given a speech criticizing Stalin at the July plenum, and Petrovskii had infuriated Stalin by publishing several editorials—one immediately after the July plenum—that endorsed Bukharin's economic program.[37] Bukharin reportedly said: "The Pitertsy [Petersburgers] on the whole were behind us, but they became scared when the talk turned to a possible replacement for Stalin."[38]

As for Kirov, his views on economic policy continued to be more in tune with those of Bukharin than with those of Stalin. Like all provincial party leaders, he was concerned about the crisis in the countryside and the crucial problem of grain supply, but he did not advocate using force to requisition grain. In a secret "informational" letter to the Central Committee written in July 1927, Kirov had described in detail the mood of the workers and peasants in the Leningrad region. He noted that anti-Soviet sentiments had increased markedly in the countryside and that a "healthy" mood among the peasants was dependent on their economic well-being. In stressing that the party in Leningrad was doing its utmost to prevent shortages of crucial products among the peasants, he clearly implied that he favored the carrot to the stick in dealing with the peasantry.[39]

Interestingly, by the summer of 1928, just as Stalin was launching his onslaught against the peasants, Kirov seemed to think that the situation did not require drastic measures. He reported to Sergo that "the mood in the factories has improved since the food problem improved: there is a lot of bread and a lot of potatoes . . . the bread is $2\frac{1}{2}$ to $3\frac{1}{2}$ times and the wheat $4\frac{1}{2}$ times more than in many years past!"[40]

▪ PRESSURE FROM STALIN

Stalin was determined to bring the wavering Kirov and his party subordinates in Leningrad into his camp. On 13 July 1928, the day after the stormy Central Committee plenum ended, Stalin accompanied Kirov to Leningrad and stayed at his apartment for two days. Stalin was so incensed about the failure of Petrovskii, Stetskii, and other Leningraders to take the proper line that he took the unusual step of reporting personally to the party organization there on what had occurred at the plenum.[41] During his stay Stalin also accompanied Kirov on a visit to a new hydroelectric station. Kirov mentioned Stalin's visit with little enthusiasm in a terse letter to Mariia L'vovna, who was vacationing in Sochi: "Dear Marusa, I received your letter and telegraphed an answer. Things are not working out very well. But it is useless to talk about it. Stalin was here with me for two or three days. I took him to the Volkhov [the hydroelectric power plant]. The day before yesterday he left."[42]

On the same day he wrote to Sergo, who was recuperating in the Caucasus from yet another illness and had been unable to attend the July plenum: "Dear Sergo, I heard about your health, of course, not from you, but from Moscow. You prefer to keep quiet about it. *I implore you to tell me what the doctors have finally determined and what they recommend be done.* The devil take them all. . . . You have doubtless already been told about the plenum. After the plenum Stalin was here in Leningrad. I went with him to Volkhov (he had never seen it before). Things here are generally in order. . . . [I will tell you] about the rest when we meet, which I hope will be soon."[43]

Kirov often implied in his letters to Mariia L'vovna and Sergo during this period that he preferred to say what he had to say in person, rather than in writing. He doubtless was aware that his letters might fall into unfriendly hands, probably those of the OGPU. Sergo's communications reflected the same guardedness. He wrote Kirov later in the summer: "Greetings, my Dear Kirov! How did your hunt go? Did you kill a lot of wildfowl? I feel nothing, except my lungs ache almost all the time. I will soon return to Moscow and we will decide what to do further. . . . I want awfully to have a chat with you on very many questions, but you can't say everything in a letter, so it is better to wait until our meeting."[44]

Clearly, both Kirov and Sergo had an intense need to share their impressions about what was happening in the party leadership. By this time, they could trust almost no one, and the internal political situation was becoming unbearably tense. One wonders whether Sergo's illness, which allowed him to avoid the confrontation with the Bukharin opposition at the July plenum, might have been exaggerated, or at least brought on by emotional distress. According to the doctors' reports, which were duly sent to the Secret Department of the Central Control Commission and always carefully scrutinized by Stalin, Sergo was suffering from an inflammation of the right kidney and the urinary tract. The doctors suspected tuberculosis, but in the end they found no evidence of it.[45] This was not the first time that Sergo missed an important plenum on account of illness and it would not be the last.

Whatever the case, Stalin was not going to put up with Sergo's ambivalence for long. Having successfully marshaled his forces against the Bukharinites, Stalin was proceeding full speed ahead with his determined campaign to oust them from all positions of influence in the party and also with his war against the countryside. As head of the Central Control Commission, which disciplined party members, Sergo was a key figure in Stalin's plans, and Stalin made every effort to secure his support. "I was over at Sergo's," Stalin wrote Molotov in August 1928. "His mood was good. He is standing firmly and decisively for the party line, against the waverers and hesitaters."[46]

As for Kirov, Stalin's victory at the July 1928 plenum put Kirov under great pressure to enforce the Central Committee's demand that the

Leningrad apparatus be brought into line. But Kirov did not cave in completely. He did his best, for example, to persuade Stalin during his Leningrad visit not to have Petrovskii removed from the editorship of *Leningradskaia pravda*, reminding Stalin how talented Petrovskii was. Stalin let matters ride for a while, but after Petrovskii's paper published further endorsements of Bukharin's program in early October 1928, Stalin decided to take action. He telephoned Kirov and announced sharply before hanging up the receiver: "Petrovskii was the chief editor of *Leningradskaia pravda*; now he will be editor of the journal *Klop* [a proposed satirical publication that never materialized]!" Kirov immediately sent a telegram to Moscow requesting that the question of *Leningradskaia pravda*'s editorship be postponed until the next Central Committee plenum. The response was a reproach from the Politburo, asking Kirov why he "did not take measures to clean up the leadership of *Leningradskaia pravda*," and a telegram from Molotov ordering him to dismiss Petrovskii on 15 October.[47]

Kirov had no choice but to obey Moscow and fire Petrovskii. He also had to go along with a Central Committee directive to regional parties, calling upon them to step up the process of self-criticism (*samo-kritika*). What this meant was endless party meetings where officials would go through the motions of confessing their shortcomings and promising to correct them. Such confessional processes were often a forerunner to substantial dismissals, or even to a complete changing of the guard. This was what happened in the Moscow organization, where the self-criticism campaign—orchestrated by the Central Committee—ended up in the ouster, in October and November, of the Bukharinite party chief there, Uglanov (replaced by Molotov), and several of his deputies. The Moscow organization had been a large stumbling block for Stalin in his drive against the right opposition, so these dismissals were an important victory for him. They not only deprived Bukharin, Tomskii, and Rykov of an important base of support. They also served as an example to other party organizations of what might happen to them if they neglected to give Stalin support.

This message cannot have been lost on Kirov and his colleagues as they witnessed Stalin's open hostility toward Bukharin's right opposition. Powerless against Stalin's superior organizational politics, the right saw public protest as their only alternative. Bukharin attacked Stalin's general line in several articles and speeches, the most sensational of which was published in *Pravda* and other leading newspapers on 24 January 1929, to mark the fifth anniversary of Lenin's death. Significantly, the speech was entitled "Lenin's Political Testament." Although Bukharin was prudent enough to restrict his comments to an analysis of Lenin's policies toward the end of his life, which ran directly counter to those of Stalin, this piece brought to mind Lenin's other, unpublished "testament," which recommended Stalin's dismissal.[48]

Livid, Stalin hauled the right opposition leaders before a joint session of the Politburo and the presidium of Sergo Ordzhonikidze's Central Control Commission to face charges of "factionalism." He wanted them out of the Politburo, but in the end, even though they refused to recant their errors, they only received a censure. A year later Sergo, who had tried to get them to compromise, was reported to have said to a group of unnamed party members: "We did everything possible to keep comrades Rykov, Bukharin, Tomskii, and Uglanov in leading posts within the party."[49] Whatever Sergo's efforts, the die was cast against the right opposition, and he went along with it. The final blow for the right came during an April 1929 Central Committee plenum, at which Stalin delivered a long attack on the Bukharin group, and the indictment of them on charges of factionalism was approved. Although the oppositionists were allowed to remain in the Politburo for a time, they were all demoted to lesser posts.

Sergo's tolerance for the right oppositionists and his reluctance to attack them—which numerous historians have remarked upon—was sincere. But it was not politically viable for a man in his position, which is doubtless why he joined the offensive against Bukharin at the plenum. Kirov, however, continued to give mixed signals. On 20 January 1929, shortly before Bukharin made his daring speech against Stalin, a long article by Kirov, also devoted to the fifth anniversary of Lenin's death, appeared in *Leningradskaia pravda.*[50] Kirov discussed Lenin's views on the importance of preserving the *smychka* (union) between the city and the countryside and stressed the need for helping the peasants with technical resources and educational work. This remarkable article was a far cry from Stalin's "extraordinary measures" and his advocacy of an all-out offensive against the peasantry. Indeed Kirov sounded like Bukharin, who had been urging the party to give meaningful aid to peasant farmers and establish civil peace between town and country.

Kirov attended the April plenum and probably was among the overwhelming majority of delegates who voted in favor of censuring the Bukharin group. But he still had doubts. The Kirov archive contains notes that he jotted down during the plenum: "Regarding fractionalism. *There wasn't any.* . . . Perhaps the opposition is justified. A clandestine struggle at the heart of the Party? I should fight against Tomskii, or better the opposite?"[51]

Kirov made no public statements criticizing the right until the spring of 1929, around the time that other Bukharinites in Leningrad began defecting from the Bukharin camp. (This may explain why there is a large gap for the year 1928 in the collections of Kirov's speeches published posthumously.) And there is little evidence that Kirov was willing to condemn the right oppositionists wholeheartedly until June 1930, when he launched a scathing invective against them at the Sixteenth Party Congress. In fact, at a stormy Central Committee plenum in November 1929, at which Stalin threatened the opposition with expulsion from the party unless they recanted their views, and others hurled insults upon them, Kirov reportedly attempted to quell the uproar. At one point he turned to Tomskii and said softly: "Misha, after all, you are not correct." He then tried to persuade him to renounce his political platform.[52] Even after Kirov finally did speak out publicly against him, Bukharin remained on friendly terms with Kirov. He continued coming to Leningrad and wrote no fewer than eight letters to him during the early 1930s, in some cases asking for his help. He would hardly have made these overtures to Kirov if he did not think of him in some way as a kindred spirit.

▪ SELF-CRITICISM IN LENINGRAD

Kirov's ambivalence about the Bukharin group and his sympathies with their economic views may have contributed to the unfortunate ordeal that he went through in the autumn of 1929, an ordeal that created an upheaval in the Leningrad party organization and seriously threatened Kirov's career. It all began on the first of September, while Kirov was on a hunting trip outside Leningrad. On that day a group of articles appeared in *Pravda* under the rubric: "Let us direct real self-criticism against distortions of the party's proletarian line, against concrete manifestations of right deviationism." The authors claimed that suppression of criticism, "criminal bureaucratism" and other negative developments were occurring in Leningrad.

Lest there be any doubt about who was to blame, *Pravda* noted pointedly that the problems were a result of weaknesses in the chain of command of the Leningrad party leadership. And, in a direct reference to Kirov, the paper observed: "There is of course a colossal difference between eradicating the suppression of self-criticism in Astrakhan [Kirov's location during the civil war], where workers with undeveloped class consciousness bring wreaths to the grave of a dead speculator and saboteur, and the Bolshevik proletariat of Leningrad. We are certain that the proletarian cadre of the Leningrad organization, uniting around its leadership . . . can quickly and energetically uncover and liquidate the branches that gave rise to these cases."

However mild the criticisms might have appeared to a reader unschooled in party parlance, *Pravda*'s commentary was a direct threat to Kirov, conveniently timed to appear in his absence. Kirov immediately cut his vacation short and returned to Leningrad, where he hastily convened a plenum of the Leningrad Regional Party Committee, the Obkom.* Damage control went into action. The next day *Leningradskaia pravda*, no longer under the editorship of Kirov's friend Petrovskii, duly reprinted the *Pravda* articles, under the rubric "Correct Mistakes," and reported on the plenum's results. The plenum passed a resolution saying that three separate commissions had been formed to investigate the charges made in *Pravda* and that the Leningrad proletariat would stand firmly behind the "general line" (Stalin's policies), making every effort to correct its mistakes. In the days that followed, party meetings were held all over Leningrad to discuss the charges made by *Pravda*. *Leningradskaia pravda* featured banner headlines about developing "Bolshevik self-criticism," and some papers even called for a "renewal [i.e., a purge] of the party leadership." The Leningrad party apparatus was thrown into a tailspin.[53]

Not surprisingly, when Kirov addressed the Leningrad Obkom on 7 September, he was on the defensive.[54] It cannot have been far from his mind that a year earlier similar charges about suppression of criticism had been leveled against Uglanov and the Moscow party organization, with the result being mass dismissals. Although Uglanov and his comrades had

---

* In late 1927 a new administrative district, called the Leningrad Oblast, was created, incorporating the five provinces of the Northwest Region, so the Leningrad Gubkom was replaced by a new, larger Obkom (regional party committee).

been outspoken Bukharinites, Kirov's organization still harbored a number of right sympathizers and he himself had been a waverer. Significantly *Pravda* had specifically mentioned that the mistakes were caused by "right deviationism."

Kirov began his address by disagreeing with the suggestion of a subordinate that the Central Committee in Moscow had been preparing this exposé for six months and had kept it a secret: "If [the Central Committee] wants to drag us through the swamp then it doesn't need a half year to think about it, but can do it at one stroke." This was a grim reminder of how vulnerable they all were. Kirov repeatedly asserted that the Leningrad Obkom and he personally were to blame for not paying more attention to problems. But he was not prepared to cave in completely. He cautioned against going too far with self-criticism: "If there are deficiencies, then they must be exposed, but in my opinion it doesn't pay to enter into some sort of a competition."

These comments, from the original stenogram, were not reprinted in the published version of his speech, which appeared a few days later. In this version, not surprisingly, Kirov was quick to acknowledge that his organization had paid insufficient attention to self-criticism. Yet he still downplayed the problem: "So it seems, well, that self-criticism became a little weak. Was that a big misfortune? Not true, comrades. Not true because developing self-criticism lies at the basis of all our work." He went out of his way to emphasize the positive achievements of Leningrad. He allowed how there were still rightist elements in the Leningrad party, but to put the problem in perspective he reminded his audience that Bukharin and his comrades were still Central Committee members (in fact Bukharin had not yet been ousted from the Politburo): "If representatives of right deviationism can be found in the Central Committee, it is easy to understand how they can also be at every factory and enterprise, at every commercial establishment."[55]

Kirov was not taking the criticisms lying down. But there was little he could do to stop the repercussions. In the immediate aftermath of the scandal, G. A. Desov, chairman of the Leningrad Control Commission, which had borne the brunt of the attack, was fired and replaced by a factory worker. This appointment reflected a new policy, dictated by Moscow to all the regional organizations, of replacing officials from the intelligentsia with those from the proletarian class and signaled the beginning of a nationwide purge or "cleansing" of party ranks. By 1931 thousands of party members in Leningrad and elsewhere would lose their jobs.[56] But the self-criticism campaign, which the press relentlessly waged, added momentum to the process.

Why had Leningrad been singled out suddenly for an attack by *Pravda*? Bukharin, it will be recalled, had lost the editorship of *Pravda* some months previously. The paper was now run by an editorial board that had been handpicked by Stalin. Judging from personal letters to Kirov and Ordzhonikidze written by party journalists who were closely involved in the affair, *Pravda* had been gathering materials on wrongdoings in Leningrad for some time. When Petr Chagin, editor of the Leningrad paper *Krasnaia gazeta*, complained to some workers in the Central Committee Agitprop Department about how the Old Leningraders controlled the press and were stifling criticism, *Pravda* smelled blood and pressured Chagin and his colleagues to come up with incriminating information.[57]

Chagin, a longtime Kirov ally, who had edited the party's official paper in Baku before following Kirov to Leningrad, was naturally reluctant to get involved in any type of a smear campaign. But, according to a letter that he sent to Kirov in early September, an agitprop official threatened him with reprisals if he did not comply. This official, the author of one of the critical articles in *Pravda*, complained later to Ordzhonikidze that he too had been pressured, by none other than the editorial staff of *Pravda*. Kirov then wrote to Molotov, a member of the CC Secretariat, sending him copies of the various letters. He told Molotov that the agitprop official could not have acted alone and asked him to investigate this "absolutely disgusting story."[58]

What was Stalin's role in the affair? Vacationing in the South at the time, he had apparently been caught off guard by the *Pravda* article and the ensuing tempest in Leningrad. But when Sergo and Molotov proposed to Stalin that the Central Committee issue a decree putting a stop to the self-criticism frenzy, he did not agree. Stalin's response on 13 September is worth quoting in full because it reveals the unique subtlety of his approach to controlling his subordinates:

> Received your coded telegram about self-criticism. Your proposal is incorrect since a special decree from the Central Committee plus a speech by Molotov may be understood (will be understood!) by the party organizations as a new course backward, as an appeal: "Rein in self-criticism," which is of course not desirable and which will undoubtedly

undermine the authority of the Central Committee (and Molotov) in the eyes of the best elements of the party in favor of all and sundry bureaucrats.

The article in *Pravda* attacking the Leningrad leadership (which means Kirov-Komarov) was a grave error (especially the *way* it was done). Someone (that is, an enemy of the party) wanted to portray the top officials in Leningrad as opposing the correction of the shortcomings (that's not true!). But those bunglers from Pravda swallowed the bait, and now "everything's in a commotion," to the delight of the party's enemies. They forgot that the Leningrad organization isn't just your Sochi or Astrakhan or Baku organization. They forgot that a blow to the chiefs of the Leningrad organization, which represents the most reliable bulwark of the Central Committee, is a blow to the very heart of the Central Committee. . . . The Central Committee's fault consists of relinquishing the rudder for a moment to *Pravda*'s editorial collegium.[59]

Stalin's reaction is instructive. Although he voiced displeasure with the *Pravda* article, it was not because *Pravda* criticized the Leningrad organization, but because the criticism was carried too far. Given that Stalin himself had been instrumental in selecting *Pravda*'s new editors, it is doubtful that they would have deliberately gone against his wishes. More likely is that they got a message from Stalin that it was time for *Pravda* to criticize Leningrad, but then, as Stalin observed, they "bungled" it and played into the hands of Kirov's enemies. Stalin may have intended to shake up the Leningrad organization and cause Kirov some discomfort, but he did not want the party leadership there to be seriously weakened, because he depended on its support.

▪ MORE ATTACKS ON KIROV

Despite his professed disapproval of the *Pravda* letter, Stalin had no intention of remedying the situation by calling a halt to the self-criticism campaign. He was not about to relinquish one of his most effective weapons against potential opposition. He had launched the campaign, along with a crusade against "bureaucratism," on the basis of the notorious 1928 Shakhty case. This case involved trumped-up charges of sabotage against a group of engineers in the Shakhty mines in the Donbass and offered Stalin the excuse to look for internal enemies everywhere under the guise of self-criticism. Nonetheless, the Central Committee did make some effort to contain the campaign in Leningrad. On 15 September, *Leningradskaia pravda* reprinted an article from *Pravda* entitled "The Leningrad Press and Self-criticism," which conveyed a message of caution. While congratulating the local press for uncovering all the problems that had arisen because of the suppression of self-criticism, the article noted that there had been exaggerations and "sensational tones" in the reporting, which might interfere with the positive aspects of the campaign.

After a few weeks Kirov decided to weigh in more forcefully on the issue. In early November 1929, in a speech to the Leningrad Obkom and Control Commission, Kirov asserted boldly that the press had printed a lot of false accusations. To be sure, Kirov said, self-criticism was essential for the party. But there was a right and a wrong kind of self-criticism. In the wrong hands self-criticism could do a lot of harm and even destroy the very individual or institution being criticized: "We, for example, are now expanding a struggle against bureaucratism. Bureaucratism is, of course, a very harmful, dangerous thing. Every institution has elements of bureaucratism. And here self-criticism must be used to fight bureaucratism, to improve the work of the institution. At the same time, in struggling against bureaucratism to strike at the institution, at all the people, mixing everyone together in the same porridge and sending them all to labor camps—this cannot be done."[60]

Kirov went on: "This is not only our opinion. This is also the opinion of the Central Committee of our party. The majority of you probably know about the decision of the CC Secretariat on this question. The CC said that, although the Leningrad press had elaborated this and that fact and raised this and that issue, nonetheless it had exhibited sensationalism and so forth. The CC said this, although of course expressing it more mildly than we have at this plenum."[61]

Although Kirov apparently had the consent of the Central Committee in putting the lid on the orgy of self-criticism in Leningrad, his vehement speech (only a sanitized version of which was published) cannot have pleased Stalin. Kirov's warning about arresting people and sending them to camps without considering the facts was a direct refutation of what Stalin and the people around him had been doing for over a year.

The "muckraking" press campaign finally died down, but it had made Kirov vulnerable. It was not just that the quality of his leadership had been called into question. There was also the problem of resentment toward him on the part of the Old Leningraders, such as Leningrad soviet chairman Nikolai Komarov, against whom much of the press criticism had been directed. Several of them lost their jobs, and they blamed Kirov. As a result, they embarked on a plan to have Kirov removed from his post. Desov, the former Leningrad Control Commission chief, who was now unemployed, spent several days in the Leningrad public library poring over old issues of the newspaper *Terek* in search of articles by Kirov that would incriminate him. With the help of "friends" in Moscow, Desov sent a letter at the end of November to the Central Committee saying that he had materials proving that Kirov had been a bourgeois liberal journalist before 1917. He had even written a patriotic article on the occasion of the 300th anniversary of the Romanov dynasty in February 1913.[62]

In a more rational world, a denunciation on such flimsy, seemingly irrelevant charges would have been dismissed out of hand as the blatant act of revenge that it was. But this was a world where everything counted, where any rumor or unfavorable report, no matter how baseless, was treated seriously. By operating on the assumption that smoke meant fire, Stalin was able to stir people up and make them vulnerable. Thus, Kirov was summoned to Moscow on 10 December, along with the entire Leningrad Party Committee, to attend a session of the Politburo and the presidium of the Central Control Commission on the subject of Desov's charges.

Judging from accounts of the two-day session, it was a real ordeal for Kirov, who was subjected to hostile remarks from his detractors. He reportedly showed great restraint. Predictably, Sergo came to Kirov's defense, writing a special report for the session, in which he described the circumstances surrounding Desov's denunciation. Desov, he said, had not quoted accurately from Kirov's writings for *Terek,* and he had taken the quotations out of context. Furthermore, while he, Sergo, by no means wanted to justify Kirov's participation on a bourgeois paper, Kirov had never made any attempt to keep it a secret. And, he went on, after the October Revolution, Kirov "never showed even the slightest sign of wavering from the Leninist line of our party." (Apparently Sergo was unaware of Kirov's continued ambivalence toward the Mensheviks in early 1918.)[63]

Stalin sat in silence for most of the session, asking only the occasional question. Finally he said: "Kirov committed mistakes while working on the paper *Terek,* but he has admitted them. And he did have the right to contribute to a liberal paper."[64] Stalin thus aided in Kirov's defense by alluding to the prerevolutionary Bolshevik regulation that allowed party members to write for liberal papers under certain circumstances. But he did not let Kirov off the hook completely. In concluding that Kirov had made mistakes, he left Kirov with another black mark on his record.

The final resolution, written by Stalin, Sergo, and others and adopted by the session on 11 December, reinforced the impression that Kirov's reputation was tainted. The resolution criticized Desov for slandering Kirov and also ordered that Komarov and other comrades who had assisted Desov be dismissed from their posts in Leningrad. But it repeatedly made reference to Kirov's mistakes, and, even worse, it compared Kirov to members of the opposition:

> The party has a complete justification for proceeding in this way toward Comrade Kirov [defending him], for it knows of the famous precedents in the history of our party, when Lenin, despite the grossest errors of Zinoviev and Kamenev before October, of Rykov on the day after October and Bukharin during the Brest peace [talks], found it possible and reasonable to allow these comrades to remain in the Central Committee and to appoint them to the Politburo. The party has the right to proceed in the same manner with Kirov, especially since the mistake of Comrade Kirov, which he never defended or tried to justify, does not even compare with the gross political errors committed by Kamenev, Zinoviev, Rykov, and Bukharin.[65]

Why such a convoluted justification for exonerating Kirov? Why compare his case to those of the oppositionists? After all, no one could miss the point that, yes, Lenin had overlooked the sins of his comrades, but in retrospect it had been a wrong decision because they ended up betraying the party line. To say that Kirov's errors were not nearly so serious was not to say that he would never betray the party line as well. Far from defending Kirov, the resolution actually raised more doubts about his political reliability.

▪ KIROV'S SECRET SPEECH

Shortly after his return to Leningrad, according to the recollections of Kirov's subordinate Mikhail Rosliakov, Kirov appeared before the Leningrad Obkom, which discussed the meeting in Moscow. As Kirov sat, agitated and silent, the second secretary of the obkom, Mikhail Chudov, went over the details and quoted Stalin's comments verbatim.[66] This meeting was not reported in the press. It may have been part of an official Leningrad Obkom plenum, on 17 December 1929, called to discuss the spring sowing campaign. Kirov gave a speech on the subject, which was reprinted in *Leningradskaia pravda* on the next day, in "condensed form." At the end of the reprinted address, it was mentioned that Kirov also spoke in honor of Stalin's fiftieth birthday, 21 December 1929.

With Stalin emerging as the single, all-powerful leader of the Soviet Union, his fiftieth birthday was used to develop his personality cult and thus became a major public event. In historian Robert Tucker's words: "Stalin was lauded in press articles as Lenin's supremely gifted disciple and rightful successor. The event was made into a symbolic coronation of him as the party's new *vozhd* [leader]."[67] Kirov attended the celebrations for Stalin in Moscow on 21 December, but he was not among the contributors to a special book published in honor of Stalin's birthday at the end of 1929.[68]

More significantly, Kirov's 17 December speech about Stalin was never published. A typewritten copy of this speech in the Kirov archive makes the reason for this strange lapse abundantly clear.[69] Kirov not only damned Stalin with faint praise but also made several unflattering, albeit subtle, references to his revolutionary past and his qualities as a leader. Thus, while others attached great significance to Stalin's early radical activities in Tbilisi, Kirov noted that "Tiflis [Tbilisi] was not much of a workers' center, but the activity of Comrade Stalin began in these first small workers' circles." Speaking of Stalin's writings at the time of the 1905 Revolution, Kirov made a point of saying that his brochures were written in Georgian and later translated into Russian, thus emphasizing that Stalin was not a native Russian speaker. As for Stalin's role in the 1917 Revolution, which was now portrayed officially as pivotal, Kirov observed only that "Stalin was one of a group of five who led the insurrection in Leningrad."

Going on to discuss the opposition within the party, Kirov noted that its leaders always struck out at Stalin: "and this is not because he has certain character traits, that he is not always easy to get along with and so on. That is rubbish. The blow goes in his direction because he is the main guard and a fierce guard at Lenin's post." Kirov also mentioned that Russian émigrés abroad characterized Stalin as "none other than a dictator."

Although he added that they were exaggerating, he gave credence to their view by noting: "The White Guards see what role in the life of our party, of our country, I would say, Stalin plays now. Although they are abroad, they too understand the significance of this man's role."

If this had been the extent of Kirov's comments, they might be dismissed as a disgruntled gesture of protest after the ordeal he had just been through in Moscow. But Kirov, it turns out, actually said more to the participants at the 17 December plenum. Buried in the archive under a cover sheet that says "stenogram of speech of S. M. Kirov on the spring sowing campaign" is another typewritten copy of his address to commemorate Stalin's birthday. This copy is identical to the other, except that it includes the following additional paragraph:

> And, finally, I don't think that it would be wrong for me to bring up what everyone is speculating about, specifically Lenin's testament, in which he characterized individual leading comrades. Ill'ich, for example, talks about Stalin, discussing what arises from all his activity. The one negative trait that Lenin saw in Stalin was that he is rude. True, he added that the rudeness was of such a quality that in certain circumstances it could lead to something. This, of course, is a minus. But aside from this minus, even Lenin, who could see through people (he knew his assistants especially well), didn't observe anything.[70]

The reason why this complete copy of Kirov's speech had been hidden is clear: it was sheer heresy on Kirov's part to bring up what Lenin said about Stalin in his testament. Never mind that Kirov feigned an effort to downplay Lenin's observation and defend Stalin. At the very time that Stalin had been raised to an infallible hero, Kirov was reminding his audience in no uncertain terms that Lenin, far from designating Stalin as his successor, had serious doubts about him.

Did Stalin find out about Kirov's speech? Typewritten stenograms of regional party committee meetings were typically forwarded to Moscow for inspection and storage. This may explain why a copy without Kirov's reference to Lenin's testament was prepared, although even this copy contained remarks that would have angered Stalin. Assuming that only an incomplete text of Kirov's remarks was sent, it is highly probable that someone reported Kirov's statements to Moscow and that Stalin eventually heard about it. If this was the case, Stalin would have been furious. Highly sensitive and insecure about his image, he could not bear criticism. According to his daughter, Svetlana Allilueva, if he was told that someone was saying bad things about him, a "psychological metamorphosis" would take place. That person would become his enemy, never to be forgiven: "Once he had cast out of his heart someone he had known a long time, once he had mentally relegated that someone to the ranks of his enemies, it was impossible to talk to him about that person anymore. He was constitutionally incapable of the reversal that would turn a fancied enemy back into a friend."[71]

But Stalin was also skilled at keeping his feelings hidden. He could hold a grudge for years, displaying such outward affection that the victim of his animosity would have no suspicion of wrath. If he was angry at Kirov, he would not have shown it. Stalin had cultivated Kirov as one of his protégés, just as he had Sergo, and he depended upon Kirov's support in Leningrad to build up his position as leader and to carry out his economic policies. Kirov had just survived a major upheaval in his organization, along with a personal attack on his revolutionary credentials. Having shown exceptional resilience in the face of these troubles, Kirov had actually gained in popularity among his subordinates, a fact that Stalin was well aware of. At the end of December 1929, Stalin made the following observation to Molotov:

> The nasty business (Desov-Komarov) against Kirov helped to accelerate the purge of bureaucratized elements from the Leningrad organization. There's no cloud without a silver lining! The Leningrad Provincial [sic] Party Committee passed the Central Committee resolution—and, according to witnesses, not without a certain enthusiasm. It's a fact! Komarov's bureaucratism played a role here, and the Central Committee's authority and the fact that Kirov has apparently earned the great respect of the Leningrad organization in recent times.[72]

If Stalin had plans to move against Kirov, this was not the time to implement them.

As for Kirov's motivations, it is difficult to understand why he made this seemingly rash attack on Stalin behind his back. To be sure, he had reason to be angry with Stalin for allowing a kangaroo court to find him guilty of compromising with liberalism before the revolution. But why would he risk incurring Stalin's wrath by retaliating in this way? Either Kirov assumed that his comments would not reach Stalin or he did not understand how severe the repercussions might be. Whatever the case, he was playing a dangerous game. In fighting back against Stalin, he had resorted to Stalin's tactics, but he was no match for the General Secretary.

6

Kirov and Stalin's Revolution

. . . .

The plan is not an abstract thing, thought up by economists, but an essential element of socialist construction. Without the plan, socialism cannot be built.

—*Sergei Kirov, 1931*

. . . .

By early 1930 Stalin's "revolution from above"—rapid industrialization, carried out according to an ambitious "five-year plan," and forced collectivization—was in full swing. In essence, this revolution was another version of war communism, a program of draconian economic measures dictated by the Kremlin and often enforced by police repression. These measures were designed to transform Russia from a peasant society to an industrial one in the shortest possible time.

As might have been expected, the new direction in Soviet economic policy put extreme pressure on Kirov and his Leningrad party organization, which oversaw the economy of both the city and the much larger Leningrad region. The first economic five-year plan, approved by the Leningrad Obkom in March 1929 but actually already in operation by late 1928, set forth a goal of industrialization at breakneck speed. The gross real output of Leningrad industry was to increase by 276 percent in the next five years. As an important industrial center, producing chemicals, machine tools, tractors, turbines, generators, and a host of other industrial products, Leningrad was a focal point of the ambitious drive to industrialize. But it was woefully unprepared for its new economic role. There were not enough skilled workers, technicians, and engineers. The city was receiving only a third of the fuel supplies necessary to run its factories. Supplies of grain were also down, largely as a result of the chaos caused by the emergency measures introduced in the countryside in 1928, and Leningrad was experiencing severe food shortages.[1]

Working sixteen hours a day, Kirov visited factories and spoke to workers and party officials, exhorting them to do all they could to speed up production, while at the same time conserving energy. In his third-floor office at the Smolnyi, Kirov consulted with economic officials and factory directors and lobbied Moscow to come up with more supplies to keep the factories going. His nerves were on edge, and everyone around him felt the pressure. "Sergei Mironovich was terribly exacting," recalls one subordinate. "If you just once did not fulfill your obligation or let him down, you could expect no mercy."[2] Another source observed: "Demanding of himself, he was demanding of others. He would not tolerate it when a worker who was needed could not be found. . . . He would not put up with even the smallest inaccuracies, including a rare mistake on a typewritten paper, which had to be corrected immediately. He could not stand it when a paper got lost, however insignificant. He himself never lost anything, everything of his was in its place."[3]

Ivan Kodatskii, chairman of the Leningrad Soviet Executive Committee and Kirov's close friend, confirmed that, while Kirov was a pleasure to work with, he drove himself very hard and insisted on following every detail: "Kirov loved to check on how his instructions were carried out at the very bottom. With this goal, he often called the shops, talked to the foreman or superintendent to see how things were going."[4] As a technician himself and a "man of the people," Kirov took an interest in the details of economic production and sought out contacts with lower-level employees.

In fact, he had a reputation for valuing technical expertise above all else. When Zinoviev ran Leningrad he had rewarded people for their party loyalty and their support for the Bolsheviks during the revolution and civil war by placing them in positions for which they were often unqualified. Kirov reversed all this. He shifted people who lacked skills into party-political positions and replaced them with experienced technicians. On one occasion, when he was visiting Khibinogorsk, a vast mining complex on the Kola Peninsula, Kirov surprised local officials by insisting on inviting nonparty specialists to a banquet held in his honor. "Here we are all Bolsheviks, all party and nonparty builders of socialism," he reportedly said. Kirov also insisted that the banquet include cognac and vodka, which had to be obtained from the coffers of the local GPU.[5]

In being such a hands-on administrator, Kirov of course put additional demands upon himself. But he was working under the watchful eyes of Moscow, and he could ill afford to make mistakes. Compounding the pressure was the steady stream of directives from the Supreme Economic Council (VSNKh) in Moscow: 100 new factories had to be built; the Red Putilovets plant had to produce 10,000 tractors in one year; and then the announcement that the production goals set for five years had to be reached in four! Because of insufficient electricity and oil, factories in Leningrad operated in shifts. Kirov had trouble maintaining the party's credibility in these circumstances and met with local resistance to what many saw as unrealistic goals. In early 1930 a factory director had the audacity to write an article, which appeared in *Leningradskaia pravda*, complaining about the "fantastic" directives, which would be impossible to fulfill. He was later arrested by the OGPU for this heresy, but his sentiments were doubtless shared by many.[6]

Support for the Kremlin's hyperaccelerated program of industrialization had to be extracted from the countryside. Peasants provided the means for investment, but often at machine-gun point. The more prosperous peasant farmers were the initial target of the regime's offensive. Local Communists, assisted by the OGPU, were ordered to confiscate their property and banish them to far-off regions. But the "war against the kulaks" soon became an assault against the entire peasantry when individual peasant households of all economic strata were forced into collective farms. Collectivization was well underway by the second half of 1929, but the real push came after Stalin's speech to commemorate the Bolshevik Revolution on 7 November 1929. Stalin declared 1929 to be the year of the "great turning point," because, he said, peasants were joining collective farms en masse. Although this was far from the truth, Stalin's statement was interpreted as a directive to step up collectivization. The human toll of what was basically an operation of terror was tremendous: there were mass deportations, and millions died of starvation or were killed for resisting collectivization.[7]

At the time of Stalin's "great turning point" speech, the Leningrad district had made little progress in collectivizing its peasants and was far behind other regions. Only 2 percent of peasant households had been collectivized there. One reason for Leningrad's laggard performance was that its poor climate and marshy or heavily forested land made agriculture less productive than in other areas and hence less conducive to collectivization. In addition, Kirov was opposed to using repressive measures against the peasants. He had continued throughout the first half of 1929 to emphasize the importance of giving economic assistance to the countryside rather than using force.[8] Prodded by Stalin toward the end of the year to step up collectivization, Kirov urged Leningrad district party and government officials to make a stronger effort to collectivize. But he warned against "chasing after percentages" and maintained that the use of repressive measures was inappropriate.[9]

Kirov was well aware of the mood of the peasants and the fact that excessive force in the countryside could be counterproductive. A letter sent in October 1929 by a group of peasants from the Luzhesk region of Leningrad to Ordzhonikidze, then head of the Worker-Peasants' Inspectorate, probably expressed the way most peasants viewed collectivization:

> Do you know that in the Luzhesk region of Leningrad they are taking away bread by force from the middle-level peasants? Do you know that in this same region they are forcibly driving us peasants into collectives, saying that if we don't go they will confiscate the land of a former landowner that we have had since 1920. . . . But we will not go into a collective, because we do not want to be slaves for someone to exhaust. . . . We did not count on the fall of the autocratic regime of Nicholas to become slaves and serfs of Comrade Stalin and his accomplices. Comrade Bukharin is right to stand for free development of agriculture and free sale of agricultural products and we congratulate him.[10]

In the peasants' view, the collective farm system was just another form of serfdom. All over the country, including the Leningrad region, peasants responded to confiscation of their grain and their forced relocation into collective farms with mass uprisings. In 1929 at least 1,300 peasant revolts were recorded in the Soviet Union, and by early 1930 there was talk of civil war. Stalin responded in March 1930 with his famous "Dizzy with Success" article in *Pravda*, in which he criticized local authorities for being overzealous in their efforts to collectivize peasants and warned them against "excesses." The party sent out directives to ease up on the collectivization process, but the revolts continued. In the end, the regime brought the situation under control only with the help of the army and the

OGPU, which sent hundreds of thousands of peasants to labor camps in Siberia and shot thousands of others.[11]

Through 1934, Kirov continued to insist publicly that repressive measures should not be used against the peasants, despite the fact that collectivization in Leningrad lagged behind other regions. By January 1931 only around 6 percent of peasant households were collectivized. To be sure, local party and OGPU officials in the Leningrad region drove the peasants into collectives, just as they did elsewhere. But, following the publication of Stalin's article in March 1930, Kirov launched a campaign against arbitrary violence against peasants and fired officials guilty of such repression. The pace of collectivization in Leningrad eventually was stepped up, so that by January 1934, 54 percent of peasant households had been collectivized.[12] But in general the process was conducted with less ruthlessness and brute force than in other regions. As Robert Tucker observed: "This was an implicit indictment of Stalin's blitzkrieg collectivization and its consequences."[13]

▪ KIROV THE STALINIST

Although he was open-minded in making economic appointments and hesitant about using excessive force against the peasants, Kirov had not become softhearted. On the contrary, there were instances where Kirov's ruthlessness called into question his reputation as a voice of moderation against the growing police dictatorship. Already during the civil war, Kirov had demonstrated that he was capable of being cruel when he deemed it necessary. Now, after ten years of imposing Bolshevik rule on a recalcitrant citizenry, he was even more hardened to human suffering.

Kirov's role in the "Case of the Academy of Sciences" is a good example of his acquiescing to repressive measures. Beginning with the notorious Shakhty trial in 1928, the OGPU had been fabricating cases against "bourgeois specialists" and members of the old intelligentsia. In the autumn of 1929, the OGPU turned its attention to the highly esteemed Academy of Sciences, headquartered in Leningrad. There a government commission to investigate the academy, headed by the old Bolshevik Iurii Figatner, found that a large number of "historically and politically significant" documents were being illegally retained by academy historians. A scandal erupted. At the end of October, Figatner and Kirov sent a series of communications to Stalin and Ordzhonikidze detailing how they had used secret agents to find out about these documents and recommending that several of the academy's leading historians be dismissed.[14]

Although hundreds of academy employees, including the renowned historian S. F. Platonov, lost their jobs, this was not the end of the affair. Predictably, the OGPU was called in to launch a criminal investigation, and many scholars were arrested on the familiar charges of "wrecking" (a form of economic sabotage). Confined in an isolation cell in a Leningrad prison, historian Platonov confessed under duress that he was a monarchist. The investigation lasted for over a year before the case went to trial and the sentences were pronounced in February 1931. Although Platonov himself was "only" sentenced to exile in Siberia, five of the defendants were shot and over seventy sent to labor camps.[15] As a result of this case, the Academy of Sciences was decimated, and the scholarly study of Russian history came to an abrupt end. Now party hacks and propagandists would step in to fill the void and rewrite that history to suit the needs of the Stalinist regime.

Kirov may not have intended that his participation in the vigilant investigation of the Academy of Sciences would lead to such a tragic end. There is no record of his involvement in the case beyond his initial communications to Moscow in October 1929. This was precisely when he was under fire from Moscow as a result of the self-criticism campaign, and thus he was not in a position to stand up to the OGPU. But he showed no signs of remorse when he mentioned Platonov at the Sixteenth Party Congress, which took place in June and July 1930.

At this congress, during which he was elected a full member of the Politburo, Kirov gave a rousing, demagogic speech against Bukharin's right opposition, a speech that bore no traces of the cautious moderation that he exhibited earlier. He observed that "a victory of the right in the party would lead in the end to a rebirth of capitalism" and that "armed with this opportunistic ideology, the right opposition has the goal of gaining the leadership of our Communist Party," thus suggesting, ominously, that the right wanted to seize power illegally. Kirov also compared the right group with the historian Platonov, at this time already under arrest: "I would recommend that Rykov and Tomskii at least read the testimony of academician Platonov. He describes the platform of the right even better than

Tomskii does. . . . The thing is, the program of the right is closely related by spirit, by ideology, by blood to the circle of all these Platonovs."[16]

Toward the end of his speech Kirov asserted that "every extra bit of speed in our industrialization, every extra collective farm—all this will be achieved not only in the struggle against the kulak and other counterrevolutionary elements in our country. It will [also] be achieved in the struggle against Bukharin, Rykov, Tomskii, and Uglanov." In general Kirov was milder toward Bukharin, who was absent from the congress, than the others, restricting his criticisms to Bukharin's failure to answer questions that the party had raised. But in suggesting that the right opposition as a whole was little different from critics of the regime who had been arrested, Kirov was taking the battle against the opposition to a new level. Of course, he was not the only speaker to make such suggestions at the congress. One speaker even accused the opposition of terrorism.[17] Nonetheless, Kirov's stance was an about-face from his earlier position.

Kirov's role in the construction of the Baltic–White Sea Canal further demonstrates that he did not shrink from draconian measures when he saw the need for them. The canal was constructed with prison camp labor, at great human cost. The project was under the control of the OGPU, but as party chief of the region, Kirov took an active role. The 227-kilometer-long canal, begun in December 1931, required the excavation of twenty million cubic meters of earth, much of it rock. Close to 100,000 of the 280,000 prison laborers are said to have lost their lives working in unspeakably harsh conditions to finish the canal in a year and a half.[18]

A local Leningrad journalist later recalled that he heard Kirov say in the early 1930s that he was opposed to the use of forced labor.[19] If this was the case, however, Kirov did not reveal his views to his superiors in Moscow. In July 1933, Stalin came to Leningrad for the canal's official opening, traveling by ship along the canal for several days with Kirov, Kliment Voroshilov, Commissar of Defense, Genrikh Iagoda, deputy chief of the OGPU, and M. D. Berman, chief of the GULAG, the notorious labor camp system. Smiling and relaxed, the proud leaders gave no hint of the suffering that was behind this "glorious Soviet achievement."[20]

At the Seventeenth Party Congress in 1934, delegates received copies of the book *The Stalin Baltic–White Sea Canal,* which Kirov declared in his speech "very useful and full of insights," although it made no reference to the fact that the canal was built with forced labor. Voroshilov made a special mention at the congress of Kirov's role in the canal's construction: "In recent years we have not only built up and strengthened our naval forces in the Baltic and Black seas. Benefiting from the fact that Comrade Kirov, together with Comrade Iagoda, at the head of a heroic army of White Sea construction workers, united the White and Baltic seas, we have transferred a few ships to the new canal in the North in order not to be defenseless in this area."[21] As for Kirov, he gave most of the credit to the OGPU: "To build such a canal in such a short time, in such a place—it is truly heroic work and we must give justice to our Chekists [original name of the political police in 1917], who led this business and who literally achieved a miracle."[22]

There are other examples of Kirov's Stalinist ruthlessness. In August 1932, as part of a propaganda campaign surrounding the introduction of a law on "misappropriating socialist property," *Pravda* reprinted a speech that Kirov delivered in Leningrad:

> It must be said frankly that our punitive policies are very liberal. We must correct this. If we condemn some embezzler . . . he is usually given amnesty quickly, and a trial never takes place. We consider cooperative and kolkhoz property to be public property. It seems to me that kolkhozes and cooperatives must be put on the same footing as government organizations, and if a person is caught stealing kolkhoz or cooperative property, then he must be sentenced to the highest form of punishment [death]. And if the punishment is mitigated, then it cannot be less than ten years' imprisonment.[23]

According to one of his biographers, Kirov was later angry that the police were applying the new law indiscriminately in the Leningrad region and chastised a group of legal authorities for "putting half of Russia into jail."[24] Was the speech published in *Pravda* just rhetoric that Kirov did not believe? It is hard to say, because we have another example of repressive measures on his direct orders. In April 1932 Kirov signed a decree authorizing the Leningrad police to "remove" 2,000 "criminal, alien class elements" (those from the intelligentsia and former merchant and noble families) and send them to an OGPU camp.[25] As in other areas of the country, Leningrad authorities "cleansed" their region of these groups in late 1932 and early 1933, in connection with the introduction of mandatory passports. Thousands were forced out of their homes and driven from the city to make housing available for the proletariat. A letter from a fifty-seven-year-old Leningrad engineer to Molotov, by this time chairman of the Council of People's Commissars, offers a glimpse of the tragic impact of this process: "The most terrible thing about what was done to me and my family and apparently to many other people like us . . . is that such important decisions, like ones on exile, on future work, on a piece of bread for very old and sick people, such as me—these are literally questions of life and death—are made secretly, irresponsibly, without consulting the interested parties."[26] To be sure, Kirov received such letters as well, but they probably lay unanswered on his desk.

▪ MORE INTRAPARTY DISSENT

Although he was consumed with administering Leningrad, Kirov could not ignore higher party politics, which continued to be fraught with intrigue and conflict, even after the decisive defeat of the right in 1930. Stalin had outmaneuvered members of the top leadership who opposed him, but he had not managed to quell discontent at lower levels of the party bureaucracy. As a result, the early 1930s witnessed a series of dramatic confrontations between Stalin and real or perceived opponents. Indeed, Stalin became so obsessed with ferreting out any vestiges of disloyalty to him that it is hard to imagine how he managed with the day-to-day governing of the country.

Kirov doubtless would have preferred to avoid the infighting and be left alone to pursue his job in Leningrad. That he quickly put the Stalin-Bukharin conflict behind him shows how little all the polemics meant to him. Despite Bukharin's disgraced status, Kirov continued on good terms with him, even inviting him on a hunting trip.[27] Bukharin's second wife, Anna Larina, recalled that her husband always had strong affection for Kirov. When she was exiled after Bukharin's arrest in 1937, she brought with her a photograph of Bukharin and Kirov, which was then confiscated: "It showed my husband with his arm around Kirov; both men were happy and smiling. The Astrakhan official who found it was clearly surprised to see the two men together in a friendly pose; it would have made more sense to him if Bukharin had been snapped pointing a revolver at Kirov."[28] (Larina was referring to the fact that, among the many false charges leveled against Bukharin after his arrest, was the charge of helping to murder Kirov.) After Kirov died, Bukharin sent Mariia L'vovna a telegram: "I grieve with you over the loss of the unforgettable Mironich. I embrace you warmly."[29]

Bukharin probably assumed, as he did with Ordzhonikidze, that Kirov's public statements about him were not necessarily a reflection of his personal views. And he seems to have been right. Although both Kirov and Sergo became outspoken defenders of Stalin's "general line" by 1930, neither had much of an appetite for going after party comrades who questioned that line. This was clearly the case with the so-called left-rightist bloc, which was organized against Stalin in 1930 by Sergei Syrtsov and Beso Lominadze and created a furor within the party.

Syrtsov, a candidate member of the Politburo and an influential economist, had been a strong supporter of Stalin during the 1920s. But Stalin's dictatorial methods and the disastrous consequences of the collectivization campaign led Syrtsov to form a group of colleagues with the aim of ousting Stalin.[30] In the autumn of 1930, Beso Lominadze, a Georgian and first secretary of the Transcaucasian party organization, met with Syrtsov and became an adherent of the group. Beso, who had worked for many years in the Caucasus and was personally close to both Sergo and Kirov, had already apprised Sergo of his dissenting views in the summer of 1929, in a letter that caused Sergo a great deal of disquiet because it placed him in an awkward position with Stalin. Sergo responded to the letter with admonishments to Beso about his disloyalty, but to no avail.[31]

Events came to a head in late October 1930, when a member of the Syrtsov-Lominadze group denounced them to Stalin. Syrtsov was arrested, along with several others, and Lominadze was called to Moscow to appear before Ordzhonikidze's Central Control Commission. Both Syrtsov and Lominadze denied that they had intended to get rid of Stalin, but admitted being dissatisfied with some aspects of his leadership. Unfortunately, however, the OGPU had managed to elicit testimony from others confirming the charges. In early November 1930, Sergo duly reported on the case to a joint session of the Politburo and the presidium of the Central Control Commission. Given his close association with Beso, this was not easy. But Sergo nonetheless did what was required of him. He condemned Syrtsov and the others for "double-dealing" and "fractionalism." Of course, he said, party members could have doubts about the general line and even voice their doubts to the Central Committee. The sin of Syrtsov and Lominadze was that they kept their disagreements secret—which amounted to antiparty activity.[32]

Sergo did not mention, of course, that he knew about Lominadze's heretical views and did not report them to the Central Committee. But we know that Stalin found out, because much later, shortly after Sergo's death in 1937, Stalin told a Central Committee plenum that Sergo had received several "anti-party" letters from Lominadze before the discovery of the group in 1930, but had kept them a secret. If they had known about Lominadze's letters, said Stalin, they never would have appointed him secretary of the Transcaucasian Regional Committee. Thus, as Stalin presented it, Sergo was guilty of deception. Indeed, although Sergo made a show of demanding that Lominadze be expelled from the party, he continued to be his friend and even supported him in his career, which cannot have made Stalin happy. In the words of one historian: "Stalin placed Lominadze in the ranks of his enemies and harbored enmity toward Ordzhonikidze, who had dared to protect Lominadze."[33]

How did Kirov figure in this controversy? Lominadze was not expelled from the party, but lost his post in Transcaucasia, as did a number of his associates. The unpleasant task of presiding over the shake-up in Transcaucasia fell to Kirov, presumably because he had been a party leader in the region until 1926. Although he had been in Leningrad for over four years, Transcaucasia was still considered his bailiwick, and the fact that he was sent there to discipline his former colleagues carried with it the implication that he was somehow responsible for their failings.

This was the impression that Kirov conveyed in an apologetic speech to a party assembly in Tbilisi in mid-November 1930.[34] Explaining why many officials would lose their jobs, Kirov emphasized that they were responsible for failing to stop Lominadze's "deviations." Even though the Politburo sent Lominadze to Transcaucasia, said Kirov, the regional committee there must answer for his wrongdoings, because they were not "watching him with both eyes." Lominadze had openly expressed his criticisms of Moscow's policies at a regional party congress and "no one slapped his hands." Significantly, Kirov added that he himself was "half Caucasian" and understood how this could have happened in a place where there was such a strong "family spirit." Lominadze had grown up in the Caucasus, and everyone knew and trusted him. Now they would have to pay the price for this misguided trust.

In Baku, where major dismissals were underway, Kirov told his party comrades: "There is no doubt that the Azerbaijan and Baku organizations in particular have to endure great ordeals, for Lominadze understood well what it meant to secure his influence in Baku, what it meant to win over the Azerbaijan organization." But again he accepted part of the blame: "Lominadze was our chap, one hundred percent Caucasian, we knew him from the time he began to climb the political ladder. . . . he was such a good fellow . . . and we see how it turned out."[35]

This was not the first purge for the Azerbaijan leadership. A year and a half earlier Kirov's close friend and protégé Levon Mirzoian had lost his job as party secretary in Baku, despite Kirov's efforts to protect him. It is not clear why he was fired, but, judging from Stalin's reaction to a letter from Mirzoian after he lost the Baku post, his malfeasance was fairly serious. In September 1929, Stalin wrote to Molotov: "I am sending you a letter I just got from Mirzoian. You know that I'm not a supporter of the policy of 'tolerance' regarding comrades who have committed grievous errors from the perspective of the party's interests. I must say, however, that it is not in the party's interests to *finish off* Mirzoian."[36] Instead of finishing Mirzoian off, Stalin sent him to the Urals to develop the oil industry and later to Kazakhstan. Mirzoian's stay of execution would last until 1939, when he would die at the hands of the secret police.

What must have caused Stalin particular concern in the case of Syrtsov and Lominadze was that their views had gained considerable sympathy within the party. Thus, the announcements of dismissals in Transcaucasia were accompanied by references to "double-dealing" and "conciliatory attitudes" toward the Syrtsov-Lominadze group. The affair made it clear that there was still dissent in the party ranks, despite Stalin's efforts to suppress all opposition and create a monolithic organization. In fact, it was precisely because dissent could not be expressed openly that "double-dealing" toward superiors arose. Officials who were forced to comply with decisions they disagreed with would express their disapproval secretly. As one historian observed: "In the Soviet Union under Stalin this phenomenon appeared in extreme form, and the charge of 'double-dealing' was brought against many later critics of the leadership. It was countered by the development of the system of informers, within as well as outside the party; and its counterpart, or mirror image, was paranoid behavior at the top."[37]

As for Kirov and Sergo, they were now full members of the Politburo and hence objects of the illegal criticism directed at the leadership. At the same time, given their close personal relations with many second-tier party officials and the propensity among members of the party hierarchy to form patron-client relationships, they were often at the receiving end of the secret complaints and appeals for help from those out of favor. In the early 1930s Sergo continued to receive letters from the disgraced Lominadze in the Urals, and Kirov kept up an active correspondence with Mirzoian. By this time, however, the OGPU was most certainly monitoring all such communications and informing Stalin, whose watchword was "guilt by association."

Of course, Stalin himself remained on outwardly cordial terms with some disgraced party members, like Bukharin, for example. Anna Larina recalled how Stalin "petted" her husband well into the 1930s, by which time he most certainly was planning Bukharin's demise. On one occasion in 1935, at a banquet for military officers, Stalin gave a toast: "Let us drink, comrades, to Nikolai Ivanovich, and let bygones be bygones." But whereas both Sergo and Kirov seem to have felt genuine compassion for their fallen comrades, in Stalin's case it was all an act. As Larina points out: "With him, everything was calculated, every step—no, every inch of every step. Of course, this is obvious *now,* but then no one, including my husband himself, suspected a thing. The toast was considered a sincere expression of Stalin's attitude toward Bukharin."[38] Stalin could trust himself and know his own motivations, but he had no way of knowing what was in the minds of Sergo and Kirov, and he was not inclined to give his subordinates the benefit of the doubt.

Whatever suspicions Stalin might have had, they did not reflect upon his outward relations with Kirov. On the contrary, Stalin sought out his companionship, inviting him to vacation with him at Sochi on the Black Sea in 1931. Kirov, who loved to fly, had asked Stalin for permission to come to Sochi by plane, but Stalin, apparently considering such travel dangerous, telegrammed him a refusal: "I have no right and I would not advise anyone to authorize flights. I most humbly request you to come by train."[39] After Kirov arrived sometime in mid-September, Stalin wrote to his wife, Nadezhda, in Moscow: "Here the weather is good for the time being. Yesterday night at 12 o'clock Kirov and I tested the temperature at the bottom at Puzanovka and above, where I live. . . . I was in the sea once (only once)! I swam. It was excellent! I think I will go again. I am having a good time with Kirov."[40] Two days later Nadezhda wrote to Stalin from Moscow: "It is very good that Kirov is staying with you and also that it is warm there at your place. Be careful with swimming."[41] It was as if Stalin and Kirov were just ordinary comrades, having a good time. But the deepening tensions within the party leadership cannot have been far from their minds.

▪ THE RIUTIN AFFAIR

If the Syrtsov-Lominadze dissent presented a challenge to Stalin, the emergence of an opposition group around Matem'ian Riutin in 1932 shook the Stalin regime to its foundations. Kirov's role in the affair is still a matter of dispute, but some see this episode as a turning point in Kirov's relationship with Stalin. Riutin was a Moscow party official who lost his job in 1928 because he spoke out against Stalin's leadership. Although Riutin soon gained another post and continued to be a candidate member of the Central Committee, he was under a shadow. In the autumn of 1930, when the Central Committee received a secret denunciation, claiming that Riutin had again criticized the General Secretary, Stalin seized upon the opportunity for vengeance. He wrote to Molotov from Sochi: "With regard to Riutin, it seems to me that it's impossible to limit ourselves to expelling him from the party. When some time has passed after his expulsion, he will have to be exiled somewhere as far as possible from Moscow. This counterrevolutionary scum should be completely disarmed."[42]

Shortly after Riutin was expelled from the party, the OGPU arrested him on charges of counterrevolutionary activity. Typically, however, Stalin decided to play games with Riutin. In early 1931, with Stalin's personal sanction, the OGPU released him because of lack of evidence, and he began working as a government economist. He also continued his opposition to Stalin's rule. In 1932, Riutin joined a group of disgruntled Old Bolsheviks called the Union of Marxist-Leninists. On behalf of the group, he wrote a lengthy brochure, "Stalin and the Crisis of the Proletarian Dictatorship," which set forth a platform, and an "Appeal to All Party Members," calling for their participation. The platform was a scathing criticism of Stalin, describing him an as unprincipled politician, capable of only intrigue and hypocrisy. Stalin, the brochure said, was not a leader, but a dictator, whose rule was disastrous for the country.[43]

As might have been expected, the OGPU's discovery of the group led to the immediate arrest of Riutin and other members in September 1932.

Their case was discussed at a Central Committee plenum called in late September, which Kirov attended. The Central Committee passed a resolution condemning the group and approving their exclusion from the Communist Party. The case was then handed back to the OGPU, which passed sentences on the accused. Riutin received ten years' imprisonment, while the other members of his group were sentenced to exile in Siberia.[44]

The rest of the story remains unclear, but several sources claim that Stalin had tried to have the Politburo approve the death sentence for Riutin (the first time a party official would receive such a punishment) and met with resistance. Kirov was reportedly the first to object, saying: "We mustn't do this. Ryutin is not a hopeless case, he's merely gone astray. . . . Who the hell knows how many hands wrote that letter [the appeal]. . . . We'll be misunderstood."[45] Sergo and Valerian Kuibyshev then endorsed Kirov's objections and others abstained, thus forcing Stalin to go back on his plan to have the OGPU sentence Riutin to death.[46]

With records of what transpired at Politburo meetings still classified secret, it is impossible to confirm this oft-repeated story. Judging from what we know about Kirov, it is perhaps surprising that he would have taken the risky step of opposing Stalin's plans so openly. Nonetheless, having seen what Stalin was doing to men like Mirzoian and Lominadze, Kirov might have realized the dangerous implications of lifting the taboo on executing party members. Also, Kirov's friend Petr Petrovskii, the former editor of *Leningradskaia pravda*, was among those arrested by the police for membership in the group. Kirov may have been anxious to protect him from a more severe punishment.[47]

Adding to the mystery is the fact that the Riutin Platform, the original text of which disappeared, actually singled out Kirov, alone of Politburo members, for special criticism. Thus, the platform read: "We can find all the genuine, most inveterate opportunists at the present time right in the ranks of Stalin's ruling clique! [names of several secondary officials] . . . Kirov, a member of the Politburo, former Kadet [a liberal party] and editor of a Kadet newspaper in Vladikavkaz. All, one might say, are pillars of the Stalinist regime. And all represent the definitive type of opportunist. These people will attach themselves to any regime, to any political system."[48] And later, in reference to "self-criticism," the platform noted: "It is well known how the efforts of the Leningraders to expose Kirov as a former Kadet and editor of a Kadet paper in Vladikavkaz turned out.

They were muzzled and told to be quiet. Stalin ... protects his own scoundrels."[49]

It is odd, to say the least, that Riutin's platform would attack Kirov in this manner. If he and his colleagues were looking for scoundrels and opportunists, there were more obvious candidates in the Politburo and in the Central Committee than Kirov. Indeed, Kirov had defended one member of Riutin's group, Petrovskii, when Stalin ordered him to be fired from his job in 1928. And why, if Riutin was truly interested in restoring democracy to the party, would he bring up the Leningrad self-criticism campaign, which was a ritual scare tactic employed by Moscow in order to shake up the regional party apparatus and possibly discredit Kirov? Yes, Kirov survived, but with a black mark on his record, which Stalin and the Politburo made no attempt to erase.

There is a possible explanation for the negative comments about Kirov. What emerged as the Riutin Platform was a typewritten version produced by the OGPU allegedly on the basis of copies or fragments the police had unearthed after Riutin was imprisoned. Thus, the OGPU may well have altered the original version.[50] Perhaps, then, the references to Kirov were a result of OGPU tampering.

If Riutin really did have it in for Kirov, it is hard to imagine that he would have the reaction he had to Kirov's murder in December 1934. He displayed no trace of contempt for Kirov in a letter written to his family from prison: "Has lightning again flashed there with you? ... Only yesterday they brought the papers with the news that Kirov was killed! For the time being everything remains unclear and puzzling. But I can already say that this is the most powerful and significant political event, full of deep meaning, which everyone must think about seriously."[51] Riutin, who was to be charged with terrorism in 1937 and later shot, understood already at this point that Stalin would use the Kirov murder as a pretext for the purges.

Whatever Kirov's involvement was, the importance of the Riutin affair cannot be underestimated. Not only did Stalin realize that there was still significant opposition to him within the party; he also was thwarted by members of the party leadership in his efforts to execute the leader of that opposition. Whether or not Kirov himself resisted the execution of a party member, the fact remains that Stalin had been restrained, which was intolerable for him.

▪ THE DEATH OF NADEZHDA ALLILUEVA

Just as the Riutin case was coming to a close, another event occurred that had an even more traumatic effect on Stalin—the suicide of his wife, Nadezhda Allilueva, on 9 November 1932. According to Stalin's daughter, Svetlana, her mother, who was almost twenty years younger than Stalin, had become increasingly unhappy in the marriage and was suffering a "terrible, devastating disillusionment" with her husband. When her dejection became unbearable after Stalin was verbally abusive to her at a dinner party, she went home and shot herself with a small revolver. Stalin never got over his shock. In Svetlana's words: "Inwardly things had changed catastrophically. Something had snapped inside my father."[52]

There can be little doubt that Nadezhda Allilueva's death contributed greatly to Stalin's growing paranoia. But it was not just a question of his grief over the loss of his wife and the mother of his two young children. Her suicide, brought on as it was by her obvious unhappiness with Stalin, was a blow to his prestige. Although the newspapers did not mention how she died, everyone knew that it was not by natural causes. And Stalin's close colleagues, including Kirov, were informed of the details. According to Mikhail Rosliakov's memoirs, Stalin was so humiliated that he talked of resigning, but was persuaded not to by other Politburo members. Although Stalin apparently had no doubts about the loyalty of yes-men like Molotov and Kaganovich, it made him uncomfortable that Ordzhonikidze, Kuibyshev, and Kirov knew his secret and had witnessed his display of weakness.[53] In fact, says Rosliakov, Kirov may have known more about Stalin's relationship with his wife than Stalin realized. Kirov was a close friend of Nadezhda's father, Sergei Alliluev, who wrote him several letters in the early 1930s. In one of these letters, written in 1931, Alliluev reportedly discussed how upset he was over the difficult situation of "poor Nadia."[54]

Kirov, as a Politburo member, of course attended the official funeral of Nadezhda Allilueva, although perhaps without Mariia L'vovna, whose name was curiously absent from the signatories to the obituary in *Pravda*. (All of the other Politburo wives except the wife of Kuibyshev were listed.) During the week after Nadezhda Allilueva's death, Kirov made five visits to Stalin's office, which was unusual for him, despite his frequent trips to Moscow.[55] Not only Stalin's sister-in-law Mariia Svanidze but also Mariia L'vovna's sister Sof'ia Markus recall that Stalin became exceptionally attached to Kirov after his wife's death. Markus has been quoted as saying that, when Kirov went to Moscow, he began staying overnight with Stalin instead of Sergo, as he had in the past.[56]

Others, however, including Sergo's wife, tell us that Kirov continued his custom of staying the night with Sergo until the very end: "Kirov always stayed with us in Moscow. Usually he would let us know in the evening that he was coming the next morning. Sergo always waited for him, so that they could breakfast together. Then they went off to work and met again late in the evening. After eating a little, they would settle in the dining room or in [Sergo's] office. Sergo would rest on the couch, Kirov would sit down next to him, and they would begin a long, heart-to-heart talk."[57] Zinaida Ordzhonikidze recalled one time when Sergo could not bear to have Kirov go back to Leningrad, so he had his driver stage a minor automobile accident on the way to the railway station, thus causing Kirov to miss his train.[58] A close colleague of Sergo's, Sof'ia Ginzburg, confirms that Kirov habitually stayed with the Ordzhonikidzes during his Moscow visits, adding that "the friendship of Sergo and Sergei Mironovich Kirov made Stalin especially suspicious."[59]

Although Kirov may have resisted Stalin's pressuring him to stay the night, it probably was not easy. Stalin wanted Kirov at his beck and call. By this time there were two telephones installed in Kirov's Leningrad apartment, one in his office and the other just outside his bedroom with a direct line to Moscow. This allowed Kirov to answer promptly when Stalin called him in the middle of the night, which he often did. Stalin was a demanding and impatient taskmaster; no subordinate would risk not answering his telephone calls, no matter what the hour.

Like his colleagues in the Politburo, Kirov now had little choice but to submit to Stalin's demands. Stalin had become a tyrant. Kirov had seen this situation coming for a long time, as his old comrade Petr Chagin later recalled. Once, at a dinner held in Kirov's apartment on the occasion of Stalin's visit to Leningrad back in 1926, Kirov gave a short speech. He said that it was difficult without Lenin, but Bolsheviks could be confident in their success because they had the Central Committee and the Politburo. Stalin then rejoined with a "tirade": the Central Committee and the Politburo were fine, he said, but the Russian people were used to having a tsar, to having only one person leading the country. According to Chagin, Kirov never again mentioned Stalin's tirade, but the meaning was clear and Kirov realized the extent of Stalin's ambitions.[60]

Later, Kirov would joke to comrades about Stalin's sensitive ego. On one occasion, in 1933, when Kirov was in Moscow with Rosliakov and other Leningraders, he recounted how Stalin had reacted when an inept official had addressed him as *khoziain* (master). Laughing, and imitating Stalin's accent and his scowl, Kirov said: "Stalin did not answer him, but was noticeably irritated, saying to me, '*Khoziain*—that sounds like a rich landowner in Central Asia. Fool!'"[61] Kirov understood that Stalin had his own vision of himself as a leader, a vision that was sacrosanct.

Significantly, Stalin never accompanied Kirov on his hunting trips, as Sergo and Kuibyshev did, but Kirov often sent him the wildfowl that he caught. Kirov's passion for hunting, with his beloved dog Strelka at his side, did not let up. Hunting gave him a connection with the world of nature that he was so close to in his childhood and allowed him to escape the increasing pressures of his job. Before 1934, when Kirov built a small house in the countryside where he could reside comfortably during his trips, he stayed in peasant huts or in a tent. Kirov loved to cook outside and enjoyed having a small feast with his friends after a day's hunt. As might be expected, there was always plenty of cognac, vodka, and merriment, with Kirov breaking into arias from his favorite operas.[62] These were the rare times when Kirov could forget about Stalin and the Kremlin.

• KIROV CARRIES ON

One of Kirov's favorite hunting companions was Leningrad GPU chief Filipp Medved, who once declared: "We are constructing Communism and we will build it until we attain our goal, whatever the difficulties and however great the number of victims."[63] Medved, a professional Chekist, arrived in Leningrad in 1929 and soon was spending a great deal of time with Kirov. Kirov was very fond of Medved's little son, Misha, and he and Mariia L'vovna doted on him when Medved brought Misha to visit their apartment. Like many Chekists, Medved was a heavy drinker. He also, according to Mikhail Rosliakov, displayed some homosexual tendencies. (At a party to celebrate the police's fifteenth anniversary, which Kirov did not attend, Medved got drunk and created a bit of a scandal by lavishing affection on one of his male guests.)[64]

Medved may not have been a very effective police chief, but Kirov trusted him, and that was important. The job of the Leningrad GPU, after all, was not just to protect party officials and hunt down spies. Like other regional OGPU branches, the Leningrad office sent secret reports to Moscow on what the local party bosses were up to. It was natural that Kirov would want a local secret police chief who was on his side. But this was not what Moscow wanted. Indeed, from Moscow's point of view, Medved was too close to Kirov to do an effective job of reporting. Medved's brother-in-law, D. B. Sorokin, recalled that in 1933 or 1934, while Kirov was out of town, either the police or the party leadership in Moscow actually sent a replacement for Medved to Leningrad—one E. G. Evdokimov. Evdokimov, who had a ruthless reputation in the secret police, had risen in its ranks during the 1920s to become police chief in the North Caucasus. He got to know Stalin well, spending time with him when Stalin vacationed in the South. According to Sorokin, when Kirov returned to Leningrad he called Stalin and insisted that Evdokimov be recalled.[65]

In fact, Moscow secret police headquarters was already "covered" in Leningrad, having managed to send one of its officers, Ivan Zaporozhets, to serve as a first deputy to Medved in April 1932. Described as "a joker and a wit, the life of the party at picnics and outings, and a connoisseur of wine and women," Zaporozhets had been a trusted aide to Genrikh Iagoda.[66] He would later become a key figure in the controversy surrounding the Kirov murder. According to Rosliakov, Zaporozhets quickly insinuated himself into a prominent role in Leningrad politics, overstepping the hapless Medved:

> He always attended the meetings of the *obkom* bureau, although he was
> not a member, and Medved himself was there. Some of us were surprised
> at this duplication of roles, but it did not bother Zaporozhets. During
> discussions, he took the floor to express his own views, despite the pres-
> ence of Medved. . . . We noticed that Zaporozhets actively established
> himself in the apparatus, as if pushing Medved aside. Medved allowed
> the reins of administration to be taken from his hands.[67]

Kirov later told Rosliakov that the Central Committee was pressuring him to have Zaporozhets replace Medved.[68]

While he was in the city Kirov was always surrounded by police guards and thus had no privacy, so it is understandable that he broke away as often as circumstances allowed. Occasionally the outings to the countryside included women, although apparently not Mariia L'vovna. One of several photographs taken of Kirov and his comrades shows a group of six, with Kirov lying relaxed, smiling, and shoeless on a hillside next to a pretty young woman, who could not be identified.[69]

Was Kirov a womanizer? He probably would have had little trouble attracting women. Although he was short, stocky, and slightly pock-marked, he still had his youthful, almost boyish good looks and energy. He was also the most powerful man in Leningrad. Rumors abounded about Kirov's attraction to the young ballerinas at the Mariinskii Theater (named the Kirov Theater in his honor after 1934) in Leningrad, and at the time of his death there were also stories about an affair between Kirov and Milda Draule, the wife of his assassin, Nikolaev.[70]

By all accounts, Kirov continued to be devoted to Mariia L'vovna, writing to her almost daily when they were separated. But they were separated much of the time. Mariia L'vovna suffered from ill health, and in the 1930s was often at sanatoriums and rest homes. By 1934, stricken by an unnamed affliction that caused headaches, difficulties with speech, and lapses of memory, she could no longer act as Kirov's personal sec-retary.[71]

With no concrete evidence, we can only speculate about whether Kirov had extramarital affairs while in Leningrad. But it is entirely possi-ble, given that he probably had an intimate relationship with Nadezhda Serebrennikova in the years of the revolution and civil war. By this time Nadezhda Serebrennikova seems to have disappeared from Kirov's life, which was now so very different from his days as a revolutionary and a ris-ing Bolshevik activist. Kirov had also lost touch with his two sisters. They did not correspond at all from 1911 until December 1932, when Kirov received a letter from his younger sister, Elizaveta, who was by then mar-ried and had children. The letter began thus: "Greetings dear brother Serezhka. I have been intending to write you for a hundred years, but I held back from doing so because I wasn't sure whether my letters would interest you and whether you would be interested in our life."[72] Elizaveta went on to tell Kirov about herself and her children, passing on greetings from their older sister, Anna.

Apparently Kirov never responded to Elizaveta's letter. Just days before he was killed, another letter from her, dated 18 November 1934, arrived at Kirov's apartment. Kirov never opened it:

Warm greetings from your two sisters Aniuta and Liza and from your nephew and niece Kostia and Emma: The last letter I received from you was in 1911 from Vladikavkaz, and then we all became confused. We thought that the government finished you off and you were no longer alive. Last summer, knowing your address, I had a strong impulse to travel to Leningrad, but business matters prevented me. . . . If I live until this summer, that is until 1935, I will come, together with Aniuta.

You speak, argue furiously to kolkhozniki [collective farm peasants] at meetings about our achievements and our better lives in the future. In our little corner, when you come home, it is vexing how godforsaken, at times wild, it is. Last year we saw an automobile in our village for the first time. . . . My son has finished technical school, has been working for a year and has never had the chance to see a train.

[signed] Elizaveta Mironovna Verkhotina[73]

Had Kirov read Elizaveta's letter, he would have understood the implicit reproach about the discrepancy between his lofty words and the grim reality. Here he was a leading party official who spoke publicly about the great successes of his government, while life was still miserable for people like his sisters, who lived in the countryside. And he had never bothered to contact them, not even to let them know that he was still alive. Kirov had clearly chosen to put his past behind him and to cut all ties with his family. Perhaps it would have been too difficult to reconcile his way of life now with the ideals and emotions he had shared with his sisters in his youth. Perhaps the letters from Elizaveta were a painful reminder of his past and how he had betrayed it.

In fact, Kirov blocked from his mind many details of his earlier life. According to one of his biographers: "It was as if everything that related to his past had been covered by a fog, although Kirov's memory for faces, books, music, facts, figures and dates was tremendous."[74] Kirov's former revolutionary comrade Mikhail Popov, who visited him in Leningrad, observed that he had completely forgotten everything that they did during his years in Tomsk. Significantly, when Kirov wrote a brief autobiography for publication by the party back in 1926, he made several mistakes. He wrote that his last arrest by tsarist police had been in 1915, when in fact it occurred in 1911, and in several questionnaires he gave his year of birth as 1888 instead of 1886, apparently forgetting that his comrades in Tomsk had changed his date of birth on his passport in order to make his sentence less severe.[75] These were curious lapses in a man with such a good memory, so it is possible that Kirov was actually trying to hide something that he thought his enemies might use against him.

▪ ECONOMIC BATTLES

Kirov had little time to think about the past anyway, because his job as Leningrad party leader during Stalin's "revolution from above" continued to be all-consuming, even after the successful completion of the First Five-Year Plan. The pressure for Leningrad to produce and meet daunting economic goals did not let up, while bread and basic foodstuffs were still scarce, as were supplies of fuel for the factories. In fact, the standard of living in the Soviet Union had been declining rapidly since 1928: in 1932–33 workers' real wages were less than half their 1928 level. According to secret party reports, members of the working-class population in Leningrad were hungry and resentful, voicing among themselves their sense of betrayal by the regime. The official rhetoric about the good life marked a sharp contrast with their deteriorating economic situation and their grim mood.[76]

As city and regional party chief,* Kirov was directly responsible for their plight. And he knew what it was like to be hungry. Yet he was not in a position to oppose the goals of Stalin's industrialization program. So he went along with the cynical propaganda campaign that portrayed Soviet leaders as benefactors of the people. By 1933, Kirov was referred to in the local press as the "beloved" (*liubimyi*) Kirov, at the same time that the term was first applied to Stalin. This reflected the Soviet practice of creating mini-cults of regional party leaders below the cult of Stalin, which had become full-blown by this time. The aim of these carefully staged propaganda efforts was to defuse discontent by arousing feelings of veneration and admiration toward the political leadership.[77] It is difficult to say how successful this strategy was, but clearly the more the economic situation declined, the fewer people would consider Kirov "beloved."

Nonetheless, Kirov did his best to cope, struggling with Moscow over economic issues. The early 1930s were a period of continuous conflict over the allocation of resources and the disbursement of state funds. Kirov

---

* The city of Leningrad became a separate administration unit in late 1931.

attended Politburo meetings only infrequently (because of the long distance between Leningrad and Moscow). But the protocols for Politburo meetings in 1932–33 show that requests from Leningrad for more supplies from the center and for reductions in procurement plans dominated the agenda. Sometimes the requests were granted and sometimes not. Thus, Leningrad was allowed 5,000 additional tons of bread (over the amount set in the plan) during the third and fourth quarters of 1933. But on the same day that this request was granted Stalin refused Kirov's application to build a department store in the city for selling high-quality goods.[78]

In defending the interests of Leningrad, Kirov ran up against opposition from Politburo member and Moscow party chief Lazar Kaganovich, who competed against Kirov in the battle for resources. More than once, Kirov complained to Molotov and Stalin about Kaganovich's heavy-handed methods. Valerian Kuibyshev, on the other hand, who was head of Gosplan (the state planning commission), was an advocate of the Leningrad leadership. Rosliakov recalls one occasion in the early 1930s when he and Ivan Kodatskii attended a meeting in Moscow to discuss their request to raise Leningrad's budget. Kirov had been unable to attend, but they had counted on Kuibyshev's support. Unexpectedly, Kuibyshev did not show up at the meeting, so they faced Kaganovich alone. They made a quick call to Kirov, who then contacted Kuibyshev. When the latter arrived, they were able to get their budget request approved.[79]

On another occasion a conflict arose with Molotov. The Leningrad government had received from Moscow several extra tons of food products, which they sold for a profit. They then diverted the extra money to a fund for developing pig farms. Although their actions were technically illegal, such diversions of funds were a common practice, without which the otherwise inflexible economic system could not function. Nonetheless, when Molotov found out about the transaction, he decided to crack down. In early 1934 he sent a telegram to Ivan Kodatskii demanding that the Leningrad Executive Committee reverse the decision to divert the funds and punish those responsible for it. Kodatskii had the decision reversed, but he prevaricated on punishing those involved, despite another angry telegram from Molotov. Presumably, Kodatskii would not have risked such insubordination without consulting Kirov. Finally, at Molotov's insistence, Kodatskii was called before the Council of People's Commissars in Moscow to account for his behavior, but in the end there were no punishments.[80]

In another case, Kirov reportedly used reserve supplies designated for the Leningrad Military District without permission from Moscow. When Commissar of Defense Kliment Voroshilov expressed displeasure about this at a Politburo meeting, Kirov responded that he had been obliged to resort to these reserves because of extreme shortages and that the supplies would be returned to the warehouse as soon as new deliveries arrived. Voroshilov is said to have retorted that Kirov "was looking for cheap popularity among the workers."[81]

Kirov was responsible for overseeing military production in the Leningrad district and was a member of the Leningrad Military Council. He was also a friend of Mikhail Tukhachevskii, commander of the Leningrad Military District from 1928 to 1931 and a civil war hero. During that war, Tukhachevskii had commanded the Eleventh Army for a time and had worked closely with Kirov. This was another dangerous friendship for Kirov. Despite his exceptional talents as a strategist, Tukhachevskii, a former tsarist army officer who joined the Bolsheviks in 1918, had never gotten on well with the General Secretary. In fact, in the autumn of 1930, while he was serving in Leningrad and seeing Kirov on a daily basis, Tukhachevskii was almost arrested as a participant in an alleged military plot to kill Stalin and seize power. After a cursory examination of the charges against Tukhachevskii, which Stalin must have known had been fabricated by the OGPU, Stalin decided to drop the matter and wrote to Molotov: "As for the T-chevskii affair, he turns out to be 100 percent clean. That's very good."[82] Tukhachevskii later returned to Moscow and played a leading role in developing new weapons for the Red Army, only to be arrested in 1937 and executed on charges of treason, as part of Stalin's sweeping purge of the Soviet military command.

Kirov did his best to meet the needs of the Soviet military in Leningrad, where much of the defense construction was centered. But it presented him with a constant challenge. Requests such as this from Tukhachevskii were typical: "Dear Sergei Mironovich, I did not manage to reach you by telephone . . . and I know that you asked Uborevich to inform you of the state of the fulfillment of our orders for aircraft at the Krasnyi Vyborjet factories. The order for aluminum is very late and we have an urgent need for your strongest support in this matter."[83]

Kirov was also under continuous pressure to develop new sources of raw materials within the Leningrad district, but was not successful. Several local scientists had told him that there were rich deposits of iron ore on the Kola Peninsula, north of the city. After considerable publicity in the press and optimistic projections of vast supplies of iron ore, the excavations began in early 1933. To the great disappointment of Kirov, the deposits proved practically worthless.[84]

By the autumn of 1933 Kirov was so shaken by the failure of this iron-ore venture that he fell ill. Other problems may have contributed to his stress. Aside from those who opposed him openly in Moscow over financial and budgetary issues, he had secret political enemies who were plotting against him. In the summer of 1933, a report reached Kirov about a group of Leningraders who were planning to have him removed from his post. At the center of the group was a person named Rekstyn, who had close ties with some of Kirov's old enemies in Moscow, such as Nikolai Komarov. Rekstyn was quoted as saying: "We will soon cut the throat of this leader Kirov. We will arrest him. We will destroy him because we have the majority of the masses on our side."[85]

Of course, denunciations, threats, and backstabbing were by now an integral feature of the Stalinist political system. All Soviet political leaders, including of course Stalin, had enemies. As for Kirov's economic troubles, he was not alone among the regional officials who had to fight battles with Moscow. Nonetheless, Kirov felt beleaguered, and this affected his health. He began suffering from severe insomnia and then nervous spasms and heart problems. He was also uncharacteristically short-tempered and more intolerant of others' mistakes than usual—all symptoms of nervous strain. In late November 1933, after Kirov returned from a trip to Moscow, during which he had a four-hour visit with Stalin in his office, his nerves were shattered.[86]

Kirov was seen by Professor G. F. Lang on 20–22 November. In his report, which was duly sent to the Kremlin, Professor Lang noted that Kirov complained of "irregular heartbeat, occurring for the last month, severe irritability, and very poor sleep." Tests, including an electrocardiogram, revealed no abnormalities, except for an enlarged aorta, which indicated sclerosis. Noting that Kirov's nervous system showed signs of strain, doctors recommended a month of complete rest.[87]

Kirov agreed to go to a rest home at Tolmachevo, a village outside Leningrad, on the condition that he would not have further examinations by doctors. Mariia L'vovna accompanied him on 23 November and they stayed until the end of the year. Viktor Val'dman, a Leningrad physician, related how he was deployed to Tolmachevo to observe Kirov's health discreetly. By the end of the month Kirov was much improved, but he again suffered a bout of ill health in early 1934, following the Seventeenth Party Congress in Moscow.[88]

There can be no doubt that Stalin was fully apprised of Kirov's illnesses, since all the medical reports reached him. Indeed, Stalin sometimes deemed it his prerogative to tell his subordinates what to do about their health problems.[89] In the early 1930s, for example, Sergo Ordzhonikidze began to suffer from circulatory and heart complaints—pains in the chest, weak pulse, occasional dizziness. The doctors' reports recommended rest, and on more than one occasion the Politburo, and Stalin personally, ordered Sergo to take time off.[90] In exhibiting such solicitous concern, Stalin was not necessarily motivated by altruism. Stalin's knowledge of intimate details about his subordinates' health reinforced his power over them. Moreover, any illness among them carried with it the possibility of incapacitation and a consequent realignment of the forces that Stalin was manipulating to assure his unchallenged authority. There can be no doubt that Kirov's health problems made him more vulnerable politically.

Stalin's revolution had taken its toll on Kirov. In the past when Kirov set himself goals, he had always shown tremendous resilience in the face of obstacles, but his goals had changed, as he himself had. Twenty years earlier, as Russia was about to enter a world war, Kirov had been an idealistic radical, healthy enough to scale a mountain peak and full of dreams for the political future of his country. Now, with his physical condition declining, he had become the very bureaucrat whom he had criticized so indignantly in his writings for *Terek*. Words like "democracy" and "freedom" had disappeared from his vocabulary, replaced by the rhetoric of party slogans and five-year plans.

Although Kirov recovered and was back on the job by the end of 1933, the tensions that doubtless contributed to his health problems did not abate. Indeed, from the very beginning of 1934, the last year of his life, Kirov found himself at the center of controversies and intrigues that would close in on him like the dark clouds that enshrouded Leningrad before a summer storm.

7

1934: Kirov's End

· · · · · · · · · · · · ·

I repeat to Thee, this very morrow Thou shalt see that obedient herd, which at a mere sign from me, will rush to heap up hot coals against that stake at which I shall burn Thee for having come to hinder us. For, if ever there was one who deserved our fire, it is Thou. Tomorrow I shall burn Thee.

—*The Grand Inquisitor in Dostoevsky's* The Brothers Karamazov

· · · · · · · · · · · · ·

It might be easier to understand the events of the year 1934 if we had a clear picture of where Kirov stood in relation to the Stalinist establishment. But Kirov's position at the beginning of this year, looked at from the outside, seemed highly ambiguous. On the one hand, Kirov's hesitations about endorsing Stalin's general line and condemning the Bukharin group, his clashes with the Politburo, and his covert slurs against Stalin suggest that he was not a "team player," that he could not be classified as a loyal Stalinist. On the other hand, his willing participation in the building of the Baltic–White Sea Canal, his acceptance of the OGPU as a pillar of the state, and his slavish public praise of Stalin make it difficult to portray him as a dissident.

Kirov was not the only Bolshevik leader to vacillate in his politics. Sergo Ordzhonikidze also gave conflicting signals. Indeed, his fluctuations between aggressive advocacy of Stalinist principles and hesitation about hard-line methods led one historian to ask: "Which of the two Ordzhonikidzes is the real one?"[1]

The apparent ambivalence of both men was a reflection of the "Asiatic politics" of the Stalinist system. Nothing was what it seemed. By 1934 the peasantry had been vanquished and was under state control, and the worst extremes of the push to industrialize were over. But the pressures inherent in political life continued to mount. Controversy over policy had become a struggle for power and position. Few dared to speak frankly, except to trusted friends. Alone together, Sergo and Kirov could share their thoughts, which doubtless included concerns about Stalin's dictatorial methods. But if Sergo and Kirov were reluctant actors in the Stalinist drama that unfolded in the 1930s, they could not get off the stage. By 1934 support for Stalin's line had become a condition for not only political but also physical survival. Whatever private reservations they had about Stalin, it was either fear or loyalty to the Bolshevik cause—or some complex combination of the two—that kept Kirov and Sergo from expressing them openly.

Anastas Mikoyan, who became a full member of the Politburo after Kirov's death and remained there throughout the Khrushchev era, offered in his memoirs some insight into the thinking of Stalin's subordinates at the time:

> Speaking about myself, I can say that I knew two Stalins. The first, whom I valued a great deal and respected as an old comrade, for the first ten years, and then a completely different person in the later period. . . . I was able to realize the full measure of Stalin's dictatorial tendencies and actions only when it was already too late to struggle against him. Ordzhonikidze and Kirov, with whom I was very close and whose attitudes I understood, ended up in the same position [as I did] of being deceived by the "first" appearance of Stalin.[2]

Was it really too late to struggle? Mikoyan does not tell us exactly when it was that he, Ordzhonikidze, and Kirov came to realize the existence of the "second" Stalin, but by 1934 others were drawing attention to it. As the events of the Seventeenth Party Congress showed, several leading party figures were so concerned about Stalin's negative characteristics that they wanted to remove him.

▪ THE CONGRESS OF VICTORS

Pravda dubbed the Seventeenth Party Congress the "Congress of Victors" when the paper announced its opening at the end of January 1934. With the crisis in the countryside having died down and industrialization in full swing, the future of socialism seemed more certain than ever before. "Socialism has won in our country," declared *Pravda* triumphantly. Ironically, however, few of the 1,966 delegates present would enjoy the fruits of that victory: 1,108 of them would eventually be arrested by the secret police.[3] Behind the atmosphere of harmony and self-congratulation another deep crisis was brewing, and Kirov was at the center of it.

A central theme of the congress was the cult of Stalin's leadership. Speaker after speaker, including vanquished enemies like Bukharin and Zinoviev, exalted the great *vozhd* (leader) to enthusiastic applause from the audience when they discussed Stalin's address to the congress, delivered on 26 January, the opening day. Kirov was the last to speak on Stalin's report—an honor, according to Soviet protocol, where the best was the last. Although Kirov had come to the congress with the flu and was still not feeling well, he delivered a rousing address on 31 January.[4] His appearance on the rostrum was greeted with a standing ovation, begun by the Leningrad delegation and taken up by the entire congress. Mikhail Rosliakov, a member of that delegation, recalls that Kirov, as usual, did not read his remarks, but spoke extemporaneously, as if sharing his immediate thoughts with the audience: "His speech reflected deep confidence in the correctness of the Leninist line; it was full of colorful expressions, passion, sincere joy over the triumph of Leninist ideas."[5]

Kirov had extravagant praise for Stalin: Stalin was "the best helmsman of our great socialist structure," whose report to the congress should be studied "down to the last comma." "Comrade Stalin," said Kirov, "opened up before us the gigantic perspectives of work for future years, a new page of our great program." Taking the cult of Stalin to its furthest degree, Kirov then proposed that, instead of following tradition and preparing a resolution on Stalin's report that would be put to a vote, the congress should "accept in full, as party law, all suggestions and conclusions in Stalin's report."

When Kirov finished his speech—"we are fulfilling that vow and will continue fulfilling it, because our great strategist of liberation of the proletariat of our country and of the whole world, Comrade Stalin, gave us that vow"—the reaction was overwhelming. According to the congress report, there was "prolonged, stormy applause, a thunderous ovation from the whole hall, everyone standing." As historian Robert Tucker observed: "The words referred to Stalin, but the huge standing ovation at the end was meant for Kirov himself and everyone there knew it."[6]

When Stalin took the floor afterward it was anticlimactic. Stalin must have been painfully aware of how poorly he compared with Kirov as a speaker. As one observer noted, his Georgian accent was "obtrusive" and his "low monotone was tiresome to the ear."[7] In other words, he completely lacked the kind of inspiration that Kirov conveyed. To the surprise of his audience, Stalin announced that, in view of the complete unanimity that the congress had shown on policy matters, he would abstain from a final address. Kirov, it seems, had elevated Stalin to unprecedented heights, but in doing so he had stolen the show.

In fact, the extremes that the Stalin cult reached at the congress gave rise to a backlash. Many Old Bolsheviks had become disenchanted with Stalin and took a dim view of all the panegyrics. According to the official *History of the Communist Party of the Soviet Union,* published in a second edition in 1963 (during the Khrushchev period): "Many congress delegates, especially those who were familiar with the testament of V. I. Lenin, thought that the time had come to move Stalin from the post of General Secretary to other work."[8] At some point during the congress they reportedly met privately—possibly at Ordzhonikidze's apartment—to discuss removing Stalin.

The sources conflict on the exact details of what happened, but apparently the group, which included Kirov's old Georgian comrade Mamia Orakhelashvili, suggested to Kirov that he take over Stalin's post. Some sources say that Stalin found out what had happened and summoned Kirov to see him.[9] Others, including Mikoyan, Khrushchev, and several congress delegates, say that Kirov opposed the idea of his replacing Stalin and promised instead to talk to Stalin and tell him what the delegates were dissatisfied about. Stalin was angry, these sources say, especially resenting the idea of Kirov taking it upon himself to be an emissary. The whole affair unnerved Kirov and left him feeling threatened.[10]

Although he was a member of the presidium of the congress, Kirov chose to disregard protocol and sit with his delegation during the sessions rather than with the presidium members. According to Filipp Medved's brother-in-law, D. B. Sorokin, Stalin became suspicious of the 132-person Leningrad delegation during the congress and wondered what they were talking about as they sat together with Kirov. At one point Stalin called Medved, who was a delegate, to see him and asked how things were going with the Leningrad delegation. Medved told him that they were all worried about Kirov's health and hoped he would take measures to get better. Medved later confided in Sorokin that he sensed Stalin's annoyance that the Leningrad delegates held Kirov in such high esteem.[11]

The real drama of the congress came with the election of the new

Central Committee. To this day, historians are still arguing about what actually happened, but they acknowledge that the circumstances were highly unusual. According to established party procedure, all 1,225 delegates eligible to vote were to receive ballots with the names of proposed candidates to the Central Committee—seventy-one for full membership and sixty-seven for provisional membership. The delegates were to strike out the names of those they opposed, leaving the names they approved of intact. They were then to deposit their ballots in one of the designated thirteen boxes. Five members of the voting commission were assigned to each box to calculate the results. Candidates needed to get a majority of affirmative votes in order to be on the Central Committee.[12]

According to Sorokin, there was an unusual innovation in the voting procedure at this congress. Although the ballots did not have the delegates' names written on them, regional delegations were assigned to specific boxes, so that it was possible, in theory at least, to determine the voting patterns of the different groups, thus undermining the principle of secrecy. The head of the voting commission complained about this change in procedure to Stalin, but to no avail. Stalin reportedly replied that it was not his idea, but that it was more efficient to do it this way.[13]

When the final tally was completed, at least 166 ballots were missing. Did the holders of these ballots simply decide not to vote (a highly unlikely possibility, given the rigorous discipline among party members), or did someone destroy the ballots after they were retrieved from the boxes? When the results of the voting were announced to the congress on 10 February, Stalin received 1,056 votes (out of 1,059) in his favor, while Kirov received 1,055 favorable votes. But three members of the voting commission (of the sixty-three members the only ones who were not shot in the purges) recalled years later that Stalin actually received a substantial number of negative votes—many more than Kirov. One member, V. M. Verkhovykh, said that Stalin received well over a hundred negative votes. Another recalled that Stalin received fewer votes in his favor than any other candidate. And the third told Mikoyan that there were at least twenty-seven ballots with votes against Stalin in just the one box that was in his charge.[14]

Olga Shatunovskaia, a party official who in 1960 served on a special commission to investigate the Kirov murder, presented an even more remarkable version of what happened. She claimed that, when she and her colleagues examined the evidence and looked at the ballots, they found

289 ballots missing. According to Shatunovskaia, voting commission member Verkhovykh told them that 292 delegates had actually voted against Stalin, but only three of the ballots with negative votes could be found. Verkhovykh also told Shatunovskaia that Stalin himself had ordered the head of the voting commission to destroy the 289 ballots and falsify the results, making it appear that only 166 ballots were missing and that Stalin received only three negative votes.[15]

Although memories of this event became blurred as the years went on, it seems clear that, whatever the exact numbers, a significant portion of the ballots were destroyed, and it is likely that these ballots registered negative votes against Stalin. Of course, Stalin would still have had the necessary majority of positive votes to be reelected to the Central Committee even if no ballots were destroyed. But if the true results had been revealed to the congress, Stalin's authority would have been seriously undermined.[16]

In the aftermath of the congress, when the new Central Committee met to elect a Secretariat and Politburo, Stalin sustained another blow. He had proposed, unexpectedly, that Kirov become a secretary of the Central Committee, which would entail his moving to Moscow. But Kirov did not like the idea. In Moscow, he would lose much of his independence and would be under Stalin's thumb, as well as under the watchful eyes of Molotov and Kaganovich. It was one thing to get telephone calls from Stalin in the middle of the night, another to be at his beck and call on a daily basis.[17]

Kirov resisted the transfer, citing his health problems and his lack of experience at the center of the party leadership. He requested that he be allowed to remain in Leningrad at least for another two years, so that he could see the second Five-Year-Plan through to completion there. When Sergo Ordzhonikidze and Kuibyshev sided with Kirov, Stalin grew angry and left the meeting in a huff. At the suggestion of his colleagues, Kirov went to talk to Stalin. They reached a compromise, whereby Kirov would in fact become a Central Committee secretary, but would remain in Leningrad for the time being. So that the Secretariat would have another Moscow-based member, Andrei Zhdanov would be transferred from Gorky to serve in that body.[18]

• AT STALIN'S CALL

The stormy Central Committee meeting that followed the Seventeenth Congress and the unpleasant confrontation with Stalin took its toll

Leningrad, 1932

Kirov and Stalin aboard the ship *Anokhin*
on the Baltic–White Sea Canal, July 1933

Members of Politburo (Kirov fourth from left)
discuss Second Five-Year Plan, Moscow, 1933

Kirov speaking at the Seventeenth Party Congress, 31 January 1934

Stalin, Kirov, and Svetlana Allilueva, Sochi, August 1934

Smolnyi building, 1998

Leonid Nikolaev, n.d.

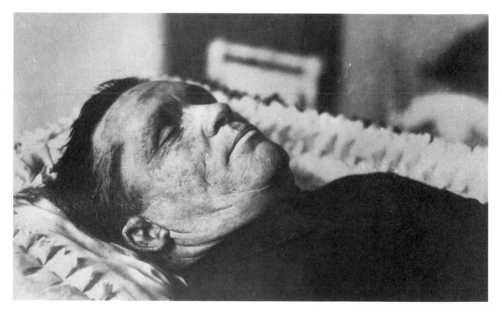

Kirov lying in state, Leningrad, December 1934

Stalin standing by Kirov's coffin, Leningrad, 2 December 1934

Stalin and Kaganovich in honor guard by Kirov's coffin,
Moscow, 5 December 1934

Soviet leaders (from left to right: Molotov, Voroshilov, Stalin, and Kalinin)
carrying urn containing Kirov's ashes, Moscow, 6 December 1934

Mariia L'vovna Kirova, 1935

Cartoon of Stalin by Lute Pease, Swann Collection

on Kirov. Perhaps he was already regretting his refusal to accept the mandate of his colleagues and oppose Stalin. Although he had refused with good reason, having witnessed many times what happened to other members of the leadership when they tried to confront Stalin, he also may have realized that he and his like-minded party colleagues had lost their last chance to oppose Stalin's ruthless course. Kirov returned to Leningrad rattled and was so sick with the flu that he could not deliver his customary report on the congress to the Leningrad party.[19] On 17 February 1934, Dr. Val'dman and Professor Lang examined Kirov and reported to Moscow (in a document marked "top secret") that he had congestion in the right lung and an elevated temperature. He had been sick with an infection for several days, but the doctors thought he was improving and that his heart seemed fine. Six days later Val'dman examined Kirov again: "He slept very badly. His mood is somewhat depressed. He is bothered by irregularities in his heartbeat (fibrillations)." By the next day Kirov was much improved. He had slept well and the heartbeat was more regular. Nonetheless, in view of the heart problem and Kirov's lung infection, the doctors recommended ten days' rest.[20]

It was not until 27 February that Kirov finally spoke to his party organization. Again, there are two versions of what he said—one, published in the press, and the original stenogram, in the Kirov archive. The published version was a standard account of the decisions of the congress with the requisite praise for Stalin. The original text was different; Kirov mentioned Stalin only a few times, and then only in passing. He spoke about the difficulties of following up on the performance of officials and the problems the Leningrad party had with Moscow when it came to accounting for their work. He also made some rather cryptic comments about what it would be like if the membership of the Central Committee were to change every month. Such a situation, he said, "would only occur with a government that was dying."[21] Whatever Kirov was referring to, the tone was out of keeping with the lofty speeches at the "Congress of Victors."

Stalin, meanwhile, became increasingly demanding of Kirov, calling him more and more frequently on the *vertushka* (the direct line from Moscow) and insisting that he visit Moscow at every opportunity. (In 1933 Kirov made only five visits to Stalin's office; in 1934, he made eighteen.) As part of his new responsibilities as a Central Committee secretary, Kirov oversaw Soviet industry—a job that was impossible to do simultaneously with his functions as Leningrad party chief. Yet Stalin persisted in giving him additional assignments. Perhaps, as Rosliakov suggests, Stalin could not reconcile himself to Kirov's refusal to move to Moscow, and this was Stalin's way of paying him back.[22] More likely is that Stalin wanted to keep Kirov "pinned down" and distracted so that he would not be a threat to Stalin's supremacy.

Judging from a letter that he sent Kirov in March, Sergo Ordzhonikidze was worried that his friend was exhausting himself from overwork. He advised Kirov to take a break:

> Dear Kirov!
> How are you doing? How are your affairs? Here I am sitting and cannot forgive myself for not having managed to get you to take a leave at least for 15 days. Listen, friend, you must rest. Really and truly, nothing is going to happen without you there for 10–15 days. In any case the world will not fall apart, and you would refresh yourself a little—this is essential and must be done.
>
> Our fellow countryman [apparently referring to Stalin] considers you a healthy man, and that is true, but nonetheless you must take a short rest!
>
> You of course won't be dragged out here. Go at least there, do it. I am resting well here, the weather is excellent, real spring. Bauman [a party official] arrived yesterday. Regards to Mariia L'vovna. With a warm handshake, Your Sergo[23]

Kirov may have taken Sergo's advice and gone hunting, but probably not for long. He was under heavy pressure to improve Leningrad's economic performance, which had dropped significantly in recent months, and to step up the process of collectivization. At a Central Committee meeting in late June 1934, Kirov sought to justify the fact that Leningrad had lagged behind in moving its peasants into collective farms: "As you know, comrades, our region was one of the last to embark on collectivization, and the process has been slower than in all the other regions. But it seems to me that there is a positive side to this in our Leningrad region. The process has proceeded and is proceeding more smoothly than in other regions."[24]

Kirov went on to note that Leningrad had not experienced the problem of peasants leaving collective farms in droves, as had happened elsewhere. And he explained the special circumstances in Leningrad that posed obstacles to collectivization. As Kirov discussed, earnestly and seriously, the difficulties of building a party organization in the countryside, Stalin interrupted him more than once with joking asides, seeming to mock him. Kirov ignored his comments, which aroused laughter, and proceeded with what he had to say.[25] This was typical behavior on Stalin's part. It was his way of keeping his subordinates on their toes.

But Kirov, perhaps emboldened by the knowledge that he was widely viewed in the party as an alternative to Stalin, continued to advocate moderation in the countryside and to pursue new initiatives. A few days later, in a report on the plenum to the Leningrad Obkom, Kirov acknowledged that their region was lagging behind significantly in livestock production. He made a point of stressing, however, that delivery plans would be met only if the authorities refrained from enforcement by illegal measures, and he warned about the need for caution in the expulsion of peasants from collective farms as a punitive measure. Such expulsions, Kirov said, were severe reprisals that threatened these peasants with starvation.[26]

Kirov's emphasis on legality was in keeping with a general policy of domestic détente that had been endorsed by Stalin in early 1934. Apparently realizing that harsh policies toward the peasantry would ultimately be counterproductive and undermine support for his leadership, Stalin had lowered delivery quotas for grain and taken other steps to give the peasants some relief. Nonetheless, Kirov was the first party official to speak out for observance of legality at this time, giving the impression that he was leading the way on this issue.

In fact, Leningrad journalist Zavalishin later claimed that by 1934 Kirov had in mind some serious reforms in agriculture and was discussing his ideas freely with his party colleagues in Leningrad. Not only did he want to return dispossessed kulaks who were languishing in labor camps to the countryside, where they could join collective farms; he also favored expanding the private plots that kolkhozniki cultivated and increasing the livestock available for their private husbandry. Another of Kirov's plans was to cut timber and allow kolkhozniki to develop the newly cleared land for their personal use. So far-reaching were the proposals discussed by Kirov and his colleagues that there were rumors in the Leningrad party apparatus of a "tactical retreat" and a "temporary move to the right."[27]

Significantly, Kirov had already taken initiatives in other areas. He was deeply concerned about the danger of war with Germany and Russia's lack of preparedness, especially because his region would be the first logical target of Nazi aggression. This was one reason why he advocated a relaxation in policies not only toward the peasantry but also toward the former Zinovievite left opposition. By 1933, Kirov was making it known that he welcomed former supporters of Zinoviev back into the fold and would encourage them in their efforts to find employment. Zavalishin noted that, whereas Kirov had been aggressively opposed to the Zinovievites in the first years of his tenure as party chief, his approach changed significantly by 1933–34. Kirov was intent on improving Leningrad's economy, and in his view it made no sense to alienate a whole group of well-educated and talented specialists. Thus, observed Zavalishin, "those very young people who had earlier supported the Zinoviev opposition and were engineers or administrators of economic production had every reason to hope for help from Kirov—a talented engineer could count on the fact that Kirov would erase his past party sins."[28] Kirov wanted to enlist all elements of society to raise Russia's economic production so the country would be better prepared to confront Germany. But Stalin, whose hatred of the former opposition continued to fester, cannot have been pleased about this open-minded approach, however practical it was in economic terms.

Already in January 1934, before the Seventeenth Party Congress occurred, Kirov had made remarkably forceful statements against Germany and fascism, statements out of keeping with what Stalin and other Kremlin politicians were saying. Addressing the Leningrad party, Kirov had the clarity of vision to label German fascism "an open, completely unmasked terrorist dictatorship of the most reactionary, chauvinistic, and imperialistic elements of finance capital." He warned of the dangers of the fascist theory of superiority of the Aryan race and its consequent anti-Semitism, asserting that Germany and Japan were the Soviet Union's greatest enemies. Thus, he concluded, "in the face of this growing military danger we must devote the most serious, most intense attention to problems of defense."[29]

As Robert Tucker has observed, Stalin was then still wavering in his policy toward Hitler, waiting for some favorable signs from him: "Between Kirov's aroused antifascist statement and Stalin's diplomatic probe of Berlin there was a political gulf."[30] Again Kirov's views had more in common with those of Bukharin, who denounced fascism in vehement terms at the Seventeenth Congress, and also with the views of Soviet writer Maxim Gorky, another outspoken antifascist.[31] Of course, Stalin soon changed his tactic and supported the idea of an antifascist Popular Front. Nonetheless, it is significant that Kirov was taking the lead in this new policy direction. Bukharin himself later acknowledged this obliquely in an article he wrote for *Izvestiia* shortly after Kirov's murder. Posing the question of who would have gained by Kirov's death, he claimed that it was the "fascist rascals" who wanted to interrupt the new course that the Soviet Union had taken in foreign and domestic policy.[32]

▪ SOCHI AND KAZAKHSTAN

By the end of July 1934, after juggling the two jobs of Leningrad party chief and Central Committee secretary for several months, Kirov was seriously in need of a respite. Unlike his Politburo colleagues, who went to sanatoriums and rest homes in the South, Kirov always preferred going hunting. His plans to do so this time, however, were disrupted by an invitation from Stalin to join him and Central Committee secretary Andrei Zhdanov at his dacha in Sochi. The invitation was not welcome. In Rosliakov's words:

> Such an "organized" vacation did not suit Kirov's free character. Moreover, if even we, the party employees, understood completely that Stalin was conducting a struggle of wills . . . then Kirov knew well both the purpose and the difficulty of such a vacation, but he could not refuse. As with chess, the game had become more intense and, given Stalin's volatile character and his unhealthy vanity, this vacation did not promise any joy.[33]

Kirov set off for Sochi via Moscow at the end of July, without getting a chance to say goodbye to Mariia L'vovna, who was on her way back to Leningrad after a visit to a rest home in the Crimea. She was suffering from numerous ailments—insomnia, headaches, and "hormonal difficulties." In mid-July, Kirov had been uncharacteristically churlish with her in a letter: "Just please don't parade about, living as you are in a TsIK [Central Executive Committee] home," a rather surprising admonition, given

Mariia L'vovna's staid countenance. But Kirov was not in the best of humor.[34]

In a letter from Moscow, marked "secret," Kirov informed his wife (now back in Leningrad) about his impending trip to Sochi:

> Dear Marusa, It so happens that I have to go south. In a few days I will be in Sochi and then soon return. I hope to be back in Leningrad by the tenth of August. I will do everything possible for this because I feel that the heat will force me away. . . . I am not in a happy mood, no better than the one when I left Leningrad. I called you several times, but in vain. If you need the car to go to Sestroretsk or somewhere else, call Iudin [the chauffeur]. I have told him already. On the rest, everything seems to be in order. Many kisses, your Sergei. It may be that I won't be home by the tenth. Regards. Kiss you once more, Sergei[35]

As it turned out, Kirov did not leave Sochi until much later than 10 August, but not because he wanted to stay. On the contrary, his letters to Mariia L'vovna indicate that he was miserable:

> I am writing from Sochi, where I have been for a few days already. It is apparently possible to have a nice vacation here, but then one must arrive much later. Now it's awfully hot. It is quite impossible to walk or play *gorodki* [similar to croquet]. I have sunburned my whole back, which cannot be touched. . . . I feel bad, and the heat prevents me from sleeping. I beg you, if everything is okay, to telegraph: "Sochi. Kirov," and at least these two words: "everything okay."[36]

On 16 August, after sending his wife another gloomy letter, Kirov wrote her: "Finally I received a short telegram from you. It was so short that I am not sure everything is okay with you. I am bored here, will try to leave on the 20th . . . My main concern is how you are, and again not a word about it. It seems that nowhere and at no time can I have a quiet vacation. To hell with it."[37]

Kirov was also in regular communication with his deputy, Second Secretary Mikhail Chudov, who did his best to set Kirov's mind at rest about the situation in Leningrad, despite the usual difficulties with meeting the production targets. In mid-August, Chudov wrote: "Work is going normally. . . . Rest, don't worry, we will do everything we can."[38] Kirov could not be reassured and expressed his impatience to Chudov: "I received your telegrams. Unfortunately they are rare and I get no information. You telegraph nothing about general business. . . . However strange, for most of the day we are busy. This is not what I expected for recreation. Well, to the devil with it. Anyhow, I will just take to my heels as soon as possible."[39]

It is significant that there is no mention of Stalin in any of Kirov's letters from Sochi, although Kirov was spending all of his time with him. Kirov and Zhdanov were ostensibly helping Stalin to review prospectuses for new history textbooks and to draft commentaries. Stalin had by this time decided to make his imprint on the way history was being written in the Soviet Union, with the underlying purpose of legitimizing his regime. Thus, for example, when one of these new history books was finally published in 1937, the tyrannical Russian tsar Ivan the Terrible was presented as a hero.[40]

It is not clear how much Kirov actually contributed to the commentaries. One of Kirov's Soviet biographers has him taken aback by having to participate in the history project, saying to Stalin: "Iosif Vissarionovich, what kind of a historian am I?" To which Stalin is said to have replied: "Never mind, sit down and listen."[41] The commentaries were signed on 8 August by Stalin, Zhdanov, and Kirov before being sent to the Politburo for approval, but it may well be that they expressed only Stalin's views and that he used the history project as a pretext to get Kirov to join him in Sochi. Whatever the case, Kirov stayed in Sochi until 20 August—almost two weeks after the textbook review had been completed.[42] Despite the fact that Kirov found the heat—and doubtless the atmosphere in general—oppressive and was desperate to leave, Stalin wanted him there, and Kirov went along with his master's wishes.

Kirov, Stalin, and Zhdanov arrived in Moscow from Sochi on 23 or 24 August, in time to attend a Politburo meeting on the 25th. A few days later Kirov returned to Leningrad. But not for long. On 3 September the Politburo dispatched him to Kazakhstan, where he remained until the end of the month. The purpose of his trip was to help party and state officials in Kazakhstan with the fall harvest campaign. All over the Soviet Union grain collection for August had dropped significantly in comparison with the previous year, threatening the country's food supply and jeopardizing the party's plan to end bread rationing in early 1935. As part of a series of measures designed to improve grain collection, Stalin and Molotov decided to send party leaders to different regions in order to administer the fall harvest on the spot. Thus Kaganovich went to Ukraine, Voroshilov to Belorussia, and Molotov himself to western Siberia.[43]

Kirov was familiar with the situation in Kazakhstan because his old friend Levon Mirzoian was now party first secretary there and had been writing Kirov regularly to report on his travails. (Stalin, as we know, had it in for Mirzoian.) Kazakhstan's problems with the fall harvest were acute and, in typical fashion, Kirov took his mission to heart. In advance of his arrival he telegraphed Mirzoian in the capital, Alma-Ata: "I heard by chance that a reception has been planned at the train station in Alma-Ata. If this is so, I categorically protest. I insist that there be no receptions, speeches, or anything. I ask you to remember the purpose of my trip."[44]

Kirov immediately plunged into his work, traveling to villages and collective farms, conducting party meetings, and making decisions on how best to implement the harvest. He requested (and received) Moscow's approval for several personnel changes among party officials in Kazakhstan whose performances were especially poor, and he also tried to curb some of the excesses of the police and judicial organs. As part of a reorganization of the Soviet police apparatus in July 1934, the OGPU had been renamed the NKVD (People's Commissariat of Internal Affairs) and had been given sweeping new powers, which its employees tended to abuse. Kirov telegraphed NKVD chief Genrikh Iagoda and complained that several NKVD staffers in Kazakhstan were violating the law by making arbitrary arrests on trumped-up charges. He also complained to Deputy USSR Prosecutor Andrei Vyshinskii about illegalities on the part of local prosecutors. Neither Iagoda nor Vyshinskii seems to have followed through with promises to address Kirov's complaints.[45]

While in Kazakhstan, Kirov tried to keep up with the situation in Leningrad, corresponding almost daily with Chudov about the numerous problems that were plaguing Leningrad. Preoccupied with his work, Kirov gave no indication that he was unhappy or anxious to leave, as he had been the previous month in Sochi. He was, however, worried about Mariia L'vovna, whose health took a sudden turn for the worse after his departure from Leningrad. On 11 September, Chudov informed Kirov: "Mariia L'vovna is resting at Tolmachevo. I spoke with Sheboldaev [a party secretary] about sending her sister here to be at our disposal. In a few days she will be in Leningrad and will go to stay with Mariia L'vovna."[46] (Chudov was referring to Mariia L'vovna's sister Rakhil' Markus, a physician, who was very close to both the Kirovs.) Mariia L'vovna was under the care of the same doctors who attended to Kirov. It is not clear from their reports exactly what was wrong with her, aside from her "female problems," but they ordered a regime of complete rest, along with medications and a restricted diet. In mid-October, they reported that she had achieved a "welcome loss of weight—one and a half kilos."[47]

In addition to the decline in his wife's health, another disturbing event occurred in Kirov's absence from Leningrad. His office was moved from the main corridor on the third floor of the Smolnyi to the end of the long left-hand corridor, close to glass doors leading to a side stairway. It is not clear who made the decision or why, but it cannot have pleased Kirov. Kirov was a creature of habit; he had that Leninist trait that Krupskaia had called "conservatism with possessions." Thus, for example, he wore an old, faded mackintosh, familiar to all of Leningrad, which he would never consider replacing. There was also his threadbare black overcoat and his visored cap, in the style of caps worn in the distant provinces.[48] He dressed this way, despite the fact that he was the most powerful man in Leningrad, because this was what he was used to.

That Kirov did not like changes in his way of life was clear from his objection to a plan to build a new home for him and his wife on Krestovskii Island. At first he forbade Mariia L'vovna even to visit the proposed site. He eventually yielded, and construction was begun in the autumn of 1934, but Kirov did not look forward to the planned move.[49] There was actually a compelling reason for the Kirovs to move to a new home. Their apartment house had no elevator, and the entrance was directly onto the street. Kirov had received more than one anonymous threat against his life, and while he was in Kazakhstan someone had reportedly attempted to kill him. Mariia L'vovna had become so worried about her husband's safety that every night she would watch nervously out the fourth-floor window until Kirov's car drove up and he was inside. Because of these threats, an additional four NKVD employees were added to Kirov's personal bodyguard during 1934, making a total of about nine.[50] Kirov was not happy about this. He hated having guards around him and on some occasions even would escape from them and go off alone (a strict violation of party regulations).

Although he went along with building a home in a more secluded place and adding more guards, Kirov refused to make other changes that might have improved his physical protection. He would not let Medved go, even though, in Rosliakov's words, "he [Medved] had gradually lost his composure and his Chekist vigilance." Nor would Kirov dismiss his fifty-year-old bodyguard, M. D. Borisov, "who wore civilian clothes and was always tired."[51] Kirov apparently felt that there were few people he could trust, so he held on to those he knew well, despite their foibles.

▪ AUTUMN 1934

Back in Leningrad after his trip to Kazakhstan, Kirov spoke in October to the district and city party committees about agricultural problems. It was his usual appeal for stronger efforts to meet economic targets. Kirov was highly critical of the economic management of the collective farms by the newly created machine-tractor stations (MTS). He was especially disparaging of the political departments attached to the MTS, which Stalin had established in 1933 to enforce laws on compulsory grain deliveries and to ensure greater party control in the countryside. Often these political departments were staffed by employees from the secret police, who ruthlessly trampled on the rights of the local party committees. Kirov had always resented the interference of the police in party affairs, and he made no secret of his contempt for these departments. As with several other issues, Kirov was the first to speak out against the political departments, even telling a local journalist that the collective farms would work better without them. It may well be that his criticisms were what led the Central Committee to pass a decree abolishing them at the plenum in November 1934.[52]

Despite his initiatives in these areas, Kirov had little to do with an even bigger reform implemented at the November plenum—the end of bread rationing, set for 1 January 1935. Rationing had been introduced in Leningrad and other industrial cities in 1928 because of the critical food shortages. In 1934, Stalin claimed that there was now plenty of bread to go around, and most members of the central leadership backed him in his proposal to end rationing. But the plan was not popular among regional party leaders like Kirov. Under the rationing system Kirov had managed to ensure that Leningrad was well supplied and that people were relatively satisfied.[53] It was not at all clear that the new policy would go down well with the public. (In fact, it did not. Leningrad workers received the news in December 1934 with openly expressed anger and even panic because they feared a price rise.)

Kirov said little publicly about the repeal of rationing. But he must have anticipated that he was in for some rough going once he announced the Central Committee's decision to Leningrad workers. Kirov was well aware of the mood of the proletariat, and it was not good. The lofty propaganda that adulated Soviet leaders and hailed the regime had little effect in this time of economic hardship. Indeed, it often evoked cynicism. Among Kirov's personal papers was a typewritten copy of a song that had been circulating around Leningrad. The song was about a dramatic event that occurred in the spring of 1934, when the icebreaker *Cheliuskin*, on a scientific expedition from Leningrad to Vladivostok, sank with over a hundred passengers. The group, which took refuge on an ice floe, was rescued over several weeks in March and April by Soviet airmen. The Soviet press reported the rescues daily, portraying the airmen as courageous and daring heroes. As usual, however, Stalin occupied center stage, getting the credit for initiating and presiding over the rescue.[54]

The song, which ridiculed the pilots and the fuss over them, was a parody of a well-known tsarist prison tune in which the names of the pilots were substituted for the names of prisoners.[55] Such irreverent treatment of the rescue, which had been presented by the press as a glorious example of the valor of the Soviet people and their leader, Stalin, reflected the bitterness and disrespect toward the regime that could not be expressed openly. Kirov must have understood why people felt this way. And he himself probably disapproved of the expensive expedition at a time of stringency, especially the vast resources that had been expended to carry out the rescue, only to have Stalin capitalize on it for propaganda purposes. But, as part of the Stalinist leadership, Kirov was identified in people's minds with all its policies. As chief of Leningrad, he would have to face the repercussions of the new bread policy, which the lofty propaganda would do little to offset.

Judging from an episode described in the diary of Stalin's sister-in-law Mariia Svanidze, Stalin was fully aware of Kirov's worries about the bread policy. Svanidze was visiting Stalin's children at his Kremlin apartment on 3 November. Stalin, having returned from Sochi just a few days earlier, showed up for dinner with Kaganovich and Zhdanov. After dinner, Svanidze notes, Stalin was in a good mood:

> He went to the intercity telephone and called Kirov; he began to joke about the repeal of rationing and the increase in the price of bread. He advised Kirov to come to Moscow immediately, in order to defend the interests of the Leningrad district from a greater increase in prices over those in other districts. Apparently Kirov was trying to get out of coming, because I[osif] gave the receiver to Kag[anovich], who talked Kirov into coming down for a day. I[osif] loved Kirov and he obviously wanted to see him after his return from Sochi, to go to the steam bath with him, and to joke around with him. The rise in bread prices was just a pretext.[56]

If Stalin thought he could persuade Kirov to come to Moscow by making threats about bread prices, then he obviously knew that this was a source of anxiety for Kirov. Kirov did not come right away, but we know that he was in Moscow at least by 12 November. Svanidze reports in her diary that he showed up together with Stalin and his son Vasilii for tea at Zubalovo, one of Stalin's dachas. After tea they watched a puppet show put on by Stalin's daughter, Svetlana, and some other children, and then played billiards. As they prepared to leave for Stalin's "nearby dacha," Svanidze noticed that Stalin was not in a good mood, but she does not say why. She only observes that, as Stalin loved to travel at top speed, they raced away by car.[57]

Kirov stayed in Moscow long enough to attend a Politburo meeting on 13 November and left for home by train that evening. A week later, on 19 November, Kirov was back in Moscow, spending several hours in Stalin's Kremlin office, along with Molotov, Kaganovich, Zhdanov, and others. They may have discussed the upcoming Central Committee plenum, scheduled to open on the 25th. At the plenum itself, which focused on the new bread policy, Kirov was uncharacteristically silent. Stalin, Molotov, and Kaganovich dominated the proceedings. Kirov's silence suggests a lack of enthusiasm for the new policy, which also is evident in the outline he wrote for his speech about the plenum to be delivered to Leningrad party activists on 1 December. Kirov was planning simply to repeat exactly what Stalin said about the importance of repealing bread rationing.[58]

As fate would have it, Kirov was not able to see Sergo Ordzhonikidze on his last visit to Moscow for the plenum, because Sergo had fallen ill while on business in Transcaucasia. It was a strange illness. Sergo had traveled with Transcaucasian party chief Lavrentii Beria to Baku, where the two dined with the head of the Azerbaijan party and former police official, Mir Dzhafar Bagirov, at the latter's apartment on 6 November. Immediately after the meal, Sergo suddenly got sick with chills and a fever. By 8 November, after returning to Tbilisi, Sergo began to experience internal bleeding and severe pain in his stomach. Unable to diagnose his illness, local doctors summoned help from Moscow, but none of the specialists could establish the cause or the nature of the problem. They advised rest and a special diet, and within a week Sergo was much improved.[59]

Considering that Beria was involved, foul play cannot be ruled out in Sergo's sudden illness. Beria, a former Chekist who would later become NKVD chief, was already notorious for his perfidy and evil deeds. It would not have been out of character for Beria to arrange for Sergo to be poisoned if he were requested to do so by Stalin.[60]

Stalin clearly was in no hurry to have Sergo return. On 19 November, just as Sergo was about to come back to Moscow, Stalin sent a telegram informing Sergo of a Central Committee decision that forbade him to leave Tbilisi without the doctors' permission, and in any case not before the 26th. Just to make sure, Stalin sent a personal message to Sergo the following day: "Better to wait until the 26th. One can't fool around with illness. Regards, Stalin." Sergo had no choice but to follow Stalin's orders. He did not arrive back in Moscow until 29 November, a day after the plenum had ended and its participants, including Kirov, had left the city. Both Kirov and Sergo were disappointed to have missed each other. According to Sergo's wife, Zinaida, Kirov had lamented: "I haven't seen Sergo in such a long time. I want to see him terribly." And Sergo himself had said to his wife when he talked to her from Tbilisi that it had been three months since he had been with Kirov, and he really missed him. The minute he arrived back in Moscow he telephoned Kirov.[61] But of course a telephone conversation could not replace a face-to-face private talk. More important, Sergo, having been away from Moscow for so long, would not have gotten wind of any impending threats to Kirov.

After arriving at the train station without the usual companionship of Sergo, Kirov boarded the Red Arrow for the return to Leningrad on the evening of 28 November. He had spent much of the afternoon in Stalin's office along with a group of about twenty. According to Rosliakov, on the way back to Leningrad, Kirov engaged in a lively conversation with him and the other delegates about Kirov's upcoming speech to party activists, scheduled for 1 December. When the train arrived in the morning they all hurried off; the decisions passed by the Central Committee at the plenum had to be implemented as soon as possible, and the next day, the 30th, was a day off.[62]

Kirov set to work immediately. However unenthusiastic he was about the new bread policy, he had to go along with it and persuade the party rank and file of its efficacy. He called Rosliakov around noon on 29 November to ask him to prepare reports on the city's trade and commercial transactions and have them sent to him no later than noon on 1 December, so that he could include them in his speech that evening. In addition to making several other calls, Kirov met with Chudov, Kodatskii, and Petr Struppe, chairman of the Leningrad Regional Executive Committee. He also presided over a meeting of the city and district committee secretariats to prepare for a plenum of the two committees, set for 2 December. Kirov worked late into the night on his report for the party *aktiv*. Mariia L'vovna was still not feeling well, so she remained with her sister Rakhil' at the rest home in Tolmachevo.[63]

On the next day, the 30th, Kirov showed up at his office at the Smolnyi, despite the fact that it was not an official workday. Several people saw him driving around the city. According to one of his chauffeurs, S. M. Iudin, he visited some construction sites and traveled around the Nevskii district, after which he returned home. One of Kirov's secretaries, who was on duty at the Smolnyi, reported that she received several calls from him that day, with requests for various things, such as the day's newspapers. The last call was at about eleven o'clock that evening. Alone at home, Kirov worked late into the night.[64]

▪ 1 DECEMBER: THE MURDER

Kirov spent much of the day of 1 December 1934 at home, preparing his speech for that evening. With his usual purposefulness, he made several telephone calls to Chudov, Rosliakov, and others at the Smolnyi requesting materials and information. The district party committee courier recalled that she made four trips to Kirov's home that day, the last being around 2:30 p.m. Kirov answered the door and told her that she would not be required to bring anything else. At 3 p.m. and then again at

3:15, Kirov called Chudov at his office, where a meeting of about twenty party officials was taking place. Rosliakov, who was present at the meeting, recalled that Kirov wanted to know how their work was coming along. It was Rosliakov's impression that Kirov gave no indication to Chudov that he planned to come to the Smolnyi before going to the Tauride Palace for his speech at 6 p.m., but of course Rosliakov could only hear one side of the conversation.[65]

Around 4 p.m. Kirov telephoned down to the garage, located at the bottom of his building, and asked a chauffeur, F. G. Ershov, to bring a car around. He then left home immediatcly and walked alone up to the Troitskii Bridge, where Ershov picked him up in the car and took him to the Smolnyi. As usual, given his penchant for mixing with people, Kirov entered the Smolnyi not through the restricted secretaries' entrance, but through the main entrance. He was met there at around 4:30 by four plainclothes NKVD guards, who had been informed of his impending arrival by the Smolnyi commandant (head of the guards), Aleksandr Mikhail'chenko.[66] (Mikhail'chenko had presumably been contacted by Kirov's chauffeur, as would have been the normal procedure.) Once in the main hallway, the group was joined by M. D. Borisov, who was responsible for guarding Kirov inside the Smolnyi. Even though the Smolnyi was a carefully protected building, the procedures for Kirov's security there were rigorous. Borisov's job was to accompany Kirov to his office and then stay in Kirov's reception room, in order to be with him every time he left his office.

Rosliakov, of course, had his reservations about Borisov's qualifications as a bodyguard. His doubts were shared by Ilia Aleksandrov, one of the NKVD guards on duty at the Smolnyi that day. Aleksandrov testified years later to the Communist Party Control Commission: "Borisov was an elderly man, physically weak, not talkative, a modest person. It seems that it would have been more appropriate to choose for a personal guard for Kirov a younger and more agile person. Why Borisov himself was chosen is unknown to me." Aleksandrov added, however, that his superiors instructed all of Kirov's guards to maintain a low profile and to stay out of Kirov's direct line of vision because "they and we knew that Kirov did not like guards."[67] In this sense, the quiet and unobtrusive Borisov was well suited for his job.

Aleksandrov recalled, in his written testimony, that his guard group went with Kirov and Borisov up to the third floor, where there was a guard post controlling access down the corridor to the offices of the regional party committee. Other sources add that, on his way up the stairs, Kirov stopped on two occasions and talked briefly to party staffers—once after reaching the second floor and again upon reaching the top of the third-floor stairs. After escorting Kirov to the control post, Aleksandrov and his fellow guards went back down the stairs, leaving Kirov as he headed down the long, wide corridor to the left with Borisov.[68]

It is at this point that accounts of what happened diverge significantly. Russian historian Alla Kirilina, an unabashed proponent of Stalin's innocence in Kirov's murder, has had access to archival files that are still closed to other researchers. Citing the assassin Leonid Nikolaev's testimony, she tells us that Kirov walked by as Nikolaev was coming out of the lavatory (*ubornaia*) on the main corridor. (It is unfortunately not clear where the lavatory was located, but it may have been next to the guard post.) Nikolaev turned around and faced the wall so Kirov would not take notice of him. He then followed Kirov as he continued to the end and turned left down another corridor to his office, which was now, since the recent move, the last one on the left. (See diagram.) Midway down this corridor, directly in front of the reception room to Chudov's office, Nikolaev pulled out a Nagan revolver and shot Kirov, from a distance of about three feet, in the back of the neck.[69]

Kirov fell against a post and then collapsed to the ground face-down. Kirilina claims that, just as Nikolaev was about to kill himself with a second shot from his gun, an electrician named S. A. Platych, who was standing on a ladder at the end of the corridor (not far from Kirov's office), hurled a screwdriver at Nikolaev and hit him in the face. This threw Nikolaev off balance, and he fell backward to the floor, the bullet from his revolver hitting just below the cornice on the opposite wall. Kirilina says that, immediately after the shots were fired, Borisov, who had been lagging significantly behind Kirov, came running up to the scene of the crime.[70]

A report on the murder by the USSR Supreme Court, published in late 1990, presents things slightly differently. The authors of this report, two military judges, rely on a joint investigation conducted by the KGB and the USSR Procurator's office in 1988–90. They recount the murder as follows:

> At 4:30 [Nikolaev] saw Kirov coming toward him in the corridor. He
> turned his back to Kirov and, after Kirov had passed, followed him at a

DIAGRAM OF THE SMOLNYI MURDER SCENE
THIRD FLOOR

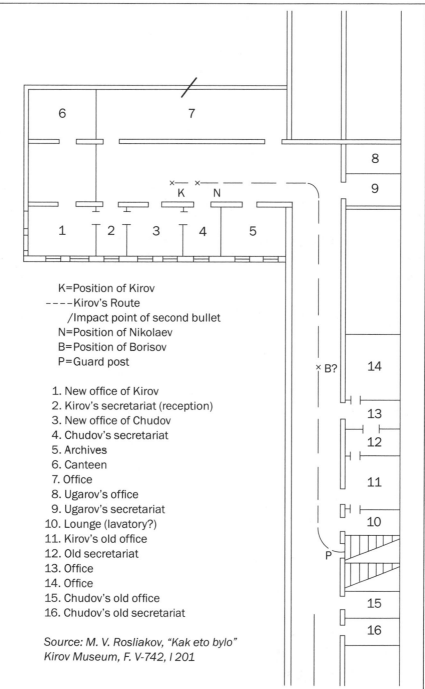

K=Position of Kirov
----Kirov's Route
/Impact point of second bullet
N=Position of Nikolaev
B=Position of Borisov
P=Guard post

1. New office of Kirov
2. Kirov's secretariat (reception)
3. New office of Chudov
4. Chudov's secretariat
5. Archives
6. Canteen
7. Office
8. Ugarov's office
9. Ugarov's secretariat
10. Lounge (lavatory?)
11. Kirov's old office
12. Old secretariat
13. Office
14. Office
15. Chudov's old office
16. Chudov's old secretariat

Source: M. V. Rosliakov, "Kak eto bylo"
Kirov Museum, F. V-742, I 201

distance of ten feet, pulled out his pistol, fired, and hit him in the back of
the neck. He [Nikolaev] immediately tried to kill himself, but at that
moment a man emerged from the office across the way, which prevented
him from firing where he had aimed. Then he felt a blow on his head and
fell to the floor. . . . Witnesses Vasil'ev, Platych, Leonik, and others saw
Nikolaev shoot the second time, and the electrician Platych testified
under questioning that he hit Nikolaev on the head with his fist and
knocked him off his feet.[71]

This version does not tell us where Nikolaev was when Kirov walked by
him; nor does it identify the man who emerged from the office across the
way or reveal what the alleged witnesses Vasil'ev and Leonik were doing at
the time.

A typewritten copy (now declassified) of electrician Platych's interrogation by NKVD official L. G. Mironov, on 2 December, does not even
mention anyone else being in the corridor at the time. Platych said that he
was walking down the corridor to close the glass door at the end, near
Kirov's office, when he heard a shot ring out. "After the first shot, I turned
and a second shot was fired. I saw right away that Comrade Kirov was
lying on the floor and another man, leaning against the wall, was slowly
sliding to the floor. I raced in the direction of this man, *guessing* [emphasis
added] that he had fired the shots. When I reached him, I picked up a
Nagan revolver lying on the floor, threw it in the corner and hit the man
twice in the face."[72]

Platych said nothing in this testimony about being on a ladder and
throwing a screwdriver. He gave no indication that he had interfered with
Nikolaev as he was firing a second shot or had caused him to slide to the
floor. (Indeed he merely "guessed" that Nikolaev had done the firing.)
When asked if there was anyone else in the corridor at the time, Platych
responded, understandably, that he was in such a state of agitation after the
murder that he could only remember seeing two people gathered around—
commandant of the Smolnyi guards Mikhail'chenko, who was pushing
away those who tried to hit the murderer, and Second Secretary Chudov.
Platych could not say whether the bodyguard Borisov was there at the
time, although he knew him well.

Also available is a copy from the archives of a brief statement by
Borisov, who was questioned by an NKVD investigator on the evening of
the murder. Borisov, who would die the next day in an alleged truck acci-

dent, said that he was following Kirov at some distance, about twenty feet. He heard the first shot just as he was about to turn left into the corridor where Kirov was. As he was taking out his revolver, he heard a second shot. "Having turned the corner, I saw two bodies lying by the door to Chudov's reception room. They were about three-quarters of a meter [two and a half feet] apart. In the corner was a Nagan. I saw the obkom electrician Platoch [sic] in the same corridor. Then the obkom employees came out the door. I don't know their names."[73]

Among those who emerged on the scene from Chudov's office, where the meeting was still going on, was Rosliakov, who recalled his memories of what happened:

> Suddenly, at five o'clock [sic] we heard shots—one, another. . . . A. Ivanchenko, who was seated closest to the door, was the first to go out into the corridor, but he came back in for a moment. Having rushed out after Ivanchenko, I saw a terrible sight: to the left of Chudov's reception in the corridor Kirov lay face-down (his head was turned to the right), his cap, the peak of which rested on the floor, raised and not touching the back part of his head; to the left of his armpit was his briefcase with materials for his report: it had not fallen completely, but his weakened hand had lost its grip on it. . . . To the right of the door, by about 15 to 20 centimeters [6 to 8 inches], lay a man on his back, his hands stretched out, and in the right hand was a revolver. . . . I ran to Kirov, picked up his head, whispered, "Kirov, Mironych." Not a sound, no reaction.[74]

Rosliakov says that he took the revolver out of the murderer's hand and gave it to A. I. Ugarov, a member of the obkom bureau. In the man's coat jacket, Rosliakov found a notebook and his party card, with the name Leonid Nikolaev on it. By this time Chudov, Kodatskii, Struppe, and the others stood in shock over Kirov's lifeless body. They called the NKVD— Medved and the medical unit. Borisov arrived out of breath, followed by medics with respiratory equipment and oxygen. Then Medved came running up "in complete confusion."[75]

▪ UNANSWERED QUESTIONS

Several questions arise from these accounts. First, Rosliakov does not mention Platych or any other witnesses, and in fact makes a point of noting what a coincidence it was that no one was in the corridor at the time.[76] It is quite possible that he simply forgot, since he wrote the account almost thirty years after it happened. Or perhaps he was too shocked to take notice of Platych, who was seen there by Borisov. Platych, on the other hand, recalled seeing Chudov and Smolnyi commandant Mikhail'chenko, but not Borisov, so it could be that Platych left shortly after people began to arrive. In any case, Platych apparently did not come forward at the time and present himself as a witness to the crime or its aftermath. Nor did Mikhail'chenko, one of the few to have had advance notice of Kirov's arrival. Mikhail'chenko was seen not only by Platych but also by a party employee named Stera Gorakova, who came out of her office after she heard the shots and saw Mikhail'chenko leaning over Nikolaev's body.[77] Yet nothing would be heard of him again.

Then there is the question of the bodyguard Borisov. Rosliakov says that Borisov arrived after the group emerged from Chudov's office and was hovering over Kirov, which makes it hard to imagine that he was only twenty feet behind Kirov, as he said during his brief questioning. Moreover, if Borisov had been that close, he could not have failed to see Nikolaev stalking after Kirov down the main corridor. As Rosliakov observes, it was a grave breach of discipline for Borisov not to have had Kirov in his sight. Why was he so far behind? Had someone detained him? According to NKVD guard Aleksandrov, Borisov was in bad shape after the murder. He, Aleksandrov, and two other guards were sent over to NKVD headquarters from the Smolnyi sometime in the evening of 1 December and spent the night—doubtless on orders of the NKVD—in one of the office rooms:

> From this office Borisov called his home and spoke with his wife. I don't remember the content of the conversation. It was a short one. I think he said that Kirov was killed and he would give the details when he returned. Borisov, like all of us, was greatly depressed by the event. We hardly talked, and he was crying all the time. Borisov told us that Kirov was killed near the office of Chudov in the Smolnyi corridor by an unknown man. He was shot point-blank. Why he couldn't prevent the attack Borisov did not tell us. He also did not tell us at what distance he was following Kirov and how the killer was able to reach the Smolnyi corridor. Maybe we didn't ask him all these questions because he was in a

severely shattered state, and it was difficult to talk or question him. Borisov didn't know Kirov's killer before. I remember that Boris said that the killer wanted . . .[78]

Here, curiously, a page is missing from the testimony, and when Aleksandrov's narrative begins again, he is talking about the next day.

Another puzzle is where the Nagan pistol was located immediately after the murder. Rosliakov says that when he came out of Chudov's office and saw the murder scene, the pistol was in Nikolaev's right hand, a claim that historian Kirilina repeats. The Supreme Court report refers only to a pistol discovered "near Nikolaev." But Platych in his questioning said he picked the gun off the floor and threw it into the corner. Was Platych lying? Or did someone retrieve the pistol and put it in the right hand of Nikolaev, who was sprawled on the floor?

It is by no means clear from any of the testimony why the second bullet ended up where it did. If it was intended for Kirov, why did the bullet go so high and so far to the right? Perhaps, as Kirilina suggests, Nikolaev, realized the hopelessness of his situation and decided to kill himself but was somehow thwarted. Or maybe he accidentally pulled the trigger as he fell backward. But who or what caused Nikolaev to fall and lie motionless on the floor?

Rosliakov points out that the press reports saying that Nikolaev was "captured" were inaccurate. Nikolaev did not try to run away. In fact he was unconscious. When someone came along and tried to kick Nikolaev, Rosliakov and Ugarov had to stop him. "It was important to have a clean investigation and not a swift destruction of the criminal."[79] The Supreme Court report confirms this, saying that Nikolaev was carried unconscious away from the scene of the crime to the medical unit of the NKVD, where he was treated.[80] For what? This was never made clear, although there are numerous references to his subsequent hysteria and uncontrolled crying.

At what point Nikolaev was carried away is also unclear. Most of the attention, quite naturally, was focused on Kirov's lifeless body. Chudov, Kodatskii, and others lifted Kirov off the floor, as Rosliakov supported his head, dripping blood from the neck. They carried him through the reception area into Chudov's office, where they placed him on the conference table. Rosliakov, a doctor by training, unfastened the collar of Kirov's shirt, took off his belt, and tried to find a pulse, but there was none. They gave

Kirov oxygen, but to no avail. Finally, one after another, the doctors arrived: the first was Professor Lang (Kirov's personal physician), followed by Professor of Surgery Vasilii Dobrotvorskii and a Georgian doctor, Dzhanelidze. In Rosliakov's words: "Their faces were guarded, without any expression of hope. Severe by nature, the harsh Dobrotvorskii was the first to declare the situation hopeless. The more delicate, milder G. F. Lang, whom I knew from our work together in 1915–18 at the 146th Petrograd Infirmary, approached me and said quietly: 'It's useless, he's dead.'"[81]

But the doctors continued to go through the motions of trying to revive Kirov. Indeed, according to the official medical report of his death, several other doctors arrived on the scene to examine and treat Kirov. They bandaged him, gave him camphor, and administered artificial respiration until almost 5:45 p.m., over an hour after he had been shot. These were tense times, and apparently no one wanted to be accused later of not having done enough for Kirov.[82]

Meanwhile Chudov telephoned Central Committee headquarters in Moscow from his office. Aleksandr Poskrebyshev, Stalin's trusted aide and the head of the Central Committee's Special Sector, picked up the receiver. Chudov asked to speak to Stalin, but Poskrebyshev could not get an answer on Stalin's line. Chudov then told Poskrebyshev what had happened, and Poskrebyshev sent Stalin's guard to find Stalin, to wake him if necessary and tell him the news about Kirov. Stalin returned Chudov's call within a few minutes. After speaking to Chudov, Stalin asked to talk to Dr. Dzhanelidze, who gave him the details about Kirov in his native Georgian. Then, on orders from the Central Committee, the doctors dictated the official medical report of his death to Kirov's stenographer, who was fighting back her tears as she wrote. The report was signed at 7:55 p.m.[83]

Curiously, although more than one source mentions specifically that Professor Lang was among the group of doctors in Chudov's office, his signature is missing from the report. And a Professor Gesse, who was not there, is among those whose signatures appear. According to the recollections of a Dr. A. G. Dembo, who was among the several physicians summoned to the Smolnyi after the murder, Leningrad police chief Medved called Lang out of Chudov's office to examine Nikolaev.[84] Perhaps, then, Lang had gone by the time of the signing of the report. But it is not clear why Gesse's signature was there, unless it was an attempt to cover up Lang's absence and the fact that Nikolaev needed medical attention.

Poskrebyshev recalled that, immediately after Stalin hung up the telephone, he went to his office and summoned members of the Politburo and Secretariat.[85] In fact, according to the log of visitors to Stalin's office that day, Molotov, Kaganovich, Voroshilov, and Zhdanov had been there since 3:05 p.m. NKVD chief Iagoda arrived at 5:50 (not long after Stalin talked to Leningrad), and numerous other party and government leaders, including Ordzhonikidze and Bukharin, showed up at varying times after six. By 8:25 everyone had departed except Iagoda, who, significantly, stayed on with Stalin alone for another five minutes.[86]

Stalin must have announced his decision to conduct a personal investigation of the murder at this meeting, because he, Molotov, Kaganovich, Voroshilov, Zhdanov, and Iagoda left for Leningrad by train that very evening. Sergo Ordzhonikidze was not included in the mission. Given that he was Kirov's closest friend and knew the details of his life better than anyone, one would have thought that Stalin would have deemed Sergo's presence in Leningrad essential, especially if he suspected that others beside Nikolaev were involved in the murder. Was Sergo still feeling ill or possibly so emotionally distraught that he was incapable of the trip? It appears more likely that he was not invited. A subordinate of Sergo in the Commissariat of Heavy Industry, Sof'ia Ginzburg, claims that Sergo wanted to go to Leningrad, but Stalin forbade him, on the grounds that Sergo had a bad heart.[87]

Back in Leningrad, NKVD officers took Nikolaev to their investigation prison, located at their headquarters, while Kirov's body was transferred to the morgue of the Sverdlov Hospital for a postmortem examination. X-rays showed that the bullet had hit the frontal bone of the skull and ricocheted back toward the neck, which suggested that it had been fired at close range. Kirov's face was distorted by a large bruise on his forehead and a severely blackened eye, the result of both internal bleeding caused by the bullet and his headfirst fall onto the floor.[88]

At around 6 p.m. a meeting of the Leningrad city and district party committees took place. Committee members discussed measures to ensure that all Kirov's papers would be secure. They also chose a funeral commission and dispatched Boris Pozern, a party secretary, to go immediately to Tolmachevo to break the news of her husband's death to Mariia L'vovna.

Pozern later recalled that, when he came to the door and stepped into the entrance way, Mariia L'vovna intuitively understood that a tragedy had occurred. She asked: "Something has happened to Sergei?" and then collapsed. The other committee members fanned out all over the city to inform people about what had happened. They were anxious to prevent any public unrest and to keep "anti-Soviet elements" from spreading harmful rumors. Rosliakov visited the May First factory and spoke to party activists there. On the way home, he recalled, "the streets were dark and silent. There was emptiness, melancholy in my heart. Kirov was gone; they didn't protect him. It had to happen, that in the corridor at the moment when that evil act was perpetrated, there was no one there. No one came out of the several contiguous rooms."[89]

Rosliakov was correct in saying that no one was there to protect Kirov as he walked to his office at 4:37 p.m. on that fateful day. But he seems to have been mistaken in assuming that no one else was in the corridor at all. Unless Platych's testimony was fabricated, along with that of Borisov, there was at least one person, Platych, in the corridor right at the time of the murder. And the report of the USSR Supreme Court mentions in passing the names of two others with Platych, but does not further identify them. None of them actually saw the first shot fired and may or may not have seen the second shot. This report also refers to an unnamed person who emerged from the office opposite Chudov's and dealt Nikolaev a blow on the head. Was this possibly Smolnyi commandant Mikhail'chenko? Once the investigation began, nothing further was heard about these witnesses, at least in any of the reports that emerged. As for the brief written testimonies of Platych and Borisov, they were buried and did not surface until the 1960s, when they were made available to a Central Committee commission, but not to the public.

As far as is known, none of the others who were on the third floor at the time of the murder were questioned by the NKVD.[90] In fact, it would have been difficult for the NKVD to establish exactly who had been there. According to historian Kirilina, it was not until Filipp Medved arrived, ten or fifteen minutes after the murder, that the entrances to and exits from the third floor were sealed, and the building itself was not surrounded by NKVD troops until 6 p.m.[91] Dr. Dembo, who arrived at the Smolnyi sometime before six, recalled: "To my surprise, there was no guard, and we went up the stairs and toward Kirov's office with no hindrance."[92] This means that someone could have easily slipped down from the third floor and out of the building after the murder. Whatever the case, the NKVD made little or no effort to track down witnesses. As events would show, no one in a position of authority wanted this investigation to establish what actually happened. That would remain for others to speculate upon, for years to come.

8

Into the Whirlwind

.   .   .   .

History has taught us that often lies serve her better than the truth;
for man is sluggish and has to be led through the desert for forty years
before each step in his development. And he has to be driven through the
desert by threats and promises, by imaginary terrors and imaginary
consolations, so that he should not sit down prematurely to rest and
divert himself by worshipping golden calves.

—*Rubashov in* Darkness at Noon, *by Arthur Koestler*

.   .   .   .

A S Rosliakov was making his sorrowful way home on the evening of
1 December, Stalin and his comrades were speeding to Leningrad by
train. They had made a hasty departure, but Stalin had nonetheless found
the time to initiate an important change in the law governing Soviet criminal procedure. He had instructed the Central Executive Committee to
draw up a resolution stating that henceforth cases of terrorism would be
conducted according to the following procedure: investigations were to be
completed within ten days; charges would be announced to the accused
twenty-four hours before the trial; the case would be heard without the
defendant or his counsel present; appeals or requests for clemency would not
be permitted; and a sentence of death would be carried out immediately.[1]

These new procedural laws would form the basis for the summary justice that Stalin and the NKVD would use in executions of innocent Soviet
citizens during their widespread purges. Beginning in December 1934,
with a "quiet terror" that lasted until late 1936, the violence gained
momentum in 1937–38, with the so-called Great Terror. By the end of
1938, close to two million victims had been arrested and tried by courts,
police boards, or military tribunals and either executed or sent to labor
camps.[2]

It all began with the murder of Kirov. The fact that Stalin took pains
to institute these new legal procedures in the brief interval between learn-

ing of Kirov's death and departing for Leningrad suggests strongly that he already had in mind that the murder investigation would lead to a terrorist organization. Indeed, Bukharin later claimed that, when Stalin first called him to the Politburo to tell him about the murder, Stalin stated flat out that the murderer was a Zinovievite. And Nikolai Ezhov, a secretary of the Central Committee with oversight of the police, who accompanied Stalin to Leningrad, recalled that Stalin had instructed him to "look for the murderers among the Zinovievites."[3]

Then, of course, there is the fact that Stalin brought with him to Leningrad, in addition to Andrei Vyshinskii, Deputy USSR Prosecutor, and Genrikh Iagoda, NKVD chief, the entire investigative apparatus of the central NKVD in Moscow. With their arrival, the ax fell on the Leningrad NKVD branch. On 4 December *Leningradskaia pravda* announced that Filipp Medved, his deputy F. T. Fomin, and six other NKVD officers from Leningrad had been dismissed from their jobs and were being prosecuted for negligence. Iagoda's deputy Ia. S. Agranov assumed Medved's post temporarily, but was soon replaced by L. M. Zakovskii, an official from the Belorussian NKVD, presumably because Agranov took charge of the murder investigation. Noticeably absent from the list of dismissed NKVD officers was Zaporozhets, Medved's other deputy, who had been sent to Leningrad by Iagoda in 1932 and who supervised investigations. Reportedly, Zaporozhets was not in Leningrad at the time of the murder. According to one account, sometime in late August or early September he had been thrown from a horse and had broken his leg. After a long hospital stay, Zaporozhets left for Sochi in mid-November to recuperate at a sanatorium, and Fomin, who was in charge of NKVD border troops, had taken over his duties until he returned, the day after the murder. Fomin later claimed that Zaporozhets was not away on leave at the time of the murder, but had simply disappeared for five days without obtaining Medved's permission. Whatever his excuse, it did not save Zaporozhets for long. A few weeks later he too was arrested.[4]

- ## WHO WAS NIKOLAEV?

Among the last documents signed by Medved before his dismissal was a short directive (dated 3 December) to some Leningrad party officials: "We inform you that, at the suggestion of the USSR NKVD, on no

account must any information of any sort about the identity of the murderer—Nikolaev, Leonid Vasil'evich—be given out to anyone, including
institutions and correspondents, especially foreign newspapers."[5] What
the public would learn about Nikolaev would be closely controlled by
those in charge of the investigation. Except for his age, thirty, and the fact
that he had once worked for the Worker-Peasants' Inspectorate, the press
revealed very little. Later, when excerpts from his testimony were published after his trial and execution in late December, a few more details
came out, tying Nikolaev to others accused in a plot to kill Kirov. But it
was not until years later, with the declassification of archival documents
relating to Nikolaev, that a fuller picture of him emerged.

Nikolaev had a hard life. His father, an alcoholic, died when he was
four, leaving his mother to support him, his two sisters, and a brother by
working as a streetcar cleaner. He suffered from rickets as a child—a common disease among the city's malnourished poor—and reportedly did not
walk properly until he was eleven. Nikolaev never grew beyond five feet
tall and, as an adult, judging from his pictures, he appeared frail. After finishing the first six grades of primary school, Nikolaev worked in a factory
as a metalworker. A malcontent who could not get along with his co-
workers or superiors, he had difficulty holding down a job, moving at least
ten times between 1919 and 1934. Nikolaev joined the party in 1924, and
in 1932 began working for the Leningrad Regional Party Committee, the
obkom. But he lasted there for only a few months. He then worked for the
regional soviet, after which he moved to the Worker-Peasants' Inspectorate and finally, in 1933, to the Institute of Party History, where he
served as an "instructor." These white-collar jobs might seem inappropriate for a man of Nikolaev's meager education. But the Communist Party
had a deliberate policy of advancing its proletarian members up the
employment ladder.[6]

Nikolaev got into trouble when he refused to accept a party assignment to work in the political department of a railway. As a result, the party
expelled him in March 1934, and he lost his job. He appealed the decision
and was reinstated in the party in May 1934, but with a severe reprimand
on his record. Nikolaev then wrote two appeals to the Moscow-based
Central Control Commission—one in June and another in August 1934.
He wanted the commission to rescind his reprimand and give him back his
job at the Institute of Party History, but he was unsuccessful.[7]

Nikolaev was married with two small children. His wife, Milda Draule, was a Latvian three years his senior. Draule, also a party member, was more successful in her career than her husband. After working in a factory, she got a job in 1930 at the Leningrad Obkom in the Smolnyi, at first in the accounting section and later as a technical secretary. In the summer of 1933 she moved to a position at the Commissariat of Heavy Industry, and by the autumn of that year had already earned a promotion. Still, Draule's salary of 275 rubles a month was not enough for the family to live on, and Nikolaev's lack of employment placed great strains on the family. Reportedly he was offered a factory job, but turned it down.[8]

These facts about Nikolaev's life and career are documented in the Leningrad party archives, and in material handed over to the party commissions investigating the murder in the 1960s. For further details about Nikolaev we must turn to a less reliable source—the NKVD, which had its own agenda for the investigation of the Kirov murder. During a search of Nikolaev's apartment the NKVD supposedly discovered Nikolaev's diary and a series of letters written to various people and institutions. Excerpts from these materials have been reproduced in the Russian press, but they must be treated with skepticism, because the NKVD might easily have doctored or even fabricated them completely in an effort to attribute a specific motive for Nikolaev's killing of Kirov.

In the writings allegedly discovered by the NKVD, the hapless Nikolaev expressed his frustration and discontent at being without a job and hinted quite explicitly that he was going to commit a terrorist act. Thus, a diary entry for July 1934 reads: "The money has run out, we will borrow. Today my supper consisted of two glasses of *prostokvasha* [sour clotted milk]." In a letter to his mother in August, Nikolaev wrote: "Soon for you there will be a lot of grief and injury, you will lose me forever." A diary entry for October reads: "I am now ready for anything and no one can stop me. I am making preparations like Zheliabov did." (Zheliabov was the terrorist who assassinated Tsar Alexander II in 1881.) And later, in November, an entry says: "If on 15 October or on 5 November I cannot do this . . . then I am ready, I will be executed. It's all nonsense—it's only easy to say."[9]

Nikolaev, we are told, wrote to Stalin and the Politburo complaining about the "heartless attitude" toward him on the part of "bureaucratic officials." He also wrote to Kirov, saying that although he had actively fought against the "new opposition" and had been a loyal son of the party, he had been "four months without work or money and no one paid any attention." In another letter to Kirov, dated 30 October, Nikolaev wrote: "I want to draw your attention to my difficult situation. I have sat for seven months without work . . . no one wants to know how difficult it is for me at this moment. I am ready to do anything if no one responds." Nikolaev is said to have sent yet another letter to Kirov on 21 November, again asking for help and saying that his children were starving.[10]

As if this were not evidence enough of Nikolaev's violent intentions, the NKVD produced a plan allegedly written by Nikolaev and found on him at the scene of the crime. The plan set forth options for carrying out the murder—on the street outside Kirov's home or in the Smolnyi Institute, at night or during the day, and, in abbreviated form, described how it would be done. Nikolaev had made things very easy for the NKVD in its investigation.[11] It is not every day that a murderer carries a written plan of his intentions with him to the scene of the crime and then falls prostrate to the floor with the murder weapon in his hand. It was almost as if the assassin had decided beforehand that he would help the NKVD out by leaving a spectacular trail of incriminating evidence.

According to NKVD records of his interrogation and also his diary, Nikolaev admitted to approaching Kirov on two previous occasions. In mid-November 1934, he had allegedly gone to the railway station to meet Kirov, who was arriving on the Red Arrow from Moscow after a Politburo meeting. On this occasion he had intended to shoot Kirov, but Kirov's guards were surrounding him.[12] Earlier, on 15 October, the militia had detained him on the street outside Kirov's home. Nikolaev had followed Kirov, but gave up the idea of approaching him when he saw Kirov together with Chudov. The militia, finding Nikolaev's behavior suspicious, took him to the Leningrad NKVD for questioning by A. A. Gubin, head of the Operative Department, and M. I. Kotomin, chief of the Guard Department. These officers later testified that they interviewed Nikolaev, but in view of the fact that he was a party member and a former employee at the Smolnyi, they did not search him. Accepting Nikolaev's statement that he had planned only to speak to Kirov about his lack of employment, they released him.[13]

Both Gubin and Kotomin were arrested, along with several other NKVD officers, in January 1935 and given three years' imprisonment for "negligence in their official duty."[14] On the surface, it would seem, this was a straightforward punishment. They should have searched Nikolaev—probably discovering a gun—and found out what he was up to. But there was an odd sequel to this story, which requires us briefly to step ahead of events. In 1938, during the notorious show trial of Bukharin, Rykov, Iagoda, and others, Iagoda (ousted as chief of the NKVD in 1936) confessed to having given instructions to NKVD deputy chief Zaporozhets "not to place any obstacles in the way of the terrorist act against Kirov." Zaporozhets, according to this account, had contacted Iagoda and told him about Nikolaev being detained, with a revolver and a map of the route Kirov traveled on, and Iagoda had ordered his release.[15]

Iagoda, who had been tortured for months by the NKVD, confessed at his trial to a host of other crimes that he could not possibly have committed. Moreover, although Zaporozhets is said to have already confirmed this story during one of his interrogations in 1937, he also admitted the far-fetched charge of spying for Germany. So we clearly cannot take either of their testimonies at face value. Nonetheless, the fact that the detention of Nikolaev in October 1934 was brought up in this manner raises some interesting questions. Recall that Zaporozhets had an alibi; he was said to be languishing in a Leningrad hospital at the time of Nikolaev's detainment before going off to Sochi in mid-November. But even if the alibi was real, it had been several weeks since Zaporozhets' accident, and he was surely in a position to give some general direction to NKVD affairs by mid-October, when Nikolaev was briefly in police custody. A telephone conversation between Zaporozhets and Gubin or Kotomin over what to do with Nikolaev cannot be ruled out. And Zaporozhets might easily have been in communication with Iagoda in Moscow as well.

▪ THE INVESTIGATION PROCEEDS

Was it unusual for someone in Nikolaev's position to have a weapon? Perhaps not. Nikolaev was a party member, and apparently a lot of young party men carried guns at this time. The archives contain copies of two permits authorizing Nikolaev to carry a Nagan revolver. The first was dated 1924, shortly after he joined the party and while he was working as a fitter at a factory. On the application form Nikolaev had requested the gun permit on the grounds that he did "social-political work." The second permit, dated April 1930, was valid for only a year.[16] This of course does not exclude the possibility that Nikolaev had it renewed and that the renewal was lost, but he may well have been carrying a gun illegally. The NKVD claimed that the serial number on the gun found at the crime scene matched the number of these permits. Amazingly, however, investigators did not bother to match the bullet found in Kirov with the Nagan until 1966, and it is not clear that the bullet in the ceiling was ever examined.[17] As for the two cartridges on the floor, in the late 1980s Gorbachev advisor Aleksandr Iakovlev found a document in the Leningrad party archives indicating that they were obtained from Dinamo, a sports organization sponsored and run by the NKVD.[18]

Nikolaev still had his party card in December 1934, so he would have had no trouble getting into the Smolnyi. He reportedly testified that he arrived around 1:30 p.m. and tried, unsuccessfully, to get a pass to attend the meeting of party activists that was scheduled for that evening at the Tauride Palace.[19] However, we do not know why Nikolaev continued to lurk around the Smolnyi for the rest of the afternoon. If he had looked for Kirov he would have found out that he was not there and was not expected.

Nor do we know how Nikolaev got beyond the guard post on the third floor, where a special employee's pass, along with a party card, was required for access. Kirilina postulates that Nikolaev still had his pass from the days when he worked for the party committee at the Smolnyi.[20] Even if this was so, the guards would not have seen him there for a long time, and his disheveled and shabby appearance must have made him look strange. This was a seriously disturbed man, we are told, who completely fell apart after he fired at Kirov. Would he not have exhibited some sign of being distraught or agitated in front of the guards?

After being carried off to NKVD headquarters for questioning by NKVD officer Fomin on the evening of 1 December, Nikolaev regained consciousness, but was reportedly hysterical and incoherent. During his interrogations on 1–2 December, we are told, he refused to talk and even tried to rip up the protocol that he was ordered to sign. According to an NKVD officer who was present during the interrogations: "This was not a person in his right mind, but only a sack of bones and meat, without any reason. . . . Nikolaev refused to answer anything for a long time. In my opinion at that point he couldn't grasp anything. . . . He just cried. . . . He literally went into hysterics every five minutes, and afterward fell into a stupor, sitting silently and staring toward one spot."[21]

Nikolaev was still in bad shape when he was interrogated by Stalin at the Smolnyi on 2 December. Not surprisingly, in the absence of an official record of this crucial interview, there are different versions of what happened. We know that Stalin arrived at the Smolnyi in the morning, after visiting the hospital where the postmortem had taken place and then going to see Mariia L'vovna. Stalin, Molotov, Voroshilov, and others ensconced themselves in Kirov's office and began calling people in. Reportedly, the first to be summoned was Filipp Medved, whom Stalin reproached sharply for not having prevented Kirov's murder. Then the guards brought in Nikolaev, "in a semiconscious state." Nikolaev did not even recognize Stalin and had to be shown Stalin's official photograph. Sobbing, Nikolaev could only repeat, "What have I done, what have I done?" He reportedly did not deny having killed Kirov but was confused about the circumstances.[22]

Stalin's bodyguard, Nikolai Vlasik, was in the outer room. He recalled thirty years later that Nikolaev was "small and shabby-looking" and seemed to be exhausted. Vlasik noted that Nikolaev was with Stalin for some time, but that he heard no shouts or loud voices.[23] Another source, an NKVD prison guard, claimed that Nikolaev had told him after he got back to his cell: "Stalin promised me my life. What rubbish, who believes a dictator? . . . He promised me my life if I named my accomplices, but I had no accomplices."[24]

After Nikolaev left, the guards brought in his wife, Milda Draule. She reportedly told Stalin that she knew nothing about the murder and had not suspected a thing beforehand. Early on in the investigation, before it became a large-scale witch-hunt, there was an attempt to portray Nikolaev's crime as motivated by jealousy. The story was circulated—doubtless by the NKVD—that Nikolaev had killed Kirov because he had found out that Draule was having an affair with him. According to a Western researcher who studied party reports in the Leningrad archives on public reaction to the murder, the rumor about Kirov and Draule caught on quickly. Party members at factories were saying such things as "Had Kirov chased after women less, he'd still be alive," and "Kirov was killed by Nikolaev because of jealousy." A Leningrad librarian was quoted as saying: "Kirov was known to the entire city as a skirt-chaser, he'd had affairs with all the female staff of the obkom, including Nikolaev's wife."[25]

We have seen that Kirov may indeed have carried on liaisons with other women. If people knew about his indiscretions, this would explain why the story about him and Draule spread so quickly. Yet, despite its persistence even today, the story lacks credibility. Draule doubtless had some contact with Kirov when she worked for the regional party committee. But she had been employed elsewhere for well over a year and would have had little occasion to see him. Also, Draule, a very plain-looking working-class woman, was an unlikely candidate as a girlfriend for Kirov, who reputedly was partial to beautiful ballerinas. This was the impression of Elizabeth Lermolo, who was in prison with some of those accused in the Kirov case and who met Draule. In her memoirs, Lermolo recounted a conversation she had with another female prisoner named Gaiderova:

> Gaiderova's voice was edged with sarcasm. "You saw Lenka's [Niko-laev's] wife, Milda Drauleh [sic], did you not? Then you know how irre-sistible she is."
>
> "Yes, she's quite a beauty," I agreed in the same ironic tone.
>
> "My feeling is that if Lenka had ever found Kirov with Milda in the bedroom the last thing he'd have wanted would have been to shoot Kirov. On the contrary, he'd have been beside himself with joy."
>
> We both laughed.[26]

Whatever the case, Stalin's intention was to portray Kirov's murder as a terrorist plot, which meant that Nikolaev's personal motives soon became irrelevant to the case.

▪ THE DEATH OF BORISOV

The next person scheduled for questioning by Stalin was Kirov's body-guard Borisov, who had spent the night of the murder in one of the NKVD offices together with Aleksandrov and other guards. In the morn-ing of 2 December, after receiving a telephone call from Medved, an NKVD officer named Maliy arrived and told Borisov to get ready quickly because he was to be interrogated by Stalin. Borisov left wearing a civilian suit and coat. Then, according to Aleksandrov: "Approximately thirty min-utes later he was delivered, dead, to the NKVD medical unit. I saw how they carried his body into the building covered by a white sheet. What were the circumstances of his death I don't know and wasn't present at the site. But there were rumors among the NKVD employees (I cannot remember from whom I heard them) that Borisov was thrown by his escort employees out of a truck and had a deadly fall."[27]

Stalin's bodyguard, Vlasik, sitting in the waiting area outside Kirov's office, had this to say: "With respect to the death of Operations Commissar Borisov, I remember the following: [NKVD officer] Pauker walked into the waiting room and told me that they were taking Borisov in a truck to be interrogated by Stalin at the Smolnyi, but there was some ice on the road, and the truck got into an accident. Borisov was taken to the hospital unconscious, and Pauker was shaken. I don't remember who told Stalin what happened to Borisov."[28]

The unfortunate Borisov, doubtless terrified by the impending confrontation with Stalin, had been in the back of the truck with an NKVD officer. In the cab was the driver and Maliy. The official story was that the men had transported Borisov in a truck because—given the arrival of Stalin and his entourage—all the cars were in use. The truck slid to the right into the wall of a house along the road, and Borisov was somehow thrown out. The report of the medical examiners, signed on 4 December, concluded that Borisov's death was caused by a brain hemorrhage received from a skull fracture: "The wound occurred because of a very strong blow to the head from a hard blunt object, for example, a brick wall. Considering the results of the postmortem examination, the absence of signs of outside force, and the circumstances of the case, it might be concluded that the death of Borisov was a result of an accident, such as a vehicle crash."[29] A mechanical expert who examined the circumstances of the accident that same day said that the truck swerved to the right when another truck came around the corner because its springs were uneven. There was no mention of ice on the road. Supposedly, a militia employee observed the accident and confirmed what had happened.[30]

This was not the end of the Borisov story by any means. In a bizarre sequence of events, Maliy, the driver, and the other passenger in the truck were hauled before the NKVD a few days later and charged with murdering Borisov. A second examination of the accident conducted on 12 December supposedly found material from Borisov's coat on a water pipe attached to the wall of the house. The conclusion was that Borisov had not in fact been murdered. Maliy and the others were freed from arrest and went back to work in the NKVD. In June 1937 the three were again arrested, as part of a general sweep of all the Iagoda men from the NKVD. They were beaten and tortured. The driver, Kuzin, testified that Borisov's death was the result of the fact that Maliy had grabbed the wheel from him and turned it sharply to the right, causing the truck to crash. Maliy and the other NKVD officer were shot and the driver was sent to prison.[31]

Less than a year later, Iagoda claimed at his trial that Zaporozhets had given orders to have Borisov killed in order to keep him quiet. Kuzin survived a lengthy prison term, followed by Siberian exile. During the 1960s, he continued to insist to the various investigative commissions that Maliy had deliberately caused the accident. But some people said that Kuzin was sticking to what he said earlier to avoid being blamed for the others' execution, and that he simply did not want to accept responsibility for causing the accident himself.[32]

Perhaps the matter would have been dropped had it not been for a letter from S. Mamushin, a physician and chief of the NKVD medical unit at the time of the Kirov assassination. He had signed Kirov's death certificate and also participated in the postmortem on Borisov. In his letter, apparently written in the early 1960s, Mamushin claimed that the results of the postmortem had been falsified and that in fact Borisov did not die because of a single blow on the head. Rather, Mamushin claimed, there were multiple radical cracks in his skull, which suggested that he had been hit several times with a blunt object. This ruled out the possibility that he died because of being thrown from the truck.[33]

The possibility that Borisov had been murdered had such implications for the Kirov case that it could not be ignored. In 1967 another "technical investigation" was conducted. Medical experts exhumed the body of Borisov and examined it yet again. The conclusion was the same as that reported in 1934: "The wounds in Borisov's head, a two-sided bruise to the lungs, and an abrasion in the area of the left shoulder blade could have occurred as a result of the road accident." For some reason, however, there were still doubts about what had happened. Amazingly, in 1989, yet another group of experts reexamined the case, studying the two earlier reports and endorsing their conclusions that Borisov's death was an accident.[34]

There were other puzzles surrounding Borisov's death. The official story was that after the accident Borisov was taken to a military hospital, where doctors tried to revive him, and he died after a few hours, never having regained consciousness. But NKVD guard Aleksandrov, in one of the few authentic handwritten testimonies available, tells us that Borisov's dead body was brought back to the NKVD medical unit—where Mamushin was in charge—thirty minutes after he had left NKVD headquarters. This of course means that Borisov died suddenly and that there was little or no attempt to revive him—a scenario more consistent with murder than with a traffic accident. There is also the question of why, if the impact of the crash was so intense, none of the other men in the truck, in particular the one in the back with Borisov, was hurt or killed. (According to one report, the truck was only going at 30 kilometers per hour.)[35]

None of the official investigations addressed these questions, although Borisov was a key figure in the Kirov case, and his failure to guard his chief remained unexplained. Did someone hold Borisov back from Kirov when he was following him down the main corridor on 1 December, or did he see something he should not have seen? If there was a conspiracy to kill Kirov, the conspirators would have had a strong motive to silence Borisov.

The story of what happened to Borisov's wife, if true, strongly suggests that the NKVD wanted to suppress anything Borisov had known about the murder. After his death his wife was reportedly placed by force into a mental hospital, but she managed to escape. She showed up at party headquarters in the Smolnyi, complaining that the hospital had tried to poison her. She also said that the NKVD had interrogated her in an effort to find out whether her husband had told her anything about the Kirov murder. (Borisov, as mentioned, had telephoned her in the presence of other NKVD guards on the night of the murder.) The authorities transferred her to a regular hospital, but she soon died, and it was rumored that the death was from poisoning.[36]

▪ THE VOLKOVA STORY

By the time Borisov was killed on 2 December, the NKVD must have been in a state of disarray. With the leading officials of the Leningrad branch about to be displaced by the team of Iagoda's deputy Agranov, the investigation was already misdirected and confused. Stalin's ominous presence there cannot have helped matters. Holed up in Kirov's office, he was issuing orders right and left. Stalin had little interest in the specifics of what had happened at the Smolnyi the day before. He was looking for conspirators further afield.

What did the senior members of the NKVD think of all this? Were they advising Stalin, approving of his strategy, or were some of them as perplexed as their junior counterparts in the Leningrad NKVD? At least one of the investigators on the team, General G. S. Liushkov, who would defect from Russia four years later, seems to have been fully convinced that Nikolaev was the murderer and that he was acting out of personal motives.[37]

Nonetheless, the idea of a terrorist plot was not out of the question. The Leningrad NKVD had a vast network of secret informers, and denunciations alleging that persons were engaged in counterrevolutionary conspiracies were not uncommon in the 1930s.[38] In 1933 Kirov himself had received a report of a group that was supposedly plotting against him, and in a note to an obkom official around that same time, Kirov had made a reference to a threatening letter he had received—"not the first—from a seemingly sick person."[39] There were doubtless other such letters.

The NKVD had some grounds for concern about plots against the regime. There was still opposition from émigrés abroad, and, although it mainly took the form of anti-Soviet propaganda, there was the occasional foray into Russia. In 1927 a member of a Paris-based organization of former White Army officers reportedly set off a bomb in a Leningrad party club. Also, in the summer of 1934, the NKVD received information about two terrorists from a so-called All-Russian Military Union, who were allegedly sent to Leningrad with the aim of killing Kirov. The NKVD is said to have launched some sort of an operation against them, even using troops, but they escaped.[40]

But often the NKVD was dealing with illusory enemies. This was the case with the story of a conspiracy to kill Kirov that came from a young woman named Mariia Volkova, whose lengthy letter to the party's Central Committee, written in 1956, is in the Moscow party archives, along with other documents relating to her case.[41] Volkova, a semiliterate domestic employee of a secretary at the Smolnyi, was one of the NKVD's multitudinous informers. In the autumn of 1934 she told both her employer and the NKVD about the existence of a secret oppositional organization called the Green Lamp, which had 700 members and was planning to kill Kirov. An NKVD officer named G. A. Petrov called Volkova in for a talk. Despite the fact that she seemed mentally imbalanced, he investigated her claims, but found no evidence to substantiate them. He passed on the information to Leningrad NKVD chief Medved, who deemed Volkova a "socially dangerous element" and had her examined at a psychiatric hospital. She was diagnosed as a schizophrenic and kept in confinement.

On 3 December, when Stalin got wind of the story, he asked to see Petrov immediately. The latter explained that Volkova was mentally ill and that her claims about a vast conspiracy had no basis. Stalin was not to be deterred. He demanded that Volkova be brought from the hospital to the Smolnyi for an interview. Although Volkova had never mentioned Nikolaev and had no idea who he was, she was persuaded, after Stalin showed her Nikolaev's picture, that she did in fact know him and several others connected with his case. Prompted by Stalin and NKVD leaders, the Leningrad NKVD acted on her denunciations and promptly arrested over fifty people. Afterward Stalin ordered the NKVD to provide Volkova with material support and medical care. The NKVD gave her a furnished apartment, money, and paid vacations for the next several years. Volkova continued to be a dependable source of denunciations for a long time, providing names of new internal enemies for the NKVD to arrest. To show his gratitude, Stalin received her in the Kremlin in August 1949.[42]

Meanwhile Petrov was arrested and sentenced to prison in January 1935 along with eleven other Leningrad NKVD officers. He was charged with failure to show "class vigilance," negligence toward his duties, and the illegal confinement of Volkova in a psychiatric hospital. One of only three of those sentenced to survive a lengthy term in the camps, Petrov wrote a letter of complaint to the USSR Prosecutor in 1956, explaining his side of the Volkova affair.[43]

The KGB, in 1956, dismissed all of what Volkova said as having no basis. Indeed, it is hard to imagine that Stalin ever took Volkova's claims seriously. The way he seized upon Volkova's story reinforces the impression that Stalin had decided from the outset to use the Kirov murder as a pretext for launching a widespread purge.

Having set the process in motion, Stalin departed for Moscow with his Politburo colleagues shortly after midnight on 4 December. It had been a long day, ending with a visit at 9:30 p.m. to the Tauride Palace, where Kirov's body, in an open casket, had been lying in state for two days so that the people of Leningrad could say their farewells to him. As protocol dictated, Stalin's group performed the final half-hour vigil over the body. Rosliakov, who was standing close by, observed them:

> I was struck by how calm and impervious Stalin's face appeared: He gave the impression that he was lost in his thoughts, his gaze fixed over the wounded Kirov, his hands, as we had often seen them before, hanging

down and his fingers clasped together. Voroshilov stood like a soldier, erect, with signs of emotion and grief on his face. Molotov appeared very calm, his face expressionless. Zhdanov's eyes were blinking, he was visibly straining to stand at attention. Without a doubt he was suffering, outwardly at least, more than the others.[44]

At 10 p.m. Stalin and his entourage, together with Central Committee members from Leningrad, carried Kirov's casket to a gun carriage. To the sounds of a funeral march, the cortege slowly began its procession along the streets of the city. Throngs of people lined the curbs. Understandably, given the tense situation, the party leaders did not feel comfortable taking part in the walk to the train station, so they slipped away, leaving the lesser politicians to make the procession. Rosliakov walked alongside Moscow regional party secretary Nikita Khrushchev, who asked a lot of questions about Nikolaev, Borisov, and the circumstances of the murder.[45] Clearly the whole case was a mystery to officials like Khrushchev.

At the station, they lifted the casket into the funeral car of the train, draped with garlands, and watched the train pull out of the station. As he was leaving, Rosliakov saw Filipp Medved standing alone, hatless and sorrowful, in the doorway of the station. He was, in Rosliakov's words "the unwitting person blamed for what had happened, who had lost his good friend and was now under house arrest."[46] Medved's fate was in Stalin's hands.

▪ FIRST REPRISALS: THE LENINGRAD CASE

Stalin left Agranov and Ezhov behind to continue with the investigation. But he followed developments closely from Moscow. Agranov sent him all the protocols of the interrogations of Nikolaev and the others who were arrested in the case. On the copy of Nikolaev's interrogation of 4 December, Agranov noted: "Nikolaev is as stubborn as a mule." Stalin wrote back to Agranov: "Nourish Nikolaev well, buy him a chicken, and other things, nourish him so that he will be strong, and then he will tell us who was leading him. And if he doesn't talk we will give it to him [*zasipim emy*] and he will tell and show everything."[47] Of course, Stalin cannot have actually believed that Nikolaev would come up with names on his own. But the NKVD had by now a list of people who were connected to

Nikolaev and could use its well-developed techniques to pressure him into testifying that they formed a terrorist organization.

On 8 December, Agranov went to Moscow with Ezhov to brief Stalin firsthand on the progress of the investigation. On that day Stalin held a meeting in his office with the party leaders who had accompanied him to Leningrad on 1 December and a group of NKVD officials, including Agranov and Iagoda. The meeting lasted well over three hours. Noticeably absent was Ordzhonikidze, who is listed as having come into Stalin's office just as others were arriving and then leaving less than a minute later. He was clearly "out of the loop" when it came to the Kirov case.[48]

Although news of the alleged conspiracy was not announced publicly until 22 December, the Leningrad party elite learned of it at a meeting on 15 December, when the new party first secretary, Andrei Zhdanov, spoke to them. Zhdanov talked about Kirov in warm terms, noting that it was difficult for him to step into the shoes of such a party leader. He then told his audience that responsibility for the murder of Kirov lay in the hands of Zinoviev and his ideological supporters. That same day, Kaganovich made a similar announcement to the Moscow party elite.[49]

On 16 December, NKVD official Agranov announced at a meeting of the Leningrad district and city party committees that the murder was organized by a group of young former Zinovievite oppositionists and gave the names of Nikolaev's thirteen co-defendants. The audience was shocked. How could the young Leningraders who had acknowledged the correctness of the party line become terrorists? And why would they kill Kirov, who had treated them with such humanity and tolerance, accepting them back into the fold after they had admitted their mistakes? According to Rosliakov, "Agranov's announcement created turmoil in the minds of many plenum participants, but of course no one expressed doubts. Back then we still believed that the party never made a mistake in its assessment of events." Shaken and tense, a few participants got up to respond to the announcement. Two party officials from the Vyborg district of the city, Petr Smorodin and Petr Struppe, were anxious to repent for their lack of vigilance—with good reason. Nikolaev and several of his co-defendants had lived in the Vyborg district and had worked for the party there.[50]

By this time the Leningrad NKVD had been rounding up suspected conspirators for two weeks. The detention cells were brimming with prisoners, and interrogators were busy day and night putting together the case against the so-called Leningrad Center. Who were the thirteen defendants accused of conspiring with Nikolaev and how were they chosen? To give the NKVD its due credit, they were not totally random suspects. Most of the defendants, all in their thirties, had been members, like Nikolaev, of the Komsomol (Communist Youth League) and most had been expelled from the party for belonging to the opposition. Several had been reinstated for having declared "complete solidarity with the policy of the party and the Soviet government." The party and the NKVD had kept close track of those who had at any point, however briefly, sided with Trotsky or Zinoviev. The NKVD used these records extensively in the arrests and trials that ensued after the Kirov murder.[51]

The first to be arrested, on 5 December, were Nikolai Shatskii and Ivan Kotolynov, both of whom knew Nikolaev personally. Shatskii, who worked as an engineer, had been an active Trotskyite and had lost his party membership in 1927. He had made no attempt to be reinstated and had removed himself from politics. Kotolynov, a student at the Leningrad Industrial Institute, had been expelled from the party for supporting the Zinoviev opposition and had been readmitted following his recantation. He had held several leading Komsomol posts, and it is probably for this reason, along with his having been a Zinovievite, that he was accused in the indictment of being a principal organizer of the plot against Kirov.[52]

The other alleged main organizer, arrested on 6 December, was Vladimir Rumiantsev, whose name had appeared, along with Shatskii's, on a list of oppositionists in the Vyborg party district, compiled for the Central Control Commission in Moscow in 1928. Rumiantsev had served as first secretary of the Leningrad City Komsomol and had been a delegate to two party congresses before losing his party membership because of his support for the Zinoviev group. Reinstated in 1928, Rumiantsev was working as a secretary of the Vyborg district soviet when he was arrested.[53]

Kirov knew Rumiantsev well, just as he knew another defendant, Vladimir Levin, who had been an active supporter of Zinoviev. When police chief Medved had approached Kirov in 1933 asking for permission to arrest Rumiantsev and Levin, along with several other former Zinovievites, on the grounds that they were again engaging in oppositional activity, Kirov had refused. He either did not believe the reports or felt that it was better to try to win over oppositionists ideologically than to arrest them.[54]

Among the other defendants was Nikolai Miasnikov, an administrator in the city soviet, who did not know Nikolaev at all. This did not prevent

Miasnikov from being immediately disavowed by friends and family. A few days after his arrest, well before he was declared guilty by the court, the secretary of a local party committee condemned Miasnikov at a large meeting of soviet and party workers. Members of the audience stood up in turn to speak out against him and disclaim their association with him. Miasnikov's colleague at the soviet, who was also his brother-in-law, had these words to say: "My situation is especially hard. Miasnikov is my relative, we are married to two sisters, but I can assure you that I had nothing to do with Miasnikov and his dirty deals. . . . Miasnikov's wife, a party member, at first did not believe her husband's crime. But when she became convinced, she denounced him to the NKVD."[55]

These thirteen defendants formed a disparate group, to say the least. There did not seem to be much holding them together, aside from Komsomol or childhood friendship with Nikolaev. Most of them had blemishes on their records, and some had been real troublemakers. But this was hardly enough to provide credible grounds that they were aligned in a conspiracy. That several were Jewish, as were Zinoviev, Kamenev, and Trotsky, might have suited Stalin's purposes. Stalin, who was to display virulent anti-Semitism toward the end of his life, had already used anti-Semitic tactics in his political battles in the 1920s.[56] Kirov, whose wife was Jewish, had never shown any inclination to go along with these tactics—which may help to explain his more conciliatory attitude toward the former Zinoviev people in Leningrad. With Kirov out of the way, Stalin could now proceed full force. There was no one to hinder him in his drive to rid Leningrad of all seeds of opposition.

▪ THE INDICTMENT AND TRIAL

Having picked the defendants out of a selection of former Zinoviev followers and acquaintances of Nikolaev, Agranov and his colleagues then pieced together a plot. They did not have an easy time of it. For the first few days Nikolaev insisted that, although he knew Kotolynov, Shatskii, and others, they had not formed a group and were not involved in the Kirov murder. Investigators stepped up the pressure, doubtless applying their standard methods of psychological and physical torture. On 6 December, after seven interrogations, Nikolaev finally affirmed that Kotolynov and Shatskii (who had been arrested the day before) conspired in the murder. He reportedly tried to commit suicide in his cell the next day.[57]

The other defendants were even more difficult to crack. Despite what was undoubtedly an all-out effort on the part of the NKVD, only two of them admitted to participating in the assassination plot. The rest confessed only to having supported the opposition, and one admitted nothing whatsoever. NKVD investigators did not rely only on the defendants' testimonies, however. They also arrested and interrogated relatives. Milda Draule, brought into NKVD headquarters on the evening of 1 December, is quoted in the indictment as saying that Nikolaev did not work after the end of March 1934 because he "dedicated himself completely to the preparation of this terrorist act." Nikolaev's brother, Petr Aleksandrovich, a soldier in the Red Army, was reported as testifying that "Leonid also told me that the overthrow of the Soviet government was possible only as a result of an attack by foreign capitalist states and that, if he were abroad, he would help in every way any capitalist state that would attack the Soviet Union in order to overthrow the Soviet government." The husband of Nikolaev's sister-in-law Olga is quoted as making a similar statement. These statements were introduced to demonstrate that the conspiracy had foreign connections.

The testimonies, doubtless falsified or elicited by torture, were all that the NKVD could produce as evidence (aside from Nikolaev's diary and plan for the murder). This was pretty thin gruel for a convincing case. The basic problem was that NKVD investigators, who initially had prepared a solid case against a crazed lone assassin, had apparently been compelled to switch gears after Stalin arrived. They now had to demonstrate that Nikolaev had conspired with others to kill Kirov for political reasons. Of course they had the advantage of total control over the investigation and trial (no defense lawyers and a secret hearing). But what were they to do with Nikolaev's diary and letters, which painted a picture of an isolated and unstable malcontent with little concern about politics?

The solution was feeble. The indictment in the case against the fourteen defendants, drawn up on 25 December, quoted Nikolaev as saying: "I was to represent the murder of Kirov as an individual act in order to conceal the participation of the Zinoviev group." According to the indictment:

> The accused Nikolaev prepared several documents (a diary, statements addressed to various institutions, etc.) in which he endeavored to portray his crime as a personal act of desperation and dissatisfaction arising out

of his straitened material circumstances and as a protest. . . . The accused Nikolaev has himself admitted the falsity and fictitiousness of this version and has explained that this version was created in preliminary agreement with members of the terrorist group, who decided to represent the murder of Comrade Kirov as an individual act and thereby to conceal the true motives for the crime.[58]

Incredibly, the indictment went on to state that Nikolaev's wife and mother had both testified that the family had plenty of money: "The fact that during this period the accused L. Nikolaev was never in material difficulties is brought out by the circumstance that Nikolaev occupied a well-appointed apartment consisting of three rooms and that, moreover, in the summer of 1934 he hired a summer apartment from a private house owner in the watering place of Sestroretsk." Nikolaev, according to the indictment, had received "considerable sums" from the Latvian consul in Leningrad.[59] The international aspect of the conspiracy, presumably introduced to appeal to public fears of foreign aggression, had little basis beyond the fact that Milda Draule, a Latvian, was acquainted with the consul. It was not developed further.[60]

This was a dizzying turn of events, to say the least. It required a great stretch of imagination to accept that Nikolaev would have written all these letters of protest, complaining about how distraught he was, and wandering around Leningrad in shabby clothes, just to cover up the fact that he was part of a terrorist group. First, in doing so, he was attracting seemingly unwanted attention to himself and determining his fate in advance. Even if he had agreed to be the sacrificial lamb, one would have thought his alleged co-conspirators would have at least encouraged him to try to escape after the murder. And why would they have chosen such an unstable and undependable person, who was bound to get caught, as the central actor of their plot in the first place?

Of course, it really did not matter whether the indictment was credible, since the NKVD was orchestrating everything, and no one was going to do anything about it. But then why even bring up the details about Nikolaev's diary? Stalin, as we have said, seems to have had the idea of drawing the Zinoviev people into the case early on in December, but apparently not before the Leningrad NKVD had produced the diary and let it be known that Nikolaev was motivated by personal reasons. The sudden change in the plot was doubtless one reason for the dismissal and arrests of those from the Leningrad NKVD branch and their replacement by their superiors from Moscow.

Stalin remained at the helm of the investigation throughout and had the final say on the list of those accused. He also edited the indictment, which he received on 25 December. On the following day, Stalin called in Deputy USSR Prosecutor Vyshinskii and chairman of the Military Collegium of the Supreme Court Vasilii Ul'rikh, instructing them to hold the trial within two days and to condemn all the defendants to death.[61] The closed court session, chaired by Ul'rikh, was held on 28–29 December. According to Ul'rikh's wife:

> When the judicial inquest came to a close and an adjournment for passing the sentence was announced, Comrade Ul'rikh, apparently dissatisfied with the proceedings, used the direct telephone line to the Kremlin to request permission for an investigation to clarify several facts that had been insufficiently illuminated, but that promised to uncover deeper involvements and clues to this evil act. He received from Comrade Stalin a sharply terse answer: "What other investigations? No other investigations. Finish it."[62]

Within an hour after their sentencing, the fourteen defendants were all shot.

True to Soviet judicial custom, their families also suffered reprisals. Milda Draule, her sister Olga, and Olga's husband were shot in March 1935. Their young children were placed in orphanages. The NKVD also executed Nikolaev's brother, Petr, and his older sister, Katia Rogacheva. His younger sister Anna Paniutkhina and her husband, his mother, and his sister-in-law received labor camp sentences of several years. Even a neighbor of Nikolaev's, Ivan Gorbachev, was sentenced to four years in the camps. The relatives of the other defendants suffered similar reprisals.[63]

▪ THE CASE OF THE MOSCOW CENTER

Leningraders were by no means the only victims. Stalin had big plans for Moscow as well. While the Leningrad NKVD was constructing a case against Nikolaev and his alleged co-conspirators, the NKVD in Moscow had begun going after those associated directly with the Zinoviev group. On 8 December the police arrested the first four of those who would be charged with membership in a group labeled the "Moscow Center." Within eight days, the NKVD apprehended the alleged ringleaders, Kamenev and Zinoviev, who were taken by complete surprise. After the police arrived at his home, Zinoviev wrote an impassioned letter to Stalin:

> Just now, at 7:30 in the evening, Molchanov [head of the NKVD Secret Political Department] and his group of Chekists showed up at my apartment and are conducting a search. I am speaking to you honestly, Comrade Stalin, from the time that I returned by order of the Central Committee from Kustan [in Kazakhstan], I have not taken a single step, not said a single word, not written a single line, not had a single thought that I would have had to hide from the party, from the Central Committee, from you personally. I think only about one thing: how to earn the trust of the Central Committee and you personally, how to get you to include me in the work. . . . I cannot imagine what might have given rise to suspicion of me. I beg you to believe my honest word. I am shaken to the depths of my soul.[64]

Iagoda passed the letter on to Stalin, who was unmoved by the pleas of his former comrade.

As with the Leningrad Center case, Stalin followed the Moscow investigation closely, scrutinizing the protocols of the interrogations of the accused on a daily basis. The Kirov murder had provided Stalin with the ideal opportunity to link the former leaders of the opposition to a real crime. But it was not easy to make the connection. Agranov put it simply to his NKVD colleagues some weeks later: "We could not prove that the Moscow Center knew about the preparation of the terrorist act against Kirov."[65]

Indeed, the NKVD was having trouble coming up with a case against Zinoviev and Kamenev. On 23 December, when the press announced the arrests of members of an anti-Soviet Zinoviev group in Moscow, it added that the cases of Zinoviev, Kamenev, and five others would not be committed to trial because of insufficient evidence. Instead, the Special Board of the NKVD would examine their cases with a view to exiling them.[66]

Thanks to the zeal of NKVD investigators, however, the situation soon changed. One of the defendants in the upcoming trial was "persuaded" to give testimony incriminating Zinoviev and the others as members of the "counterrevolutionary Moscow Center." Zinoviev and Kamenev continued to deny that they had participated in such a center up through 13 January, when the indictment was drawn up and the case sent for trial. On the next day, the investigators altered the original text of the indictment (keeping the date the same) to show that Zinoviev and Kamenev had admitted their guilt, which they had not. The published indictment charged all defendants with membership in the Moscow Center and with "political and moral responsibility" for the murder of Kirov.[67]

After a two-day closed session of the Supreme Court Military Collegium on 15–16 January, the defendants were found guilty and sentenced to varying periods of imprisonment. Zinoviev, as the alleged leader of the group, received ten years, and Kamenev five years. According to the sentences, the trial had not revealed evidence that members of the Moscow Center had directly ordered the Kirov murder. But, the court said, "the trial has confirmed the fact that the members of the counterrevolutionary 'Moscow Center' were aware of the terrorist sentiments of the Leningrad group and inflamed these sentiments."[68]

Why did Stalin decide to hold back and not have the Zinoviev group charged directly with conspiracy to kill Kirov? The NKVD had already falsified the testimonies of the defendants. Why not have them admit to arranging the murder? Perhaps Stalin calculated that it would be too risky at this point to execute Zinoviev, Kamenev, and their supporters. He might have worried about resistance from other members of the party leadership. More likely is that he already had it in his mind to change the story of the conspiracy, so as to bring in a host of new characters to play the role of villains. For that he needed further testimonies from Zinoviev and his group.

Stalin gave a clear indication that this was his intention in an ominous secret letter, which he himself drafted in the name of the Central Committee and circulated to all the party organizations on 18 January 1935.[69] The letter, entitled "on the lessons of the events connected to the evil murder of Comrade Kirov," asserted that Zinoviev's oppositional group was the "most treacherous and despicable of all fractional groups in the history of our country. . . . masking itself in the form of a White Guard organization, and completely deserving to have its members treated like White Guards." "Therefore," the letter went on, "with such double-dealers we cannot restrict ourselves to their exclusion from the party; they must be arrested and isolated in order to prevent them from undermining the might of the proletarian dictatorship."

In this letter, Stalin put the party elite on notice that the arrests would not stop with the Leningrad and Moscow Centers. All former left oppositionists had to be put behind bars. It was a mistake, he said, to be complacent about the oppositionists and to accept their assertions that they had embraced socialism. The more hopeless their situation was, the more they would resort to extreme measures: "The events linked to the murder of Comrade Kirov show that the failure to understand this truth played an evil joke on the workers of the NKVD in Leningrad. Let this be a lesson to us."

▪ THE FATE OF THE LENINGRAD NKVD

Stalin's letter pointed a finger at the Leningrad NKVD for underestimating the dangers of "alien class elements and former oppositionists" in the city. But there was no suggestion of any NKVD responsibility for the murder itself. Indeed, the letter even said that the Leningrad NKVD should not be "run down groundlessly."[70] Nonetheless, as mentioned, a group of twelve NKVD officers, including Medved, Fomin, and, somewhat later, Zaporozhets, were prosecuted for criminal negligence. On 23 January their case went to trial, and their sentences were announced three days later. Medved, Zaporozhets, and Petrov were sentenced to three years in labor camps, as were Kotomin and Gubin, the two NKVD officers who had released Nikolaev from custody in October 1934. Six others received two years. Only one officer received a lengthy sentence—ten years.[71] In all, the sentences were surprisingly light. As one observer put it: "Genuine negligence on the part of the NKVD officers in preventing assassinations, of which [Stalin] himself was an obvious potential target, would inevitably have resulted in the summary execution of all concerned."[72]

Significantly, Filipp Medved's brother-in-law Sorokin recalled that Medved and his NKVD colleagues, although charged in early December, were not put in prison until early January—which would explain why Rosliakov had seen Medved at the Leningrad railway station the night that Kirov's body was sent to Moscow. According to Sorokin, Medved arrived in Moscow around 10 December. He had planned to go to Sorokin's home for a party on New Year's Eve, but did not show up until just before midnight because he had been at Stalin's place. Sorokin later recounted what Medved told him about the meeting:

> After reproaching him for not protecting Kirov, Stalin asked Medved what he should do with him. Medved said that he deserved his punishment and was obliged to serve it. Then Stalin took him to a map and asked him to point out the place where he would like to go. Medved pointed to Kolyma [the site of forced labor camps in the Soviet Far East]. Stalin agreed to it. Naturally, I asked Medved if Stalin revealed any interest by asking him the details of Kirov's assassination. In reply, Medved cursed and answered: "Why in hell should he ask, if he knows better than myself the story of Kirov's assassination and that its organizers were Iagoda and Zaporozhets." I was shocked by what he said and couldn't take in the meaning of his message.[73]

Sorokin, whose recollections have been buried in the Moscow party archives since the early 1960s, had good reason to be shocked. He had heard a clear statement from someone with inside information that Iagoda and Zaporozhets had organized the Kirov murder and Stalin knew about it!

Sorokin went to visit Medved in prison twice before his trial. Medved and his colleagues were not incarcerated in the basement of Lubianka, where prisoners were usually held, but in well-furnished rooms on the third floor. According to Sorokin: "They were held in good conditions, one could scarcely believe that they were under arrest." On the eve of the trial, Sorokin went to see the prosecutor, Ul'rikh, at the Metropol Hotel. Over a glass of vodka Ul'rikh said: "Tomorrow the bear will be tried together with his cubs." (Medved is the Russian word for bear.) When Sorokin asked him what the punishment would be, Ul'rikh responded: "Nothing serious. They will receive short terms and will work in Kolyma."[74]

Medved insisted that Sorokin not try to attend the trial or see him off at the Kazan railway station, where he and his colleagues boarded a special railway car, rather than a prison car, for the trip. But Sorokin did write and sent him books. Sometime in 1936, Deputy NKVD chief Mikhail Frinovskii took an inspection trip to the Far East and met Medved at Kolyma. On his return he telephoned Sorokin and asked him to come to his dacha for a visit with Medved's son Misha. Frinovskii told them that Medved was doing well and that his work was easy, adding that he, Frinovskii, would gladly go there for a change of scene.[75]

Other reports from Kolyma confirm that the NKVD officers were having an easy time of it. All received administrative positions in the camps and were able to live comfortably, some even having their families join them.[76] However, with the onset of the Great Terror of 1937–38, things would change for Medved and his colleagues. In 1937, most of them would be mowed down in the wave of arrests that swept the NKVD when its new chief, Nikolai Ezhov, began routing out the Iagoda men. Only three of the twelve Leningrad NKVD officers convicted in January 1935 survived the camps: F. T. Fomin, who substituted for Zaporozhets in the latter's absence; P. I. Lobov, Secret Political Department chief; and G. A. Petrov, who, as we saw, interviewed the NKVD informer Mariia Volkova.[77] Even Medved's son Misha, so beloved of Kirov, would be arrested at age thirteen and would perish.

Why, in early 1935, did Stalin treat these Leningrad NKVD officers with kid gloves? According to one source, the defendants pled in court that their laxness was largely a result of Kirov's lack of concern for his own safety—his refusal to sanction the arrest of oppositionists in 1933 and his dislike of having guards in his presence.[78] But, given that people were being executed for mere connections with Nikolaev or Zinoviev, this was hardly a persuasive argument if the NKVD really had been negligent. Indeed, if it had been a question of negligence, then why were other NKVD officers not tried on this charge? Take, for example, Aleksandr Mikhail'chenko, commander of the Smolnyi guard on the day Kirov was killed, who was at the scene of the crime. Was he not responsible for the failure of his guards? Mikhail'chenko, whose fate is unknown, may well have been arrested at some point during the purges, but he was never publicly blamed in the Kirov case.

The token sentences meted out to officers of the Leningrad NKVD suggest that their punishment was just a show—intended only to cover up the real circumstances of the crime. Of course, if there was an NKVD plot to kill Kirov, not all of these men were in on it. Medved, for one, would have been in the dark, only after the fact learning that Zaporozhets, at Iagoda's instigation, had organized the murder, with Stalin's sanction. Others apparently heard the same thing. Rosliakov points out that immediately after the murder there were rumors circulating to the effect that Zaporozhets had released Nikolaev from arrest during the autumn of 1934.[79] This was long before Iagoda testified at his show trial that he had told Zaporozhets to set Nikolaev free.

It is significant that Soviet authorities never rehabilitated Zapo-rozhets—who was tried again in 1937 on charges of killing Kirov and Borisov and shot—despite repeated requests by his family to reconsider his sentence. During the period from 1989 to 1991, judicial authorities reviewed thousands of cases of those who were punished for crimes during the Stalinist purges. They found that the charges were groundless in most cases, including those of Nikolaev's alleged accomplices in the Leningrad Center. But in October 1991 a Soviet military prosecutor wrote to Zaporozhets' widow: "In connection with supplemental investigations into the case of I. V. Zaporozhets, it was established that while he was first deputy chief of the Leningrad NKVD he violated socialist legality—as a result of which many innocent Soviet citizens were persecuted. Thus there can be no reconsideration of his case."[80]

▪ WEIGHING THE EVIDENCE

The light sentences originally meted out to members of the Leningrad NKVD were one more link in a long chain of circumstances that suggested a cover-up. But even with Medved's statement to his brother-in-law, does this chain amount to a convincing argument that certain members of the Leningrad NKVD, on orders from the central NKVD and Stalin, orga-nized the crime? The evidence that has been presented thus far falls roughly into three categories. First, there are the numerous occurrences leading up to the murder that, taken together, suggest an effort to under-mine Kirov's security and conceal NKVD involvement: the attempt to get rid of Kirov's loyal comrade, Leningrad NKVD chief Medved, and to replace him with someone more reliable to Moscow, such as Zaporozhets; the surprising release of Nikolaev from police custody in October 1934 without searching him; the illness and subsequent absence of Zaporozhets from Leningrad exactly at the time of the murder, which gave him an alibi; the transfer of Kirov's office (in Kirov's absence) from the main corridor of the Smolnyi to the end of the side corridor; the addition of guards to Kirov's duty with whom he was unfamiliar; and Sergo Ordzhonikidze's strange illness, which kept him away from Kirov before the murder and served as a pretext for preventing him from going to Leningrad afterward.

Second, there are the puzzles surrounding Nikolaev and the scenario of the murder itself, puzzles that raise doubts about the theory that he acted alone. Proponents of the single assassin theory have argued that the NKVD could not have arranged the murder because Kirov arrived completely unexpectedly at the Smolnyi and the NKVD would have had no time to prepare. We now know that the NKVD was advised at least a half hour in advance of Kirov's arrival. This was not a great deal of time, but it would have been enough for NKVD employees to prepare for a murder if they had been waiting all along for the opportunity.

Let us, for the sake of argument, assume that Nikolaev himself knew nothing of Kirov's impending arrival and just happened to be in the Smolnyi, wandering around trying unsuccessfully to get a ticket to the party meeting that evening. Would it not be a surprising coincidence that he was in the corridor with a gun and a written plan of how he would kill Kirov at the very moment Kirov appeared on the third floor? Equally hard to understand is how Nikolaev, who did not have the requisite employee pass, managed to get by the third-floor guard post unnoticed. The Soviet Union, after all, was in 1934 a police state, where security procedures were extremely rigorous. And why was no one else in the corridor at this busy time except the electrician Platych (and possibly two others)? Most puzzling of all is why Borisov was lagging so far behind that he did not see the assassin stalking Kirov.

Then there is the second bullet and Nikolaev's unexplained collapse to the floor. How did the bullet end up in the upper corner of the corridor wall? And what or who caused Nikolaev to fall to the floor and lie there unconscious, requiring medical attention? (Recall that the electrician Platych and Borisov saw the gun lying in the corner and Rosliakov subsequently found it in Nikolaev's hand.) Alla Kirilina has theorized that Nikolaev was trying to kill himself and that Platych prevented him from doing so by throwing a screwdriver at him, causing him to misfire his gun and fall down in the process. The USSR Supreme Court study has a somewhat similar explanation. But this contradicts the testimony of Platych himself, given immediately after the murder when his memory was still fresh. Platych says he turned around as the second bullet was fired and Nikolaev was sliding to the floor.

As it turns out, no one actually witnessed the shooting of Kirov. It is not inconceivable, therefore, that someone else fired at Kirov and then tried to kill Nikolaev—who just happened to be in the corridor at the time—with the bullet only wounding him slightly and ricocheting upward, perhaps as a result of a struggle between Nikolaev and the assailant. Or maybe Niko-laev was not wounded by a shot, but was somehow knocked down by the killer, who then placed the gun in Nikolaev's hand and either went back into one of the rooms or escaped down the stairs located near Kirov's office. But if Nikolaev was just an unlucky scapegoat, then how do we account for Nikolaev's permit matching the Nagan gun, the plan to kill Kirov found on Nikolaev, the diary and the other letters he wrote? It is quite possible that they were fabricated by the NKVD, which, operating without the constraints of a free press or an honest judicial system, could concoct whatever story was convenient. As for Nikolaev's detention in October 1934, which seems to be an established fact, maybe he was simply trying to have a talk with Kirov about his employment, as those who arrested him originally claimed.

Another possible scenario is that someone from the NKVD went to Nikolaev, who was known to have been stalking Kirov and was in the Smolnyi when the NKVD learned that Kirov was coming, and instructed Nikolaev to murder Kirov. After the deed was done, an NKVD operative might then have tried unsuccessfully to kill Nikolaev, causing him to fall to the floor and drop his gun—which the agent might have placed in his hand before fleeing, apparently escaping the notice of the shocked Platych. Or Nikolaev might have somehow fallen by himself, causing the gun to go off a second time by accident. Whatever the case, with the murder plan in his pocket, a gun in his hand, and an incriminating diary at home, Niko-laev was the ideal suspect.

Both of these scenarios would explain the gun cartridges from the NKVD sports society, the NKVD's lack of interest in either examining the bullets or interviewing witnesses, and, most important, Borisov's absence and subsequent death the next day. They would also account for the lapse in security that allowed Nikolaev to get to the third-floor corridor.

Given the discrepancies in the accounts of those who were at the Smolnyi that fateful day and the incredible contradictions in the NKVD's various versions of events, the precise circumstances of the murder can only be speculated upon. In this sense, it might be argued that the evidence against Stalin and the NKVD is still inconclusive. But the case against Stalin and the NKVD goes well beyond the details of the crime itself. A crucial category of evidence is that relating to Stalin and his motives. As we have said, it is inconceivable that Iagoda and the NKVD would have arranged the murder of Kirov without Stalin's knowledge and sanction. The NKVD was firmly in Stalin's hands. He decided personally all top NKVD appointments and gave the NKVD its marching orders. No police official, least of all Iagoda, would have dared to commit such a crime independently. Thus, no matter how much evidence there is to suspect an NKVD conspiracy, the crucial issue is whether Stalin had a reason for ordering the murder of Kirov.

Even discounting some of the traditionally cited reasons for Stalin's revenge, such as the Riutin affair, on the grounds that they have not been completely substantiated, our narrative thus far has revealed the existence of deep antagonisms between Stalin and Kirov. It is clear that Kirov not only disagreed with Stalin on a number of key issues but also "stonewalled" instead of following Stalin's line. Moreover, both he and Sergo continued their contacts with the men whom Stalin considered his enemies. This was intolerable to Stalin, who got back at Kirov by undermining him—albeit subtly—at every opportunity. But this strategy, doubtless abetted by people like Molotov and Kaganovich, was unsuccessful. By 1934, with Kirov so popular at the Seventeenth Congress that his name was being suggested as Stalin's replacement and, with a significant number of delegates rejecting Stalin's candidacy for the Central Committee, Stalin must have seen Kirov as a real threat. But Kirov, who had voiced no open opposition to Stalin, had too much support within the party for Stalin to destroy him the way he did his lesser enemies. The route of arranging an assassination would have been a logical choice for Stalin. Granted, it was not a venture without risk, but Stalin had taken plenty of risks before, and this would have been a chance worth taking. As events would show, Kirov's murder not only freed Stalin of his nemesis but also gave him the ideal opportunity for launching a purge.

Finally, let us suppose that Kirov's murder was just a convenient coincidence for Stalin, who was pleased to have a rival gone and to be able to use the tragedy for his own purposes, but was not involved in the crime. Why then would Medved tell his brother-in-law Sorokin that Stalin knew that the NKVD had organized the murder? How do we account for the painstaking efforts to hide and destroy evidence? Why did large bits of the correspondence among Kirov, Stalin, and Ordzhonikidze, gathered together by Mamia Orakhelashvili at the request of the party, disappear?[81] What happened to the crucial page of NKVD guard Aleksandrov's

testimony, where he talks about Borisov and the assassin? Why did someone go through the Kirov archive and label certain documents, often per-
taining to Kirov and Stalin, "secret, not for access in the reading room"? Is
it not logical to assume that, if Nikolaev really had acted alone, the authorities would have wanted to quell rumors about Stalin's connivance in the
murder by releasing evidence instead of suppressing it? It is difficult to
avoid the conclusion that the NKVD had something to hide.

The concealment of the evidence did not end with Stalin and the
NKVD. As will be seen, the Soviet leadership kept the Kirov case a mystery well after Stalin's death. It was as if the truth was so damning that it
would destroy not only Stalin's legacy but the legitimacy of the leaders that
followed him.

9

Stalin Consolidates Power: 1935–38

The nausea rises to my throat when I hear how calmly people can say it: He was shot, someone else was shot, shot, shot. The word is always in the air; it resonates through the air. People pronounce the words completely calmly, as though they were saying, "He went to the theater." I think that the real meaning of the word doesn't reach our consciousness—all we hear is the sound. We don't have a mental image of those people actually dying under the bullets.

—*From the diary of Lyubov Shaporina, Leningrad, 1937,*
in Intimacy and Terror: Soviet Diaries of the 1930s

The story of Kirov's murder did not end with the trials of January 1935. On the contrary, the murder and its aftermath marked the beginning of a nightmare that would consume the Soviet Union for the next four years. Some historians insist that the police terror that unfolded after Kirov's assassination was not the product of any grand strategy of Stalin's, but rather a haphazard, frenzied process that fed on itself. But when one considers how Stalin meticulously pored over transcripts of interrogations and indictments and how he systematically meted out retribution to his real or perceived enemies, a picture of a carefully planned vendetta emerges.

Stalin was deliberate and thorough, ordering the NKVD to round up entire groups of people, even if there was only one suspected oppositionist among them. Never forgetting offenses, however minor, committed against him in the past, Stalin kept careful track of potential enemies, although they might be left dangling for months before the NKVD came knocking at their doors in the middle of the night. And he wove Kirov into the plot of all the conspiracies; the man and his murder are the narrative thread that connects an endless parade of arrests, trials, executions, and labor camps. No one, it seems, was untouched by what had happened on the first of December 1934.

Stalin's aim in carrying out his vendetta was far from irrational: he wanted to eliminate once and for all anyone who might challenge his absolute power. But while avenging himself on the party bureaucracy, the intelligentsia, and other suspect elements of society, he could not neglect the rest of the country. The workers and peasants had endured a great deal of economic misery, and many were discontented with their lot. Aware that he could ill afford a purge of the party if he was unpopular with the masses, Stalin developed a plan to broaden his base of popular support. First, he turned the death of Kirov, a potentially destabilizing event, into an opportunity to shore up loyalty for the regime by creating a posthumous cult of the former leader. Second, Stalin continued the policy of conciliation toward workers and peasants that had begun in 1934.

After ration cards were revoked in 1935, more bread was made available in the cities. Collective farm peasants were allowed to have small private plots for themselves, along with some livestock, and they could sell their surpluses on the open market. Soviet authorities also bestowed a cascade of awards and honors upon workers, soldiers, and technocrats. Heroes of the Soviet Union were created; Orders of the Red Banner and other decorations were handed out at an increasing rate. In the words of one observer: "While beginning the desecration of the Party, Stalin was assembling a host of new supporters who should be dependent on him for a suddenly acquired eminence in Soviet life."[1]

Thus, simultaneous with the repression, an active propaganda effort was launched. Its purpose was to convince the country at large that the good life had begun and that the only threats to this life were the ever present saboteurs lurking around under the guise of good citizens. The result was surreal. On any given day the press might report that the NKVD had arrested a number of people who were part of a terrorist conspiracy (inevitably linked to the Kirov murder), while at the same time featuring an inspiring story about a "Stakhanovite" (a worker who exceeded labor norms). It was as if life in the country was occurring in two completely separate dimensions.

The success of Stalin's strategy was a testimony more to the NKVD's effectiveness at suppressing dissent than to the party's skill at manipulating public opinion. Although it served its purpose, the propaganda was not believed by everyone. There were a lot of cynics, even among the more backward workers and peasants. But those who were not convinced by the propaganda were often intimidated by Stalin's awesome powers. This was particularly the case with members of the party bureaucracy, who knew much more about Stalin and the Kirov case than the general population did. If they expressed their suspicions at all, it was only in whispers.

As for Stalin's fellow Politburo members, it is unlikely that they considered resisting his systematic destruction of the party old guard. Molotov (who did nothing when his own wife was arrested in 1949), Kaganovich, and Voroshilov were stalwart Stalinists, as were Supreme Soviet President Mikhail Kalinin, and Central Control Commission chairman Aleksei Andrccv. Evcn Anastas Mikoyan, Kirov's old acquaintance from the Caucasus and a full member of the Politburo since early 1935, seemed resigned to Stalin's tyranny.[2] Kuibyshev, who had been an ally of Kirov and took his side in the numerous disputes within the leadership, might have offered some resistance, but he died suddenly of a heart attack in January 1935. (Rumors that he had been murdered were never substantiated, but doubtless contributed to the atmosphere of fear that engulfed the party bureaucracy.[3])

This left Sergo Ordzhonikidze as the only one of Stalin's immediate subordinates who was clearly distraught about what his boss was doing. But Sergo was crumbling under the pressure. In fact, he never really recovered from the death of Kirov. After the murder he did not show up for work at the Commissariat of Heavy Industry for several days. When he finally did reappear, his colleagues "did not recognize the usually energetic and cheerful Sergo. His hair had become grayer, he had aged noticeably during these days. He was often deep in thought, with his face dark from grief." One colleague even claimed that Sergo had been stricken with a heart attack when he heard the news of Kirov's murder, but this is doubtful, given that he was well enough to appear in Red Square less than five days later. Whatever the case, as a result of Kirov's murder, Sergo "was a completely changed man."[4]

Sergo must have had private doubts about the official story, but it would have been impossible to express them publicly. His sense of powerlessness probably grew as he saw what was happening to his close comrades. Although arrests did not become widespread until late 1936, those associated in any way with the former opposition began to feel panic and despair almost immediately after the indictments of Zinoviev, Kamenev, and their supporters were announced. It was clear that the slightest connection with the former opposition meant blame for the Kirov murder. For example, in late December 1934, Sergo received a letter from an old comrade, secretary of the Taganrog Party Committee, Stepa Vardanian. Vardanian was terribly worried about his association with one of those under prosecution in the Zinoviev case and wanted to limit the damage: "I started to reckon with my remorse, although it was only for a slight, but superficial trust in a former oppositionist, or too little mistrust—the latter would be correct now."[5] Apparently Sergo sympathized with his situation and made an effort to help him, because much later, in a speech to the Central Committee made after Sergo's death in 1937, Stalin made a scornful reference to Sergo's "needless concern" about a group of comrades that included Vardanian, "who turned out to be scoundrels."[6] Sergo's efforts did not save Vardanian for long. (In fact, they may well have offered additional impetus for Stalin in his perverse way to go after Vardanian.) In October 1936 Stalin wrote to the new NKVD chief Ezhov: "About Vardanian—he is now secretary of the Taganrog City Party Committee. He is without doubt a secret Trotskyite, or in any case a protector and concealer of Trotskyites. He must be arrested."[7]

Sergo most certainly received other entreaties for protection from the NKVD. By this time he had a well-deserved reputation as a defender of his own subordinates against the police and the punitive bodies. As Commissar of Heavy Industry, Sergo had objected time and again to the prosecution of plant directors and other economic officials because of deficiencies in their performances. On more than one occasion, he had defeated the efforts of the NKVD to organize trials of those engaged in production.[8]

But Sergo's position had weakened as Stalin grew increasingly distrustful, and even contemptuous of him. Also, the Kirov murder brought about a dramatic change in the political atmosphere. The stakes involved in protesting injustices and protecting people from the NKVD were suddenly much higher. This may explain why Sergo's old Georgian friend Beso Lominadze could not turn to him for help when the arrests of former oppositionists began, although Sergo had been instrumental in getting him a prestigious job as secretary of the Magnitogorsk party organization and had been regularly corresponding with him. After his sensational removal from the Central Committee in 1930 for forming a clandestine oppositional group, Lominadze had recanted his heretical views and continued his party career. But Stalin never forgave Lominadze, and the Kirov murder gave Stalin the opportunity to pay him back.

Among the testimonies that the NKVD extorted from those arrested in December 1934 in the case of the Moscow Center was the claim that Lominadze had participated in a counterrevolutionary group in 1932, two years after he had recanted his oppositional views. When he heard about the accusation, Lominadze wrote to Stalin and professed his innocence, but he did not receive an answer. Repressions began in Magnitogorsk, and then the sentences in the Moscow Center case were announced. Realizing that he too would be implicated in the Kirov murder, Lominadze was thrown into despair. On 18 January, while being driven in his car outside Magnitogorsk, Lominadze wrote a suicide letter and then shot himself. He did not die right away, but only after he was taken to the hospital and operated upon unsuccessfully.

During the operation, Lominadze's deputy called Moscow and dictated the contents of the suicide note, intended for Sergo, to Sergo's assistant:

> I had decided long before to choose this end in the event that they would not believe me. Apparently some scoundrel like Safarov [accused in the Moscow Center case] and others said things about me. I would have had to show the foolishness and untruthfulness of this talk, to defend myself and persuade them, and they still might not have believed me. I am in no condition to go through all that. Nothing serious occurred with me in 1932. I gave the correct explanation to Stalin and Ryndin [a party official]. But apparently it was not enough. I face a trial, which I am in no condition to endure. Despite all my mistakes, I devoted my entire conscious life to the cause of communism, the cause of our party. Only one thing is clear—that I will not live to see the struggle on the international arena. And it is not far away. I die with full faith in the victory of our cause. Give Sergo Ordzhonikidze the contents of this letter. I ask for help for my family.[9]

Lominadze's suicide must have been a crushing blow for Sergo. For the second time in less than two months he had lost a close comrade as a result of gunshot wounds. Although Lominadze died in public disgrace—the NKVD labeled him a traitor and instituted a case against his colleagues in Magnitogorsk—Sergo carried out his last request, managing to protect his family and secure a pension for his widow. It was not until after Sergo's own death in 1937 that the pension was cut off. A year later the NKVD arrested Lominadze's widow as "a family member of a traitor."[10]

▪ REMEMBERING KIROV

Meanwhile, as the NKVD was moving in on selected members of the party, the propaganda machine was set into motion—at remarkable speed. Not only was there an instant outpouring of detailed information about the deceased leader in all the newspapers; by the end of December 1934, several books had appeared. Among them were: *Writers on Kirov: A Collection,* comprised of over 200 pages of tributes to Kirov by well-known figures like Maxim Gorky and Nikolai Bukharin; *S. M. Kirov, 1886–1934: Material for a Biography,* which included documents and reminiscences about him by old friends; and even a book in English, *S. M. Kirov, 1886–1934, In Memoriam,* published by the Society of Foreign Workers in the USSR. Individual speeches by Kirov appearing in separate booklets flooded the bookstores, and were translated into foreign languages for distribution abroad. In 1935 the first edition of his collected works appeared, to be followed by several others. By 1940 so much had been published by and about Kirov that a bibliography appearing in that year was over forty pages long, and this excluded most of the publications that came out before 1938 because their authors (or editors) had been purged.[11] In terms of posthumous public veneration, Kirov was running a close second to Lenin.

Stalin was an active sponsor of the elevation of Kirov to the status of martyr and saint. On the first anniversary of Kirov's death, Stalin sent telegrams to all the local party organizations, instructing them to "show Kirov as one of the greatest leaders of our party," thus making the observance of the anniversary an official ritual.[12] By this time towns, villages, streets, and other places were named after Kirov, along with Leningrad's Mariinskii Theater, home of what would be the world-famous Kirov Ballet. Stalin probably had concerns about the destabilizing influence of Kirov's sudden death, which interrupted the conservative, rather static portrayal of the leadership and led some people to expect change. Making Kirov into a cult figure raised his death to a more abstract level and gave constancy to his image as part of the official culture.[13] But, as in the case of the extravagant posthumous cult of Lenin, Stalin also wanted to capitalize on Kirov's popularity, channeling feelings of veneration for Kirov in his direction. Most important, his sponsorship of the Kirov cult helped allay suspicions about his role in the murder.

Krupskaia had strongly disapproved of the way Lenin was deified after his death, especially the embalming of his body for display in a mausoleum. But she was powerless against Stalin. Whatever Mariia L'vovna thought of the official efforts to sanctify her husband, she too was powerless and had no role in the process. According to the already established Soviet ritual, cults of personality deliberately ignored the private lives of leaders. They were meant to be above ordinary human involvements, such as families, and their wives maintained a low profile. In Mariia L'vovna's case, she was so frail and so overcome with grief that she quietly disappeared from the picture anyway.

Indeed, Mariia L'vovna had a difficult time getting through the events surrounding her husband's funeral in Moscow. Zinaida Ordzhonikidze brought her to stay with her and Sergo in Moscow for the duration. Also staying at the Ordzhonikidzes' were Kirov's two sisters and his former teacher Iulia Konstantinovna, who had apparently come all the way from Urzhum. When Stalin's sister-in-law Mariia Svanidze stopped by the Ordzhonikidzes' on 9 December, the group from Urzhum had left, but Mariia L'vovna was still there, along with her sisters, the physician Rakhil' and the Old Bolshevik Sof'ia. The atmosphere was awkward. Zinaida Ordzhonikidze fussed nervously over tea, and Mariia L'vovna did not emerge from her room. Perhaps she did not wish to see one of Stalin's close relatives at this stressful time. According to Svanidze, Mariia L'vovna's sisters were thinking of having her move to Moscow, where they lived, because she was now a "complete invalid."[14] But in the end the sisters moved to Leningrad.

Despite her relative obscurity among the population as a whole, Mariia L'vovna, as the wife of a prominent leader, was well known in party circles and apparently highly regarded. She received telegrams of condolences from all over the country. Many were from official groups, like the women workers of the Red Banner factory in Leningrad and the Political Department of the Kirov State Farm, but quite a few were from personal friends, such as Levon Mirzoian and his family and Nikolai Bukharin.

Among the sympathy letters Mariia L'vovna received was one from a friend named Tamara Rezakova, who had known the Kirovs in Vladikavkaz before and during the Bolshevik Revolution. She recalled how splendid and enlightening Kirov's speeches were and urged Mariia L'vovna to let the "brilliant memory of Sergei Mironovich" sustain her. In the spring of 1935, Mariia L'vovna dictated her thoughts about Kirov to Rezakova, who typed them out in three pages under the title "Memories of a Dear Friend and Comrade." They were apparently intended for publication in one of the many books about Kirov that were now rolling off the press or in one of the journals, but they never made it.[15]

It is not difficult to figure out why. Mariia L'vovna, like her husband on certain occasions, had her small moment of rebellion. Although her memoir appeared to be acceptable for public distribution, written as it was in formalistic Bolshevik style with all the requisite paeans to the party, it had one egregious omission. Whereas Mariia L'vovna made a point of mentioning her husband's tremendous devotion to Lenin, she had not a word to say about the great leader Stalin, supposedly Kirov's devoted friend, the source of inspiration for Kirov and the model Kirov loyally followed. To omit Stalin was unacceptable, and even dangerous, but Kirov's wife apparently drew the line at portraying her husband's relationship with Stalin falsely. As a result, Rezakova apparently did not show the memoirs to anyone until 1949 (after Mariia L'vovna's death), when she sent them discreetly to the Institute of Marxism-Leninism.

As far as is known, Mariia L'vovna never again recorded her thoughts about her husband. She lived out the remaining years of her life together with her sisters at her home on Krasnykh Zor'. Her silence meant that she was well provided for: in January 1935, the Leningrad soviet passed a decree authorizing payment for her rent and all her expenses. She had a car and a chauffeur at her disposal, as well as a dacha outside Leningrad.[16] But she never regained her health. After surviving the terrible 900-day siege of Leningrad by the Germans, which began in September 1941, she died in 1945.

None of Kirov's family seems to have been persecuted by the NKVD during the purges, but they did not escape the shadow of Stalin's vengeance. Having moved to Leningrad sometime in 1935, Mariia L'vovna's sister Sof'ia Markus became director of the Kirov Museum, set up in 1938 as part of the official effort to keep her brother-in-law's memory alive and remind the Soviet people of his intimate connection to Stalin. A staunch and unquestioning Bolshevik, Markus loyally went along with the official line that Kirov and Stalin were the closest of comrades. Nonetheless, she seems to have come dangerously close to arrest in 1939, when her lifelong friend, a woman named Vlasova, with whom she had lived in Moscow, was taken away by the NKVD. When she learned of Vlasova's arrest, Markus—doubtless fearful for her life—immediately wrote a statement to the party denouncing Vlasova and confessing her lack of vigilance: "The party committee was right to exclude Vlasova from the party. The committee showed more political farsightedness than I, who blindly trusted her until the last minute. My guilt before the party is heavy. I cannot find any justification for myself. This realization especially anguishes and oppresses me: do I have the right at the present time to remain as a leading worker in the Kirov Museum?"[17] Luckily for Markus, the authorities chose to overlook her injudicious friendship with an enemy of the people.

▪ REACTIONS FROM BELOW

We know that Kirov's family and his party comrades mourned his death and kept silent about their thoughts on the murder. What about the public at large? How effective was the official propaganda? Did people accept the version put forth by the leadership? In the view of Valentin Bliumenfel'd, a young Leningrad University mathematics student at the time, people were terribly shaken by the death of Kirov because Leningraders loved and respected him. Bliumenfel'd recalled that the wait for people lined up to pay their respects to Kirov while his body was lying in state in the Uritskii Palace was nearly ten hours long. He also remembered seeing tears on the faces of many people who watched the procession accompanying Kirov's body to the train station.[18] Historian Roy Medvedev, a child in Leningrad at the time, concurs: "Among the majority of Soviet young people the assassination aroused profound grief and anger, feelings that also prevailed among the working class of Leningrad, where Kirov was quite popular."[19]

Their impression is reinforced to some extent by secret reports from the NKVD and the party, who were monitoring reaction to the murder. The Leningrad militia estimated that a million and a half people, more than half the population of the city, viewed Kirov's body, and many others, after waiting for hours in freezing temperatures, were turned away. Judging from the spontaneous statements recorded in the reports, Kirov was highly regarded by a substantial element of the working class, who saw him as their advocate: "Kirov was close to us, simple, completely one of us" was one view. Workers recalled that he went out among the people and used public transportation: "He was brave, he went everywhere alone, did not hide himself behind thick walls, [as] we have seen other *vozhdi* do." Significantly, he was portrayed as being more concerned about the people, "much more softhearted" than Stalin. An indication of the veneration for Kirov among Leningraders is the fact that the poem "Kirov Is with Us," published in 1942, was one of the most popular poems during the siege of Leningrad.[20]

It would be a mistake, however, to assume that Kirov was universally admired. According to more than one study, the elaborate official display of grief over his death aroused contempt among some members of the working class, whose main concern was where the next meal would come from. Statements such as "Kirov was killed because the Leningrad workers are unhappy about the repeal of the rationing system for bread" were not atypical. There were allusions to Kirov's portliness. One factory employee asked rhetorically: "What did Kirov ever do for workers, except develop a paunch?"[21] And there were even reports of people expressing disrespect for the deceased Kirov by joking about his death—a sad commentary on his years of working sixteen-hour days as Leningrad party chief. While going through the cafeteria line at her plant, a young female worker observed that "brains" were on the menu and joked that they might belong to the dead Kirov. The joke was spread around the plant by the Komsomol organizer, who was later reprimanded.[22]

Some people resented what they saw as vast sums being spent on Kirov's funeral, as well as the requests for donations to the government in his memory. They also complained about the endless meetings called to discuss Kirov's death and the need for more vigilance. Party reports from Leningrad include examples of people "protesting the fact that they were wasting time on useless chatter about Kirov that would have no effect on price changes." When told to attend a meeting to mourn Kirov, one female worker in Leningrad responded: "Let those who have butter to guzzle down go to the meeting."[23]

Such diverse reactions to Kirov's murder are not all that surprising. It could hardly be expected, given the grim economic situation, that Kirov would be loved by all. As with most political leaders, Kirov aroused different feelings from different elements of the population. But from the point of view of Stalin and the Politburo, there was a much more disturbing aspect to the secret reports. Some "ordinary people" said such things as: "They killed Kirov; now let them kill Stalin." There were other comments: "To murder one is not enough, more should be killed." "It is great that they killed Kirov, but if they murdered Stalin, very well, I would sacrifice a day and work for the cause; they killed one dog, Kirov, now one dog is left, Stalin."[24]

As a corollary to this, people began harking back to Lenin, saying that things would be much better if he were still alive. Rank-and-file party members began discussing Lenin's testament and his recommendation that Stalin be removed from his post as General Secretary. They remembered that Stalin was never as prominent in the revolution as Trotsky, Bukharin, and Kamenev, and expressed doubts about the story that Zinoviev-backed terrorists had killed Kirov. As one Russian historian expressed it: "Despite the energetic propaganda efforts to discredit the fallen leaders, to portray them as minor figures in the revolution, and to exalt Stalin, people in many cases told each other their perceptions of party history, especially since many still remembered the former attitude toward the now damned oppositionists."[25]

Even more disturbing for the Kremlin, some people expressed the opinion that Stalin and the NKVD were behind the murder. According to Leningrader Bliumenfel'd: "Early on there were persistent rumors that Stalin did not like Kirov or Leningrad and that an unpleasant blow for Leningraders was about to follow."[26] People wondered aloud how someone like Nikolaev could have gained entrance into the heavily guarded Smolnyi and why, if he was the murderer, he would not have done it on the street, where Kirov was easily accessible. Versions that deviated from the official accounts proliferated among the workers and the party rank and file, making it difficult for local party officials to make a convincing case. The party organizer at one Leningrad technical institute complained to his superiors: "What can I say about the murder of Comrade Kirov—that he was killed by the class enemy?—when the papers are silent on the subject; and therefore I am unable to refute and rebuff all manner of rumors on the murder."[27]

Local party secretaries reported such comments as "Kirov was killed by agents of Comrade Stalin; he was seen as competition" and "they wanted to replace Stalin with Kirov, but there was no place to put Stalin and therefore they shot Kirov." One white-collar worker in a village outside the city was quoted as saying: "Kirov was a genius, and he enjoyed great authority, which grew with each day, among the workers as well as the peasants. Stalin was afraid that Kirov was competing for his position and thus dispatched the murderer."[28] Such views were by no means restricted to Leningrad. Party secretaries elsewhere in the Soviet Union noted comments such as "Stalin ordered the murder of Kirov, because they had political disagreements and Stalin wanted to remove him."[29]

It goes without saying that such remarks were reported immediately to the NKVD, which in most cases arrested the people in question. But presumably many negative comments went unreported, and others kept such thoughts to themselves. The implications of these reports for the Stalin leadership were serious. Here was irrefutable evidence that disloyalty toward the regime, Stalin in particular, was not limited to former oppositionists or to small pockets of disgruntled workers and peasants. It seemed to be much more widespread.

▪ STALIN'S WAR AGAINST LENINGRAD

Of course, there was a great difference between individual expressions of contempt for the regime and organized resistance. The police state that was the Soviet Union kept any form of dissent in check. Most of those who voiced antiregime sentiments were downtrodden, poverty-stricken workers and peasants, who were unlikely to become politically active. But this may not have been how Stalin and his colleagues saw it. It is quite possible, as one historian has suggested, that the hundreds of "counterrevolutionary" statements reported to the leadership in the wake of Kirov's death may have contributed to the escalation of terror.[30] In other words, Stalin may have reacted to the reports by deciding to repress a much broader segment of Soviet society than he had originally intended.

The initial focus, however, was on Leningrad. Recall the secret letter that Stalin sent to party members in late January 1935, after two months of public reactions to the Kirov murder. Most of the reactions that Stalin learned about were presumably in Leningrad, where people were directly affected by the murder and its aftermath and where the party paid special attention to monitoring people. Leningrad, Stalin's letter pointed out, was a unique city, where the greatest number of former tsarist officials and policemen lived. And its proximity to the border enabled criminal elements to escape from persecution. The Leningrad NKVD would need help in increasing its vigilance.

With these words Stalin launched an all-out war against Leningrad, which he portrayed as a hostile place, teeming with enemies. This was the city to which he had sent Kirov nine years earlier, with the purpose of destroying the opposition. But Kirov had not accomplished the task. To be sure, he had forced the Zinoviev people out of leading positions in the party apparatus, and he had presided over the exile of "alien class elements" from Leningrad. But his general strategy toward the opposition had been one of moderation. He had tried to bring many rank-and-file Zinoviev supporters back into the fold by persuading them to support Stalin's line. Now, with Kirov out of the way, Stalin could unleash his vengeance against those who had dared to oppose him in the past. As Isaac Deutscher put it: "Stalin now acted on the principle that it was not enough to hit his real opponents; he rooted out the environment that bred them. He vented his wrath on Leningrad, whose *genius loci* had seemed to defy him for the last ten years."[31]

During the first two and a half months after the Kirov murder the police arrested 843 persons in the city of Leningrad. And from 1935 through 1938 more than 90,000 persons in the Leningrad district as a whole found themselves in NKVD prisons.[32] Initially the police targeted those who had actually been members of the Zinoviev opposition. But they soon became less selective in their choice of victims.

There were also mass deportations, primarily of former nobility, tsarist officers, and merchants who had escaped earlier sweeps. According to Roy Medvedev: "The relocation process was carried out on the basis of the following principle: an old directory or social register entitled *Ves' Petersburg* (All of St. Petersburg) was examined, and any surviving persons listed in it were deported."[33] By order of the Central Committee, close to a thousand Leningrad residents were exiled in January 1935, to be followed by thousands more. One eyewitness to the deportations was struck by the tragedy of forcing innocent, often elderly people from their lifelong homes: "I had never seen such despair, such horror. The procedure was as follows. A person was arrested and then after two days was released with instructions to come back with his or her passport; the passport was taken away, and in its place a document was issued, ordering the person to leave for a particular locality within twenty-four hours."[34]

The story of Olga Krupovich illustrates how this vendetta affected "ordinary people." Krupovich, who lived with her husband, a bookkeeper, in Leningrad and worked as a teacher in a nursery school, recalled years later what happened to her:

> We lived well, happily, because we were happy, cheerful, contented people. And suddenly everything collapsed. On 1 December 1934 Sergei Mironovich Kirov was murdered, and, although we had no connection to this event, we and many others (close to 100,000) were exiled from Leningrad to various places—in our case to Ufa [in the Ural Mountains] for five years, as "murderers of Kirov." . . . They took my husband during the night of March 8 [1935]. I had on that day [International Women's Day] to give a performance with the children, and you can imagine my mood. But we had the celebration. My husband returned in five days. . . . We began packing and selling our things, since we had no money for the trip.[35]

The couple had only a short time to prepare for their sad journey. The train to Ufa, Olga Krupovich said, they called the "train of tears," because all the passengers were crying. Once in Ufa, living with several others in one room of a peasant hut, she and her husband managed, after great difficulty, to find work. In August 1937, just as they had begun to get used to their new place of residence—where temperatures dipped to −40 degrees Fahrenheit in winter—and feel themselves at home, the police took Krupovich's husband away. As a result of his arrest, Krupovich immediately lost her job. Within a short time she too was arrested and sentenced to ten years in the camps.[36]

The intelligentsia was hit particularly hard by Stalin's vendetta. Lyubov Shaporina, founder of the Puppet Theater and wife of the famous composer Iurii Shaporin, kept a diary of life in Leningrad at this time and chronicled the wave of arrests and deportations that began after the Kirov murder. At the end of March 1935, she wrote: "The month of March, it was like some terrible, nightmarish avalanche coming through, destroying families and homes in its path. It is all so unreal: it came, and it's still here, right before your eyes, but you still can't believe it." Shaporina described the bizarre contrast between what was portrayed in the press and what was really happening. The *Red Evening Gazette,* for example, carried a sentimental story about how schoolchildren in Leningrad were building starling houses for birds, so that when they arrived they would find shelter awaiting them. Meanwhile, Shaporina wrote, "tens of thousands of people of all ages, from newborn babies to old women in their eighties, are being thrown out in the most literal sense of the word onto the street and their nests are destroyed. And here we get STARLING HOUSES."[37]

These reprisals in Leningrad—random as they seemed in the choice of victims—were conducted under the guise of routing all remnants of the Zinoviev opposition. But Stalin did not stop there. With the help of the new Leningrad party secretary, Andrei Zhdanov, he set out to destroy, albeit gradually, the entire party apparatus that had worked under Kirov, the very men who had moved in to replace the Zinoviev supporters after Kirov had come to Leningrad in early 1926. From Stalin's point of view, their loyalty to Kirov made them suspect. Or perhaps they knew too much about the circumstances of Kirov's murder.

Nadezhda Kodatskaia remembers well what happened to her father, Leningrad city soviet chief Ivan Kodatskii, after Kirov died. Kodatskii had worked closely with Kirov ever since the latter's arrival in Leningrad in 1926. Living together in the same building, Kirov and Kodatskii saw a great deal of each other. They would get together with their families on holidays, and Kodatskii frequently accompanied Kirov on his hunting trips. Nadezhda, around ten years old at the time, recalled that her parents did not discuss the details of the murder, but it was clear that they were deeply concerned about the implications for them.[38]

Kirov's replacement, Zhdanov, made changes in the Leningrad party and government bureaucracy that Kodatskii disapproved of. He had trouble working with Zhdanov, so he found a new position in Moscow, as a department chief in the Commissariat of Heavy Industry under Sergo Ordzhonikidze, who had apparently taken him, as a friend of Kirov, under his wing. In early 1937, shortly before Kodatskii was to arrive in Moscow, Sergo died. Kodatskii took up his new job anyway, while his family stayed behind in Leningrad. But by the spring of 1937 he was under arrest. Two months later, the NKVD took away Kodatskii's wife, leaving young Nadezhda and her teenage brother by themselves in the family's apartment. Finally, in December 1937, the police came for her brother, whom she never saw again. He did not survive his five-year labor camp sentence. Nadezhda, who ended up in an orphanage, did not find out until many years later, after she wrote countless letters to her father without receiving a response, that he had been shot not long after his arrest.[39]

Kirov's deputy in Leningrad, Mikhail Chudov, suffered a fate similar to that of Kodatskii. Chudov was removed from his post as second secretary of the Leningrad party apparatus in July 1936 in the wake of a virulent press campaign against "Trotskyites and Zinovievites" in one of the Leningrad party districts. Like Kodatskii, Chudov was transferred to Moscow, where he took up a minor trade union post. The die was cast against him: in May 1937 Leningrad party chief Zhdanov announced to a meeting of stunned party officials that Chudov and Kodatskii had been exposed as enemies of the people. One of those present, party worker Dora Lazurkina, recalled that "it was as if our tongues were tied." When she courageously went up to Zhdanov after the session to protest Chudov's innocence, Zhdanov warned her: "Lazurkina, stop this talk, otherwise things will end badly for you."[40] As it turned out, Lazurkina was arrested some months later and spent the next twenty years in labor camps. As for Chudov, he was shot, along with Kodatskii, in October 1937.

In fact, Chudov was actually not a Kirov loyalist in the sense that Kodatskii was, but that made no difference to Stalin. Although he was outwardly a team player, Chudov was not above the typical party intrigues, and Kirov apparently had not trusted him completely. (In his letters to Chudov when he was away from Leningrad in September 1934, Kirov implied that information was being deliberately kept from him.)[41] Perhaps because people knew about tensions in Chudov's relationship with Kirov, they spread rumors about his having been involved in Kirov's murder. The fact that Chudov had called a meeting of party officials on the third floor of the Smolnyi on 1 December, thereby clearing the corridors of people that fateful afternoon, may also have struck some as more than a coincidence, especially if Kirov had given Chudov advance notice that he planned to show up there. But Mikhail Rosliakov, who knew both Kirov and Chudov well, insists that Chudov had no role in Kirov's murder, which is probably true. Chudov had little to gain—in fact everything to lose, it turned out—by Kirov's death. Zhdanov, an unflinching follower of the Stalinist line, was a far worse boss than Kirov had been. Also, it is unlikely that the NKVD, with its own chain of command separate from the party, would have confided its plans in Chudov.

In fact, Chudov surmised early on that Stalin and the NKVD were behind the crime. His wife, arrested soon after her husband was taken away, said as much to Anna Larina, whom she ran into in the camps in early 1938. Larina, who had been arrested in June 1937, recalls in her memoirs the conversation that took place after she asked Chudov's wife what had really happened:

> She looked at me for a long time, her face reddened, nervous and distraught. Finally, she exclaimed, "What questions you put to me! Can one really talk about this?"
>
> "I think we can, Lyudmila Kuzminichna. We can!"
>
> "Yes, yes, I'm going to die anyway, but you must go on living. I'm not afraid for myself, but for you. However . . . can you keep as silent as the grave?"
>
> Naturally, I insisted I could. She was persuaded.
>
> "Zinoviev didn't need to get Kirov. This came down from the very top, on orders from the Boss." [That's exactly how she put it.] "After Kirov was shot, many Leningraders understood this. Chudov did, too."[42]

Mikhail Rosliakov, who also "knew too much," was one of the few former subordinates of Kirov in Leningrad who survived the purges and the camps, probably as a result of a rare oversight. After being transferred in 1935 to the city of Gorky to work in the finance department there, Rosliakov was arrested in November 1937 on charges of being a member of a terrorist group. He spent three years in prison before being sent to a labor camp in 1940. It was not until 1956, almost twenty years after his arrest, that Rosliakov returned from the camps to Leningrad and began writing his memoirs about Kirov (which could not be published until Gorbachev instituted glasnost).[43]

▪ BUKHARIN AND THE KIROV MURDER

Anna Larina recalled how shocked she was when she heard from Chudov's wife that Stalin had ordered the murder: "When Kirov was murdered, in December 1934, I was not able to think my way through to a conclusion. But after my arrest, while in Astrakhan prison, I found myself entertaining the most terrible thoughts. Even so, now that my rising suspicions were confirmed, I could only gasp, 'How horrible!'"[44] Larina insists in her memoirs that neither she nor her husband had suspected that Stalin was behind the murder. "Bukharin," she says, "could not then plumb Stalin's intentions, even though he recognized the man's love of political intrigue, pathological suspicion, and thirst for revenge. Although Bukharin was therefore confident that the Gensek [General Secretary] could remove any opponent, any potential candidate for his post, by political means, he never imagined that Stalin might eliminate him physically."[45]

According to Larina, Bukharin refused to discuss the Kirov murder with her. Perhaps, as his biographer Stephen Cohen suggests, he simply did not want to burden his young wife, only twenty years old at the time, with the immense implications of his suspicions about Stalin.[46] In any case, by 1936, after the widespread arrests in connection with the murder and the first trial of Kamenev and Zinoviev, Bukharin cannot have been under any illusions about Stalin. In the spring of that year, Bukharin traveled to Paris on business, and met several times with the prominent Menshevik Boris Nicolaevsky. The details of these meetings are unknown. But when Nicolaevsky published his anonymous "Letter of an Old Bolshevik" in an émigré journal at the end of 1936, he used information that Bukharin related to him.[47]

In a long section on Kirov and his murder, this now famous letter described Kirov as a "one hundred percent supporter" of the party's general line, who could not be accused of "undue tenderness in the manner in which he disposed of human lives." But, the letter went on, Kirov was also someone who was flexible and independent, which annoyed Stalin. He had spoken out against the death penalty for Riutin, and stood clearly for the abolition of terror in both the party and the country. The letter discussed Kirov's prestige in Leningrad and the tremendous reception he had received at the Seventeenth Party Congress, thus implying that he was somehow a political threat to Stalin. In recounting the details of the murder, the letter pointed out several suspicious circumstances, including the absence of guard protection, and then asked "Who had an interest in the removal of Kirov before he was to have moved to Moscow?"[48]

The letter was a remarkable document, because it put forth an insider's view of the Soviet leadership at a time when it was shrouded in secrecy. More important, it was one of the first sources to claim that Kirov was a moderate (in Soviet terms) and that Stalin might have viewed him as a rival, thus fueling suspicions in the West that Stalin had ordered the murder. It was not until years later, in 1964, that Nicolaevsky revealed that he had written the document after a conversation between himself and Bukharin in Paris. He also acknowledged that he incorporated other sources into the letter. This may account for some factual errors that Bukharin would never have made, such as the statement that Ordzhonikidze accompanied Stalin to Leningrad on 1 December and that Nikolaev had been employed by the secret police.[49]

Because of these errors, some Western historians raised doubts about the letter's authenticity, especially after Anna Larina denied in her memoirs that the letter represented the substance of Nicolaevsky's conversations with Bukharin.[50] But Larina, who did not learn of the letter until the 1960s, was with her husband in Paris for only part of his 1936 visit, and she had no way of knowing everything that was said between him and Nicolaevsky. Also, some parts of the letter do seem strikingly consistent with Bukharin's views. Recall, for example, that Bukharin's article in *Pravda* in December 1934 asked the very same question raised in the letter: Who would have gained by Kirov's death? And Bukharin's answer— those who want to crush internal reforms and provoke a crisis—also accords with the letter.[51]

Larina's anger about the letter stems partly from her belief that Nicolaevsky deliberately incriminated Bukharin and that the NKVD used the letter to strengthen their case against Bukharin after his arrest in February 1937. Yet, while it may be that the NKVD and Stalin found out about the letter and suspected that Bukharin was the author, they cannot have received a copy of it until late 1936 or early 1937, by which time Bukharin's fate had already been decided. When Bukharin was away from Moscow in August 1936, the press published testimonies of Zinoviev and Kamenev at their public trial there. To Bukharin's great dismay, they admitted to having had ties with leaders of the former right opposition— Bukharin, Tomskii, and Rykov. On 21 August, USSR Prosecutor Vyshinskii announced that he had initiated an investigation regarding these testimonies, and on the next day Tomskii committed suicide. When the death sentences against the defendants in the trial were announced, Bukharin telegraphed Stalin in desperation, requesting that he delay the executions until he could have a face-to-face encounter with Zinoviev. Of course, there was no response.[52]

Kamenev and Zinoviev had been languishing in prison since their arrests in the Moscow Center case in December 1934. NKVD chief Iagoda had suggested to Stalin that the pair be disposed of quickly by trying them secretly. But Stalin had insisted on a large public trial. As with the earlier cases, Stalin followed the investigation carefully, studying the interrogation reports and even adding new defendants to the list. In early August the prosecutor, Vyshinskii, sent Stalin a copy of the indictment for editing.[53]

The charges against Zinoviev and Kamenev had expanded significantly since their first trial in January 1935, when they were accused of merely "inspiring" the murder of Kirov. Now they were charged, along with fourteen other defendants, of being part of a terrorist group that was receiving instructions from Trotsky and plotting the assassination of Kirov and several Soviet leaders, including Stalin. Worn down physically by the constant interrogation and unbearable prison conditions and assured personally by Stalin that their lives would be spared if they confessed, the accused agreed to go to trial. This was the first trial in the Kirov murder to be held publicly, with representatives from the Western press and diplomatic corps in the audience, and it generated considerable publicity.

What this audience witnessed—and apparently believed—were complete confessions from Zinoviev, Kamenev, and the other accused. Both gave lurid details of how they had planned the murder and organized a terrorist group to kill other Bolshevik leaders. One wonders about the reaction of those familiar with the Kirov murder when they heard the testimony of one defendant: "Nikolaev gave me the impression of being a determined and convinced terrorist. He told me that he had succeeded in finding out the exact time when Kirov traveled from his apartment to the Smolnyi, that he could kill Kirov either near the Smolnyi or in the Smolnyi."[54] Since Nikolaev can only have learned about Kirov's unplanned arrival at the Smolnyi that day from one source—the NKVD, which controlled his bodyguard—the testimony implicated the NKVD. This may not have been an oversight on the part of the prosecution. Within a year and a half Iagoda would be publicly tried for taking part in the murder. In fact, the very next month Stalin fired Iagoda from his job as NKVD chief, for being "incapable of unmasking the Trotskyite-Zinovievite bloc," and replaced him with Central Committee secretary Nikolai Ezhov.[55]

In the "Letter of an Old Bolshevik," Nicolaevsky wrote: "Iagoda has been deposed because he made some mild opposition to the staging of the [Zinoviev–Kamenev] trial, of which he learned only after the preparations had been completed, and urged that the case be discussed in the 'Politburo.'"[56] According to archival documents published years later, when Iagoda received copies of testimonies from the growing list of defendants, who drew Trotsky into the plot, he wrote such things as "impossible" and "a lie."[57]

Not surprisingly, Iagoda was becoming uneasy about Stalin's insistence on bringing in more and more accomplices to the Kirov murder. He probably foresaw that the net would eventually draw him in, a possibility that became all the more likely with the incriminating comments made at the August 1936 show trial about Bukharin and the rightists. In fact, unbeknownst to Iagoda, Tomskii had written a suicide note to Stalin in which he said that his wife would name those persons responsible for leading him on the path of "right deviationism." When interviewed subsequently by Ezhov, Tomskii's wife said that Tomskii was referring to Iagoda.[58]

Thus Iagoda now was being shifted from the role of executioner on Stalin's behalf to that of Stalin's victim, although the process, as was customary with Stalin, would be subtle. The story of his connection to Bukharin and the rightists and his role in the Kirov murder would not be revealed until March 1938, with his appearance as a defendant in the notorious show trial of Bukharin. In fact, despite the tantalizing hint of reprisals against Bukharin and other rightists offered by Vyshinskii, the plan got stalled. On 10 September the press had announced that their investigation had been suspended and the charges dropped because of lack of evidence. Some historians have speculated that, with Stalin at this time in Sochi, the Politburo members in Moscow may have opposed the idea of going after Bukharin. But this apparent retreat may simply have been a tactical maneuver. Bukharin and Rykov were still party members, as well as candidate members of the Central Committee, who enjoyed wide respect. It was thus expedient to prepare the party for their arrests by attacking them in the press beforehand.[59]

▪ THE FATE OF ORDZHONIKIDZE

Realizing that things were closing in on him, Bukharin wrote Sergo in October 1936. On at least two earlier occasions he had asked Sergo to intervene on his behalf to prevent reprisals against him by the party. By this time, however, Bukharin was more fatalistic. He explained to Sergo that, although he was still an editor of *Izvestiia*, he would not be able to have his article published there to commemorate Sergo's fiftieth birthday, as might have been expected:

> I am not writing to complain, but to ensure that you don't draw the wrong conclusions. The slanderers are trying to hold me at their fingertips. And there are still people here who are trying to torment and torture me.
>
> I only want to convey to you my most sincere, heartfelt, fervent, kind congratulations, which are based on my deep love for you. My entire soul trembles as I am writing you this letter. Be healthy, strong and hearty.[60]

Sergo was not able to prevent the onslaught against Bukharin, although he did demonstrate some passive resistance to it. When Stalin and Ezhov pilloried Bukharin at a Central Committee plenum in December 1936, shortly before his arrest, Sergo did not chime in, as Molotov, Kaganovich, Beria, and others did. In fact, the only words he spoke were to affirm something that Bukharin had said. After the plenum, when Sergo received a copy of the stenogram for his approval, he returned it to the Secretariat with the notation "Comrade Sergo will not correct this."[61]

But Sergo could do no more. In fact, he had already been compelled to stand by helplessly as his trusted deputy Iurii Piatakov was arrested in September 1936. Sergo cannot have possibly believed the extravagant charges of sabotage against Piatakov, even when he saw copies of Piatakov's interrogation, in which he admitted his guilt. Then, in October 1936, just as he was about to celebrate his fiftieth birthday while vacationing in the North Caucasus, Sergo heard that his brother Papulia had been arrested in Georgia. Not surprisingly, he was so upset that he refused to attend the special celebration in his honor. Georgian party chief Beria had ordered the arrest, and Sergo was reportedly furious at him. But Beria would not have taken such an initiative without Stalin's sanction. Thus, when Sergo appealed to Stalin for his brother's release, he came up against a stone wall. Upon his return from the Caucasus, Sergo faced more trouble: the NKVD had begun new arrests of his subordinates in the Commissariat of Heavy Industry.[62]

Sergo did his best to buy time for some of his factory directors who were implicated in cases of sabotage and even tried to persuade Prosecutor Vyshinskii to drop charges, but to no avail. By early 1937 Piatakov had been executed, and the staggering numbers of arrests among his subordinates, friends, and relatives were clearly overwhelming Sergo. On 5 February 1937, just a few days after the execution of Piatakov, Sergo gave a speech to officials at the Commissariat of Heavy Industry, who by this time were aware of their impending doom. The transcript of his speech, which was never published, but was retained in the Ordzhonikidze archive, is a testimony to Sergo's bitter and confused state:

> A very interesting question plagues me: how can this have occurred? We have been working together for so many years, and not so badly, the results are not bad. We fulfilled the Five-Year Plan in four years. How could it be that Piatakov was with us and no one realized anything? You'll tell me: "He was your deputy, we didn't realize." But in this case, then why have we gathered here? . . . Why did it happen? Was it because we have been blind? We must ask ourselves this question. If we will not be tried in a court, it is we who must try ourselves, before our own consciences.[63]

This time, however, Sergo's despair did not prevent him from acting. After promising that the party would surely continue to differentiate between real criminals and innocent party servants, he urged his department heads to defend their employees against false accusations. The factory directors and workers needed to be assured, Sergo said, that they were not responsible for Piatakov's deeds, that they were not criminals, but excellent employees.[64]

In an amazing gesture of defiance, Sergo took things one step further. He formed a series of commissions from his employees to visit the factories and investigate what was happening there, thus undercutting the NKVD's reports on sabotage. His commissariat would conduct its own on-site investigations of the NKVD charges of sabotage at the factories. He planned to present their findings at the upcoming Central Committee plenum, scheduled to take place on 20 February.[65]

On that same day, 5 February, Sergo gave the Secretariat the draft of a speech he was to deliver at the upcoming plenum. The plenum was to consider, among other things, the case of Bukharin and Rykov, and the "lessons of the sabotage, diversion, and espionage of the Trotskyites." Stalin had ordered Politburo members to give reports on sabotage within their own jurisdictions, the drafts of which he would approve. In his draft on the Commissariat of Heavy Industry, Sergo kept references to sabotage as formal as possible and emphasized instead technical and economic problems. Stalin was not happy with the report, covering it with notations and marks.[66]

Sergo's resistance to a witch-hunt in the Commissariat of Heavy Industry, only recently revealed from declassified archival documents, is remarkable indeed. To be sure, it was very much a case of "too little too late." If Sergo had seriously intended to do anything to stop the momentum of Stalin's terror, he should have done it two years earlier, when Stalin initiated the arrests in the Kirov case. By this time nothing could stop Stalin, or even jolt people out of their pattern of passive, unquestioning acceptance of his terror. Nonetheless, given the circumstances, Sergo's defiance was a courageous challenge, a challenge Stalin could not tolerate.

As it turned out, Sergo never delivered his speech at the plenum. On 18 February 1937, at 5:30 in the afternoon, he died from a gunshot wound. The circumstances of his death—namely, the question of whether it was murder or suicide—have never been resolved. Sergo had spent the day before busily preparing for the plenum. After a long meeting with Stalin in the morning, he had arrived at his office shortly after noon, remaining there until he went over to the Kremlin for a Politburo meeting. After a late supper at his apartment, Sergo returned to his office, where he met with some subordinates and set up appointments for the next day. There was no sign of an impending tragedy. It was business as usual.

However, upon arriving home about 1:30 a.m. on the 18th, Sergo heard disturbing news from his wife, Zinaida: the NKVD had just searched their apartment. Highly agitated, Sergo telephoned Stalin to protest. According to what Zinaida Ordzhonikidze later recounted to one of Sergo's deputies, Stalin said calmly to Sergo: "Sergo, what are you so upset about? This organ [the NKVD] can search me at any moment too." To this remark Sergo responded: "That means that above the government and party stands the state security service, which directs them?" "Listen," Stalin answered, "you had better come over here and we will talk." Sergo flew out the door without his coat and hat, which Zinaida carried, running after him. She ended up waiting an hour and a half for her husband outside Stalin's apartment. He emerged very upset.[67]

On the morning of 18 February, Sergo did not get out of bed and he refused breakfast. He stayed in his room, requesting that he not be disturbed. His wife overheard a brief, angry conversation with someone (probably Stalin) in Georgian over the telephone, but aside from that Sergo talked to no one. When a visitor arrived at his apartment in the afternoon, Sergo refused to see him. As the afternoon wore on, Zinaida became concerned about her husband and decided to go to his room. On her way she heard a shot explode. She found Sergo lying lifeless on the bed in a pool of blood. Zinaida immediately telephoned Stalin, who arrived a few minutes later with other Politburo members. Stalin informed her that the official cause of death would be reported as a heart attack and warned her not say a word to anyone about what had really happened.[68]

Given Sergo's history of heart trouble, the story that he died of a heart attack was not implausible and may have been believed by some.[69] But after Stalin's death, at the Twentieth Party Congress in 1956, Khrushchev announced publicly that Sergo's death was a suicide. Ordzhonikidze apparently knew what was in store for his comrades and relatives, as well as possibly himself. In poor health and depressed by the executions and arrests that had already occurred, he must have decided that he could not live any longer.

Although Sergo had planned to assert himself at the plenum and oppose further NKVD investigations into sabotage in heavy industry, the NKVD search of his apartment and his confrontation with Stalin may have made him realize what he was up against. He may have decided that opposition to Stalin and NKVD chief Ezhov at the plenum was pointless and that suicide was the only form of protest left. He would follow in the footsteps of Lominadze, Tomskii, and others and, in doing so, he would at the very least throw Stalin off balance. Sergo had observed at a December 1936 Central Committee meeting Stalin's emotional outburst against these Bolshevik suicide victims, in which he called them traitors and conspirators, so Sergo knew that his suicide would have an impact.[70]

Given the murky circumstances of Sergo's death, including the publication of a false medical report citing a heart attack as the cause, it is not surprising that speculation about murder arose. Clearly, Stalin had a motive for killing Sergo, who was about to oppose his policies at the plenum. But there was no credible explanation of how a murderer could have entered his apartment and then escaped while Sergo's wife was there. Whatever really happened, one thing is clear: Stalin had already determined Sergo's fate. If he had not died in February 1937, he would have faced NKVD executioners sooner or later.

Sergo's death, like that of Kirov, shook party members to the core. Again, Mariia Svanidze recorded her impressions in her diary, the entries of which were becoming increasingly intermittent, no doubt because she too had premonitions of her impending doom. In contrast to her entries after Kirov died, she expressed no concern about how Stalin was taking Sergo's death, even though he had been close to Sergo and she, as a family member, was still seeing Stalin regularly. It is interesting that, although the official report was that Sergo died of a heart attack, Mariia Svanidze, in a sort of stream-of-consciousness raving, attributed Sergo's death to the same forces that were alleged to have killed Kirov. After a reference to the recent trial of Sergo's deputy Piatakov on charges of being a Trotskyite, she went on:

> They prepared for the terrible end of our country, they wanted to kill our husbands and sons. They killed Kirov and they killed Sergo. Sergo died on 18 February, killed by the baseness of Piatakov and his minions. We are enduring the passing of Sergo gravely and tearfully. The hall of columns, the wreaths, the music, the smell of flowers, the tears, the honor guards, the thousands and thousands of people passing by the grave . . . all this comes into the ears and in front of our eyes, but Sergo is gone.[71]

Did Svanidze know that Sergo had died from a gunshot wound? In any case, she seems to have assumed that there would be a new version of Sergo's death, with more accusations of terrorism and murder by Zinovievites and Trotskyites.

After a visit to Sergo's widow, Svanidze remarked on how heroic she was: "She herself directed the funeral, was continuously by the coffin. She reads the letters and telegrams calmly and rationally. She goes to work and quietly discusses her future life. She said at first that with Sergo gone there was nothing to live for and that she didn't want to live like M[ariia] L['vovna] Kirova, but then she got hold of herself and will live just like Sergo would have wanted."[72] Unlike Svanidze, who would soon be arrested along with her husband (the brother of Stalin's first wife) and shot, Zinaida Ordzhonikidze had her life spared. Stalin and Ezhov had no qualms about going after Sergo's siblings and close friends, but for some reason they left his wife alone.

▪ THE END OF OPPOSITION

It is ironic that just a few days before Sergo died Bukharin, knowing that he was about to be arrested, had written Sergo a farewell letter, expressing his fears that, once in prison, he would be forced by the NKVD to make false confessions, just like Sergo's deputy Piatakov and the others. He was certain, Bukharin wrote, that Sergo understood that the testimonies were all false, concocted by the NKVD. Bukharin declared his innocence, asked Sergo to understand him, and ended, like Lominadze did in his final letter to Sergo, by asking him to take care of his family in the event of his arrest. Specifically, he asked Sergo to look after their little son until Anna Larina could pull herself together and find work.

This latter request displeased Anna Larina, who considered herself completely capable of caring for her baby. For this reason, Larina put off sending the letter, and within a short time, there was no one to receive it. Thinking back on this letter, Larina observed that it was naive of Bukharin to make a request for help from Sergo, who even if he had stayed alive would not have been in a position to do anything.[73] Indeed, it is curious that, even at this stage, Bukharin did not seem to realize that Sergo too was doomed, that no one in the Kremlin could offer him protection from Stalin's wrath.

Bukharin's arrest, along with that of Rykov, came just nine days after Sergo's death, during a session of a Central Committee plenum, the opening of which had been postponed because of the tragedy. Their arrests were not unexpected. The two had been accused of a raft of heinous crimes by plenum participants and shouted down when they sought to defend themselves—an even worse spectacle than the December 1936 plenum. The specifics of the charges had not been spelled out, but the ties that Bukharin and Rykov were accused of having with "Zinovievite-Trotskyite terrorists" made it apparent that eventually they would be linked to Kirov's murder. In view of the fact that Bukharin and Rykov had advocated rightist policies, diametrically opposed to those of the leftists Zinoviev and Kamenev, the accusations of an alliance with this group might have seemed farfetched (although Bukharin reportedly did make an approach to Kamenev in 1928). By this time, however, all elements of rationality had disappeared from political discussions, and the talk was only of conspiracy and betrayal.[74]

The dramatic show trial of Bukharin and Rykov, as members of a so-called Bloc of Rightists and Trotskyites, took place in Moscow in March 1938, tying up the loose ends of the Kirov case. The details of the trial, which served as the inspiration for Arthur Koestler's novel *Darkness at Noon* and ended with the executions of ten defendants, including Bukharin,

Rykov, and Iagoda, have been recounted by others.[75] Suffice it to say that, among the many charges leveled at the rightists was their role, through Iagoda and the NKVD, in arranging the murder of Kirov. Bukharin and Rykov steadfastly denied any complicity in the murder, but, as noted earlier, Iagoda confessed to having given secret directions to Leningrad NKVD deputy Zaporozhets, executed a year before. He also stated that Zaporozhets had arranged to have Kirov's guard Borisov killed in an automobile accident because Borisov had been involved in the assassination of Kirov, and Zaporozhets was afraid that he might betray him.

It was implausible, however, to have Iagoda, who had no logical motive for wanting to kill Kirov, directing the whole crime. So a new character was dredged up to take on the role of the ringleader—Avel' Enukidze, Stalin's old Georgian comrade who had been secretary of the Central Executive Committee before his arrest and execution in late 1937. Enukidze was portrayed as the one who gave Iagoda his marching orders, overriding Iagoda's objections. In Iagoda's words: "I tried to object, I marshaled a series of arguments about this terrorist act being inexpedient and unnecessary. I even argued that I, as a person responsible for guarding members of the government, would be the first to be held responsible in case a terrorist act was committed against a member of the government. Needless to say, my objections were not taken into consideration and had no effect."[76]

While it was convenient to choose someone who was dead as the ultimate villain, Enukidze was an unlikely candidate. He had enjoyed far less authority than Iagoda and would never have been able to compel Iagoda to do anything. According to Trotsky, Enukidze had been on Stalin's blacklist because he protested the fierce reprisals against the Leninist old guard, even telephoning members of the Politburo. There was also a rumor that Enukidze was the author of "Letter of an Old Bolshevik," but Trotsky considered that ridiculous because "Avel' wasn't up to this." After his arrest, Enukidze refused to cooperate and confess to ties with the rightists, which would have given him a place in the dock during the March 1938 trial. Instead he was quietly shot.[77]

Iagoda may have objected to arranging the Kirov murder, as he said at his trial, but the only person who could have ordered him to do so against his will would have been Stalin, not Enukidze. Why did Stalin and Ezhov have Iagoda stand trial to begin with? First of all, he served as a useful means for implicating the rightists, because the claim about Iagoda's ties to

Bukharin and the rightists was not completely without foundation.[78] Also, Stalin probably realized, particularly after the publication of the "Letter of an Old Bolshevik," that suspicions about NKVD involvement in the Kirov murder were running high. Thus it made sense to have Iagoda admit publicly to the murder. As for Iagoda himself, he had little choice but to confess. Having been in prison for almost a year, he had been tortured and otherwise worn down to the point where he was compliant. As with all the defendants, Ezhov had spent many hours with Iagoda rehearsing his testimony. Like the others, Iagoda was no doubt promised his life in exchange for his cooperation.[79]

In fact, Iagoda hinted in his testimony that he was not telling the whole story. Under questioning by Vyshinskii he responded several times with qualifications like "that's not quite how it was" and "it was not like that." But those nuances were probably lost on the courtroom audience, whose attention was captured by the terrible accusations against venerable old Bolsheviks and the humiliation and degradation they were subjected to. Most of the charges must have seemed preposterous. No one could have possibly believed that Bukharin and Rykov were capable of murdering not only Kirov but also, as the charges read, Kuibyshev, Soviet writer Maxim Gorky, and others.[80] Yet defendant upon defendant abjectly confessed. Bukharin was the only one to attempt to defend himself and expose the real purpose of the trial, although he too was guarded in what he said, presumably because he wanted to protect his family.[81]

With the executions of the defendants in this final show trial, Stalin had destroyed all of his real or perceived Bolshevik opponents except one—Trotsky, who was accused at the trial of having directed the entire conspiracy from abroad. Sentenced to death in absentia by a Soviet court, Trotsky was a marked man. After two unsuccessful attempts, the sentence was carried out in Mexico in 1940 by an NKVD-recruited assassin named Ramon Mercader.

Shortly after the Kirov murder, a group of American Communists had cabled Trotsky requesting him to give his opinion on the assassination, which he did in a thirty-page pamphlet.[82] He had scoffed at the idea that Zinoviev and Kamenev would have wanted to kill Kirov: "The implication that Kirov may have been the victim of vengeance for depriving Zinoviev of leading posts in Leningrad is manifestly absurd. Eight years have since gone by. Zinoviev himself and his friends have had time enough to repent twice, the 'grievances' of 1926 have long ago paled in the face of events of infinitely greater importance." Nonetheless, although he suggested that the NKVD was involved in Kirov's murder, he did not directly implicate Stalin. He assumed instead that the NKVD had only encouraged Nikolaev as a provocation and had intended to thwart the murder at the last moment, accusing Stalin's political opponents of making an attempt on Kirov's life through Nikolaev.

Although Trotsky, who was forming his hypothesis on the basis of incomplete information from the Soviet Union, seems to have misjudged Stalin's role in the Kirov murder, he immediately grasped the broader implications of the case. Stalin's goal, he wrote, was "to terrorize completely all critics and oppositionists, and this time not by expulsion from the party nor by depriving them of their daily bread, nor even by imprisonment or exile, but by the firing squad. *To the terrorist act of Nicolaiev, Stalin replies by redoubling the terror against the party.*" With these words, written at the end of December 1934, Trotsky predicted the future of the Soviet Communist Party more accurately than any of his former colleagues who were directly involved in these events.

10

The Kirov Legacy

Those same hands which once screwed tight our handcuffs now hold out their palms in reconciliation: "No, don't! Don't dig up the past! Dwell on the past and you'll lose an eye." But the proverb goes on to say: "Forgive the past and you'll lose both eyes."

—*Aleksandr Solzhenitsyn in* The Gulag Archipelago

Death scenes of political leaders, even without the drama of assassination, are often controversial events when remembered later. The celebrated British historian Lord Macaulay realized this when he tried to reconstruct the details of the seemingly straightforward death of Charles II from natural causes in 1685:

> It should seem that no transactions in history ought to be more accurately known to us than those which took place round the deathbed of Charles the Second. We have several relations written by persons who were actually in his room. We have several relations written by people who, though not themselves eyewitnesses, had the best opportunity of obtaining information from eyewitnesses. Yet, whoever attempts to digest this vast mass of materials into a consistent narrative will find the task a difficult one.[1]

Lord Macaulay's complaint was not that he lacked information about Charles II's death, but rather that there were inconsistencies in the accounts. People's memories, distorted by time and emotion, can never be counted on for complete accuracy when the trauma of human death is involved.

Lord Macaulay might well have been daunted by the task of piecing together what happened at Kirov's death scene. Rather than finding reports of eyewitnesses sincerely attempting to recall what they saw, he would have encountered what the writer Michael Ignatieff has termed the "administrative memory of the totalitarian state." As Ignatieff observed, this memory was based on "fastidious record-keeping."[2] But the records, while observing the outward forms of judicial norms, were constructed on falsehoods, on the version of Stalin and the NKVD, which was intended for consumption not only by the people they ruled at the time but also by future generations.

The post-Stalin leadership colluded in the immense cover-up by keeping the archives closed until the late 1980s, when Mikhail Gorbachev initiated the policy of "openness." Before this time the evidence implicating Stalin in the murder rested almost entirely upon hearsay—stories repeated by defectors and by survivors of the labor camps, who quietly passed on what they had heard through second- and thirdhand sources. And it was not until after 1991 that the authorities began to release—on a selected basis—correspondence among members of the Politburo, records of party plenums, personal archives of men like Ordzhonikidze and Kirov, and materials from the commissions that studied the Kirov murder.

Behind the scenes, however, the Kirov murder had been a burning issue that the Communist leadership could not ignore. Indeed, one of the most remarkable and fascinating aspects of the case is how it has been played out in the forty-six years since Stalin's death. Nikita Khrushchev, who had been part of the delegation accompanying Stalin to Leningrad in December 1934 and had asked Mikhail Rosliakov several questions about the murder, first raised the issue publicly in October 1961, in a speech to the Twenty-second Party Congress. He claimed that Kirov's bodyguard Borisov had been "liquidated" on the way to his meeting with Stalin because "someone" had wanted to hide the facts of the murder and he suggested obliquely that Stalin was behind the Kirov crime by saying that there was "much to be revealed" about the case. In fact, behind closed doors, the party leadership had already launched several investigations into the Kirov case before Khrushchev made his statement.

In late December 1955, the Central Committee's Presidium (as the Politburo came to be called after Stalin's death) had a heated discussion about the repressions of the 1930s, and the question of Kirov's murder came up. When someone suggested that the NKVD might have been involved, the Presidium members decided to examine the cases of former NKVD officials Iagoda, Ezhov, and Medved. At this same meeting they formed a commission, headed by Petr Pospelov, a member of the Central Committee Secretariat, to look into the fate of the delegates to the Seventeenth Party Congress, and within a month the commission had produced a seventy-page report. But, not surprisingly, the report was never released, and it is not clear what it said, if anything, about the Kirov case.[3]

In 1956, at the time that Khrushchev began his de-Stalinization campaign, designed to dismantle the cult of Stalin, a special commission headed by Molotov was looking into the Kirov affair. A year later the commission reached the conclusion that Nikolaev had acted alone in committing the murder. Designating Molotov to head the commission was of course like putting the fox in charge of the chicken coop. Already part of Stalin's inner circle in 1934, Molotov had been with Stalin when he interrogated Nikolaev and others on 2–3 December 1934. If Stalin was involved in the Kirov murder, then Molotov was surely an accessory to the crime.

Obviously the investigation was more a political gambit than a search for the truth. Khrushchev had initiated the anti-Stalin campaign to garner public support and discredit his opponents in the leadership, but he did not want it to go too far. Although he had ended the terror and sent a message to the Soviet people that he was different from Stalin and disapproved of him, he was too closely associated with the Stalin regime to be completely honest about Stalin's crimes. In fact, a leading Russian historian has claimed that in early 1955 Khrushchev had eleven bags of documents belonging to Stalin and other leaders destroyed. He also had his KGB chief, Ivan Serov, purge the archives of any materials that might incriminate him.[4]

Whatever Khrushchev's motives, he could not in any event proceed fully with de-Stalinization as long as men like Molotov, Voroshilov, and Kaganovich were still in the Presidium. But in 1957 Khrushchev succeeded in ousting Molotov and Kaganovich from the leadership and in discrediting Voroshilov for being a member of their "anti-party group." This action helped to pave the way for a deeper, although still by no means comprehensive, investigation of the Kirov case. In 1960, another commission, under the direction of Control Commission chairman Nikolai Shvernik, looked into the case, interviewing hundreds of witnesses, eliciting written testimony from others, and examining thousands of documents. This time the commission concluded (in a report that is still classified secret) that the murder of Kirov was organized by Stalin and the NKVD and that the NKVD had killed Borisov.[5]

But some members of the party leadership, taking their cue from the KGB (a successor to the NKVD), were not satisfied with these results. In May 1961 Shvernik was instructed to launch a new investigation, together with representatives from the KGB, the Procuracy (prosecutor's office), and the Central Committee. The conclusion was the same as in 1957—that Nikolaev had acted alone and Borisov's death was an accident. This is perhaps not surprising. According to Olga Shatunovskaia, a member of the original Shvernik Commission, many key documents were destroyed or disappeared after they had reached their conclusion that Stalin was behind the murder.[6]

Meanwhile more and more witnesses were coming forth to give testimony on the Kirov affair and additional evidence was cropping up. The matter could not be dropped. In 1963, a year before Khrushchev's ouster, yet another commission, headed by Presidium member Arvid Pelshe, began the investigation anew, continuing its work until 1967. The conclusion of the Pelshe Commission reaffirmed that of the previous one—that Nikolaev had acted alone, without the involvement of Stalin or the NKVD.[7]

By this time, 1967, Leonid Brezhnev had been Communist Party chief for three years and had effectively consolidated his power. Although he was from a younger generation that had no direct association with Stalin, Brezhnev was not disposed to the idea of dredging up Stalin's past sins. An honest public reckoning with the terror would destroy the historical basis for the legitimacy of the Soviet regime. A conservative neo-Stalinist in his policies, Brezhnev made every effort to reestablish Stalin's good name in history. Further attempts to get to the bottom of the Kirov murder would have to wait until after Brezhnev and his two equally pro-Stalinist successors, Konstantin Chernenko and Iurii Andropov, had passed from the scene.

Inevitably, when Gorbachev and his colleagues condemned the purges and permitted a public discussion of their consequences, the debate over the Kirov case was reopened. This time it was not restricted to party circles, but was carried openly in the press. Personal accounts of the case by people like Rosliakov and others began to appear. Anti-Stalinist historians, like Anton Antonov-Ovseenko, whose writings had been suppressed, were suddenly coming out and saying that Stalin was the culprit, while party historians and former secret policemen were insisting on Stalin's innocence.[8] As a result, a great many new details about the Kirov case emerged, but because the archives were only opening slowly and selectively, these details could not all be documented as true.

Gorbachev's approach to the past was in some ways similar to that of Khrushchev. Although he was clearly prepared to take the de-Stalinization process much further than Khrushchev had done, he was still ambivalent about a wholesale condemnation of the Stalin period. In the words of one scholar: "the passage of decades could not destroy the corrosive potential of negative history on the regime's legitimacy."[9] To reveal that Stalin and the NKVD were behind the Kirov murder would have laid bare the cynicism and moral depravity of the entire Stalinist, and hence Soviet, system.

Given the debate that had begun in the press, however, Gorbachev could not ignore the Kirov issue. Like Khrushchev, he initiated an official investigation of the case, this time by a working group from the KGB and the USSR Procuracy. But when the working group presented its conclusions exonerating Stalin in 1990, not everyone was satisfied. Gorbachev's Politburo colleague Aleksandr Iakovlev, for one, felt that the group had, as in the past, only superficially looked at the Kirov case and had left many questions unanswered. Iakovlev himself was at the time directing a Politburo commission to study the Stalinist repressions of the 1930s, 1940s, and early 1950s, so he had a special interest in the KGB report on the Kirov case. In March 1990 Iakovlev wrote a letter (now declassified) to other members of his commission laying out his objections to the report.[10]

First, Iakovlev observed, former NKVD chief Iagoda gave testimony at closed sessions of the March 1938 trial at which he was accused of killing Kirov. Yet the working group made no attempts to find out what he said at those sessions or to ascertain why Iagoda took the blame for arranging Kirov's murder. Second, no one tried to track down records (probably located in the KGB archives) relating to the two trials of officials from the Leningrad NKVD in January 1935 and in 1937. This was a surprising omission, given that the Leningrad NKVD was central to the Kirov case. Iakovlev went on to point out that the report ignored the evidence that a special pass, which Nikolaev presumably did not have, was needed to gain access to the third floor at the Smolnyi. And he complained that the report devoted very little time to explaining Nikolaev's motives or analyzing the murder itself. In sum, Iakovlev said, "the major emphasis has been to show first of all that Stalin did not know of and had no connection of any kind with planning Kirov's assassination."[11]

Two members of the KGB working group, interviewed in *Pravda* in late 1990, insisted that they had scoured all the available evidence and that there was nothing whatsoever to suggest Stalin's involvement in the murder. On the contrary, they said, Stalin and Kirov were the closest of friends, as exemplified by the fact that Kirov had vacationed with Stalin in Sochi the summer before the murder. (Apparently they had not seen the letters that the miserable Kirov had written to his wife and others from Sochi.) This interview prompted an indignant response from Iakovlev, in the form of a long *Pravda* article in early 1991.[12] He had not intended, he said, to bring the complicated and murky Kirov case out into the open. But he felt compelled to do so in light of the earlier interview.

Iakovlev expanded on the points he had made in his secret letter to the Politburo commission and raised several additional questions, including one about correspondence between Stalin and Kirov. Immediately after the murder, Kirov's close friend Mamia Orakhelashvili had been placed in charge of gathering together all of Kirov's documents and personal papers in his office and his home. According to Iakovlev, these materials included the most recent correspondence between Kirov and Stalin. What happened to these crucial letters, he asked, and what did they say? Had they been destroyed, or did the KGB choose not to use them as evidence? In either case, the implication was that they incriminated Stalin.

The unhappy sequel to the story of officially sanctioned efforts to unravel the Kirov mystery is that, even under Yeltsin's political leadership, the authorities have remained selective in releasing archival documents, preventing the whole story from coming out. The keepers of the archives are former Communist and KGB officials schooled in the habits of secrecy that the Soviet system engendered. Moreover, they are not inclined to provide further ammunition to those who condemn the past Soviet system of which they were a part.[13]

Ironically, the Russian people themselves no longer seem so preoccupied with finding the answers anyway. After the initial flurry of interest in their past when the Soviet regime collapsed, people stopped pounding on the doors of the archives in search of historical truth. They were, it seems, worn out by all the political struggles and overwhelmed with economic concerns. It was easier just to erase the Soviet past completely by removing all the Bolshevik names—including those of hallowed figures like Lenin and Kirov—from places and monuments and bringing back the old names from the tsarist period. Rather than come to terms with the Soviet past, it was simpler to forget it—a sort of reverse version of the "administrative memory" of the Stalinist state.

But why is knowing the truth about the Kirov case so important anyway, especially now, when Russia has made substantial progress toward democracy? Is it really necessary to demonstrate, yet again, how terrible Stalin was? We already knew of his paranoia, his ruthlessness, his ability to manipulate his subordinates, his endless capacity for cruelty. He ordered the execution of millions. Does it matter whether or not he committed the additional crime of having Kirov killed?

When President Yeltsin acknowledged, in July 1998, the shameful truth about the Bolsheviks' murder of Russia's royal family, *The Economist* observed that it was somewhat off the point: "The murder of the tsar and his family was but a tiny speck on the vast canvas of horror painted in Russian blood for more than half a century." In a sense, the Kirov murder could also be viewed as just another such speck, especially since Kirov was a culprit as well as a victim. He had, after all, been an accomplice in the crimes that the young Bolshevik regime perpetrated upon its people, and he had contributed to Stalin's rise to power.

What is so significant about the Kirov case is not just the compelling evidence pointing to Stalin's complicity in the murder but the fact that this evidence was ignored. In attempting to understand why, it is necessary to look not only at Stalin but also at his victims, men like Sergo, Bukharin, and other members of the party leadership who were later purged. The ultimate blame for the success of Stalin's audacious crime—if such it was—lies with them. It was not just fear of the secret police that kept them silent. Also—and this goes back to the argument made about Bukharin earlier in the book—they doubtless thought that, if they created an open conflict by opposing Stalin, they would bring the system crashing down.

By 1934, they were probably right. We know now, from the secret reports of reactions among the workers and peasants to Kirov's murder, how widespread was the resentment toward the regime. Mikhail Rosliakov even recalled that, immediately after the murder, Leningrad party officials held a meeting to discuss how to contain the public response and prevent an outbreak of unrest. The propaganda machine was set into motion with the purpose of channeling people's emotions into loyalty toward the regime.[14]

In these circumstances, however strong their suspicions were about Stalin's role in the murder, Stalin's subordinates chose to keep quiet. They had helped to build the cult of Stalin, upon which the edifice of the state rested, and they would have thrown the entire regime into jeopardy if they questioned the official version of what happened to Kirov. It was this concern, more than fear of the NKVD, that helped to ensure the silence of people like Bukharin and Sergo Ordzhonikidze. Their situation was the inevitable consequence of having created a system that excluded all but a small elite from decision making. When one member of that elite became a tyrant and imposed himself on the others, there was no recourse. Factional struggles turned into mass bloodletting.

How, one might ask, would Kirov have reacted to Stalin's terror if he had not been murdered when he was? It is possible that he would have backed down and toed the line as the others did when their colleagues were being arrested. And he might even have eventually taken his own life in despair, as Sergo apparently did—although this is doubtful, given Kirov's temperament. On the other hand, had Kirov lived, he might have stiffened his resolve and actually shown the audacity to challenge Stalin, perhaps serving as a rallying point for those who wanted to oppose his dictatorship. Clearly Stalin thought this was a possibility, and it gave him a strong motive, as 1934 wore to a close, to have Kirov murdered. Kirov was not a rebel, but, as this book demonstrates, he was much more independent-minded than most of his Politburo colleagues, and possessed his own, solid base of support within the party. One also suspects that he would not have been a willing accomplice when the full force of Stalin's terror was unleashed on Leningrad.

The murder of Kirov in 1934, then, represented effectively the end of any possible alternatives to Stalin or to the ultimate catastrophe of the Great Terror. But its significance goes beyond what it meant for Stalin's generation. The Kirov case—not just the murder, but the investigation, trials, and propaganda that followed—served as a prototype for all future cases that the secret police would investigate. Marking the beginning of a collusion between the party leadership and the secret police in a travesty of justice for the Soviet people, it incorporated all the elements of the Soviet system of repression that would be refined in the decades to come—falsified testimonies, scapegoats, arbitrary punishments, physical and psychological torture, intimidation and threats, and meaningless judicial jargon.

Although the post-Stalin Soviet leadership put a stop to mass arrests and executions, the other essential features of the system remained in place. Read the accounts of dissidents in the 1970s and early 1980s about their encounters with Soviet justice and you will see how expertly the KGB had honed the methods of the NKVD and how well it coordinated its efforts with the goals of the party. No wonder, then, that the KGB staffers who ran the archives and their bosses in the party wanted to keep the Kirov case a secret. It laid bare the total hypocrisy of the Soviet system.

But once the archives had been opened, however slightly, it was impossible to control completely what secrets about the past were revealed. The keepers of the archives did not realize, as they carefully began screening materials for declassification, that even seemingly insignificant documents or files could contain revelations. As the story of the Kirov murder shows, the pieces of evidence, however small, can mount up to form a convincing case. Take, for example, Kirov's outwardly innocuous letters to his wife and to Sergo, written with the knowledge that they would be read by the secret police. The expression and the tone of these letters, what they say and do not say, make it quite obvious that Kirov, especially by 1934, was not well disposed toward Stalin.

In fact, the signs of conflict between him and Stalin that the censors were so intent upon hiding could be seen much earlier in documents like his 1929 speech for Stalin's birthday, where he mentions Lenin's testament. This speech, delivered at a regional party meeting and never published, was apparently overlooked by the screeners of Kirov's archive because the cover page said it was a speech on the sowing campaign.

For the time being, given the economic and political turmoil that Russia is now going through, the implications of the Kirov case and of the other crimes committed in the name of communism may be lost on the Russian people. But sooner or later, they will have to do what people of other nations with dark pasts have done and confront head-on the horrors of what their country went through under Stalin. Only then will Russia be able to rediscover its full identity as a nation. The prominent Russian historian Yuri Afanasyev described this process:

Today, as we structure our identity, we also begin to study our past. We begin with a void, with what is not there, with the investigation of emptiness and the absence of speech. . . . The newfound ability to look at facts without prejudice, without an a priori construct into which facts must be fitted presents us with an opportunity to reclaim our history. Memory is an element of social consciousness, which fundamentally must be historical in nature. By straining our memories we seek to find meaning in our lives, to understand our place in history, and ultimately to know ourselves.[15]

Afanasyev saw this new understanding of the past as already having begun in late 1996. Perhaps now that Russia is going through a period of instability and uncertainty, with the Communists regaining their influence, he might not be so optimistic. But even if the doors to the archives are again closed, the truth will continue to seep out through the cracks, and the Russian people will eventually begin to care again about their past.

Appendix I

CHRONOLOGY OF KEY EVENTS IN THE LIFE OF SERGEI KIROV

27 March 1886	Born, Urzhum, Viatka Province.
August 1901	Enrolls in Kazan Industrial School.
August 1904	Leaves for Tomsk.
November 1904	Joins Russian Social Democratic Labor Party (RSDRP).
January–February 1905	Bloody Sunday begins 1905 Revolution; Kirov arrested.
January 1906	Second arrest and imprisonment.
May 1909	Arrives in Vladikavkaz and begins work on *Terek*.
1911–12	Third arrest and imprisonment.
1917	February and October revolutions.
1918	Organizes military expedition to North Caucasus.
1919–20	Leads Bolshevik military administration in Astrakhan.
April 1920	Joins Central Committee's Caucasian Bureau; arrives in Baku, Azerbaijan, with invading Red Army.

May 1920	Appointed Russian ambassador to Georgia.
October 1920	Attends peace talks with Poland in Riga; returns to Vladikavkaz.
February 1921	Participates in Soviet invasion of Georgia.
July 1921	Becomes secretary of Communist Party of Azerbaijan; moves to Baku.
April 1923	Twelfth Party Congress in Moscow: elected member of Central Committee.
January–February 1926	Moves to Leningrad; elected first secretary of Leningrad Gubkom and Northwest Regional Bureau.
July 1926	Fourteenth Party Congress: elected candidate (nonvoting) member of Politburo.
July 1930	Sixteenth Party Congress: elected member of Politburo.
February 1934	Seventeenth Party Congress: elected secretary of Central Committee.
1 December 1934	Assassinated.

Appendix II

. . . .

GOVERNING HIERARCHY OF THE SOVIET UNION

(late 1920s–early 1930s)

Communist Party of the Soviet Union (CPSU)

Politburo
(policy decisions)

General Secretary
Secretariat
(administration and personnel)

Orgburo
(subsidiary to Politburo and Secretariat)

CPSU Central Committee
*(deliberative body meeting
a few times a year)*

Central Control Commission
(party discipline)

Party Congress
(large body of several hundred delegates meeting every two to four years)

Regional (Oblast)
Committees
or
Republic Central Committees
*(both run day-to-day by
smaller bureaus)*

Regional and Republic Control
Commissions

District and City Committees

District and City Control
Commissions

State Government

Council of People's Commissars *(Sovnarkom) (day-to-day functions)*	Central Executive Committee (VTsIK) *(large body with general government oversight)*
Commissariats: Internal Affairs (NKVD), Defense, Foreign Affairs, National Economy, Worker-Peasants' Inspectorate (RKI), etc.	All-Russian Congress of Soviets
Republic Commissariats	Republic, regional, city, and local soviets *(run by executive committees)*

Appendix III

SELECTED GLOSSARY OF NAMES

Agranov, Ia. S. (1893–1938). First deputy chief of the NKVD, 1934–37; investigated the Kirov murder. Arrested in 1937 and executed.

Anisimov, N. A. Attended historic Second All-Russian Congress of Soviets with Kirov in October 1917; military commander of Astrakhan, 1918.

Atarbekov, G. S. (1891–1925). Chief of the Cheka in the North Caucasus, 1918; worked with Kirov in Astrakhan, 1919, and later in Azerbaijan. Died in a plane crash, March 1925.

Bagirov, Mir Dzhafar (1896–1956). Chief of Azerbaijan Cheka/GPU, 1920–30 (with interruptions); from 1930, party chief in Azerbaijan.

Barmine, Alexander. Soviet diplomat; defected to the West in 1937 and later wrote memoirs.

Beria, Lavrentii (1899–1953). Official of the Cheka/GPU in Transcaucasia, 1921–31; later chief of Georgian Communist Party and in 1938 appointed head of NKVD.

Borisov, M. D. NKVD bodyguard for Kirov; died 2 December 1934.

Buachidze, Samuil. Georgian Bolshevik and comrade of Kirov in Vladikavkaz at the time of the 1917 Revolution; assassinated there in June 1918.

Bukharin, Nikolai (1888–1938). Politburo member and leading party theoretician, 1924–29; leader of right opposition; tried and executed in 1938.

Butiagin, Iurii. Kirov's deputy in Astrakhan, 1919, and later temporary commander of Eleventh Army.

Chagin, Petr. Worked under Kirov in the party apparatus in Baku; later moved to Leningrad and became editor of the paper *Krasnaia gazeta.*

Chudov, Mikhail (1893–1937). Member of Central Committee, 1925–37; second secretary of the Leningrad party organization, 1928–36. Arrested and executed in 1937.

Desov, G. A. (1884–?). Chairman of the Leningrad Control Commission, 1926–29; opponent of Kirov.

Enukidze, Avel' (1877–1937). Old Georgian Bolshevik and chairman of the Central Executive Committee at the time of Kirov's death. Arrested in 1936 and charged with, among other things, ordering the murder of Kirov.

Ezhov, Nikolai (1895–1940). Central Committee secretary, 1930–36; oversaw initial investigation of Kirov case; head of NKVD, 1936–38. Arrested, 1939.

Frunze, M. V. (1885–1925). Central Committee member from 1921 and Politburo candidate member from 1924; Commissar of Defense, from January 1925.

Iagoda, Genrikh (1891–1938). Member of the Cheka since 1919; rose to post of deputy chairman of the OGPU in 1923; chairman of OGPU/NKVD, 1934–36; arrested in 1937 and executed in 1938.

Iakovlev, Aleksandr (1923–   ). Secretary of CPSU Central Committee, 1986–91; member of Politburo, 1987–91; historian and member of the Academy of Sciences; head of a Politburo Commission in the late 1980s to study the repressions under Stalin.

Kaganovich, L. M. (1893–1991). First secretary of Moscow Party Committee, 1930–35; Politburo member, 1930–52. Expelled from the Central Committee in 1957, after trying to oust Khrushchev.

Kamenev, Lev (1883–1936). Deputy chairman of Council of People's Commissars, Politburo member, 1919–26; arrested in connection with Kirov murder for being part of the Moscow Center, December 1934. Tried and executed in 1936.

Khrushchev, N. S. (1894–1971). Held mid-level party and economic posts in the 1920s and early 1930s. In 1935 became chief of Moscow party apparatus and later of the Ukrainian party. First secretary of the CPSU Central Committee, 1953–64.

Kodatskii, Ivan Fedorovich (1893–1938). From 1925 to 1934, Leningrad party posts, then chairman of the Leningrad Regional and City Executive Committees; member of the Leningrad Regional and City Party Committee Bureaus; and member of the CPSU Central Committee. Arrested in 1937.

Komarov, N. P. (1886–1937). Chairman of the Leningrad Regional Executive Committee, 1926–29; worked in economic posts in Moscow after 1929; executed in 1937.

Kuibyshev, Valerian (1888–1935). Politburo member, 1927–35; chairman of the Supreme Economic Council, 1926–30; deputy chairman and chairman of Gosplan, 1930–35.

Larina, Anna. Bukharin's widow and the author of memoirs, *This I Cannot Forget.*

Lominadze, Beso (1897–1935). Georgian Bolshevik; chief of the party organization in Transcaucasia in 1930, but soon dismissed because of his role in an opposition group. Later worked as party secretary in Magnitogorsk before committing suicide in early 1935.

Medved, Filipp (1899–1937). Chief of Leningrad GPU/NKVD, 1929–34; arrested, 1934; executed, 1937.

Mikoyan, Anastas (1895–1978). Revolutionary activity in the Caucasus until mid-1920; party secretary in regional organizations, 1920–26; various national economic posts, 1926–35; Politburo member, 1935–66.

Mirzoian, Levon (1897–1939). Secretary of Central Committee of Azerbaijan Communist Party, 1925–29; then party secretary in Kazakhstan; close friend of Kirov. Arrested in 1937.

Molotov, Viacheslav (1890–1986). Central Committee secretary, 1921–36; member of Politburo, 1926–57; chairman of Council of People's Commissars, 1930–41; later Minister of Foreign Affairs; fell out with Khrushchev and disgraced, 1957.

Orakhelashvili, Mamia (1881–1937). Georgian Bolshevik; worked with Kirov in the North Caucasus at the time of the 1917 Revolution; party chief of Transcaucasia, 1926–31; tried for treason and shot, 1937.

Petrovskii, Petr. Editor of *Leningradskaia pravda*, 1926–28; in 1932 suspended from party and arrested for membership in Bukharin's right opposition and for connections with the Riutin group. Later released, but arrested again in 1937. Executed in 1941.

Piatakov, Iurii (1890–1937). Central Committee member, 1923–36, and Deputy Commissar of Heavy Industry (under Ordzhonikidze), 1931–36. Tried and executed, 1937.

Pozern, Boris (1882–1939). Commissar in the Red Army during the civil war; then employed in economic and party work in Leningrad. Edited two volumes of Kirov's collected articles and speeches. Killed during the purges.

Riutin, M. M. (1890–1937). Regional party secretary; candidate member of Central Committee; in 1931 sentenced to ten years in prison for writing program of anti-Stalinist opposition group, the so-called Riutin Platform. Executed in 1937.

Rosliakov, Mikhail Vasil'evich (1897–1991). From 1926 to 1934, headed the regional and city financial departments of the Leningrad Planning Commission; candidate member of the Leningrad Regional and City Party Bureaus. Arrested in 1937. After returning from many years in the camps, wrote a book about the Kirov case.

Rykov, A. I. (1881–1938). Politburo member, 1922–30; chairman of the Council of People's Commissars, 1924–30; connected with Bukharin's right opposition; expelled from the party in 1937; defendant with Bukharin in the show trial of March 1938.

Sorokin, D. B. Brother-in-law of Leningrad NKVD chief Filipp Medved, employee of the Central Committee Secretariat, 1918–26.

Stetskii, A. I. (1896–1938). Head of party's agitprop department in Leningrad until 1930; then head of Central Committee agitprop department. Arrested and executed, 1938.

Svanidze, Mariia (1889–1942). Married to A. S. Svanidze, the brother of Stalin's first wife. A part of Stalin's inner circle until she was arrested in 1939. Shot in 1942.

Syrtsov, S. I. (1893–1937). Candidate member of Politburo, chairman of the Supreme Council of the National Economy, 1929–30; expelled from the Central Committee for "fractional activity," December 1930; executed, 1937.

Tomskii, Mikhail (1880–1936). Politburo member, 1922–30; chairman of the All-Union Central Executive Committee, 1922–29; from 1929, chairman of the All-Union Association of the Chemical Industry; allied with Bukharin's right opposition; committed suicide, 1936.

Tukhachevskii, Mikhail (1893–1937). Bolshevik military commander; served as commander of troops of Leningrad Military District, 1928–31; later transferred back to Moscow. Executed for treason, 1937.

Ul'rikh, V. V. (1889–1951). Chairman, Military Collegium of the Supreme Court, 1926–48.

Voroshilov, Kliment (1881–1969). Red Army commander; Commissar of Military Affairs/Defense, 1925–40; member of Politburo, 1934–40; occupied key military posts throughout the Stalin period and afterward.

Vyshinskii, A. Ia. (1883–1954). Prosecutor at various levels, 1921–33; Deputy USSR Prosecutor from 1933, and from 1935 USSR Prosecutor General. Later Minister of Foreign Affairs.

Zaporozhets, I. V. (1895–1938). Cheka/OGPU official; deputy chief, Leningrad GPU/NKVD, 1932–34. Executed, 1938.

Zhdanov, Andrei (1896–1948). Party chief in Gorky before being elected Central Committee secretary and candidate Politburo member in early 1934. Succeeded Kirov as party chief of Leningrad in December 1934.

Zinoviev, Grigorii (1883–1936). Member of the Central Committee, 1912–27; member of the Politburo, 1917–26; chairman of the Petrograd/Leningrad soviet, 1919–26; prominent leader of the so-called left opposition to Stalin; arrested, December 1934; tried and sentenced to death, 1936.

Notes

. . . .

1. A December Tragedy

1. They included: Politburo members Viacheslav Molotov and Kliment Voroshilov, NKVD chief Genrikh Iagoda, and Central Committee secretaries Nikolai Ezhov and Andrei Zhdanov.

2. Alexander Barmine, *One Who Survived. The Life Story of a Russian Under the Soviets* (New York: G. P. Putnam's Sons, 1945), p. 251. Barmine defected to the United States in 1937.

3. *The New York Times*, 2 December 1934, pp. 1; 30.

4. Ibid., 3 December 1934, p. 9.

5. Described by Mariia Svanidze in her diary, excerpts of which appeared in Iu. G. Murin, comp., *Iosif Stalin v ob'iatiiakh sem'i (Spornik dokumentov)* (Moscow, 1993), p. 165.

6. Ibid., pp. 165–66.

7. For some reason, events began an hour and a half earlier than had been previously announced. On 4 December *Pravda* had reported that the Hall of Columns would be open until 1:30 p.m. and the funeral in Red Square would start at 2:30.

8. *Iosif Stalin v ob'iatiiakh sem'i*, p. 164; Anna Kirilina, *Rikoshet, ili skol'ko chelovek bylo ubito vystrelom v Smol'nom* (St. Petersburg: Znanie, 1993), p. 35.

9. John Biggart, "Kirov Before the Revolution," *Soviet Studies*, Vol. 23 (January 1972), pp. 345–73 (p. 371).

10. *Nedelia*, no. 46, 1961, p. 9.

11. Isaac Deutscher, *Stalin: A Political Biography*, 2nd edition (New York: Oxford University Press, 1967), p. 102.

12. See Lesley A. Rimmel, "Another Kind of Fear: The Kirov Murder and the End of Bread Rationing in Leningrad," *Slavic Review*, Vol. 56, no. 3 (Fall 1997).

13. Interview with Valentin Bliumenfel'd, St. Petersburg, 11 April 1997.

14. Roy Medvedev, *Let History Judge: The Origins and Consequences of Stalinism* (New York: Columbia University Press, 1989), p. 336.

15. *The New York Times*, 3 December 1934, p. 9.

16. Interview with Nadezhda Kodatskaia, St. Petersburg, 9 April 1997.

17. Barmine, *One Who Survived*, p. 251.

18. *Pravda*, 3 December 1934, p. 1.

19. Elizabeth Lermolo, *Face of a Victim*, translated by I. D. W. Talmadge (New York: Harper & Brothers, 1956), pp. 40–47.

20. *Izvestiia TsK KPSS* (published by the CPSU Central Committee in Moscow), no. 8, 1989, pp. 95–100.

21. Medvedev, *Let History Judge*, p. 344.

22. Ibid.

23. *Bulleten' oppozitsii*, no. 1–2, July 1929, p. 2.

24. Robert Conquest, *Stalin and the Kirov Murder* (New York: Oxford University Press, 1989).

25. These arguments have been forcefully put forth by Western historians who downplay Stalin's role in implementing the purges. See, for example, J. Arch Getty, "The Politics of Repression Revisited," in J. Arch Getty and Roberta T. Manning, eds., *Stalinist Terror: New Perspectives* (Cambridge: Cambridge University Press, 1993). In Getty's words: "According to persistent oral tradition, Stalin had organized the assassination; only a few anomalies remained. Now, at least in the former Soviet Union, this assumption is not officially supported. . . . The secondhand stories are inconsistent with known facts about the circumstances of the crime. There was always reasonable doubt about Stalin's participation, and now there is more than before" (p. 49).

26. Adam Ulam, *Stalin: The Man and His Era* (Boston: Beacon Press, 1972), p. 385.

27. Oleg Khlevniuk, *1937-i: Stalin, NKVD i Sovetskoe obshchestvo* (Moscow: Respublika, 1992), p. 52.

28. *Iosif Stalin v ob'iatiiakh sem'i,* pp. 160–61.

29. Ibid., p. 168.

30. *Dvadtsat' vtoroi s'ezd KPSS. Stenograficheskii otchet* (Moscow: Politizdat, 1962), Vol. 2, p. 584.

31. Iakovlev subsequently presented a detailed summary of his reservations about the commission's findings in an article, "O Dekabr'skoi tragedii 1934 goda," *Pravda,* 28 January 1991, p. 3. He left open the question of Stalin's guilt, saying it was impossible to reach any conclusion on the basis of the available evidence.

32. Ibid.

33. The guests included Politburo members Molotov and Voroshilov, Georgian party chief Lavrentii Beria, the Svanidzes, and Stalin's brother-in-law Stanislav Redens and his wife, Anna.

34. *Iosif Stalin v ob'iatiiakh sem'i,* p. 170.

2. THE BOY FROM URZHUM

1. Sergei Kostrikov's (Kirov's) departure for Tomsk in 1904 is described by his sisters in their memoirs about him: A. M. Kostrikova and E. M. Kostrikova, *Eto bylo v Urzhume. Vospominaniia o S. M. Kirove* (Kirov: Volgo-Viatskoe Knizhnoe Izdatel'stvo, 1967), pp. 100–1.

2. Descriptions of Urzhum and Kirov's childhood appear in Kostrikova, *Eto bylo v Urzhume,* pp. 1–40; Semen Sinel'nikov, *Kirov* (Moscow: Molodaia gvardiia, 1964), pp. 1–20; and S. V. Krasnikov, *Sergei Mironovich Kirov: Zhizn' i deiatel'nost'* (Moscow: Politizdat, 1964), pp. 5–10.

3. V. Topor, *Tovarishch Kirov* (Moscow: Profizdat, 1935), p. 15.

4. Kostrikova, *Eto bylo v Urzhume,* p. 5.

5. Ibid., p. 6.

6. Ibid.

7. The details of his death are reported in a letter written some years later by a local resident of the area. See RTsKhIDNI (Russian Center for the Preservation and Study of Documents of Contemporary History), Fond (Archive) 80 (Kirov archive), opis (inventory) 19, delo (file) 21, ll. (pages) 1–2.

8. Topor, *Tovarishch Kirov,* p. 15.

9. Kostrikova, *Eto bylo v Urzhume,* pp. 21–22.

10. Ibid., pp. 23–24; Topor, *Tovarishch Kirov,* p. 17.

11. It is worth noting that Stalin also had intense exposure to Russian Orthodox theology as a young student at a seminary in Tbilisi. See Mikhail Agursky, "Stalin's Ecclesiastical Background," *Survey,* Vol. 28, no. 4 (1984), pp. 1–14.

12. Kostrikova, *Eto bylo v Urzhume,* pp. 27–34.

13. Ibid., pp. 55–56.

14. RTsKhIDNI, Fond 80, opis 1, dela 55–57.

15. Kostrikova, *Eto bylo v Urzhume,* pp. 68–70.

16. Sinel'nikov, *Kirov,* pp. 46–47.

17. Kostrikova, *Eto bylo v Urzhume,* p. 74.

18. Topor, *Tovarishch Kirov,* p. 27.

19. Sinel'nikov, *Kirov,* pp. 40–43; 65.

20. Kostrikova, *Eto bylo v Urzhume,* p. 76.

21. Sinel'nikov, *Kirov,* pp. 50–60; Biggart, "Kirov Before the Revolution," pp. 348–49; Topor, *Tovarishch Kirov,* pp. 19–20.

22. Richard Pipes, *The Russian Revolution* (New York: Alfred A. Knopf, 1990), pp. 4–9.

23. Sinel'nikov, *Kirov,* pp. 58–64; Kostrikova, *Eto bylo v Urzhume,* pp. 76–77.

24. Kostrikova, *Eto bylo v Urzhume,* pp. 86–101; Sinel'nikov, *Kirov,* pp. 65–66.

25. Sinel'nikov, *Kirov,* pp. 67–69.

26. On Sergei's early experiences in Tomsk, see Sinel'nikov, *Kirov,* pp. 69–75; Krasnikov, *Sergei Mironovich Kirov,* pp. 17–25.

27. Ibid.

28. See Biggart, "Kirov Before the Revolution," pp. 351–55.

29. Topor, *Tovarishch Kirov,* pp. 37–39.

30. Reproduced in *Krasnaia letopis',* no. 6 (63), 1934, p. 19.

31. *Deiateli SSSR i Revoliutsionnogo Dvizheniia Rossii. Entsiklopedicheskii Slovar' Granat* (Moscow: "Sovetskaia Entsiklopediia," 1989), p. 188.

32. Topor, *Tovarishch Kirov,* pp. 44–45.

33. See John Biggart, "Kirov Before the Revolution," pp. 353–55.

34. RTsKhIDNI, Fond 80, opis 19, delo 18 (memoirs of a Taiga worker named Nosov).

35. Ibid.; Topor, *Tovarishch Kirov,* p. 49.

36. Topor, *Tovarishch Kirov,* pp. 50–60; Krasnikov, *Sergei Mironovich Kirov,* pp. 30–31.

37. Biggart, "Kirov Before the Revolution," pp. 369–70; Kirov autobiography, *Deiateli SSSR,* p. 188.

38. *Tovarishch Kirov,* pp. 60–68; Biggart, "Kirov Before the Revolution," p. 356.

39. V. Dubrovin, *Povest' o plamennom publitsiste: S. M. Kirov i pechat'* (Leningrad: Lenizdat, 1969), p. 16.

40. Topor, *Tovarishch Kirov,* pp. 69–74; Sinel'nikov, *Kirov,* pp. 112–17.

41. Ibid.

42. Ibid.

43. Kostrikova, *Eto bylo v Urzhume,* pp. 105–6; Krasnikov, *Sergei Mironovich Kirov,* pp. 37–38.

44. RTsKhIDNI, Fond 80, opis 1, delo 54k.

45. Sinel'nikov, *Kirov,* pp. 118–19.

46. RTsKhIDNI, Fond 80, opis 19, delo 25, ll. 5–6. (From a letter written by Sof'ia L'vovna to the Cultural Department of the Communist Party Central Committee in 1956.)

47. Ibid.

48. RTsKhIDNI, Fond 80, opis 19, delo 22, l. 1.

49. Biggart, "Kirov Before the Revolution," p. 358.

50. On the ethics of Kirov's writing for the bourgeois press, see Dubrovin, *Povest',* pp. 19–20.

51. Kirov autobiography, *Deiateli SSSR,* p. 190.

52. RTsKhIDNI, Fond 80, opis 19, delo 20, ll. 1–9; Biggart, "Kirov Before the Revolution," pp. 363–64; Richard Douglas King, *Sergei Kirov and the Struggle for Soviet Power in the Terek Region, 1917–1918* (New York and London: Garland Publishing, 1987), pp. 34–36.

53. B. M. Mostiev, *Revoliutsionnaia publitsistika S. M. Kirova, 1909–1917 gg.* (Ordzhonikidze: "Ir," 1973), p. 21.

54. Dubrovin, *Povest'*, pp. 22–25.

55. Reprinted in *Krasnaia nov'*, no. 10–12, 1939, pp. 145–47.

56. Ibid., p. 152.

57. Mostiev, *Revoliutsionnaia publitsistika S. M. Kirova*, p. 18.

58. As cited in Biggart, "Kirov Before the Revolution," p. 360.

59. As cited in Sinel'nikov, *Kirov*, p. 129.

60. Reprinted in *Nedelia*, no. 46, 1961, p. 6.

61. Ibid.

62. RTsKhIDNI, Fond 80, opis 19, delo 12, l. 1.

63. RTsKhIDNI, Fond 80, opis 20, delo 10.

64. *Nedelia*, no. 46, 1961, p. 7.

65. RTsKhIDNI, Fond 80, opis 1, delo 12.

66. Topor, *Tovarishch Kirov*, pp. 77–78.

67. Dubrovin, *Povest'*, p. 28.

68. Ibid.

69. Ibid., p. 37; Topor, *Tovarishch Kirov*, pp. 78–79.

3. The Triumph of Bolshevism

1. In 1901, Stalin adopted the name Koba, after a heroic outlaw and a people's avenger in a famous Georgian poem. He first began using the name Stalin, from the Russian word for steel, in 1913. See Deutscher, *Stalin*, pp. 46; 121.

2. Ibid., p. 26.

3. See Richard Pipes, *The Formation of the Soviet Union: Communism and Nationalism, 1917–1923*, revised edition (Cambridge, MA: Harvard University Press, 1997), pp. 93–96.

4. *Terek*, 3 November 1912, reprinted in S. M. Kirov, *Stat'i i rechi*, Vol. 1 (1912–21) (Moscow: Partizdat, 1935), pp. 3–5.

5. Biggart, "Kirov Before the Revolution," p. 361.

6. Sinel'nikov, *Kirov*, p. 141.

7. RTsKhIDNI, Fond 80, opis 20, delo 24, ll. 1–3.

8. Biggart, "Kirov Before the Revolution," p. 376.

9. As cited in ibid. Two of Kirov's more interesting articles in 1914 addressed the problem of suicide: "Ukhodiashchie iz zhizni," *Terek,* 22 February 1914; "K bor'be s samoubiistvami," *Terek,* 20 April 1914; RTsKhIDNI, Fond 80, opis 19, delo 20, ll. 2–3.

10. King, *Sergei Kirov*, p. 35.

11. G. K. Dolunts, *Kirov na Severnom Kavkaze* (Moscow: Politizdat, 1973), pp. 15–25; 60–61.

12. Biggart, "Kirov Before the Revolution," pp. 361–62.

13. RTsKhIDNI, Fond 80, opis 20, delo 27. Presumably when Iakov Markus arrived in Vladikavkazin in 1916, he was there illegally.

14. Dolunts, *Kirov na Severnom Kavkaze,* pp. 64–65; King, *Sergei Kirov,* pp. 36–38.

15. King, *Sergei Kirov,* pp. 40–41.

16. Ibid., pp. 82–91; Biggart, "Kirov Before the Revolution," p. 362.

17. As quoted in Pipes, *The Russian Revolution,* pp. 386–87.

18. G. K. Dolunts, *Kirov v revoliutsii. Rol' S. M. Kirova v bor'be za pobedu sotsialisticheskoi revoliutsii* (Krasnodar: Krasnodarskoe Knizhnoe Izdatel'stvo, 1967), pp. 16–26.

19. Dubrovin, *Povest',* pp. 87–88; King, *Sergei Kirov,* p. 73.

20. Dubrovin, *Povest',* p. 88.

21. A. I. Kozlov, *Stalin: Bor'ba za vlast'* (Rostov-na-Donu, 1991), pp. 159–60.

22. Leonard Schapiro, *The Communist Party of the Soviet Union* (New York: Vintage Books, 1971), p. 166.

23. Mostiev, *Revoliutsionnaia publitsistika S. M. Kirova,* pp. 252–53.

24. Dolunts, *Kirov v revoliutsii,* p. 45.

25. King, *Sergei Kirov,* pp. 93–94.

26. Ibid., pp. 94–97; Dolunts, *Kirov na Severnom Kavkaze*, pp. 116–17.

27. M. Orakhelashvili, "Prekrasnyi Chelovek," *Krasnaia letopis'*, no. 6 (63), 1934, pp. 49–51.

28. Ibid.

29. King, *Sergei Kirov*, pp. 125–28.

30. Dolunts, *Kirov v revoliutsii*, p. 109.

31. See Pipes, *The Russian Revolution*, pp. 440–67. Pipes shows that in fact Kornilov never intended to carry out a putsch against the Kerenskii government. He was reacting initially to false reports of an impending Bolshevik takeover.

32. Dolunts, *Kirov v revoliutsii*, pp. 133–35.

33. Ibid., pp. 136–48.

34. See Kirov, *Stat'i i rechi*, Vol. 1 (1935), p. XIX.

35. Schapiro, *The Communist Party of the Soviet Union*, pp. 171–72; Dolunts, *Kirov v revoliutsii*, pp. 149–50.

36. Dolunts, *Kirov v revoliutsii*, p. 136.

37. King, *Sergei Kirov*, pp. 147–48, citing several sources. The introduction to a collection of Kirov's speeches and writings says that the Vladikavkaz soviet passed into the hands of the Bolsheviks at the end of September or the beginning of October. See Kirov, *Stat'i i rechi*, Vol. 1 (1935), p. XVIII.

38. N. A. Efimov, "Sergei Mironovich Kirov," *Voprosy istorii*, no. 11–12, 1995, p. 52.

39. Pipes, *The Russian Revolution*, pp. 489–505.

40. Kirov, *Stat'i i rechi*, Vol. 1 (1935), pp. 9–12.

41. Ibid., pp. XVIII–XIX.

42. S. M. Kirov, *Stat'i, rechi, dokumenty*, Vol. 1 (1912–21) (Leningrad: 1936), pp. 9–16.

43. S. I. Avvakumov, ed., *Sergei Mironovich Kirov: Spornik materialov dlia dokladchikov i besedchikov* (Leningrad: Izdatel'stvo Leningradskogo Soveta PK i KD, 1938), pp. 25–30.

44. Kirov, *Stat'i i rechi*, Vol. 1 (1935), p. 12; King, *Sergei Kirov*, pp. 181–82.

45. Writing from Piatigorsk for a local paper, Kirov observed that "the Terek region has actually plunged itself into an abyss of lawlessness and anarchy." RTsKhIDNI, Fond 80, opis 2, delo 15.

46. Kirov, *Stat'i i rechi,* Vol. 1 (1935), pp. 17–18.

47. Ibid., pp. 19–20.

48. It did, however, appear in the 1936 edition, referred to above, pp. 19–26.

49. Jacob Marschak, "Recollections of Kiev and the Northern Caucasus, 1917–1918: An Interview Conducted by Richard A. Pierce," University of California Oral History Collection, Microfilm Corporation of America, Glen Rock, NJ, 1978, pp. 35; 38.

50. Ibid., p. 39.

51. For a detailed account of the Piatigorsk congress, see King, *Sergei Kirov,* pp. 310–72.

52. Robert Service, *A History of Twentieth Century Russia* (Cambridge, MA: Harvard University Press, 1998), p. 102.

53. Pipes, *The Formation of the Soviet Union,* p. 197.

54. Sinel'nikov, *Kirov,* pp. 174–75.

55. Efimov, "Sergei Mironovich Kirov," p. 53, citing RTsKhIDNI, Fond 7, opis 84, delo 196, ll. 4–6.

56. King, *Sergei Kirov,* pp. 389–90; Iu. I. Koniev, ed., *S. M. Kirov i G. K. Ordzhonikidze na Severnom Kavkaze* (Ordzhonikidze: "IR," 1986), p. 28.

57. RTsKhIDNI, Fond 80, opis 21, delo 1.

58. RTsKhIDNI, Fond 80, opis 19, delo 3, l. 6. On the certificate of identification, see John Biggart, "The Astrakhan Rebellion: An Episode in the Career of Sergey Mironovich Kirov," *The Slavonic and East European Review,* Vol. 54, no. 2, April 1976, p. 238.

59. RTsKhIDNI, Fond 80, opis 19, delo 3, l. 1; delo 21, ll. 41–46.

60. *Pravda,* 2 July 1918, p. 3.

61. Krasnikov, *Sergei Mironovich Kirov,* pp. 64–65.

62. RTsKhIDNI, Fond 80, opis 19, delo 21, ll. 45–51.

63. Deutscher, *Stalin*, pp. 196–97.

64. RTsKhIDNI, Fond 80, opis 19, delo 21, ll. 45–51.

65. On Stalin in Tsaritsyn, see Robert C. Tucker, *Stalin as Revolutionary, 1879–1929: A Study in History and Personality* (New York: W. W. Norton, 1973), pp. 192–96.

66. Sinel'nikov, *Kirov*, pp. 176–80; 211–16.

67. RTsKhIDNI, Fond 80, opis 19, delo 21, ll. 77–80; *Tovarishch Kirov*, pp. 109–13 (recollections of Iurii Butiagin).

68. Ibid.

69. RTsKhIDNI, Fond 80, opis 3, delo 19.

70. As cited in Krasnikov, *Sergei Mironovich Kirov*, pp. 72–73.

71. Kirov's dispute with Shliapnikov was not the only reason for the latter's recall. Ordzhonikidze, who was in command of the Eleventh Army before it fell apart, had also complained about Shliapnikov, accusing him of treachery and of diverting supplies for the Eleventh Army. See Biggart, "The Astrakhan Rebellion," p. 238.

72. Efimov, "Sergei Mironovich Kirov," p. 54.

73. Protocol of the session, file no. 0371, Kirov Museum, St. Petersburg.

74. RTsKhIDNI, Fond 80, opis 3, delo 3.

75. Efimov, "Sergei Mironovich Kirov," pp. 55–56. Efimov's casualty figures, which are much higher than those mentioned by Soviet historians, are based on documents in the archives of the Central Committee and in the state archives.

76. Efimov, "Sergei Mironovich Kirov," p. 56.

77. Kirov Museum, St. Petersburg, document no. 0625.

78. As cited in Biggart, "The Astrakhan Rebellion," p. 238, n. 42.

79. RTsKhIDNI, Fond 80, opis 19, delo 12, l. 6.

80. As quoted in Biggart, "The Astrakhan Rebellion," p. 245.

81. As cited in Koniev, *S. M. Kirov i G. K. Ordzhonikidze na Severnom Kavkaze*, p. 92.

82. RTsKhIDNI, Fond 80, opis 3, delo 4, ll. 24–47.

83. RTsKhIDNI, Fond 80, opis 3, delo 54/c.

84. In explaining why Stalin appeared to be a "Great Russian chauvinist," Isaac Deutscher points out: "He was not, either then or even in later days, prompted by any of the ordinary emotions and prejudices that go with nationalism. What he represented was merely the principle of centralization, common to all modern revolutions. To that principle he gave an exaggerated and brutal expression." Deutscher, *Stalin*, pp. 240–41.

85. Stephen Blank, "Bolshevik Organizational Development in Early Soviet Transcaucasia: Autonomy vs. Centralization, 1918–1924," in Ronald Grigor Suny, ed., *Transcaucasia: Nationalism and Social Change. Essays in the History of Armenia, Azerbaijan and Georgia* (Ann Arbor: Michigan Slavic Publications, 1983), pp. 314–25.

86. RTsKhIDNI, Fond 80, opis 3, delo 20.

87. *The Memoirs of Anastas Mikoyan*, Vol. 1: *The Path of Struggle*, ed. by Sergo Mikoyan, trans. by Katherine T. O'Connor and Diane L. Burgin (Madison, CT: Sphinx Press, 1988), pp. 502–3.

88. As cited in Alla Kirilina, *L'Assassinat de Kirov: Destin d'un Stalinien, 1888–1934*, adapted from the Russian by Pierre Forgues and Nicolas Werth (Paris: Seuil, 1995), p. 21. This book is an expanded and rewritten version of Kirilina's book in Russian, *Rikoshet*.

89. Blank, "Bolshevik Organizational Development," p. 318.

90. Biggart, "The Astrakhan Rebellion," pp. 245–46.

4. Building Soviet Power

1. RTsKhIDNI, Fond 80, opis 3, delo 1, l. 59.

2. RTsKhIDNI, Fond 80, opis 3, delo 3, ll. 48–49.

3. RTsKhIDNI, Fond 80, opis 4, delo 31, letter dated 20 January 1920.

4. RTsKhIDNI, Fond 80, opis 4, delo 29, l. 40.

5. On the details of the invasion, see *The Memoirs of Anastas Mikoyan*, pp. 527–38.

6. Efimov, "Sergei Mironovich Kirov," pp. 56–57.

7. M. G. Iskenderov, *Iz istorii bor'by kommunisticheskoi partii Azerbaidzhana za pobedu Sovetskoi vlasti* (Baku: Azerbaidzhanskoe Gosudarstvennoe Izdatel'stvo, 1958), pp. 488–89.

8. Victor Chernov, as quoted in Martin Malia, *A Soviet Tragedy: A History of Socialism in Russia, 1917–1991* (New York: The Free Press, 1994), p. 136.

9. Blank, "Bolshevik Organizational Development," p. 327; James P. Nichol, *Diplomacy in the Former Soviet Republics* (Westport: Praeger, 1995), p. 138.

10. Sinel'nikov, *Kirov,* pp. 241–43.

11. RTsKhIDNI, Fond 80, opis 4, delo 57.

12. RTsKhIDNI, Fond 85, opis 15, delo 28.

13. Letter dated 20 July 1920, Kirov Museum, no. III/728.

14. Letter dated 6 August 1920, RTsKhIDNI, Fond 80, opis 4, delo 106, l. 2.

15. Letter dated 20 July 1920, Kirov Museum, no. III/729.

16. Letter dated 24 August 1920, Kirov Museum, no. III/1257.

17. See his letters to Lenin, Stalin, and Chicherin, cited above.

18. Krasnikov, *Sergei Mironovich Kirov,* p. 100, citing the memoirs of Central Committee secretary Elena Stasova.

19. RTsKhIDNI, Fond 80, opis 19, delo 12, l. 11.

20. RTsKhIDNI, Fond 80, opis 4, dela 3, 93, 94.

21. RTsKhIDNI, Fond 80, opis 4, delo 93.

22. RTsKhIDNI, Fond 80, opis 4, delo 94.

23. Portions of the stenographic record of the meeting are in RTsKhIDNI, Fond 80, opis 4, delo 3, ll. 1–27.

24. Ibid.

25. See RTsKhIDNI, Fond 80, opis 18, delo 146, l. 63, which cites a press report from *Kommunist* in Vladikavkaz. Also see Biggart, "The Astrakhan Rebellion," p. 246, n. 90.

26. RTsKhIDNI, Fond 80, opis 4, delo 3, l. 18.

27. *The Memoirs of Anastas Mikoyan,* pp. 415–16.

28. As cited in Oleg Khlevniuk, *Stalin i Ordzhonikidze: Konflikty v Politbiuro v 30-e gody* (Moscow: "Rossiia Molodaia," 1993), p. 9.

29. As cited in Biggart, "The Astrakhan Rebellion," p. 247.

30. RTsKhIDNI, Fond 85, opis 15, delo 68.

31. RTsKhIDNI, Fond 80, opis 5, delo 13.

32. *The Memoirs of Anastas Mikoyan*, pp. 417–18.

33. Ibid.

34. Schapiro, *The Communist Party of the Soviet Union*, p. 207.

35. The speech is reprinted in Kirov, *Stat'i i rechi*, Vol. 1 (1935), pp. 195–204.

36. Ibid., p. 198.

37. As quoted in RTsKhIDNI, Fond 80, opis 18, delo 146, l. 68.

38. See *Tovarishch Kirov*, p. 166; and Krasnikov, *Sergei Mironovich Kirov*, p. 104.

39. *The Memoirs of Anastas Mikoyan*, p. 68.

40. As quoted in Sinel'nikov, *Kirov*, pp. 279–80.

41. RTsKhIDNI, Fond 80, opis 19, delo 12, l. 14.

42. Efimov, "Sergei Mironovich Kirov," p. 57.

43. RTsKhIDNI, Fond 80, opis 19, delo 20, ll. 9–10.

44. RTsKhIDNI, Fond 85, opis 24, delo 121, l. 3. The telegram was undated.

45. As quoted in Dubrovin, *Povest' o plamennom publitsiste*, p. 122.

46. *Krasnaia letopis'*, no. 6 (63), 1934, p. 51.

47. *Tovarishch Kirov*, pp. 165–66.

48. Ibid., p. 167; Sinel'nikov, *Kirov*, pp. 263–68.

49. *Tovarishch Kirov*, p. 169.

50. Krasnikov, *Sergei Mironovich Kirov*, pp. 105–13.

51. RTsKhIDNI, Fond 80, opis 7, delo 29K, ll. 1–2.

52. Ibid., ll. 5–6.

53. Ibid., l. 8.

54. A copy of the protocol of the Kavburo plenum is in RTsKhIDNI, Fond 85, opis 18, delo 58, ll. 21–22.

55. Krasnikov, *Sergei Mironovich Kirov*, p. 108.

56. See Khlevniuk, *Stalin i Ordzhonikidze*, pp. 11–12.

57. *Izvestiia TsK KPSS*, no. 9, 1990, p. 149.

58. Khlevniuk, *Stalin i Ordzhonikidze*, pp. 11–13; *Izvestiia TsK KPSS*, no. 9, 1990, pp. 147–54.

59. See Kirilina, *L'Assassinat de Kirov*, pp. 26–27.

60. See Amy Knight, *Beria: Stalin's Chief Lieutenant* (Princeton: Princeton University Press, 1993), p. 23.

61. Kirov Museum, document nos. III/442 (telegram from Kirov and Ordzhonikidze to Bagirov) and III/0502 (protocol of a September 1925 Zakkraikom plenum).

62. RTsKhIDNI, Fond 85, opis 2C, delo 3, ll. 34; 68.

63. RTsKhIDNI, Fond 80, opis 19, delo 1.

64. *Izvestiia TsK KPSS*, no. 1, 1990, pp. 157; 159.

65. Deutscher, *Stalin*, pp. 255–57; *Izvestiia TsK KPSS*, no. 4, 1991, p. 198.

66. Khlevniuk, *Stalin i Ordzhonikidze*, p. 13.

67. See Deutscher, *Stalin*, pp. 258–70; and Schapiro, *The Communist Party of the Soviet Union*, pp. 280–89.

68. Schapiro, *The Communist Party of the Soviet Union*, p. 286.

69. RTsKhIDNI, Fond 80, opis 8, delo 1, l. 2.

70. RTsKhIDNI, Fond 80, opis 8, delo 11, l. 15. The date of and occasion of this speech were not given.

71. See Deutscher, *Stalin*, pp. 279–94.

72. RTsKhIDNI, Fond 80, opis 9, delo 3, ll. 17–20.

73. See ibid. and Avvakumov, *Sergei Mironovich Kirov*, p. 68.

74. RTsKhIDNI, Fond 80, opis 9, delo 7, ll. 1–2.

75. See Knight, *Beria*, pp. 35–36.

76. RTsKhIDNI, Fond 85, opis 25, delo 112.

77. Kirov Museum, document no. III/0864.

78. RTsKhIDNI, Fond 558, opis 1, delo 3334. The exact date on this letter is unclear. Some sources have 30 March, but, judging from other correspondence, it was probably June or July.

79. Kirilina, *Rikoshet,* p. 69.

80. For details, see Schapiro, *The Communist Party of the Soviet Union,* pp. 297–300.

81. As cited in Efimov, "Sergei Mironovich Kirov," p. 58.

82. RTsKhIDNI, Fond 80, opis 25, delo 8.

83. RTsKhIDNI, Fond 80, opis 26, delo 55.

5. Leader of Leningrad

1. For an overview of the city's cultural heritage, see Solomon Volkov, *St. Petersburg: A Cultural History* (New York: The Free Press, 1995).

2. RTsKhIDNI, Fond 80, opis 26, delo 56, ll. 1–2.

3. Ibid. ll. 3–5.

4. Dubrovin, *Povest',* pp. 146–47.

5. RTsKhIDNI, Fond 80, opis 9, delo 38. Also see Sinel'nikov, *Kirov,* p. 285.

6. Mikhail Rosliakov, *Ubiistvo Kirova. Politicheskie i ugolovnye prestupleniia v 1930-x godakh: svidetel'stva ochevidtsa* (Leningrad: Lenizdat, 1991), p. 99.

7. Krasnikov, *Sergei Mironovich Kirov,* p. 133; Rosliakov, *Ubiistvo Kirova,* p. 99.

8. Rosliakov, *Ubiistvo Kirova,* pp. 98–100.

9. RTsKhIDNI, Fond 85, opis 25, delo 119.

10. RTsKhIDNI, Fond 80, opis 26, delo 40, l. 4.

11. RTsKhIDNI, Fond 85, opis 25, delo 120.

12. RTsKhIDNI, Fond 80, opis 26, delo 40.

13. Ibid.

14. Kirov Museum, document no. III/369C, undated.

15. The details of this incident are recounted in Khlevniuk, *Stalin i Ordzhonikidze*, pp. 16–17.

16. Ibid.; *Izvestiia TsK KPSS*, no. 7, 1991, pp. 130–31.

17. Sinel'nikov, *Kirov*, p. 360.

18. Open exhibit, Kirov Museum.

19. Ibid.

20. Ibid.

21. Dubrovin, *Povest'*, pp. 153–63; Efimov, "Sergei Mironich Kirov," p. 58.

22. Dubrovin, *Povest'*, pp. 162–63.

23. S. M. Kirov, *Stat'i, rechi, dokumenty*, Vol. 3 (1925–27) (Moscow: Partizdat, 1936), p. 221.

24. Ibid., p. 389.

25. As quoted in Krasnikov, *Sergei Mironovich Kirov*, p. 137.

26. Kirov, *Stat'i*, Vol. 3, p. 377.

27. Ibid., pp. 471–81.

28. Miklosh Kun, *Bukharin: ego druz'ia i vragi* (Moscow: Respublika, 1992), pp. 172; 215.

29. Ibid., p. 199.

30. Stephen Cohen, *Bukharin and the Bolshevik Revolution: A Political Biography, 1888–1938* (Oxford: Oxford University Press, 1980), p. 268.

31. Ibid., p. 240.

32. Kun, *Bukharin*, p. 175.

33. Krasnikov, *Sergei Mironovich Kirov*, p. 137.

34. This was the Georgian Communist Beso Lominadze, who would soon find himself on the wrong side of Stalin.

35. See Schapiro, *The Communist Party of the Soviet Union*, pp. 368–70.

36. As cited in Kun, *Bukharin*, p. 257.

37. V. M. Podugol'nikov, ed., *Oni ne molchali* (Moscow: Politizdat, 1991), pp. 179–98.

38. Kun, *Bukharin*, p. 255.

39. RTsKhIDNI, Fond 80, opis 11, delo 34.

40. RTsKhIDNI, Fond 85, opis 27, delo 98, l. 7.

41. Podugol'nikov, *Oni ne molchali*, pp. 183–86. Stalin reportedly stayed up all night at Kirov's, working on his speech to the Leningraders.

42. RTsKhIDNI, Fond 80, opis 26, delo 60, l. 1.

43. RTsKhIDNI, Fond 85, opis 25, delo 125, ll. 1–2.

44. RTsKhIDNI, Fond 85, opis 29, delo 440. This was an undated postcard. The Kirov Museum puts the date at 3 July 1928, whereas another source says it was written in 1934. See O. V. Khlevniuk et al., eds., *Stalinskoe Politbiuro v 30-e gody. Spornik dokumentov* (Moscow: "AIRO—XX," 1995), p. 139. Given the history of Sergo's health troubles, it is more likely to have been written in 1928, although after Kirov's hunting trip in early August.

45. RTsKhIDNI, Fond 85, opis 1, delo 144, ll. 1–21.

46. As cited in O. V. Khlevniuk, *Politbiuro. Mekhanismy politicheskoi vlasti v 30-e gody* (Moscow: "Rossiiskaia politicheskaia entsiklopedia," 1996), p. 22.

47. Podugol'nikov, *Oni ne molchali*, pp. 185–88.

48. See Cohen, *Bukharin and the Bolshevik Revolution*, pp. 302–4; and Schapiro, *The Communist Party of the Soviet Union*, pp. 374–77.

49. As cited in Cohen, *Bukharin and the Bolshevik Revolution*, p. 452, n. 162. Also see Khlevniuk, *Politbiuro*, p. 22, where he cites an émigré source as saying that Ordzhonikidze, Kalinin, and Voroshilov had all urged Stalin to make concessions to the right.

50. *Leningradskaia pravda*, 20 January 1929, p. 3.

51. As cited in Kirilina, *L'Assassinat de Kirov*, pp. 60–61.

52. Kun, *Bukharin*, p. 296.

53. See *Leningradskaia pravda*, 3–7 September 1929; and Iurii Pompeev, *Khochet-sia zhit' i zhit'. Dokumental'naia povest' o S. M. Kirove* (Moscow: Politizdat, 1987), pp. 100–4.

54. The uncorrected stenogram is in the Kirov archive, RTsKhIDNI, Fond 80, opis 26, delo 10.

55. *Leningradskaia pravda*, 12 September 1929, p. 2.

56. See Dubrovin, *Povest'*, pp. 234–35.

57. RTsKhIDNI, Fond 85, opis 27, delo 108, ll. 6–7.

58. Ibid., ll. 1–2, 8–11.

59. Reprinted in Lars Lih, Oleg Naumov, and Oleg Khlevniuk, eds., *Stalin's Letters to Molotov: 1925–1936* (New Haven and London: Yale University Press, 1995), p. 180.

60. RTsKhIDNI, Fond 80, opis 13, delo 35.

61. Ibid.

62. Rosliakov, *Ubiistvo Kirova*, pp. 107–8; RTsKhIDNI, Fond 17, opis 163, delo 814, ll. 7–11.

63. Sergo ended his report by angrily denying Desov's assertion that he, Sergo, had remarked to Desov: "Even Comrade Stalin was wavering [on the question of relations with the Provisional Government in 1917] for a short time." RTsKhIDNI, Fond 17, opis 163, delo 814, ll. 7–11.

64. As cited in Rosliakov, *Ubiistvo Kirova*, p. 109.

65. RTsKhIDNI, Fond 17, opis 162, delo 8, ll. 24–25.

66. Rosliakov, *Ubiistvo Kirova*, pp. 108–9.

67. Robert C. Tucker, *Stalin in Power: The Revolution from Above, 1928–1941* (New York: W. W. Norton, 1990), p. 128.

68. See Kirilina, *L'Assassinat de Kirov*, p. 188. Among the contributors were Ordzhonikidze, Kalinin, Kaganovich, Voroshilov, Mikoyan, and others. Kuibyshev, Rudzutak, and Rykov, who were full members of the Politburo, also did not contribute.

69. RTsKhIDNI, Fond 80, opis 13, delo 37.

70. RTsKhIDNI, Fond 80, opis 13, delo 7.

71. As cited in Robert C. Tucker, "Svetlana Alliluyeva as Witness of Stalin," *The Slavic Review*, no. 2, 1968, pp. 302–3.

72. *Stalin's Letters to Molotov*, p. 185.

6. Kirov and Stalin's Revolution

1. Krasnikov, *Sergei Mironovich Kirov*, pp. 138–45.

2. Ibid., p. 157.

3. Sinel'nikov, *Kirov,* p. 353.

4. As quoted in Pompeev, *Khochetsia zhit' i zhit',* p. 61.

5. V. K. Zavalishin, "Leningrad i Leningradskaia Oblast' posle Ubiistva Kirova," unpublished manuscript, Nicolaevsky Collection, Hoover Institution Archives, Stanford, CA, undated, p. 18. I am grateful to Dr. Robert Conquest for sending me a copy of this manuscript.

6. Krasnikov, *Sergei Mironovich Kirov,* pp. 145–52.

7. See Robert Conquest, *The Harvest of Sorrow: Soviet Collectivization and the Terror Famine* (London and Oxford: Hutchinson, 1986). Also see Tucker, *Stalin in Power,* pp. 172–80.

8. See, for example, two speeches delivered by Kirov in Leningrad and published in *Leningradskaia pravda,* 14 March and 21 May 1929.

9. Krasnikov, *Sergei Mironovich Kirov,* pp. 174–75; Sinel'nikov, *Kirov,* pp. 310–11.

10. RTsKhIDNI, Fond 85, opis 1C, delo 179.

11. Khlevniuk, *Politbiuro,* pp. 17–19.

12. See Kirov's speech to Leningrad party members, reprinted in *Pravda,* 19 July 1934; Sinel'nikov, *Kirov,* p. 310; and *Ocherki istorii Leningradskoi organizatsii KPSS, chast' II, Noiabr' 1927–1945* (Leningrad: Lenizdat, 1968), pp. 426–37.

13. Tucker, *Stalin in Power,* p. 240.

14. "Ostalos' eshche nemalo khlama v liudskom sostave; Kak nachinalos' 'delo Akademii Nauk,'" *Vestnik Arkhiva Presidenta Rossiiskoi Federatsii,* no. 3, 1997, pp. 105–26; and no. 4, 1997, pp. 103–29. Also see V. S. Brachev, "'Delo' Akademika S. F. Platonova," *Voprosy istorii,* no. 5, 1989, pp. 117–29.

15. Ibid.

16. S. M. Kirov, *Izbrannye stat'i i rechi, 1912–1934* (Moscow: OGIZ, 1939), pp. 351–61.

17. On this point, see Kun, *Bukharin,* pp. 301–2. The speaker in question was Emelian Iaroslavskii, who had masterminded the *Pravda* attack against Kirov in 1929.

18. RTsKhIDNI, Fond 17, opis 3, delo 898, l. 14; Krasnikov, *Sergei Mironovich Kirov*, pp. 180–81; Zhak Rossi, *Spravochnik po GULAG*, part 1 (Moscow: Prosvet, 1991), pp. 26–27.

19. Zavalishin Manuscript, pp. 33–34. Kirov had said this in reference to the use of imprisoned kulaks, who were employed at the Khibinogorsk complex.

20. Open Exhibit, Kirov Museum.

21. *XVII S'ezd Vsesoiuznoi Kommunisticheskoi partii (B), 26 Ianvaria–10 Fevralia 1934 g. Stenograficheskii otchet* (Moscow, 1934), p. 230.

22. Ibid., p. 255. Kirov had already expressed his gratitude to the Leningrad branch of the OGPU in a December 1932 speech honoring the fifteenth anniversary of the founding of the political police. He praised the achievements of this organization, saying that "when we must move forward and solve important tasks, especially when they need to be solved exactly, decisively, and quickly, the Cheka occupies first place in the resolution of these questions." Kirov Museum, document no. III/0605.

23. *Pravda*, 6 August 1932.

24. Sinel'nikov, *Kirov*, p. 355.

25. As cited in Khlevniuk, *Politbiuro*, p. 77.

26. Ibid., p. 78.

27. To be sure, there was occasional tension. In a March 1933 letter to Kirov requesting that he reconsider the dismissal of an economic official, Bukharin wrote: "I ask you, as chief of Leningrad, not to permit on your territory such abuses, which could cost us dearly . . ." Cited in *Leningradskaia pravda*, 1 December 1989, p. 3.

28. Anna Larina, *This I Cannot Forget: The Memoirs of Nikolai Bukharin's Widow*, trans. by Gary Kern (New York: W. W. Norton, 1994), p. 180.

29. RTsKhIDNI, Fond 80, opis 18, delo 143, l. 46.

30. Podugol'nikov, *Oni ne molchali*, pp. 125–44; Khlevniuk, *Stalin i Ordzhonikidze*, pp. 21–29; and Khlevniuk, *Politbiuro*, pp. 40–50.

31. Ibid.; RTsKhIDNI, Fond 85, opis 1C, delo 115, ll. 1–17.

32. RTsKhIDNI, Fond 85, opis 1C, delo 130.

33. Khlevniuk, *Stalin i Ordzhonikidze*, p. 29. It is not clear when Stalin actually saw Lominadze's "anti-party" letters to Sergo. He claimed at the Central Com-

mittee plenum following Sergo's death that Sergo had approached him (probably in 1929) and told him about one such letter but had refused to give it to him or to take it to the Central Committee. See Khlevniuk, ibid., pp. 24–25. It is possible, however, that Stalin was lying and that he heard about the letters from the OGPU, which routinely opened mail.

34. RTsKhIDNI, Fond 80, opis 14, delo 9.

35. RTsKhIDNI, Fond 80, opis 14, delo 10, ll. 40; 45.

36. *Stalin's Letters to Molotov*, p. 177.

37. R. W. Davies, "The Syrtsov-Lominadze Affair," *Soviet Studies*, Vol. 33, no. 1 (January 1981), pp. 29–50 (p. 46).

38. Larina, *This I Cannot Forget*, pp. 64–65.

39. *Iosif Stalin v ob'iatiiakh sem'i*, p. 42.

40. Ibid., p. 37.

41. Ibid., p. 38.

42. *Stalin's Letters to Molotov*, p. 215.

43. See A. N. Iakovlev, ed., *Reabilitatsiia: Politicheskie protsessy 30–50-x godov* (Moscow: Politizdat, 1991), pp. 92–104, and, for the full text of Riutin's platform, pp. 334–446. Also see *Izvestiia TsK KPSS*, no. 3, 1990, pp. 150–78.

44. Ibid.

45. Dmitri Volkogonov, *Stalin: Triumph and Tragedy*, edited and translated by Harold Shukman (New York: Grove Weidenfeld, 1991), pp. 205–6; also see *Sotsialisticheskii vestnik*, no. 23/24, 1936, pp. 20–21 (from Boris Nikolaevskii's "Letter of an Old Bolshevik"); and Podugol'nikov, *Oni ne molchali*, pp. 170–71.

46. Ibid.

47. Podugol'nikov, *Oni ne molchali*, pp. 179–97. Petrovskii, who was exiled to Siberia, was arrested again and imprisoned a year later.

48. *Reabilitatsiia*, pp. 362–63.

49. Ibid., p. 421.

50. See *Izvestiia TsK KPSS*, no. 8, 1990, p. 200.

51. Ibid., no. 3, 1990, p. 175.

52. As cited in Tucker, *Stalin in Power*, pp. 216–17.

53. Rosliakov, *Ubiistvo Kirova*, pp. 116–17.

54. Ibid., p. 118. Unfortunately, these letters could not be located in the Kirov archive.

55. See Stalin's visitor log for 1932 reproduced in *Istoricheskii arkhiv*, no. 2, 1995, pp. 155–56.

56. Kirilina, *L'Assassinat de Kirov*, pp. 188–89. Kirilina cites memoirs by Markus that are apparently still classified secret.

57. As cited in Khlevniuk, *Stalin i Ordzhonikidze*, p. 44.

58. Ibid., p. 43.

59. S. Z. Ginzburg, "O gibeli Sergo Ordzhonikidze," *Voprosy istorii KPSS*, no. 3, 1991, p. 89.

60. I. Kurilov and N. Mikhailov, *Tainy spetsial'nogo khraneniia: O chem rasskazali sekretnye arkhivy 30–50-x godov* (Moscow: Sovetskaia Sibir', 1992), pp. 102–3. The authors cite Chagin's memoirs in the party archives.

61. Rosliakov, *Ubiistvo Kirova*, p. 119. Another source reported that Kirov once remarked about Stalin: "He's an hysteric." Tucker, *Stalin in Power*, p. 240.

62. Open Exhibit, Kirov Museum; S. Sinel'nikov, comp. *Sto Stranits o Kirove* (Moscow: Politizdat, 1968), pp. 97–99; *Iosif Stalin v ob'iatiiakh sem'i*, p. 162.

63. As cited in Kirilina, *L'Assassinat de Kirov*, p. 41.

64. Rosliakov, *Ubiistvo Kirova*, pp. 68–71.

65. RTsKhIDNI, Fond 560, opis 1, delo 47, ll. 107–8; on Evdokimov's background, see Robert Conquest, *Inside Stalin's Secret Police: NKVD Politics, 1936–39* (Stanford: Hoover Institution Press, 1985), p. 25.

66. Conquest, *Stalin and the Kirov Murder*, p. 39.

67. Rosliakov, *Ubiistvo Kirova*, pp. 70–71, citing the Leningrad party archives for background on Zaporozhets. Kirilina, *Rikoshet*, p. 131, mistakenly claims that Zaporozhets did not arrive in Leningrad until the summer of 1934. In fact he was a delegate from Leningrad to the Seventeenth Party Congress in January 1934.

68. Ibid.

69. Open Exhibit, Kirov Museum. For a copy of the photograph, see photo no. 12.

70. Efimov, "Sergei Mironovich Kirov," pp. 64–65; Pavel and Anatolii Sudoplatov, *Special Tasks: The Memoirs of an Unwanted Witness—a Soviet Spymaster* (Boston

and New York: Little, Brown, 1994), pp. 50–54. See below, Chapter 8, pp. 207–8, for further discussion of this issue.

71. Sinel'nikov, *Kirov*, p. 356.

72. Open Exhibit, Kirov Museum.

73. *Leningradskaia pravda*, 1 December 1989, p. 3.

74. Sinel'nikov, *Kirov*, pp. 350–51.

75. Ibid.

76. Sarah Davies, *Popular Opinion in Stalin's Russia: Terror, Propaganda and Dissent, 1934–1941*(Cambridge: Cambridge University Press, 1997), pp. 23–25.

77. Ibid., pp. 147–54.

78. Khlevniuk, *Politbiuro*, p. 123.

79. Rosliakov, *Ubiistvo Kirova*, pp. 112–15.

80. Khlevniuk, *Politbiuro*, pp. 123–25.

81. Ibid., pp. 122–23.

82. *Stalin's Letters to Molotov*, p. 223; Khlevniuk, *Politbiuro*, pp. 36–37.

83. *Krasnaia zvezda*, 12 November 1988.

84. Krasnikov, *Sergei Mironovich Kirov*, pp. 166–68.

85. RTsKhIDNI, Fond 80, opis 17, delo 70. The letter was dated 16 July 1933.

86. Sinel'nikov, *Kirov*, p. 357; Krasnikov, *Sergei Mironovich Kirov*, p. 168.

87. RTsKhIDNI, Fond 80, opis 18, delo 138, ll. 1–2.

88. A. N. Pazi, ed., *Nash Mironych: Vospominaniia o zhizni i deiatel'nosti S. M. Kirova v Leningrade* (Leningrad: Lenizdat, 1969), pp. 412–18.

89. In 1925, when Commissar of Defense Mikhail Frunze developed a stomach ulcer, Stalin insisted that he have an operation, despite the fact that Frunze was opposed to the idea. Unfortunately, the operation resulted in Frunze's untimely death. The fact that Frunze was a sympathizer of the Zinovievites led to rumors that the operation was unnecessary and speculation that he was murdered, none of which was ever substantiated. See Robert Conquest, *Stalin: Breaker of Nations* (New York: Viking, 1991), pp. 123–24.

90. RTsKhIDNI, Fond 85, opis 1, delo 144.

7. 1934: KIROV'S END

1. Francesco Benvenuti, "A Stalinist Victim of Stalinism: 'Sergo' Ordzhoni-kidze," *Soviet History, 1917–53: Essays in Honour of R. W. Davies,* ed. by Julian Cooper et al. (London: St. Martin's Press, 1995), p. 144.

2. A. I. Mikoyan, "V pervyi raz bez Lenina," *Ogonek,* no. 50, 1987, p. 6.

3. See Tucker, *Stalin in Power,* pp. 247–48.

4. Reprinted in full in *Leningradskaia pravda,* 3 February 1934, p. 1.

5. Rosliakov, *Ubiistvo Kirova,* pp. 26–27.

6. Tucker, *Stalin in Power,* p. 251.

7. Barmine, *One Who Survived,* p. 260.

8. B. N. Ponomarev et al., eds., *Istoriia Kommunisticheskoi Partii Sovetskogo Soiuza,* 2nd edition (Moscow: Politizdat, 1963), p. 486. Interestingly, this phrase is omitted in the 3rd edition, published after Khrushchev, who was committed to de-Stalinization, had been ousted.

9. O. G. Shatunovskaia, "Vokrug tragedii v Smol'nom," *Sel'skaia zhizn',* 23 September 1990, p. 3.

10. Sorokin memoirs, RTsKhIDNI, Fond 560, opis 1, delo 47, ll. 4–8; Mikoyan, "V pervyi raz bez Lenina"; and N. Mikhailov and V. N. Naumov, "Skol'ko delegatov XVII s'ezda partii golosovalo protiv Stalina?" *Izvestiia TsK KPSS,* no. 7, 1989, pp. 114–21.

11. RTsKhIDNI, Fond 560, opis 1, delo 47, l. 11.

12. Mikhailov and Naumov, "Skol'ko delegatov."

13. RTsKhIDNI, Fond 560, opis 1, delo 47, ll. 11–14.

14. Mikoyan, "V pervyi raz bez Lenina," p. 6; Mikhailov and Naumov, "Skol'ko delegatov." Also see Kurilov and Mikhailov, *Tainy spetseal'nogo khraneniia,* pp. 99–114. Actually, Mikhailov and Naumov say that the third commission member in question, N. V. Andreasian, recalled only three cases where Stalin's name was crossed out, but Mikoyan, who had known and worked with Andreasian for years, is probably more reliable on this point, citing Andreasian's claim of twenty-seven ballots against Stalin in Andreasian's box.

15. Shatunovskaia, "Vokrug tragedii v Smol'nom," p. 3.

16. Interestingly, Russian historian Oleg Khlevniuk, who is not convinced of Stalin's complicity in the Kirov murder, makes only a very brief reference to the

story about Stalin's receiving negative votes at the congress and says simply that "documents that would help us conclusively to refute or confirm this version are unknown." (Khlevniuk, *Politbiuro,* p. 120.) Khlevniuk ignores the fact that archival records of the voting show conclusively that, at the very least, 166 ballots were missing, a highly unusual circumstance. Taken together with the testimonies of several of those present, this amounts to strong evidence that Stalin received a large number of negative votes.

17. Rosliakov, *Ubiistvo Kirova,* pp. 28–30; RTsKhIDNI, Fond 560, opis 1, delo 47, ll. 13–14 (Sorokin memoirs).

18. Ibid. Khlevniuk downplays this controversy as well, saying that such disputes with Stalin occurred often in the early 1930s and were proof that he did not have absolute power. (Khlevniuk, *Politbiuro,* pp. 113–14.)

19. Rosliakov, *Ubiistvo Kirova,* pp. 28–30.

20. RTsKhIDNI, Fond 80, opis 18, delo 138, ll. 3–7.

21. S. M. Kirov, *Stat'i i rechi* (1934) (Moscow: Partizdat, 1934), pp. 76–85; Kirov Museum, document no. III/0612.

22. Rosliakov, *Ubiistvo Kirova,* pp. 30–33. On the visits, see *Istoricheskii arkhiv,* nos. 2 and 3, 1995.

23. RTsKhIDNI, Fond 85, opis 29, delo 439, ll. 1–2.

24. RTsKhIDNI, Fond 80, opis 18, delo 11, ll. 1–7.

25. Ibid.

26. S. M. Kirov, *Itogi iun'skogo plenuma TsK VKP(b): doklad na rashurennom plenume Leningradskogo oblastnogo plenuma VKB(b), 4 Iulia 1934 g.* (Leningrad: Leningradskoe oblastnoe izdatel'stvo, 1934).

27. Zavalishin Manuscript, pp. 34–39. When asked what Stalin would think of enlarging private plots, Second Secretary Chudov is said to have replied: "Well, so what? The party will say to him, Comrade Stalin you have great achievements, but you are hot-tempered and stubborn." Zavalishin, p. 39.

28. Ibid., pp. 44–45.

29. Kirov, *Stat'i i rechi* (1934), pp. 39–41; 46.

30. Tucker, *Stalin in Power,* p. 258. Also see Francesco Benvenuti, "Kirov in Soviet Politics: 1933–1934," *Soviet Industrialization Series,* SIPS, no. 8 (Center for Russian and East European Studies, University of Birmingham, 1977), pp. 27–29.

31. Benvenuti noted that a whole passage of Kirov's speech in Leningrad appeared to have been taken from a speech Gorky had made in Moscow a few days before. Benvenuti, "Kirov in Soviet Politics," p. 28.

32. On this point, see ibid., pp. 7–8.

33. Rosliakov, *Ubiistvo Kirova*, p. 35.

34. RTsKhIDNI, Fond 80, opis 26, delo 61, l. 1. On Mariia L'vovna's health, see Kirilina, *Rikoshet*, p. 83.

35. RTsKhIDNI, Fond 80, opis 26, delo 67.

36. RTsKhIDNI, Fond 80, opis 26, delo 68, ll. 1–3.

37. Ibid., ll. 6–7.

38. RTsKhIDNI, Fond 80, opis 18, delo 122.

39. RTsKhIDNI, Fond 80, opis 18, delo 61.

40. Tucker, *Stalin in Power*, p. 281.

41. Krasnikov, *Sergei Mironovich Kirov*, p. 196.

42. Kirilina, *Rikoshet*, pp. 85–88.

43. Ibid., pp. 91–93.

44. RTsKhIDNI, Fond 80, opis 18, delo 67, l. 63.

45. Kirilina, *Rikoshet*, pp. 92–94.

46. As cited in ibid., p. 94.

47. RTsKhIDNI, Fond 80, opis 18, delo 138, l. 8.

48. Rosliakov, *Ubiistvo Kirova*, pp. 36–37.

49. Ibid.

50. On the reported attempt to kill Kirov in Kazakhstan, see Roy Medvedev, *Let History Judge*, p. 336. On the guards, see Library of Congress Russian Archive Collection (hereafter LCRAC), LC A12.5w; A12.511–A12.5 (from materials gathered by the commission investigating the Kirov murder, 1990). The LCRAC recently became available in English: *Revelations from the Russian Archives: Documents in English Translation*, ed. by Diane P. Koenker and Ronald D. Bachman (Washington, D.C.: Library of Congress, 1997).

51. Rosliakov, *Ubiistvo Kirova*, p. 37.

52. See RTsKhIDNI, Fond 80, opis 18, delo 15, for the original copy of his speech. Also see Benvenuti, "Kirov in Soviet Politics," pp. 17–18; and Zavalishin Manuscript, pp. 24–26.

53. Khlevniuk, *Politbiuro*, pp. 125–26.

54. See Tucker, *Stalin in Power*, p. 285.

55. RTsKhIDNI, Fond 80, opis 18, delo 136.

56. Svanidze, *Iosif Stalin v ob'iatiiakh sem'i*, pp. 158–59.

57. Ibid., p. 160.

58. Khlevniuk, *Politbiuro*, p. 127; *Istoricheskii arkhiv*, no. 3, 1995, p. 143.

59. Khlevniuk, *Stalin i Ordzhonikidze*, pp. 44–45.

60. In addition to the executions he carried out in his capacity as a police official, Beria is thought to have been responsible for several mysterious deaths of party officials—including that of Nestor Lakoba, head of the Communist Party in Abkhazia. Lakoba died in 1936, ostensibly of a heart attack. It was later claimed that Beria had poisoned him. Beria also murdered A. G. Khandzhian, party chief of Armenia. See Knight, *Beria*, pp. 70–72.

61. Khlevniuk, *Stalin i Ordzhonikidze*, pp. 45–46.

62. Rosliakov, *Ubiistvo Kirova*, pp. 38–39

63. Ibid., pp. 39–40; Kirilina, *Rikoshet*, pp. 20–21.

64. Ibid.

65. Kirilina, *Rikoshet*, pp. 21–22; Rosliakov, *Ubiistvo Kirova*, p. 40.

66. Kirilina, *Rikoshet*, p. 22; LCRAC, LC A12.511–00.

67. LCRAC, LC A12.5ww.

68. LCRAC, LC A12.5rr–Al2.5vv; Rosliakov, *Ubiistvo Kirova*, p. 51; Kirilina, *Rikoshet*, pp. 22–23.

69. Kirilina, *Rikoshet*, pp. 22–24.

70. Ibid.

71. N. Petukhov and V. Khomchik, "Delo o 'Leningradskom Tsentre,'" *Vestnik Verkhovnogo Suda SSSR*, nos. 5 & 6, 1991 (no. 5, p. 16).

72. LCRAC, LC A.12.5ii–LC A.12.5jj. (Record of interrogation of S. A. Platych, 2 December 1934.)

73. LCRAC, LC A.12.5hh.

74. Rosliakov, *Ubiistvo Kirova*, p. 41.

75. Ibid.

76. Ibid., p. 54.

77. Kirilina, *Rikoshet*, p. 36.

78. LCRAC, LC A.12.5tt.

79. Rosliakov, *Ubiistvo Kirova*, pp. 41; 45.

80. *Vestnik Verkhovnogo Suda SSSR*, no. 5, p. 18.

81. Rosliakov, *Ubiistvo Kirova*, p. 42.

82. LCRAC, LC A.12.5mm (from the Leningrad party archives, Fond 24, opis 2-v, delo 927).

83. Rosliakov, *Ubiistvo Kirova*, pp. 41–45; LCRAC, LC A.12.5h–i (written testimony of Poskrebyshev to N. M. Shvernik, chairman of CPSU Committee of Party Control, 28 July 1961). Rosliakov had the impression that Chudov first talked with Kaganovich, but it was in fact with Poskrebyshev.

84. A. G. Dembo, "Kirov Meshal Prestupnikam iz NKVD," *Vestnik*, no. 6, 1995 (written in 1988), pp. 139–45.

85. LCRAC, LC A.12.5h.

86. *Istoricheskii arkhiv*, no. 3, 1995, p. 144.

87. Ginzburg, "O gibeli Sergo Ordzhonikidze," p. 89.

88. Dembo, in *Vestnik*, no. 6, 1995, p. 142; Kirov Museum, document no. III 294/c.

89. Rosliakov, *Ubiistvo Kirova*, p. 43.

90. Ibid., p. 44.

91. Kirilina, *Rikoshet*, p. 24.

92. Dembo in *Vestnik*, no. 6, 1995, p. 141. NKVD guard Aleksandrov recalled in 1966 that "moments after [the murder] all the entrances and exits in the Smolnyi were closed and the building surrounded by NKVD people and the military" (LCRAC, LC A.12.5.rr), but this appears to have taken longer than Aleksandrov remembered.

8. INTO THE WHIRLWIND

1. Resolution dated 1 December 1934, published in *Pravda*, 5 December 1934.

2. See Peter Solomon, *Soviet Criminal Justice Under Stalin* (Cambridge: Cambridge University Press, 1996), pp. 232–36. Earlier estimates on the numbers of purge victims, which ranged up to seven million, have now been shown by archival data to be inflated. Although the figures are still by no means exact, the lower number cited here is doubtless more accurate.

3. These statements are cited by Aleksandr Iakovlev, "O Dekabr'skoi tragedii." In fact, Bukharin said that Stalin told him about the murder on the day after it happened, apparently forgetting (this was two years later) that Stalin was already in Leningrad on 2 December and that he had been called to Stalin's office on the evening of 1 December. Stalin later acknowledged having made this comment to Bukharin, but claimed that he made it a week later.

4. Rosliakov, *Ubiistvo Kirova*, pp. 72–74; *Vestnik Verkhovnogo Suda*, no. 6, 1991, p. 21; Kirilina, *Rikoshet*, p. 110.

5. Davies, *Popular Opinion in Stalin's Russia*, p. 115, citing the Leningrad party archives, 24/2V/935/2.

6. LCRAC, LC A.12.5f; Rosliakov, *Ubiistvo Kirova*, pp. 78–80; *Vestnik Verkhovnogo Suda*, no. 5, 1991, p. 16. It is not clear why Nikolaev's employment at the Institute of Party History was never revealed in the press, but this was clearly an element of Nikolaev's past that the authorities wanted to keep hidden. Perhaps it was simply considered to reflect so negatively on the party that it could not be acknowledged.

7. Ibid.

8. Kirilina, *Rikoshet*, pp. 41–44.

9. *Vestnik Verkhovnogo Suda*, no. 5, 1991, pp. 16–18; Kirilina, *Rikoshet*, pp. 48–50; *St. Peterburgskie vedomosti*, 4 December 1993, p. 3.

10. Ibid.

11. *Vestnik Verkhovnogo Suda*, no. 5, 1991, pp. 17–18.

12. Kirilina, *Rikoshet*, p. 103; *St. Peterburgskie vedomosti*, 4 December 1993, p. 3.

13. *Vestnik Verkhovnogo Suda*, no. 6, 1991, p. 20. Kirilina (see ibid.) suggests that Nikolaev was searched on this occasion and that nothing was found. But this contradicts official documents unearthed during the USSR Supreme Court investigation.

14. *Pravda,* 24 January 1935.

15. *Report of Court Proceedings in the Case of the Anti-Soviet "Bloc of Rightists and Trotskyites"* (Moscow, 1938), pp. 356; 376; 572; 678.

16. Copies from the Kirov Museum, Nikolaev's personal file.

17. *Vestnik Verkhovnogo Suda,* no. 5, 1991, p. 16.

18. See Iakovlev, "O Dekabr'skoi tragedii."

19. *Vestnik Verkhovnogo Suda,* no. 5, 1991, p. 16.

20. Kirilina, *Rikoshet,* p. 15. Also see Iakovlev, "O Dekabr'skoi tragedii."

21. *Vestnik Verkhovnogo Suda,* no. 5, 1991, p. 18.

22. Rosliakov, *Ubiistvo Kirova,* p. 46.

23. LCRAC, L CA. 12.5gg.

24. *Vestnik Verkhovnogo Suda,* no. 6, 1991, p. 19.

25. Lesley A. Rimmel, "The Kirov Murder and Soviet Society: Propaganda and Popular Opinion in Leningrad, 1934–35," Ph.D. Dissertation, University of Pennsylvania, 1995, pp. 58–60.

26. Lermolo, *Face of a Victim,* pp. 83–84. A documentary on Russian television, NTV, 13 April 1997, dredged up the story about Kirov and Draule again, but was unconvincing. That the story emanated from the NKVD is made clear by former NKVD official Pavel Sudoplatov in his book *Special Tasks* (New York: Little, Brown, 1994), pp. 50–55. Sudoplatov cites the Kirov-Draule affair as a true story, but mistakenly has Draule employed as a waitress for Kirov and the party secretariat at the Smolnyi.

27. LCRAC, LC A.12.5vv–ww.

28. LCRAC, LC A.12.5.gg.

29. Kirilina, *L'Assassinat de Kirov,* p. 233, citing documents from the Leningrad party archives; *Vestnik Verkhovnogo Suda,* no. 6, 1991, p. 21.

30. Ibid.

31. *Vestnik Verkhovnogo Suda,* no. 6, 1991, p. 21.

32. Ibid.

33. Iakovlev, "O Dekabr'skoi tragedii."

34. Kirilina, *L'Assassinat de Kirov,* pp. 235–36.

35. Iakovlev, "O Dekabr'skoi tragedii."

36. Roy Medvedev, *Let History Judge,* p. 340.

37. Liushkov later observed: "Nikolaev lacked balance, he had many problems. In short, he was dissatisfied with life. He was convinced that he was capable of any work. He also felt he was hard to understand. He was always discontented. . . . This discontent in turn drove him into his scheme to assassinate some important figure in the party." As cited in Conquest, *Stalin and the Kirov Murder,* p. 12 (from a magazine published in Tokyo, where Liushkov first went).

38. On the subject of denunciations, see Sheila Fitzpatrick, "Signals from Below: Soviet Letters of Denunciation of the 1930s," *The Journal of Modern History,* no. 68, December 1996, pp. 831–66.

39. RTsKhIDNI, Fond 80, opis 17, delo 22.

40. Kirilina, *L'Assassinat de Kirov,* pp. 66–69; Iakovlev, "O Dekabr'skoi tragedii."

41. TsKhSD (Center for the Preservation of Contemporary Documents, Moscow), Fond 5, opis 30, delo 141. Most of these documents were published in *Istochnik,* no. 2, 1994, pp. 58–70.

42. Ibid.

43. Ibid.

44. Rosliakov, *Ubiistvo Kirova,* p. 48.

45. Ibid.

46. Ibid., p. 49.

47. *Vestnik Verkhovnogo Suda,* no. 6, 1991, p. 19.

48. Ibid.; *Istoricheskii arkhiv,* no. 3, 1995, p. 146.

49. Rosliakov, *Ubiistvo Kirova,* p. 57.

50. Ibid., pp. 57–58.

51. Some of these lists are in the party archives in Moscow. See, for example, RTsKhIDNI, Fond 17, opis 71, delo 19, a document in the party organs department listing biographies of Leningrad party oppositionists in the years 1927–28.

52. Kirilina, *L'Assassinat de Kirov,* pp. 160–63.

53. Ibid.

54. Kirilina, *Rikoshet,* pp. 121–24; Roy Medvedev, *Let History Judge,* p. 343.

55. Kirilina, *L'Assassinat de Kirov*, p. 171.

56. See Robert Tucker, *Stalin in Power*, p. 41.

57. Kirilina, *L'Assassinat de Kirov*, pp. 151–52.

58. *The Crime of the Zinoviev Opposition: The Assassination of S. M. Kirov* (Moscow: Co-operative Publishing Society of Foreign Workers in the USSR, 1935), pp. 19–20.

59. Ibid., pp. 20–21.

60. See Conquest, *Stalin and the Kirov Murder*, p. 56.

61. *Vestnik Verkhovnogo Suda*, no. 6, 1991, p. 19, citing Fomin's testimony; Roy Medvedev, *Let History Judge*, pp. 343–44. Ezhov was also present at the meeting in Stalin's office on 26 December. The three men left five minutes before Ordzhonikidze came in—which again shows that Stalin was not letting him in on the Kirov case.

62. LCRAC, LC A.12.9 (from RTsKhIDNI, Fond 629, opis 1, delo 150, l. 29). Ul'rikh's former wife, Aristova-Litkene, said this in a letter written much later to the Control Commission.

63. Kirilina, *Rikoshet*, pp. 126–30. Elizabeth Lermolo, the young woman mentioned in Chapter 1 above who was arrested because she had a brief acquaintance with Nikolaev, recalled in her memoirs meeting some of Nikolaev's relatives in prison before and after the trial. See Lermolo, *Face of a Victim*. Among those listed by the NKVD as having been sentenced in connection with the Leningrad Center is one E. F. Yermolayeva (see *The Crime of the Zinoviev Opposition*, p. 49). It is possible that this was Lermolo. Unfortunately, Lermolo's memoirs, published more than twenty years after the Kirov murder, do not always accord with the facts, so they cannot be relied upon completely.

64. *Izvestiia TsK KPSS*, no. 7, 1989, p. 70.

65. Ibid.

66. *Pravda*, 23 December 1934.

67. *Izvestiia TsK KPSS*, no. 7, 1989, pp. 82–84.

68. *The Crime of the Zinoviev Opposition*, pp. 46–48.

69. Reproduced for the first time in *Izvestiia TsK KPSS*, no. 8, 1989, pp. 95–100.

70. Ibid., p. 99.

71. This officer was M. S. Bal'tsevich, from the NKVD Operative Department. It is not clear why, but, in addition to criminal negligence, Bal'tsevich was charged with "illegal actions during the investigations." Robert Conquest suggests several possible reasons for the severe punishment, including that Bal'tsevich may have been overzealous in trying to extract testimony from one of the prisoners and had somehow botched things. Conquest, *Stalin and the Kirov Murder,* pp. 70–71.

72. Conquest, *Stalin and the Kirov Murder,* p. 71, citing the NKVD defector Alexander Orlov.

73. Sorokin memoirs, RTsKhIDNI, Fond 560, opis 1, delo 47, l. 101.

74. Ibid., ll. 110–11.

75. Ibid., ll. 110–12.

76. Conquest, *Stalin and the Kirov Murder,* pp. 72–75.

77. Fomin's memoir, *Notes of an Old Chekist* [*Zapiski starogo chekista*], was published in Moscow in 1962, but it did not discuss the Kirov case. He gave some testimony to one of the party commissions in the 1960s (small parts of which have been cited in Soviet sources), but it remains classified. Petrov, as mentioned, talked later about the Volkova affair, and Lobov gave testimony to a party commission which still has not been released.

78. *Letter of an Old Bolshevik: The Key to the Moscow Trials* (New York: Rand School Press, 1937), p. 34

79. Rosliakov, *Ubiistvo Kirova,* pp. 70–74.

80. Kirilina, *Rikoshet,* pp. 130–31.

81. On the disappearance of the letters, see Iakovlev, "O Dekabr'skoi tragedii."

9. Stalin Consolidates Power: 1935–38

1. Barmine, *One Who Survived,* p. 253.

2. Two other members of the Politburo, Stanislav Kossior and Vlas Chubar, were not unswerving Stalinists, but they were about to be purged themselves.

3. Kuibyshev's son Vladimir raised this issue again when he claimed that his father was in fact murdered: *Moskovskie novosti,* no. 5, 22–29 January 1995, p. 14.

4. Iakovlev, "O Dekabr'skoi tragedii," p. 1.

5. RTsKhIDNI, Fond 85, opis 29, delo 455.

6. Transcripts of this Central Committee meeting were declassified after 1991 and appear in numerous issues of *Voprosy istorii*, from issue no. 2–3, 1992, through issue no. 2, 1995. For Stalin's comment, see no. 11–12, 1995, p. 14.

7. Khlevniuk, *Politbiuro*, p. 173.

8. In the summer of 1933, Sergo went so far as to have the Politburo censure Deputy Prosecutor Vyshinskii after he had conducted a highly publicized trial of economic administrators in the city of Kharkov. Stalin, who was vacationing in the South at the time, was furious, labeling the action of Sergo as "nothing other than anti-party, since it had the objective aim of defending reactionary elements of the party against the Central Committee." *Kommunist*, no. 11, 1990, p. 105.

9. Khlevniuk, *Stalin i Ordzhonikidze*, p. 54.

10. Ibid., pp. 54–55.

11. See *Sergei Mironovich Kirov: Ukazatel' literatury* (Moscow: Vsesoiuznaia Knizhnaia Palata, 1940).

12. Davies, *Popular Opinion in Stalin's Russia*, p. 154.

13. This point is made by Sarah Davies, ibid.

14. *Iosif Stalin v ob'iatiiakh sem'i*, p. 169.

15. RTsKhIDNI, Fond 80, opis 19, delo 22.

16. Kirov Museum, Open Exhibit.

17. Kirilina, *Rikoshet*, pp. 96–97.

18. Personal communication from Valentin Bliumenfel'd, 13 May 1997.

19. Medvedev, *Let History Judge*, p. 336.

20. Davies, *Popular Opinion in Stalin's Russia*, pp. 127; 164; 178.

21. Rimmel, "Another Kind of Fear," p. 489.

22. Rimmel, "The Kirov Murder and Soviet Society," p. 114.

23. Rimmel, "Another Kind of Fear," pp. 490–92.

24. Khlevniuk, *1937-i*, pp. 52–53.

25. Ibid., p. 54.

26. Personal communication from Bliumenfel'd, 13 May 1997.

27. Rimmel, "The Kirov Murder and Soviet Society," pp. 57–58.

28. Ibid., pp. 55–56.

29. Khlevniuk, *1937-i*, p. 55.

30. Rimmel, "The Kirov Murder and Soviet Society," p. 15.

31. Deutscher, *Stalin*, pp. 357–58.

32. *Vestnik Verkhovnogo Suda SSSR*, no. 6, 1991, p. 20.

33. Medvedev, *Let History Judge*, p. 348.

34. Ibid.

35. O. F. Krupovich, "Moi Vospominaniia o Vstrechakh i Liudiakh." Manuscript, RTsKhIDNI, Fond 560, opis 1, delo 20.

36. Ibid.

37. *Intimacy and Terror: Soviet Diaries of the 1930s,* ed. by Veronique Garros, Natalia Korenevskaya, and Thomas Lahusen, trans. by Carol A. Flath (New York: The New Press, 1995), pp. 336–37.

38. Interview with Nadezhda Kodatskaia, St. Petersburg, 9 April 1997.

39. Ibid.

40. *Pravda*, 31 October 1961.

41. Chudov was close to Molotov, close enough to address him using the familiar *ty* instead of the formal *vy*. Moreover, Chudov's wife, Liudmilla Shaposhnikova, and Molotov's wife were the best of friends. Rosliakov speculates that Chudov may have been secretly informing Molotov (who in turn of course would inform Stalin) about Kirov. See Rosliakov, *Ubiistvo Kirova*, pp. 82–84.

42. Larina, *This I Cannot Forget*, p. 46.

43. Rosliakov, *Ubiistvo Kirova*, pp. 14–15.

44. Larina, *This I Cannot Forget*, p. 46.

45. Ibid., p. 265.

46. Introduction to Larina, *This I Cannot Forget*, pp. 30–31.

47. *Letter of an Old Bolshevik.* The letter was first published in Russian in *Sotsialis-ticheskii Vestnik*, no. 23–24, December 1936, and no. 1, January 1937.

48. Ibid., p. 33.

49. J. D. Zagoria, ed., *Power and the Soviet Elite: The Letter of an Old Bolshevik and Other Essays by Boris Nicolaevsky* (New York: Praeger, 1966), p. 8.

50. See, for example, Getty, "The Politics of Repression Revisited," p. 44. Getty says: "With her [Larina's] discrediting of the 'Letter,' the original source for an anti-Stalinist, moderate Kirov and for a Stalin opposing him is seriously weakened." But, as shown here, there exists documented evidence of Kirov's moderate views from several other sources, including Kirov's own unpublished statements, made at Leningrad party meetings and in letters.

51. This is pointed out by Francesco Benvenuti, "Kirov in Soviet Politics," p. 7.

52. Larina, *This I Cannot Forget*, pp. 286–88.

53. *Izvestiia TsK KPSS*, no. 8, 1989, pp. 84; 90–93.

54. *Report of the Court Proceedings in the Case of the Trotskyite-Zinovievite Terrorist Center* (New York: Howard Fertig, 1967), p. 61.

55. *Reabilitatsiia*, p. 32.

56. "Letter of an Old Bolshevik," pp. 60–61. Also see a letter from Kaganovich to Ordzhonikidze, dated 30 September 1936, reproduced in *Stalinskoe politbiuro*, pp. 148–49.

57. *Izvestiia TsK KPSS*, no. 8, 1989, p. 85.

58. Khlevniuk, *Politbiuro*, pp. 204–5.

59. *Reabilitatsiia*, pp. 245–46.

60. *Voprosy istorii*, no. 11, 1988, p. 49.

61. Khlevniuk, *Stalin i Ordzhonikidze*, pp. 109–10.

62. Knight, *Beria*, pp. 73–75.

63. RTsKhIDNI, Fond 85, opis 29, delo 156, ll. 5, 6–7, 9–10.

64. Khlevniuk, *Stalin i Ordzhonikidze*, pp. 96–103.

65. F. G. Seiranian, ed., *O Sergo Ordzhonikidze: Vospominania, ocherki, stat'i sovremennikov* (Moscow: Politizdat, 1986), pp. 292–96.

66. Khlevniuk, "Ordzhonikidze—Kirov—Stalin," *Svobodnaia mysl'*, no. 13, 1991, pp. 59–60.

67. Ginzberg, "O gibeli Sergo Ordzhonikidze," pp. 92–93.

68. Ibid.; Roy Medvedev, *Let History Judge*, pp. 400–2.

69. On Sergo's health problems, see RTsKhIDNI, Fond 85, opis 1, delo 144, ll. 40–51.

70. Stalin had said: "A person commits suicide because he is afraid that everything will come out in the open, and he doesn't want to be a witness to his own universal disgrace." "Fragmenty stenograma dekabr'skogo plenuma TsK VKP(B) 1936 goda," *Voprosy istorii,* no. 1, 1995, p. 11.

71. *Iosif Stalin v ob'iatiiakh sem'i,* p. 191.

72. Ibid.

73. Larina, *This I Cannot Forget,* pp. 316–17. Larina recalls that shortly before Bukharin wrote the letter, she happened to run into Sergo as she was out taking a walk. He had squeezed her hand and said: "Stand firm." Larina, justifiably, found this "cold comfort."

74. In fact, some oblique references to Bukharin's involvement in the Kirov murder had already been made at the December 1936 plenum. See *Voprosy istorii,* no. 1, 1995, p. 14.

75. The entire transcript of the trial was published and translated into English: *Report of Court Proceedings in the Case of the Anti-Soviet "Bloc of Rightists and Trotskyites"* (Moscow, 1938).

76. Ibid., p. 572.

77. *Novaia Rossiia,* no. 60, 1939, pp. 7–10. Also see "Letter of an Old Bolshevik," pp. 52–53, which gives a somewhat different interpretation, saying that Stalin tried to defend Enukidze from Ezhov, which is highly unlikely.

78. On Iagoda's views toward Bukharin and collectivization, also see Conquest, *Inside Stalin's Secret Police,* pp. 12–13; and Kun, *Bukharin,* p. 451.

79. On the preparations for the trial and the treatment of the defendants, see *Reabilitatsiia,* pp. 238–40.

80. But it is not entirely out of the question that Iagoda and the NKVD (hence Stalin) had a hand in these deaths. Kuibyshev's son suspected this in the case of his father. See note 3 above. As for Gorky, his relationship with Stalin and the circumstances of his death have been the subject of much speculation. Although he was an active propagandist for the Bolshevik regime in the 1920s and early 1930s, he reportedly supported Kirov's policy of reconciling with the former oppositionists and bringing them back into the fold. After Kirov's death, which devastated Gorky, his relations with Stalin deteriorated. The officially reported cause of Gorky's death in June 1936 was influenza, but some people have claimed that it

was murder. See V. V. Ivanova, "Pochemu Stalin ubil Gor'kogo?" *Voprosy literatury,* no. 1, 1993, pp. 91–134; and Lidiia Spiridonova, "Gorky and Stalin (According to New Materials from A. M. Gorky's Archive)," *The Russian Review,* Vol. 54, no. 3 (1995), pp. 413–23.

81. See Cohen, *Bukharin and the Bolshevik Revolution,* pp. 376–80.

82. *Leon Trotsky on the Kirov Assassination* (New York: Pioneer Publishers, 1956). This is a reprint of a pamphlet originally written by Trotsky at the end of 1934.

10. The Kirov Legacy

1. *The Works of Lord Macaulay,* Vol. 1 (London: Longmans, Green, 1866), p. 343.

2. Michael Ignatieff, "Whispers from the Abyss," *The New York Review of Books,* 2 October 1996, p. 4.

3. Vladimir Naumov, "Utverdit' dokladchikom tovarishcha Khrushcheva," *Moskovskie novosti,* no. 5, 4–11 February 1996, p. 34.

4. Ibid.

5. *Vestnik Verkhovnogo Suda,* no. 5, 1991, pp. 15–16.

6. Shatunovskaia, "Vokrug tragedii v Smol'nom."

7. Ibid.

8. See, for example, Shatunovskaia, "Vokrug tragedii v Smol'nom"; V. Lordkipanidze, "Ubiistvo Kirova. Nekotorye podrobnosti," *Argumenty i fakty,* no. 6, 11–17 February 1989; and Anton Antonov-Ovseenko, "Ubiitsy Kirova," *Gudok,* 11–13 April 1989, for the anti-Stalinist version. Historian Dmitrii Volkogonov also weighed in with his assessment, concluding in his 1989 biography of Stalin that he had a role in the murder. See the English translation, Volkogonov, *Stalin,* pp. 207–8. Meanwhile, Alla Kirilina, a senior researcher at the Institute of Party History in Leningrad, was publishing article after article (several of which have been cited in these notes) exonerating Stalin. For a defense of Stalin on the part of the police, see A. T. Rybin, *Kto ubil Kirova?* (*Zapiski telokhranitelia*) (Moscow, 1996).

9. Kathleen E. Smith, *Remembering Stalin's Victims: Popular Memory and the End of the USSR* (Ithaca and London: Cornell University Press, 1996), p. 197.

10. LCRAC, LC A.12.5a.

11. Ibid.

12. *Pravda,* 4 November 1990; Iakovlev, "O Dekabr'skoi tragedii."

13. Another factor may be the profit motive: documents are sometimes withheld from general access because they are believed to have a market value.

14. The young Leningrad journalist V. K. Zavalishin, for example, said that he was asked by his paper, *Krestianskaia pravda* (The Peasants' Truth), to cover a funeral meeting at a village in the Leningrad district which was located along the railway line. Kirov's casket was taken off the train there and opened up so that the peasants could bid farewell to their leader. The local NKVD, orchestrating everything, instructed journalists to depict a scene of great mourning. Zavalishin Manuscript, pp. 5–7. Zavalishin at first refused to go along with this "farce," but he was advised by his boss to comply with the NKVD's request.

15. Yuri Afanasyev, "Reclaiming Russian History," *Perspective,* Vol. 7, no. 1 (September–October 1996), p. 1.

Index